THE LOST CONTINENT
and
NEITHER HERE NOR THERE

Also by Bill Bryson
Mother Tongue

BILL BRYSON

The Lost Continent

Travels in Small Town America

and

Neither Here Nor There

Travels in Europe

SECKER & WARBURG
London

The Lost Continent first published in Great Britain in 1989
Neither Here Nor There first published in Great Britain in 1991
This edition first published in Great Britain in 1992 by
Secker & Warburg
Random House, 20 Vauxhall Bridge Road,
London SW1V 2SA

18 20 19 17

Random House Australia (Pty) Limited
20 Alfred Street, Milsons Point, Sydney,
New South Wales 2061, Australia

Random House New Zealand Limited
18 Poland Road, Glenfield,
Auckland 10, New Zealand

Random House South Africa (Pty) Limited
Endulini, 5A Jubilee Road, Parktown 2193, South Africa

Random House UK Limited Reg. No. 954009

A CIP catalogue record for this book
is available from the British Library

ISBN 0 436 20130 5

The song on p. 40 is from 'Child Support' by Tom Schuyler,
reprinted by kind permission of Screen-Gems-EMI Music Inc.,
Hollywood, California; the extract on p. 266 is reprinted by kind
permission of Unwin Hyman, part of HarperCollins Publishers;
part of *Neither Here Nor There* first appeared in *Granta*

Papers used by Random House UK Limited are natural,
recyclable products made from wood grown in sustainable forests.
The manufacturing processes conform to the environmental
regulations of the country of origin.

Printed and bound in Great Britain by
Mackays of Chatham PLC

The Lost Continent

To my father

Acknowledgement

I would like to thank the following people for their kind and various assistance in helping me during the preparation of this book: Hal and Lucia Horning, Robert and Rita Schmidt, Stan and Nancy Kluender, Mike and Sherry Bryson, Peter Dunn, Cynthia Mitchell, Nick Tosches, Paul Kingsbury, and, above all, my mother, Mary Bryson, who still has the best legs in Des Moines.

PART ONE

East

ONE

I come from Des Moines. Somebody had to.

When you come from Des Moines you either accept the fact without question and settle down with a local girl named Bobbi and get a job at the Firestone factory and live there for ever and ever, or you spend your adolescence moaning at length about what a dump it is and how you can't wait to get out, and then you settle down with a local girl named Bobbi and get a job at the Firestone factory and live there for ever and ever.

Hardly anyone ever leaves. This is because Des Moines is the most powerful hypnotic known to man. Outside town there is a big sign that says WELCOME TO DES MOINES. THIS IS WHAT DEATH IS LIKE. There isn't really. I just made that up. But the place does get a grip on you. People who have nothing to do with Des Moines drive in off the interstate, looking for gas or hamburgers, and stay for ever. There's a New Jersey couple up the street from my parents' house whom you see wandering around from time to time looking faintly puzzled but strangely serene. Everybody in Des Moines is strangely serene.

The only person I ever knew in Des Moines who wasn't serene was Mr Piper. Mr Piper was my parents' neighbour, a leering, cherry-faced idiot who was forever getting drunk and crashing his car into telephone poles. Everywhere you went you encountered telephone poles and road signs leaning dangerously in testimony to Mr Piper's driving habits. He distributed them all over the west side of town, rather in the way dogs mark trees. Mr Piper was the nearest possible human equivalent to Fred Flintstone, but less charming. He was a Shriner and a Republican – a Nixon Republican – and he appeared to feel he had a mission in life to spread offence. His favourite pastime, apart from getting drunk and crashing his car, was to get drunk and insult the neighbours, particularly us because we were Democrats, though he was prepared to insult Republicans when we weren't available.

Eventually, I grew up and moved to England. This irritated Mr Piper almost beyond measure. It was worse than being a Democrat. Whenever I was in town, Mr Piper would come over and chide me. 'I don't know what you're doing over there with all those Limeys,' he would say provocatively. 'They're not clean people.'

'Mr Piper, you don't know what you're talking about,' I would reply in my affected English accent. 'You are a cretin.' You could talk like that to Mr Piper because (1) he *was* a cretin and (2) he never listened to anything that was said to him.

'Bobbi and I went over to London two years ago and our hotel room didn't even have a *bath*room in it,' Mr Piper would go on. 'If you wanted to take a leak in the middle of the night you had to walk about a mile down the hallway. That isn't a clean way to live.'

'Mr Piper, the English are paragons of cleanliness. It is a well-known fact that they use more soap per capita than anyone else in Europe.'

Mr Piper would snort derisively at this. 'That doesn't mean diddly-squat, boy, just because they're cleaner than a bunch of Krauts and Eyeties. My God, a *dog's* cleaner than a bunch of Krauts and Eyeties. And I'll tell you something else: if his Daddy hadn't bought Illinois for him, John F. Kennedy would never have been elected President.'

I had lived around Mr Piper long enough not to be thrown by this abrupt change of tack. The theft of the 1960 presidential election was a long-standing plaint of his, one that he brought into the conversation every ten or twelve minutes regardless of the prevailing drift of the discussion. In 1963, during Kennedy's funeral, someone in the Waveland Tap punched Mr Piper in the nose for making that remark. Mr Piper was so furious that he went straight out and crashed his car into a telephone pole. Mr Piper is dead now, which is of course one thing that Des Moines prepares you for.

When I was growing up I used to think that the best thing about coming from Des Moines was that it meant you didn't come from anywhere else in Iowa. By Iowa standards, Des Moines is a Mecca of cosmopolitanism, a dynamic hub of wealth and education, where people wear three-piece suits and dark socks, often simultaneously. During the annual state high school basketball tournament, when the hayseeds from out in the state would flood into the city for a week, we used to accost them downtown and snidely offer to show them how to ride an escalator or negotiate a revolving door. This wasn't always so far from reality. My friend Stan, when he was about sixteen, had to go and stay with his cousin in some remote, dusty hamlet called Dog Water or Dunceville or some such improbable spot – the kind of place where if a dog gets run over by a truck everybody goes out to have a look at it. By the second week, delirious with boredom, Stan insisted that he and his cousin drive the fifty miles into the county town, Hooterville, and find something to do. They went bowling at an alley with warped lanes and chipped balls and afterwards had a chocolate soda and looked at a *Playboy* in a drugstore, and on the way home the cousin sighed with immense satisfaction and said, 'Gee thanks, Stan. That was the best time I ever had in my whole life!' It's true.

I had to drive to Minneapolis once, and I went on a back road just to see the country. But there was nothing to see. It's just flat and hot, and full of corn and soya beans and hogs. Every once in a while you come across a farm or some dead little town where the liveliest thing is the flies. I remember one long, shimmering stretch where I could see a couple of miles down the highway and there was a brown dot beside the road. As I got closer I saw it was a man sitting on a box by his front yard, in some six-house town with a name like Spigot or Urinal, watching my approach with inordinate interest. He watched me zip past and in the rear-view mirror I could see him still watching me going on down the road until at last I disappeared into a heat haze. The whole thing must have taken about five minutes. I wouldn't be surprised if even now he thinks of me from time to time.

He was wearing a baseball cap. You can always spot an Iowa man because he is wearing a baseball cap advertising John Deere or a feed company, and because the back of his neck has been lasered into deep crevasses by years of driving a John Deere tractor back and forth in a blazing sun. (This does not do his mind a whole lot of good either.) His other distinguishing feature is that he looks ridiculous when he takes off his shirt because his neck and arms are chocolate brown and his torso is as white as a sow's belly. In Iowa it is called a farmer's tan and it is, I believe, a badge of distinction.

Iowa women are almost always sensationally overweight – you see them at Merle Hay Mall in Des Moines on Saturdays, clammy and meaty in their shorts and halter tops, looking a little like elephants dressed in children's clothes, yelling at their kids, calling out names like Dwayne and Shauna. Jack Kerouac, of all people, thought that Iowa women were the prettiest in the country, but I don't think he ever went to Merle Hay Mall on a Saturday. I will say this, however – and it's a strange, strange thing – the teenaged daughters of these fat women are always utterly delectable, as soft and gloriously rounded and naturally fresh-smelling as a basket of fruit. I don't know what it is that happens to them, but it must be awful to marry one of those nubile cuties knowing that there is a time bomb ticking away in her that will at some unknown date make her bloat out into something huge and grotesque, presumably all of a sudden and without much notice, like a self-inflating raft from which the stopper has been yanked.

Even without this inducement, I don't think I would have stayed in Iowa. I never felt altogether at home there, even when I was small. In about 1957, my grandparents gave me a Viewmaster for my birthday and a packet of discs with the title 'Iowa—Our Glorious State'. I can remember thinking even then that the selection of glories was a trifle on the thin side. With no natural features of note, no national parks, no battlefields or famous birthplaces, the Viewmaster people had to stretch their creative 3-D talents to the full. Putting the Viewmaster to your eyes and clicking the white handle gave you, as I recall, a shot of Herbert Hoover's birthplace, impressively three-dimensional, followed by Iowa's other great treasure, the Little Brown Church in the Vale (which inspired the song whose tune nobody ever quite knows), the highway bridge over the Mississippi River at Davenport (all the cars seemed to be hurrying towards Illinois), a field of waving corn, the bridge over the Missouri River at Council Bluffs and the Little Brown Church in the Vale again, taken from another angle. I can remember thinking even then that there must be more to life than that.

Then one grey Sunday afternoon when I was about ten I was watching TV and there was a documentary on about movie-making in Europe. One clip showed Anthony Perkins walking along some sloping city street at dusk. I don't remember now if it was Rome or Paris, but the street was cobbled and shiny with rain and Perkins was hunched deep in a trench coat and I thought, 'Hey, *c'est moi!*' I began to read – no, I began to *consume* – *National Geographics*, with their pictures of glowing Lapps and mist-shrouded castles and ancient cities of infinite charm. From that moment, I wanted to be a European boy. I wanted to live in an apartment across from a park in the heart of a city, and from my bedroom window look out on a crowded vista of hills and roof-tops. I wanted to ride trams and understand strange languages. I wanted friends named Werner and Marco who wore short pants and played soccer in the street and owned toys made of wood. I cannot for the life of me think why. I wanted my mother to send me out to buy long loaves of bread from a shop with a wooden pretzel hanging above the entrance. I wanted to step outside my front door and *be* somewhere.

As soon as I was old enough I left. I left Des Moines and Iowa and the United States and the war in Vietnam and Watergate, and settled across the world. And now when I came home it was to a foreign country, full of serial murderers and sports teams in the wrong towns (the Indianapolis Colts? the Toronto Blue Jays?) and a personable old fart who was President. My mother knew that personable old fart when he was a sports caster called Dutch Reagan at WHO Radio in Des Moines. 'He was just a nice, friendly, kind of dopey guy,' my mother says.

Which, come to that, is a pretty fair description of most Iowans. Don't get me wrong. I am not for a moment suggesting that Iowans are mentally deficient. They are a decidedly intelligent and sensible people who, despite their natural conservatism, have always been prepared to elect a conscientious, clear-thinking liberal in preference to some cretinous conservative. (This used to drive Mr Piper practically insane.) And Iowans, I am proud to tell you, have the highest literacy rate in the nation: 99·5 per cent of grown-ups there can read. When I say they are kind of dopey I mean they are trusting and amiable and open. They are a tad slow, certainly – when you tell an Iowan a joke, you can see a kind of race going on between his brain and his expression – but it's not because they're incapable of high-speed mental activity, it's only that there's not much call for it. Their wits are dulled by simple, wholesome faith in God and the soil and their fellow man.

Above all, Iowans are friendly. You go into a strange diner in the South and everything goes quiet, and you realise all the other customers are looking at you as if they are sizing up the risk involved in murdering you for your wallet and leaving your body in a shallow grave somewhere out in the swamps. In Iowa you are the centre of attention, the most interesting thing to hit town since a tornado carried off old Frank Sprinkel and his tractor last May. Everybody you meet acts like he would gladly give you his last beer and let you sleep with his sister. Everyone is happy and friendly and strangely serene.

The last time I was home, I went to Kresge's downtown and bought a bunch of postcards to send back to England. I bought the most ridiculous ones I could find – a sunset over a feed lot, a picture of farmers bravely grasping a moving staircase beside the caption 'We rode the escalator at Merle Hay Mall!', that sort of thing. They were so uniformly absurd that when I took them up to the check-out, I felt embarrassed by them, as if I were buying dirty magazines, and hoped somehow to convey the impression that they weren't really for me. But the check-out lady regarded each of them with interest and deliberation – just as they always do with dirty magazines, come to that.

When she looked up at me she was almost misty-eyed. She wore butterfly glasses and a beehive hairdo. 'Those are real nice,' she said. 'You know, honey, I've bin in a lot of states and seen a lot of places, but I can tell you that this is just about the purtiest one I ever saw.' She really said purtiest. She really meant it. The poor woman was in a state of terminal hypnosis. I glanced at the cards and to my surprise I suddenly saw what she meant. I couldn't help but agree with her. They *were* purty. Together, we made a little pool of silent admiration. For one giddy, careless moment, I was almost serene myself. It was a strange sensation, and it soon passed.

II

My father liked Iowa. He lived his whole life in the state, and is even now working his way through eternity there, in Glendale Cemetery in Des Moines. But every year he became seized with a quietly maniacal urge to get out of the state and go on vacation. Every summer, without a whole lot of notice, he would load the car to groaning, hurry us into it, take off for some distant point, return to get his wallet after having driven almost to the next state, and take off again for some distant point. Every year it was the same. Every year it was awful.

The big killer was the tedium. Iowa is in the middle of the biggest plain this side of Jupiter. Climb onto a roof-top almost anywhere in the state and you are confronted with a featureless sweep of corn for as far as the eye can see. It is 1,000 miles from the sea in any direction,

400 miles from the nearest mountain, 300 miles from skyscrapers and muggers and things of interest, 200 miles from people who do not habitually stick a finger in their ear and swivel it around as a preliminary to answering any question addressed to them by a stranger. To reach anywhere of even passing interest from Des Moines by car requires a journey that in other countries would be considered epic. It means days and days of unrelenting tedium, in a baking steel capsule on a ribbon of highway.

In my memory, our vacations were always taken in a big blue Rambler station-wagon. It was a cruddy car – my dad always bought cruddy cars, until he got to the male menopause and started buying zippy red convertibles – but it had the great virtue of space. My brother, sister and I in the back were miles away from my parents up front, in effect in another room. We quickly discovered during illicit forays into the picnic hamper that if you stuck a bunch of Ohio Blue Tip matches into an apple or hard-boiled egg, so that it resembled a porcupine, and casually dropped it out the tailgate window, it was like a bomb. It would explode with a small bang and a surprisingly big flash of blue flame, causing cars following behind to veer in an amusing fashion.

My dad, miles away up front, never knew what was going on and could not understand why all day long cars would zoom up alongside him with the driver gesticulating furiously, before tearing off into the distance. 'What was that all about?' he would say to my mother in a wounded tone.

'I don't know, dear,' my mother would answer mildly. My mother only ever said two things. She said, 'I don't know, dear.' And she said, 'Can I get you a sandwich, honey?' Occasionally on our trips she would volunteer other pieces of intelligence like, 'Should that dashboard light be glowing like that, dear?' or, 'I think you hit that dog/man/blind person back there, honey,' but mostly she wisely kept quiet. This was because on vacations my father was a man obsessed. His principal obsession was with trying to economise. He always took us to the crummiest hotels and motor lodges, and to the kind of roadside eating-houses where they only washed the dishes weekly. You always knew, with a sense of doom, that at some point before finishing you were going to discover someone else's congealed egg-yolk lurking somewhere on your plate or plugged between the tines of your fork. This, of course, meant cooties and a long, painful death.

But even that was a relative treat. Usually we were forced to picnic by the side of the road. My father had an instinct for picking bad picnic sites – on the apron of a busy truck stop or in a little park that turned out to be in the heart of some seriously deprived ghetto, so that groups of children would come and stand silently by our table and watch us eating Hostess Cupcakes and crinkle-cut potato chips – and it always became incredibly windy the moment we stopped, so that my mother spent the whole of lunch-time chasing paper plates over an area of about an acre.

In 1957 my father invested $19·98 in a portable gas stove that took an hour to assemble before each use and was so wildly temperamental that we children were always ordered to stand well back when it was being lit. This always proved unnecessary, however, because the stove would flicker to life only for a few seconds before puttering out, and my father would spend many hours turning it this way and that to keep it out of the wind, simultaneously addressing it in a low, agitated tone normally associated with the chronically insane. All the while my brother, sister and I would implore him to take us some place with air-conditioning, linen table-cloths and ice-cubes clinking in glasses of clear water. 'Dad,' we would beg, 'you're a successful man. You make a good living. Take us to a Howard Johnson's.' But he wouldn't have it. He was a child of the Depression and where capital outlays were involved he always wore the haunted look of a fugitive who has just heard bloodhounds in the distance.

Eventually, with the sun low in the sky, he would hand us hamburgers that were cold and raw and smelled of butane. We would take one bite and refuse to eat any more. So my father would lose his temper and throw everything into the car and drive us at high speed to some roadside diner where a sweaty man with a floppy hat would sling hash while grease-fires danced on his grill. And afterwards, in a silent car ·filled with bitterness and unquenched basic needs, we would mistakenly turn off the main highway and get lost and end up in some no-hope hamlet with a name like Draino, Indiana, or Tapwater, Missouri, and get a room in the only hotel in town, the sort of run-down place where if you wanted to watch TV it meant you had to sit in the lobby and share a cracked leatherette sofa with an old man with big sweat circles under his arms. The old man would almost certainly have only one leg and probably one other truly arresting deficiency, like no nose or a caved-in forehead, which meant that although you were sincerely intent on watching *Laramie* or *Our Miss Brooks*, you found your gaze being drawn, ineluctably and sneakily, to the amazing eaten-away body sitting beside you. You couldn't help yourself. Occasionally the man would turn out to have no tongue, in which case he would try to engage you in lively conversation. It was all most unsatisfying.

After a week or so of this kind of searing torment, we would fetch up at some blue and glinting sweep of lake or sea in a bowl of pine-clad mountains, a place full of swings and amusements and the gay shrieks of children splashing in water, and it would all almost be worth it. Dad would become funny and warm and even once or twice might take us out to the sort of restaurant where you didn't have to watch your food being cooked and where the glass of water they served you wasn't autographed with lipstick. This was living. This was heady opulence.

It was against this disturbed and erratic background that I became gripped with a curious urge to go back to the land of my youth and make what the blurb writers like to call a journey of discovery. On another continent, 4,000 miles away, I became quietly seized with that nostalgia that overcomes you when you have reached the middle of your life and your father has recently died and it dawns on you that when he went he took some of you with him. I wanted to go back to the magic places of my youth – to Mackinac Island, the Rocky Mountains, Gettysburg – and see if they were as good as I remembered them. I wanted to hear the long, low sound of a Rock Island locomotive calling across a still night and the clack of it receding into the distance. I wanted to see lightning bugs, and hear cicadas shrill, and be inescapably immersed in that hot, crazy-making August weather that makes your underwear scoot up every crack and fissure and cling to you like latex, and drives mild-mannered men to pull out hand-guns in bars and light up the night with gunfire. I wanted to look for Ne-Hi Pop and Burma Shave signs and go to a ball game and sit at a marble-topped soda-fountain and drive through the kind of small towns that Deanna Durbin and Mickey Rooney used to inhabit in the movies. I wanted to travel around. I wanted to see America. I wanted to come home.

So I flew to Des Moines and acquired a sheaf of road-maps, which I studied and puzzled over on the living-room floor, drawing an immense circular itinerary that would take me all over this strange and giant semi-foreign land. My mother, meantime, made me sandwiches and said, 'Oh, I don't know, dear,' when I asked her questions about the vacations of my childhood. And one September dawn in my thirty-sixth year I crept out of my childhood home, slid behind the wheel of an ageing Chevrolet Chevette lent me by my sainted and trusting mother and guided it out through the flat, sleeping streets of the city. I cruised down an empty freeway, the only person with a mission in a city of 250,000 sleeping souls. The sun was already high in the sky and promised a blisteringly hot day. Ahead of me lay about a million square miles of quietly rustling corn. At the edge of town I joined Iowa Highway 163 and with a light heart headed towards Missouri. And it isn't often you hear anyone say that.

TWO

In Britain it had been a year without summer. Wet spring had merged imperceptibly into bleak autumn. For months the sky had remained a depthless grey. Sometimes it rained, but mostly it was just dull, a land without shadows. It was like living inside Tupperware. And here suddenly the sun was dazzling in its intensity. Iowa was hysterical with colour and light. Roadside barns were a glossy red, the sky a deep, hypnotic blue; fields of mustard and green stretched out before me. Flecks of mica glittered in the rolling road. And here and there in the distance mighty grain elevators, the cathedrals of the Middle West, the ships of the prairie seas, drew the sun's light and bounced it back as pure white. Squinting in the unaccustomed brilliance, I followed the highway to Otley.

My intention was to retrace the route my father always took to my grandparents' house in Winfield – through Prairie City, Pella, Oskaloosa, Hedrick, Brighton, Coppock, Wayland and Olds. The sequence was tattooed on my memory. Always having been a passenger before, I had never paid much attention to the road, so I was surprised to find I kept coming up against odd turns and abrupt T-junctions, requiring me to go left here for a couple of miles, then right for a few miles, then left again, and so on. It would have been much more straightforward to take Highway 92 to Ainsworth and then head south to Mount Pleasant. I couldn't imagine by what method of reasoning my father had ever settled on this route, and now of course I never would know. This seemed a pity, particularly as there was almost nothing he would have liked better than to cover the dining-room table with maps and consider at length possible routings. In this he was like most Midwesterners. Directions are very important to them. They have an innate need to be oriented, even in their anecdotes. Any story related by a Midwesterner will wander off at some point into a thicket of interior monologue along the lines of 'We were staying at a hotel that was eight blocks north-east of the state capitol building. Come to think of it, it was north-west. And I think it was probably more like nine blocks. And this woman without any clothes on, naked as the day she was born except for a coonskin cap, came running at us from the south-west . . . or was it the south-east?' If there are two Midwesterners present and they both witnessed the incident, you can just about write off the anecdote because they will spend the rest of the afternoon arguing points of the compass and will never get back to the original story. You can always tell a Midwestern couple in Europe because they will be standing on a traffic island in the middle of a busy intersection looking at a wind-blown map and arguing over which way is west. European cities, with their wandering streets and undisciplined alleys, drive Midwesterners practically insane.

This geographical obsession probably has something to do with the absence of landmarks throughout middle America. I had forgotten just how flat and empty it is. Stand on two phone books almost anywhere in Iowa and you get a view. From where I was now I could look out on a sweep of landscape about the size of Belgium, but there was nothing on it except for a few widely-separated farms, some scattered stands of trees and two water-towers, brilliant silver glints signifying distant, unseen towns. Far off in the middle distance a cloud of dust chased a car up a gravel road. The only things that stood out from the landscape were the grain elevators, but even they looked all the same, and there was nothing much to distinguish one view from another.

And it's so quiet. Apart from the ceaseless fidgeting of the corn, there is not a sound. Somebody could sneeze in a house three miles away and you would hear it ('Bless you!' 'Thank you!'). It must nearly drive you crazy to live a life so devoid of stimulus, where no passing aeroplane ever draws your gaze and no car horns honk, where time shuffles forward so slowly that you half expect to find the people still watching *Ozzie and Harriet* on TV and voting for Eisenhower. ('I don't know how far you folks in Des Moines have got, but we're only up to 1958 here in Fudd County.')

Small towns are equally unhelpful in offering distinguishing features. About all that separates them are their names. They always have a gas station, a grocery store, a grain elevator, a place selling farm equipment and fertilisers, and something improbable like a micro-wave oven dealer or a dry cleaner's, so you can say to yourself as you glide through town, 'Now what would they be doing with a dry cleaner's in Fungus City?' Every fourth or fifth community will be a county town, built around a square. A handsome brick courthouse with a Civil War cannon and a monument to the dead of at least two wars will stand on one side of the square and on the other sides will be businesses: a five and dime, a luncheonette, two banks, a hardware store, a Christian bookstore, a barber's, a couple of hairdressers, a place selling the sort of men's clothing that only someone from a very small town would wear. At least two of the businesses will be called Vern's. The central area of the square will be a park, with fat trees and a bandstand and a pole with an American flag and scattered benches full of old men in John Deere caps sitting around talking about the days when they had something else to do other than sit around and talk about the days when they had something else to do. Time in these places creaks along.

The best county town in Iowa is Pella, forty miles south-east of Des Moines. Pella was founded by Dutch immigrants and every May it still holds a big tulip festival for which they get somebody important like the mayor of The Hague to fly in and praise their bulbs. I used to like Pella when I was little because many of the residents put little windmills in their front yards, which made it kind of interesting. I wouldn't say it made it *outstandingly* interesting, but you learned from an early age to take what pleasures you could find on any trip across Iowa. Besides, Pella had a Dairy Queen on the edge of town where my father would sometimes stop and buy us ice-cream cones dipped in chocolate, and for this alone I have always felt a special fondness for the place. So I was pleased to note, as I rolled into the town on this fine September morn, that there were still windmills whirling in many a front yard. I stopped at the square and got out to stretch my legs. Being a Sunday, the old men from the square had the day off – they would be on sleeping-in-front-of-the-TV duty all day – but in every other respect Pella was as perfect as I remembered it. The square was thick with trees and flower-beds of blazing salvias and glowing marigolds. It had its own windmill, a handsome green one with white blades, nearly full-sized, standing on one corner. The stores around the square were of the cereal box architecture favoured by small-town stores throughout the Midwest, but with gingerbread cornices and other cheery embellishments. Every business had a solid, trustworthy Dutch name: Pardekooper's Drug Store, Jaarsma Bakery,

Van Gorp Insurers, Gosselink's Christian Book Store, Vander Ploeg Bakery. All were shut, of course. Sundays are still closely observed in places like Pella. Indeed, the whole town was eerily quiet. It was steeped in that kind of dead silence that makes you begin to wonder, if you are of a suitably hysterical nature, if perhaps everybody has been poisoned in the night by a leak of odourless gas – which even now could be taking insidious control of your own central nervous system – turning Pella into a kind of Pompeii of the plains. I briefly imagined people from all over coming to look at the victims and being especially enthralled at the worried-looking young man in spectacles on the town square, forever clutching his throat and trying to get his car door open. But then I saw a man walking a dog at the far end of the square and realised that any danger was safely past.

I hadn't intended to linger, but it was such a splendid morning that I wandered off down a nearby street, past neat wooden-framed houses with cupolas and gables and front porches with two-seater swings that creaked in the breeze. There was no other sound, apart from the scuffling of my feet through dried leaves. At the bottom of the street, I came across the campus of Central College, a small institution run by the Dutch Reformed Church, with a campus of redbrick buildings overlooking a serpentine with an arching wooden footbridge. The whole place was as tranquil as a double dose of Valium. It looked like the sort of tidy, friendly, clean-thinking college that Clark Kent would have attended. I crossed the bridge and at the far side of the campus found further evidence that I was not the only living person in Pella. From an open window high up in a dormitory building came the sound of a stereo turned up far too loud. It blared for a moment – something by Frankie Goes to Hollywood, I believe – and then from someplace indiscernible there came a booming voice that said, 'IF YOU DON'T TURN THAT THING THE FUCK OFF RIGHT NOW I'M GONNA COME OVER THERE AND POUND YOUR HEAD IN!' It was the voice of a large person – someone, I fancied, with the nickname Moose. Immediately the music stopped and Pella slept again.

I continued on east, through Oskaloosa, Fremont, Hedrick, Martinsburg. The names were familiar, but the towns themselves awoke few memories. By this stage on most trips I was on the floor in a boredom-induced stupor, calling out at fifteen-second intervals, 'How much longer? When are we going to be there? I'm bored. I feel sick.

How much longer? When are we going to be there?' I vaguely recognised a bend in the road near Coppock, where we once spent four hours caught in a blizzard waiting for a snow-plough to come through, and several spots where we had paused to let my sister throw up, including a gas station at Martinsburg where she tumbled out of the car and was lavishly sick in the direction of a pump attendant's ankles (boy did that guy dance!), and another at Wayland where my father nearly left me at the side of the road after discovering that I had passed the time by working loose all the rivets on one of the back door panels, exposing an interesting view of the interior mechanism, but unfortunately rendering both the window and door forever inoperable. However, it wasn't until I reached the turning off for Winfield, just past Olds, a place where my father would announce with a sort of delirious joy that we were practically there, that I felt a pang of recognition. I had not been down this road for at least a dozen years, but its gentle slopes and isolated farms were as familiar to me as my own left leg. My heart soared. This was like going back in time. I was about to be a boy again.

Arriving in Winfield was always thrilling. Dad would turn off Highway 78 and bounce us down a rough gravel road at far too high a speed, throwing up clouds of white dust, and then to my mother's unfailing alarm would drive with evident insanity towards some railroad tracks on a blind bend in the road, remarking gravely, 'I hope there's not a train coming.' My mother didn't discover until years later that there were only two trains a day along those tracks, both in the dead of night. Beyond the tracks, standing alone in a neglected field, was a Victorian mansion like the one in the Charles Addams cartoons in the *New Yorker*. No one had lived in it for decades, but it was still full of furniture, under dank sheets. My sister and brother and I used to climb in through a broken window and look through trunks of musty clothes and old *Collier's* magazines and photographs of strangely worried-looking people. Upstairs was a bedroom in which, according to my brother, lay the shrivelled body of the last occupant, a woman who had died of heartbreak after being abandoned at the altar. We never went in there, though once, when I was about four, my brother peered through the keyhole, let out a howl, cried 'She's coming!' and ran headlong down the stairs. Whimpering, I followed, squirting urine at every step. Beyond the mansion was a wide field, full of black and white cows, and beyond that was my grandparents' house, pretty and white beneath a canopy of trees, with a big red barn and acres of lawn. My grandparents were always waiting at the gate. I don't know whether they could see us coming and raced to their positions or whether they just waited there hour after hour. Quite possibly the latter because, let's face it, they didn't have a whole lot else to do. And then it would be four or five days of fun. My grandfather had a Model T Ford, which he let us kids drive around the yard, to the distress of his chickens and the older women. In the winter he would attach a sleigh to the back and take us for long cold rides down snowy roads. In the evenings we would all play cards around the kitchen table and stay up late. It was always Christmas at my grandparents' house, or Thanksgiving, or the Fourth of July, or somebody's birthday. There was always happiness there.

When we arrived, my grandmother would scuttle off to pull something fresh-baked out of the oven. This was always something unusual. My grandmother was the only person I ever knew – possibly the only person who ever lived – who actually made things from the recipes on the backs of food packets. These dishes always had names like 'Rice Krispies 'n' Banana Chunks Upside-Down Cake' or 'Del Monte Lima Bean 'n' Pretzels Party Snacks'. Generally they consisted of suspiciously large amounts of the manufacturer's own products, usually in combinations you wouldn't think of except perhaps in an especially severe famine. The one thing to be said for these dishes was that they were novel. When my grandmother offered you a steaming slab of cake or wedge of pie it might contain almost anything – Niblets sweet corn, chocolate chips, Spam, diced carrots, peanut butter. Generally it would have some Rice Krispies in it somewhere. My grandmother was particularly partial to Rice Krispies and would add a couple of shovelfuls to whatever she made, even if the recipe didn't call for it. She was about as bad a cook as you can be without actually being hazardous.

It all seems so long ago now. And it was. It was so long ago, in fact, that my grandparents had a crank telephone, the kind that hung on the wall and had a handle you turned and said, 'Mabel, get me Gladys Scribbage. I want to ask her how she makes her Frosted Flakes 'n' Cheez Whiz Party Nuggets.' And it would turn out that Gladys Scribbage was already listening in, or somebody else listening in would know how to make Frosted Flakes 'n' Cheez Whiz Party Nuggets. Everybody listened in. My grandmother often listened in when things were slow around the house, covering the mouthpiece with a hand and relaying to the rest of the room vivid accounts of colonic irrigations, prolapsed wombs, husbands who ran off to Burlington with the barmaid from Vern's Uptown Tavern and Supper Club, and other crises of small-town life. We always had to maintain the strictest silence during these sessions. I could never entirely understand why, because if things got really juicy my grandmother would often butt in. 'Well, I think Merle's a real skunk,' she would say. 'Yes, that's right, it's Maude Bryson here, and I just want to say that I think he's an absolute stinker to do that to poor Pearl. And I'll tell you something else, Mabel, you know you could get those support bras a dollar cheaper in Columbus Junction.' In about 1962 the telephone company came and put a normal phone without a party line in my grandmother's house, possibly at the request of the rest of the town. It drove a hole right through her life from which she never entirely recovered.

I didn't really expect my grandparents to be waiting for me at the gate, on account of them both having been dead for many years. But I suppose I had vaguely hoped that another nice old couple might be living there now and would invite me in to look around and share my reminiscences. Perhaps they would let me be their grandson. At the very least, I had assumed that my grandparents' house would be just as I had last seen it.

It was not to be. The road leading to the house was still gravelled with gleaming gypsum pebbles and still threw up satisfying clouds of dust, but the railroad tracks were gone. There was no sign that they had ever been there. The Victorian mansion was gone too, replaced by a ranch-house-style home with cars and propane gas cylinders scattered around the yard like a toddler's playthings. Worse still, the field of cows was now an estate of box houses. My grandparents' home had stood well outside the town, a cool island of trees in an ocean of fields. Now cheap little houses crowded in on it from all sides. With shock, I realised that the barn was gone. Some jerk had torn down my barn! And the house itself – well, it was a shack. Paint had abandoned it in chunks. Bushes had been pointlessly uprooted, trees chopped down. The grass was high and littered with overspill from the house. I stopped the car on the road out front and just gaped. I cannot describe the sense of loss. Half my memories were inside that house. After a moment a hugely overweight woman in pink shorts, talking on a phone with an apparently endless cord, came and stood in the open doorway and stared at me, wondering what I was doing staring at her.

I drove on into the town. When I was growing up, Main Street in Winfield had two grocery stores, a variety store, a tavern, a pool hall, a newspaper, a bank, a barbershop, a post office, two gas stations – all the things you would expect of any thriving little town. Everyone shopped locally; everyone knew everyone else. Now all that was left was a tavern and a place selling farm equipment. There were half a dozen vacant lots, full of patchy grass, where buildings had been torn down and never replaced. Most of the remaining buildings were dark and boarded up. It was like an abandoned film set which had long since been left to decay.

I couldn't understand what had happened. People now must have to drive thirty miles to buy a loaf of bread. Outside the tavern a group of young thuggy-looking motorcyclists were hanging out. I was going to stop to ask them what had happened to their town, but one of them, seeing me slow down, gave me the finger. For no reason. He was about fourteen. Abruptly, I drove on, back out towards Highway 78, past the scattered farms and gentle slopes that I knew like my own left leg. It was the first time in my life that I had turned my back on a place knowing that I would never see it again. It was all very sad, but I should have known better. As I always used to tell Thomas Wolfe, there are three things you just can't do in life. You can't beat the phone company, you can't make a waiter see you until he's ready to see you, and you can't go home again.

THREE

I drove on, without the radio or much in the way of thoughts, to Mount Pleasant, where I stopped for coffee. I had the Sunday *New York Times* with me – one of the greatest improvements in life since I had been away was that you could now buy the *New York Times* out of machines on the day of publication in a place like Iowa, an extraordinary feat of distribution – and I spread out with it in a booth. Boy, do I love the Sunday *New York Times*. Apart from its many virtues as a newspaper, there is just something wonderfully reassuring about its very bulk. The issue in front of me must have weighed ten or twelve pounds. It could've stopped a bullet at twenty yards. I read once that it takes 75,000 trees to produce one issue of the Sunday *New York Times* – and it's well worth every trembling leaf. So what if our grandchildren have no oxygen to breathe? Fuck 'em.

My favourite parts of the *Times* are the peripheral bits – the parts that are so dull and obscure that they exert a kind of hypnotic fascination, like the home improvements column ('All You Need to Know About Fixings and Fastenings') and the stamps column ('Post Office Marks 25 Years of Aeronautic Issues'). Above all, I love the advertising supplements. If a Bulgarian asked me what life was like in America, I would without hesitation tell him to get hold of a stack of *New York Times* advertising supplements. They show a life of richness and variety beyond the wildest dreams of most foreigners. As if to illustrate my point, the issue before me contained a gift catalogue from the Zwingle Company of New York offering scores of products of the things-you-never-knew-you-needed variety – musical shoe-trees, an umbrella with a transistor radio in the handle, an electric nail buffer. What a great country! My favourite was a small electric hotplate you could put on your desk to keep your coffee from going cold. This must be a real boon to people with brain damage, the sort of injuries that lead them to wander off and neglect their beverages. And epileptics all over America must be feeling equally grateful. ('Dear Zwingle Company: I can't tell you how many times I have come around from a *grand mal* seizure to find myself lying on the floor thinking, "Oh God, I bet my coffee's gone cold again." ') Really, who buys these things – silver toothpicks and monogrammed underpants and mirrors that say Man of the Year on them? I have often thought that if I ran one of these companies I would produce a polished mahogany plaque with a brass plate on it saying 'Hey, how about me? I paid $22·95 for this completely useless piece of crap'. I'm certain they would sell like hot cakes.

Once in a deranged moment I bought something myself from one of these catalogues, knowing deep in my mind that it would end in heartbreak. It was a little reading light that you clipped on to your book so as not to disturb your bedmate as she slumbered beside you. In this respect it was outstanding because it barely worked. The light it cast was absurdly feeble (in the catalogue it looked like the sort of thing you could signal ships with if you got lost at sea) and left all but the first two lines of a page in darkness. I have seen more luminous insects. After about four minutes its little beam fluttered and failed altogether, and it has never been used again. And the thing is that I knew all along that this was how it was going to end, that it would all be a bitter disappointment. On second thought, if I ever ran one of those companies I would just send people an empty box with a note in it saying 'We have decided not to send you the item you've ordered because, as you well know, it would never properly work and you would only be disappointed. So let this be a lesson to you for the future.'

From the Zwingle catalogue I moved on to the food and household products advertisements. There is usually a wodge of these bright and glossy inducements to try out exciting new products – things with names like Hunk o' Meat Beef Stew 'n' Gravy ('with rich 'n' meaty chunks of beef-textured fibre') and Sniffa-Snax ('An Exciting New Snack Treat You Take Through the Nose!') and Country Sunshine Honey-Toasted Wheat Nut 'n' Sugar Bits Breakfast Cereal ('Now with Vitamin-Enriched Chocolate-Covered Raisin Substitute!'). I am endlessly fascinated by these new products. Clearly, some time ago makers and consumers of American junk food passed jointly through some kind of sensibility barrier in the endless quest for new taste sensations. Now they are a little like those desperate junkies who have tried every known drug and are finally reduced to mainlining toilet bowl cleanser in an effort to get still higher. All over America you can see countless flabby-butted couples quietly searching supermarket shelves for new combinations of flavours, hoping to find some untried product that will tingle in their mouths and excite, however briefly, their leaden tastebuds.

The competition for this market is intense. The food inserts not only offered 50¢ discounts and the like, but also if you sent off two or three labels the manufacturers would dispatch to you a Hunk o' Meat Beach Towel, or Country Sunshine Matching Apron and Oven Mitt, or a Sniffa-Snax hotplate for keeping your coffee warm while you slipped in and out of consciousness from a surfeit of blood sugar. Interestingly, the advertisements for dog food were much the same, except that they weren't usually chocolate-flavoured. In fact, every single product – from the lemon-scented toilet bowl cleansers to the scent-o-pine trash bags – promised to give you a brief buzz. It's no wonder that so many Americans have a glazed look. They are completely junked out.

I drove on south on Highway 218 to Keokuk. This stretch of the road was marked on my map as a scenic route, though these things are decidedly relative. Talking about a scenic route in south-east Iowa is like talking about a good Barry Manilow album. You have to make certain allowances. Compared with an afternoon in a darkened room, it wasn't bad. But compared with, say, the coast road along the Sorrentine peninsula, it was perhaps a little tame. Certainly it didn't strike me as being any more or less scenic than any of the other roads I had been on today. Keokuk is a Mississippi River town where Iowa, Illinois and Missouri face each other across a broad bend in the river. I was heading towards Hannibal in Missouri and was hoping to see a bit of the town *en route* to the bridge south. But before I knew it, I found myself on a bridge going east to Illinois. I was so disconcerted by this that I only caught a glimpse of the river, a glistening smear of brown stretching off in two directions, and then, chagrined, I was in Illinois. I had really looked forward to seeing the Mississippi. Crossing it as a child had always been an adventure. Dad would call, 'Here's the Mississippi, kids!' and we would scramble to the window to find ourselves on a bridge practically in the clouds, so high it made our breath catch, and the silvery river far, far below, wide, majestic, serene, going about its timeless business of just rolling on. You could see for miles – a novel experience in Iowa. You could see barges and islands and riverside towns. It looked wonderful. And then, abruptly, you were in Illinois and it was flat and full of corn and you realised with a sinking heart that that was it. That was your visual stimulation for the day. Now you had hundreds more miles of arid cornland to cross before you would experience even the most fractional sense of pleasure.

And now here I was in Illinois, and it was flat and full of corn and boring. A childlike voice in my head cried, 'When are we going to be there? I'm bored. Let's go home. When are we going to be there?' Having confidently expected at this stage to be in Missouri, I had my book of maps opened to the Missouri page, so I pulled over to the side of the road, in a state of some petulance, to make a cartographical adjustment. A sign just ahead of me said BUCKLE UP. ITS THE LAW IN ILLINOIS. Clearly, however, it was not an offence to be unable to punctuate. Frowning, I studied my maps. If I turned off at Hamilton, just down the road, I could drive along the east bank of the river and cross into Missouri at Quincy. It was even marked on the map as a scenic route; perhaps my blundering would turn out to be no bad thing.

I followed the road through Warsaw, a run-down little river town. A steep hill plunged down towards the river, but then turned inland and again I caught no more than a glimpse of the river. Almost immediately, the landscape spread out into a broad alluvial plain. The sun was sinking in the sky. To the left hills rose up, flecked with trees that were just beginning to show a blush of autumn colour. To the right the land was as flat as a table-top. Teams of combine harvesters laboured in the fields, kicking up dust, working late to bring in the harvest. In the far distance, grain elevators caught the fading sun and glowed an opalescent white, as if lit from within. Somewhere out there, unseen, was the river.

I drove on. The road was completely unsignposted. They do this to you a lot in America, particularly on country roads that go from nowhere to nowhere. You are left to rely on your own sense of direction to find your way – which in my case, let us not forget, had only recently delivered me to the wrong state. I calculated that if I were going south the sun should be to my right (a conclusion I reached by imagining myself in a tiny car driving across a big map of America), but the road twisted and wandered, causing the sun to drift teasingly in front of me, first to this side of the road, then to that. For the first time all day, I had a sense of being in the heart of a vast continent, in the middle of nowhere.

Abruptly the highway turned to gravel. Gypsum nuggets, jagged as arrowheads, flew up against the underside of the car and made a fearful din. I had visions of hosepipes rupturing, hot oil spraying everywhere, me rolling to a steamy, hissing halt out here on this desolate road. The wandering sun was just settling on to the horizon, splashing the sky with faint pinks. Uneasily I drove on, and steeled myself for the prospect of a night spent beneath the stars, with dog-like animals sniffing at my feet and snakes finding warmth up a trouser leg. Ahead of me on the road an advancing storm of dust became after a moment a pickup truck, which passed in a hell-bent fashion, spraying the car with rocky projectiles, which thumped against the sides and bounced off the windows with a cracking sound, and then left me adrift in a cloud of dust. I trundled on, peering helplessly through the murk. It cleared just in time to show me that I was twenty feet from a T-junction with a stop sign. I was going fifty miles an hour, which on gravel leaves you with a stopping distance of about three miles. I jumped on the brakes with all my feet and made a noise like Tarzan missing a vine as the car went into a skid. It slid sideways past the stop sign and out onto a paved highway, where it came to a halt, rocking gently from side to side. At that instant an enormous semi-trailer truck – all silver horns and flashing lights – blared mightily at me as it swept past, setting the car rocking again. Had I slid out on to the highway three seconds earlier it would have crushed the car into something about the size of a stock cube. I pulled on to the shoulder and got out to examine the damage. It looked as if the car had been dive-bombed with bags of flour. Bits of raw metal showed through where the paint had been pinged away. I thanked God that my mother was so much smaller than me. I sighed, suddenly feeling lost and far from home, and noticed ahead a road sign pointing the way to Quincy. I had come to a halt facing in the right direction, so at least something had come of it.

It was time to stop. Just down the road stood a little town, which I shall call Dullard lest the people recognise themselves and take me to court or come to my house and batter me with baseball bats. On the edge of town was an old motel which looked pretty seedy, though judging by the absence of charred furniture in the front yard it was clearly a step up from the sort of place my dad would have chosen. I pulled on to the gravel drive and went inside. A woman of about seventy-five was sitting behind the desk. She wore butterfly glasses and a beehive hairdo. She was doing one of those books that require you to find words in a mass of letters and circle them. I think it was called 'Word Puzzles for Morons'.

'Help yew?' she drawled without looking up.

'I'd like a room for the night, please.'

'That'll be thirty-eight dollars and fifty cents,' she replied, as her pen fell greedily on the word YUP.

I was nonplussed. In my day a motel room cost about $12. 'I don't want to *buy* the room,' I explained. 'I just want to sleep in it for one night.'

She looked at me gravely over the tops of her glasses. 'The room is thirty-eight dollars and fifty cents. Per night. Plus tax. You want it or not?' She had one of those disagreeable accents that add a syllable to every word. 'Tax' came out as 'tayax'.

We both knew that I was miles from anywhere. 'Yes, please,' I said contritely. I signed in and crunched across the gravel to my *suite du nuit*. There appeared to be no other customers. I went into my room with my bag and had a look around, as you do in a new place. There was a black and white TV which appeared to get only one channel and three bent coat-hangers. The bathroom mirror was cracked, and the shower curtains didn't match. The toilet seat had a strip of paper across it saying 'Sanitized For Your Protection', but floating beneath it was a cigarette butt, adrift in a little circle of nicotine. Dad would have liked it here, I thought.

I had a shower – that is to say, water dribbled onto my head from a nozzle in the wall – and afterwards went out to check out the town. I had a meal of gristle and baked wiffle ball at a place called – aptly – Chuck's. I didn't think it was possible to get a truly bad meal anywhere in the Midwest, but Chuck managed to provide it. It was the worst food I had ever had – and remember, I've lived in Britain. It had all the attributes of chewing-gum, except flavour. Even now when I burp I can taste it.

Afterwards I had a look around the town. There wasn't much. It was mostly just one street, with a grain silo and railroad tracks at one end and my motel at the other, with a couple of gas stations and grocery stores in between. Everyone regarded me with interest. Years ago, in the midst of a vivid and impressionable youth, I read a chilling story by Richard Matheson about a remote hamlet whose inhabitants waited every year for a lone stranger to come to town so that they could roast him for their annual barbecue. The people here watched me with barbecue eyes.

Feeling self-conscious I went into a dark place called Vern's Tap and took a scat at thc bar. I was thc only customer, apart from an old man in the corner with only one leg. The barmaid was friendly. She wore butterfly glasses and a beehive hairdo. You could see in an instant that she had been the local good-time girl since about 1931. She had 'Ready for Sex' written all over her face, but 'Better Bring a Paper Bag' written all over her body. Somehow she had managed to pour her capacious backside into some tight red toreador pants and to stretch a clinging blouse over her bosom. She looked as if she had dressed in her granddaughter's clothes by mistake. She was about sixty. It was pretty awful. I could see why the guy with one leg had chosen to sit in the farthest corner.

I asked her what people in Dullard did for fun. 'What exactly did you have in mind, honey?' she said, and rolled her eyes suggestively. The 'Ready for Sex' signs flickered, an occurrence I found unsettling. I wasn't used to being hustled by women, though somehow I had always known that when the moment came it would be in some place like downstate Illinois with a sixty-year-old grandmother. 'Well, perhaps something in the way of legitimate theatre or maybe an international chess congress,' I croaked weakly. However, once we established that I was only prepared to love her for her mind, she became quite sensible and even rather charming. Shc told mc in grcat and frank dctail about hcr life, which seemed to have involved a dizzying succession of marriages to guys who were now in prison or dead as a result of shoot-outs, and dropped in breathtakingly candid disclosures like: 'Now Jimmy kilt his mother, I never did know why, but Curtis never kilt nobody except once by accident when he was robbing a gas station and his gun went off. And Floyd – he was my fourth husband – he never kilt nobody either, but he used to break people's arms if they got him riled.'

'You must have some interesting family reunions,' I ventured politely.

'I don't know what ever became of Floyd,' she went on. 'He had a little cleft in his chin rot year' – after a moment I realised that this was Downstate Illinois for 'right here, on this very spot indicated' – 'that made him look kind of like Kirk Douglas. He was real cute, but he had a temper on him. I got a two-foot scar right across my back where he cut me with an ice-pick. You wanna see it?' She started to hoist up her blouse, but I stopped her. She went on and on like that for ages. Every once in a while the guy in the corner, who was clearly eavesdropping, would grin, showing large yellow teeth. I expect Floyd had torn his leg off in a moment of high spirits. At the end of our conversation, the barmaid gave me a sideways look, as if I had been slyly trying to fool her, and said, 'Say, where do you come from anyway, honey?'

I didn't feel like giving her my whole life story, so I just said, 'Great Britain.'

'Well, I'll tell you one thing, honey,' she said, 'for a foreigner you speak English real good.'

Afterwards I retired with a six-pack to my motel, where I discovered that the bed, judging by its fragrance and shape, had only recently been vacated by a horse. It had a sag in it so severe that I could only see the TV at its foot by splaying my legs to their widest extremity. It was like lying in a wheelbarrow. The night was hot and the air conditioner, an aged Philco window unit, expended so much energy making a noise like a steelworks that it could only manage to emit the feeblest and most occasional puffs of cool air. I lay with the six-pack on my chest, effectively immobilised, and drank the beers one by one. On the TV was a talk show presided over by some smooth asshole in a blazer whose name I didn't catch. He was the kind of guy for whom personal hair care was clearly a high priority. He exchanged some witless banter with the bandleader, who of course had a silvery goatee, and then turned to the camera and said in a solemn voice, 'But seriously, folks. If you've ever had a personal problem or trouble at work or you just can't seem to get a grip on life, I know you're gonna be real interested in what our first guest has to tell you tonight. Ladies and gentlemen: Dr Joyce Brothers.'

As the band launched into a perky tune and Joyce Brothers strode onstage, I sat up as far as the bed would allow me and cried, 'Joyce!

Joyce Brothers!' as if to an old friend. I couldn't believe it. I hadn't seen Joyce Brothers for years and she hadn't changed a bit. Not one hair on her head had altered a fraction since the last time I saw her, droning on about menstrual flow, in 1962. It was as if they had kept her in a box for twenty-five years. This was as close as I would ever come to time travel. I watched agog as she and Mr Smoothie chattered away about penis envy and Fallopian tubes. I kept expecting him to say to her, 'Now seriously, Joyce, here's a question all America has been wanting me to ask you: what sort of preparations do you take to keep yourself looking like that? Also, when are you going to do something about that hairstyle? And finally, why is it, do you think, that talk show bozos like me all over America keep inviting you back again and again?' Because, let's be frank, Joyce Brothers is pretty dull. I mean, if you turn on the *Johnny Carson Show* and she is one of the guests you know that absolutely everybody in town must be at some really big party or première. She is like downstate Illinois made flesh.

Still, like most immensely boring things, there is something wonderfully comforting about her. Her cheery visage on the glowing box at the foot of my bed made me feel strangely warm and whole and at peace with the world. Out here in this crudbucket motel in the middle of a great empty plain I began for the first time to feel at home. I somehow knew that when I awoke I would see this alien land in a new but oddly familiar light. With a happy heart, I fell asleep and dreamt gentle dreams of southern Illinois and the rolling Mississippi River and Dr Joyce Brothers. And it's not often you hear anyone say that either.

FOUR

In the morning I crossed the Mississippi at Quincy; somehow it didn't look as big or majestic as I had remembered it. It was stately. It was imposing. It took whole minutes to cross. But it was also somehow flat and dull. This may have had something to do with the weather, which was likewise flat and dull. Missouri looked precisely the same as Illinois, which had looked precisely the same as Iowa. The only difference was that the car licence plates were a different colour.

Near Palmyra, I stopped at a roadside café for breakfast and took a seat at the counter. At this hour, just after eight in the morning, it was full of farmers. If there is one thing farmers sure do love it is to drive into town and spend half a day (a whole day in winter) sitting at a counter with a bunch of other farmers drinking coffee and teasing the waitress in a half-assed sort of way. I had thought that this was the busiest time of their year, but they didn't seem to be in any rush. Every once in a while one of them would put a quarter on the counter, get up with the air of a man who has just loaded six gallons of coffee into his belly, tell Tammy not to do anything he wouldn't do, and depart. A moment later we would hear the grip of his pickup truck's wheels on the gravel drive, someone would say something candid about him, provoking appreciative laughter, and the conversation would drift lazily back to hogs, state politics, Big Eight football and – when Tammy was out of earshot – sexual predilections, not least Tammy's .

The farmer next to me had only three fingers on his right hand. It is a little-noticed fact that most farmers have parts missing off them. This used to trouble me when I was small. For a long time I assumed that it was because of the hazards of farming life. After all, farmers deal with lots of dangerous machinery. But when you think about it, a lot of people deal with dangerous machinery, and only a tiny proportion of them ever suffer permanent injury. Yet there is scarcely a farmer in the Midwest over the age of twenty who has not at some time or other had a limb or digit yanked off and thrown into the next field by some noisy farmyard implement. To tell you the absolute truth, I think farmers do it on purpose. I think working day after day beside these massive threshers and balers with their grinding gears and flapping fan belts and complex mechanisms they get a little hypnotised by all the noise and motion. They stand there staring at the whirring machinery and they think, 'I wonder what would happen if I just stuck my finger in there a little bit.' I know that sounds crazy. But you have to realise that farmers don't have a whole lot of sense in these matters because they feel no pain.

It's true. Every day in the *Des Moines Register* you can find a story about a farmer who has inadvertently torn off an arm and then calmly walked six miles into the nearest town to have it sewn back on. The stories always say, 'Jones, clutching his severed limb, told his physician, "I seem to have cut my durn arm off, Doc."' It's never 'Jones, spurting blood, jumped around hysterically for twenty minutes, fell into a swoon and then tried to run in four directions at once', which is how it would be with you or me. Farmers simply don't feel pain – that little voice in your head that tells you not to do something because it's foolish and will hurt like hell and for the rest of your life somebody will have to cut up your food for you doesn't speak to them. My grandfather was just the same. He would often be repairing the car when the jack would slip and he would call out to you to come and crank it up again as he was having difficulty breathing, or he would run over his foot with the lawn-mower, or touch a live wire, shorting out the whole of Winfield but leaving himself unscathed apart from a ringing in the ears and a certain lingering smell of burnt flesh. Like most people from the rural Midwest, he was practically indestructible. There are only three things that can kill a farmer: lightning, rolling over in a tractor, and old age. It was old age that got my grandfather.

I drove on forty miles south to Hannibal, and went to see Mark Twain's boyhood home, a trim and tidy whitewashed house with green shutters set incongruously in the middle of the downtown. It cost $2 to get in and was a disappointment. It purported to be a faithful reproduction of the original interiors, but there were wires and water sprinklers clumsily evident in every room. I also very much doubt that young Samuel Clemens's bedroom had Armstrong vinyl on the floor (the same pattern as in my mother's kitchen, I was interested to note) or that his sister's bedroom had a plywood partition in it. You don't actually go in the house; you look at it through the windows. At each window there is a recorded message telling you about that room as if you were a moron: 'This is the kitchen. This is where Mrs Clemens would prepare the family's meals . . .'. The whole thing is pretty shabby, which wouldn't be so awful if it were owned by some underfunded local literary society and they were doing the best they could with it. In fact, it is owned by the city of Hannibal and it draws 135,000 visitors a year. It's a little gold mine for the town.

I proceeded from window to window behind a bald fat guy, whose abundant rolls of flesh made him look as if he were wearing an assortment of inner tubes beneath his shirt. 'What do you think of it?' I asked him. He fixed me with that instant friendliness Americans freely adopt with strangers. It is their most becoming trait. 'Oh, I think it's great. I come here whenever I'm in Hannibal – two, three times a year. Sometimes I go out of my way to come here.'

'Really?' I tried not to sound dumbfounded.

'Yeah. I must have been here twenty, thirty times by now. This is a real shrine, you know.'

'You think it's well done?'

'Oh, for sure.'

'Would you say the house is just like Twain described it in his books?'

'I don't know,' the man said thoughtfully, 'I've never read one of his books.'

Next door, attached to the house, was a small museum, which was better. There were cases of Twain memorabilia – first editions, one of his typewriters, photographs, some letters. There was precious little to link him to the house or the town. It is worth remembering that Twain got the hell out of both Hannibal and Missouri as soon as he could, and was always disinclined to come back. I went outside and looked around. Beside the house was a white fence with a sign saying TOM SAWYER'S FENCE. HERE STOOD THE BOARD FENCE WHICH TOM SAWYER PERSUADED HIS GANG TO PAY HIM FOR THE PLEASURE OF WHITE-WASHING. TOM SAT BY AND SAW THAT IT WAS WELL DONE. Really wakes up your interest in literature, doesn't it? Next door to the Twain house and museum – and I mean absolutely right next to it – was the Mark Twain Drive-In Restaurant and Dinette, with cars parked in little bays and people grazing off trays attached to their windows. It really lent the scene a touch of class. I began to understand why Clemens didn't just leave town but also changed his name.

I strolled around the business district. The whole area was a dispiriting combination of auto parts stores, empty buildings and vacant lots. I had always thought that all river towns, even the poor ones, had something about them – a kind of faded elegance, a raffish air – that made them more interesting than other towns, that the river served as a conduit to the larger world and washed up a more interesting and sophisticated brand of detritus. But not Hannibal. It had obviously had better days, but even they couldn't have been all that great. The Hotel Mark Twain was boarded up. That's a sad sight – a tall building with every window plugged with plywood. Every business in town appeared to trade on Twain and his books – the Mark Twain Roofing Company, the Mark Twain Savings and Loan, the Tom 'n' Huck Motel, the Injun Joe Campground and Go-Kart Track, the Huck Finn Shopping Center. You could even go and be insane at the Mark Twain Mental Health Center – a possibility that would, I imagine, grow increasingly likely with every day spent in Hannibal. The whole place was sad and awful. I had been planning to stay for lunch, but the thought of having to face a Tom Sawyer Burger or Injun Joe Cola left me without any appetite for either food or Hannibal.

I walked back to the car. Every parked car along the street had a licence plate that said 'Missouri—the Show Me State'. I wondered idly if this could be short for 'Show Me the Way to Any Other State'. In any case, I crossed the Mississippi – still muddy, still strangely unimpressive – on a long, high bridge and turned my back on Missouri without regret. On the other side a sign said BUCKLE UP. ITS THE LAW IN ILLINOIS. Just beyond it another said AND WE STILL CAN'T PUNCTUATE.

I plunged east into Illinois. I was heading for Springfield, the state capital, and New Salem, a restored village where Abraham Lincoln lived as a young man. My dad had taken us there when I was about five and I thought it was wonderful. I wondered if it still was. I also wanted to see if Springfield was in any way an ideal town. One of the things I was looking for on this trip was the perfect town. I've always felt certain that somewhere out there in America it must exist. When I was small, WHO TV in Des Moines used to show old movies every

afternoon after school, and when other children were out playing kick
the can or catching bullfrogs or encouraging little Bobby Birnbaum to
eat worms (something he did with surprising amenability), I was alone
in a curtained room in front of the TV, lost in a private world, with a
plate of Oreo cookies on my lap and Hollywood magic flickering on
my glasses. I didn't realise it at the time, but the films WHO showed
were mostly classics – *The Best Years of Our Lives, Mr Smith Goes to
Washington, Never Give a Sucker an Even Break, It Happened One
Night*. The one constant in these pictures was the background. It was
always the same place, a trim and sunny little city with a tree-lined
Main Street full of friendly merchants ('Good morning, Mrs Smith!')
and a courthouse square, and wooded neighbourhoods where fine
houses slumbered beneath graceful elms. There was always a paper-
boy on a bike slinging papers onto front porches, and a genial old fart
in a white apron sweeping the sidewalk in front of his drugstore and
two men striding briskly past. These two background men always
wore suits, and they always strode smartly, never strolled or ambled,
but strode in perfect harmony. They were really good at it. No matter
what was going on in the foreground – Humphrey Bogart blowing
away a bad guy with a ·45, Jimmy Stewart earnestly explaining his
ambitions to Donna Reed, W. C. Fields lighting a cigar with the
cellophane still on it – the background was always this timeless,
tranquil place. Even in the midst of the most dreadful crises, when
monster ants were at large in the streets or buildings were collapsing
from some careless scientific experiment out at State University, you
could still generally spot the paper-boy slinging newspapers somewhere in the background and those two guys in suits striding along like
Siamese twins. They were absolutely imperturbable.

And it wasn't just in the movies. Everybody on TV – Ozzie and
Harriet, Wally and Beaver Cleaver, George Burns and Gracie Allen –
lived in this middle-class Elysium. So did the people in the
advertisements in magazines and on the commercials on television and
in the Norman Rockwell paintings on the covers of the *Saturday
Evening Post*. In books it was the same. I used to read Hardy Boys
mysteries one after the other, not for the plots, which even at the age of
eight I could see were ridiculously improbable ('Say, Frank, do you
suppose those fellows with the funny accents that we saw at Moose
Lake yesterday weren't really fishermen, but German spies, and that

the girl in the bottom of their canoe with the bandage around her mouth wasn't really suffering from pyorrhea but was actually Dr Rorshack's daughter? I've got a funny feeling those fellows might even be able to tell us a thing or two about the missing rocket fuel!'). No, I read them for Franklin W. Dixon's evocative, albeit incidental, descriptions of Bayport, the Hardy Boys' home town, a place inexpressibly picturesque, where houses with porch swings and picket fences peeked out on a blue sweep of bay full of sail-boats and skimming launches. It was a place of constant adventures and summers without end.

It began to bother me that I had never seen this town. Every year on vacation we would drive hundreds and hundreds of miles across the country, in an insane pursuit of holiday happiness, toiling over blue hills and brown prairies, through towns and cities without number, but without ever going through anywhere even remotely like that dreamy town in the movies. The places we passed through were hot and dusty and full of scrawny dogs, closed-down movie theatres, grubby diners and gas stations that looked as if they would be grateful to get two customers a week. But I felt sure that it must exist somewhere. It was inconceivable that a nation so firmly attached to small-town ideals, so dedicated in its fantasies to small-town notions, could not have somewhere built one perfect place – a place of harmony and industry, a place without shopping malls and oceanic parking lots, without factories and drive-in churches, without Kwik-Kraps and Jiffi-Shits and commercial squalor from one end to the other. In this timeless place Bing Crosby would be the priest, Jimmy Stewart the mayor, Fred Macmurray the high school principal, Henry Fonda a Quaker farmer. Walter Brennan would run the gas station, a boyish Mickey Rooney would deliver groceries, and somewhere at an open window Deanna Durbin would sing. And in the background, always, would be the kid on a bike and those two smartly striding men. The place I was looking for would be an amalgam of all those towns I had encountered in fiction. Indeed, that might well be its name – Amalgam, Ohio, or Amalgam, North Dakota. It could exist almost anywhere, but it had to exist. And on this trip, I intended to find it.

I drove and drove, through flat farming country and little towns devoid of life: Hull, Pittsfield, Barry, Oxville. On my map, Springfield was about two inches to the right of Hannibal, but it seemed to take hours to get there. In fact, it does take hours to get there. I was only slowly adjusting to the continental scale of America, where states are the size of countries. Illinois is nearly twice as big as Austria, four times the size of Switzerland. There is so much emptiness, so much space between towns. You go through a little place and the dinette looks crowded, so you think, 'Oh, I'll wait till I get to Fuddville before I stop for coffee,' because it's only just down the road, and then you get out on the highway and a sign says FUDDVILLE 102 MILES. And you realize that you are dealing with another scale of geography altogether. There is a corresponding lack of detail on the maps. On British maps every church and public house is dutifully recorded. Rivers of laughable minuteness – rivers you can step across – are landmarks of importance, known for miles around. In America whole towns go missing – places with schools, businesses, hundreds of quiet little lives, just vanish, as effectively as if they had been vaporised.

And the system of roads is only cruelly hinted at. You look at the map and think you spy a short cut between, say, Weinerville and Bewilderment, a straight grey line of county road that promises to shave thirty minutes from your driving time. But when you leave the main highway, you find yourself in a network of unrecorded back roads, radiating out across the countryside like cracks in a pane of broken glass.

The whole business of finding your way around becomes laden with frustration, especially away from the main roads. Near Jacksonville I missed a left turn for Springfield and had to go miles out of my way to get back to where I wanted to be. This happens a lot in America. The highway authorities are curiously reluctant to impart much in the way of useful information, like where you are or what road you are on. This is all the more strange when you consider that they are only too happy to provide all kinds of peripheral facts – NOW ENTERING BUBB COUNTY SOIL CONSERVATION DISTRICT, NATIONAL SPRAT HATCHERY 5 MILES, NO PARKING WED 3 A.M. TO 6 A.M., DANGER: LOW-FLYING GEESE, NOW LEAVING BUBB COUNTY SOIL CONSERVATION DISTRICT. Often on country roads you will come to a crossroads without signposts and then have to drive twenty miles or more without having any confidence in where you are. And then abruptly, without warning, you round a bend and find yourself at an eight-lane intersection with fourteen traffic lights and the most bewildering assortment of signs, all with arrows pointing in different directions. Lake Maggot State Park this way. Curtis Dribble Memorial Expressway over there. US Highway 41 South. US Highway 53 North. Interstate 11/78. Business District this way. Dextrose County Teachers' College that way. Junction 17 West. Junction 17 Not West. No U-Turn. Left Lane Must Turn Left. Buckle Your Seat Belt. Sit Up Straight. Did You Brush Your Teeth This Morning?

Just as you realise that you should be three lanes to the left, the lights change and you are swept off with the traffic, like a cork on a fast river. This sort of thing used to happen to my father all the time. I don't think Dad ever went through a really big and important intersection without getting siphoned off to somewhere he didn't want to be – a black hole of one-way streets, an expressway into the desert, a long and expensive toll bridge to some offshore island, necessitating an embarrassing and costly return trip. ('Hey, mister, didn't you come through here a minute ago from the other direction?') My father's particular speciality was the ability to get hopelessly lost without ever actually losing sight of the target. He never arrived at an amusement park or tourist attraction without first approaching it from several directions, like a pilot making passes over an unfamiliar airport. My sister and brother and I, bouncing on the back seat, could always see it on the other side of the freeway and cry, 'There it is! There it is!' Then after a minute we would spy it from another angle on the far side of a cement works. And then across a broad river. And then on the other side of the freeway again. Sometimes all that would separate us from our goal would be a high chain-link fence. On the other side you could see happy, carefree families parking their cars and getting ready for a wonderful day. 'How did they get in there?' my dad would cry, the veins on his forehead lively. 'Why can't the city put up some signs, for Christ's sake? It's no wonder you can't find your way into the place,' he would add, conveniently overlooking the fact that 18,000 other people, some of them of decidedly limited mental acuity, had managed to get on to the right side of the barbed wire without too much difficulty.

Springfield was a disappointment. I wasn't really surprised. If it were a nice place, someone would have said to me, 'Say, you should go to Springfield. It's a nice place.' I had high hopes for it only because I had always thought it sounded promising. In a part of the world where so many places have harsh, foreign-sounding names full of hard consonants – De Kalb, Du Quoin, Keokuk, Kankakee – Springfield is a little piece of poetry, a name suggesting grassy meadows and cool waters. In fact, it was nothing of the sort. Like all small American cities, it had a downtown of parking lots and tallish buildings surrounded by a sprawl of shopping centres, gas stations and fast food joints. It was neither offensive nor charming. I drove around a little bit, but finding nothing worth stopping for, I drove on to New Salem, twelve miles to the north.

New Salem had a short and not very successful life. The original settlers intended to cash in on the river trade that passed by, but in fact the river trade did just that – passed by – and the town never prospered. In 1837 it was abandoned and would no doubt have been lost to history altogether except that one of its residents from 1831 to 1837 was a young Abraham Lincoln. So now, on a 620-acre site, New Salem has been rebuilt just as it was when Lincoln lived there, and you can go and see why everybody was pretty pleased to clear off. Actually it was very nice. There were about thirty or forty log cabins distributed around a series of leafy clearings. It was a gorgeous autumn afternoon, with a warm breeze and soft sunlight adrift in the trees. It all looked impossibly quaint and appealing. You are not allowed to go in the houses. Instead you walk up to each one and peer through the windows or front door and you get an idea of what life was like for the people who lived there. Mostly it must have been pretty uncomfortable. Every house had a sign telling you about its residents. The historical research was impressively diligent. The only problem was that it all became a little repetitive after a while. Once you have looked through the windows of fourteen log cabins, you find yourself approaching number fifteen with a certain diminution of enthusiasm, and by the time you reach number twenty it is really only politeness that impels you onward. Since they've taken the trouble to build all these cabins and scour the country digging out old rocking-chairs and chamber-pots, you feel that the least you can do is walk around and feign interest at each one. But in your heart you are really thinking that if you never saw a log cabin again you'd be pretty damn pleased. I'm sure that was what Lincoln was thinking when he packed his cases and decided not to be a backwoods merchant any more, but to take up a more rewarding career emancipating Negroes and being President.

Down at the far end of the site, I met an older couple plodding towards me, looking tired. The man gave me a sympathetic look as he passed and said, 'Only two more to go.' Down the path from where they had come I could see one of the two remaining cabins, looking distant and small. I waited until the older couple were safely out of sight around a bend, and then sat down beneath a tree, a handsome oak into whose leaves the first trace of autumn gold was delicately bleeding. I felt a weight lifting from my shoulders and wondered why it was that I had been so enchanted by this place when I was five years old. Were childhoods so boring back then? I knew my own little boy, if driven to this place, would drop to the ground and start hyperventilating at the discovery that he had spent a day and a half sealed in a car only to come and see a bunch of boring log cabins. And looking at it now, I couldn't have blamed him. I mused for a few moments on the question of which was worse, to lead a life so boring that you are easily enchanted or a life so full of stimulus that you are easily bored.

But then it occurred to me that musing is a pointless waste of anyone's time, and instead I went off to see if I could find a Baby Ruth candy bar, a far more profitable exercise.

After New Salem, I took Interstate 55 south, and drove for an hour and a half towards St Louis. It was boring, too. On a road as straight and as wide as an American interstate, fifty-five miles an hour is just too slow. It feels like walking speed. Cars and trucks coming towards you on the opposite carriageway seem to be travelling on one of those pedestrian conveyor belts you find in airports. You can see the people inside, get a long, lingering glimpse into their lives, as they slide past. And there's no sense of driving. You need to put a hand to the wheel occasionally just to confirm your course, but you can take time out to do the most intricate things – count your money, brush your hair, tidy up the car, use the rear-view mirror to search-and-destroy blackheads, read maps and guidebooks, put on or discard articles of clothing. If your car possessed cruise control you could just about climb in the back and take a nap. It is certainly quite easy to forget that you are in charge of two tons of speeding metal, and it is only when you start to scatter emergency cones at roadworks sites or a truck honks at you as you drift into its path that you are jolted back to reality and you realise that henceforth you probably shouldn't leave your seat to search for snack food.

The one thing that can be said is that it leaves you time to think, and to consider questions like why is it that the trees along highways never grow? Some of them must have been there for forty years by now, and yet they are still no more than six feet tall and with only fourteen leaves on them. Is it a particular low-maintenance strain, do you suppose? And here's another one. Why can't they make cereal boxes with pouring spouts? Is some guy at General Foods splitting his sides at the thought that every time people pour out a bowl of cornflakes they spill some of it on the floor? And why is that when you clean a sink, no matter how long you let the water run or how much you wipe it with a cloth there's always a strand of hair and some bits of wet fluff left behind? And just what *do* the Spanish see in flamenco music?

In a forlorn effort to keep from losing my mind, I switched on the radio, but then I remembered that American radio is designed for people who have already lost their minds. The first thing I came across was a commercial for Folger's Coffee. An announcer said in a confidential whisper, 'We went to the world famous Napa Valley Restaurant in California and – without telling the customers – served them Folger's instant coffee instead of the restaurant's usual brand. Then we listened in on hidden microphones.' There followed an assortment of praise for the coffee along the lines of 'Hey, this coffee is fantastic!', 'I've never tasted such rich, full-bodied coffee before!', 'This coffee is so good I can hardly stand it!' and that sort of thing. Then the announcer leapt out and told the diners that it was Folger's coffee, and they all shared a good laugh – and an important lesson about the benefits of drinking quality instant coffee. I twirled the dial. A voice said, 'We'll return to our discussion of maleness in sixty seconds.' I twirled the dial. The warbling voice of a female country singer intoned:

> His hands are tiny
> His arms are short
> But I lean upon him
> For my child support.

I twirled the dial. A voice said, 'This portion of the news is brought

to you by the Airport Barber Shop, Biloxi.' There was then a
commercial for the said barber shop, followed by thirty seconds of
news, all of it related to deaths by cars, fires and gunfire in Biloxi in the
last twenty-four hours. There was no hint that there might be a wider,
yet more violent world beyond the city limits. Then there was another
commercial for the Airport Barber Shop, in case you were so
monumentally cretinous that you had forgotten about it during the
preceding thirty seconds of news. I switched the radio off.

At Litchfield, I left the interstate vowing not to get on one again if I
could possibly help it, and joined a state highway, Illinois 127, heading
south towards Murphysboro and Carbondale. Almost immediately
life became more interesting. There were farms and houses and little
towns to look at. I was still going fifty-five miles an hour, but now I
seemed to be fairly skimming along. The landscape flashed past, more
absorbing than before, more hilly and varied, and the foliage was a
darker blur of green. Signs came and went: TEE PEE MINI MART, B-RITE
FOOD STORE, BETTY'S BEAUTY BOX, SAV-A-LOT FOOD CENTER,
PINCKNEYVILLE COON CLUB, BALD KNOB TRAILER COURT, DAIRY
DELITE, ALL U CAN EAT. In between these shrines to dyslexia and free
enterprise there were clearings on the hillsides where farmhouses
stood. Almost every one had a satellite dish in the yard, pointed to the
sky as if tapping into some life-giving celestial force. I suppose in a
sense they were. Here in the hills, the light failed more quickly. I
noticed with surprise that it was past six o'clock and I decided that I
had better find a room. As if on cue, Carbondale hove into view.

It used to be that when you came to the outskirts of a town you
would find a gas station and a Dairy Queen, maybe a motel or two if it
was a busy road or the town had a college. Now every town, even a
quite modest one, has a mile or more of fast food places, motor inns,
discount cities, shopping malls — all with thirty-foot-high revolving
signs and parking lots the size of Shropshire. Carbondale appeared to
have nothing else. I drove in on a road that became a two-mile strip of
shopping centres and gas stations, K-Marts, J. C. Penneys, Hardees
and McDonald's. And then, abruptly, I was in the country again. I
turned around and drove back through town on a parallel street that
offered precisely the same sorts of things but in slightly different
configurations and then I was in the country again. The town had no
centre. It had been eaten by shopping malls.

I got a room in the Heritage Motor Inn, then went out for a walk to try once more to find Carbondale. But there was nothing there. I was perplexed and disillusioned. Before I had left on this trip I had lain awake at night in my bed in England and pictured myself stopping each evening at a motel in a little city, strolling into town along sidewalks, dining on the blue plate special at Betty's Family Restaurant on the town square, then plugging a scented toothpick in my mouth and going for a stroll around the town, very probably stopping off at Vern's Midnite Tavern for a couple of draws and a game of eight-ball with the boys or taking in a movie at the Regal or looking in at the Val-Hi Bowling Alley to kibitz the Mid-Week Hairdressers' League matches before rounding off the night with a couple of games of pinball and a grilled cheese sandwich. But here there was no square to stroll to, no Betty's, no blue plate specials, no Vern's Midnite Tavern, no movie theatre, no bowling alley. There was no town, just six-lane highways and shopping malls. There weren't even any sidewalks. Going for a walk, as I discovered, was a ridiculous and impossible undertaking. I had to cross parking lots and gas station forecourts, and I kept coming up against little white-painted walls marking the boundaries between, say, Long John Silver's Seafood Shoppe and Kentucky Fried Chicken. To get from one to the other, it was necessary to clamber over the wall, scramble up a grassy embankment and pick your way through a thicket of parked cars. That is if you were on foot. But clearly from the looks people gave me as I lumbered breathlessly over the embankment, no one had ever tried to go from one of these places to another under his own motive power. What you were supposed to do was get in your car, drive twelve feet down the street to another parking lot, park the car and get out. Glumly I clambered my way to a Pizza Hut and went inside, where a waitress seated me at a table with a view of the parking lot.

All around me people were eating pizzas the size of bus wheels. Directly opposite, inescapably in my line of vision, an overweight man of about thirty was lowering wedges into his mouth whole, like a sword swallower. The menu was dazzling in its variety. It went on for pages. There were so many types and sizes of pizza, so many possible permutations, that I felt quite at a loss. The waitress appeared. 'Are you ready to order?'

'I'm sorry,' I replied, 'I need a little more time.'

·'Sure,' she said. 'You take your time.' She went off to somewhere out of my line of vision, counted to four and came back. 'Are you ready to order now?' she asked.

'I'm sorry,' I said, 'I really need just a little more time.'

'OK,' she said, and left. This time she may have counted as high as twenty, but when she returned I was still nowhere near understanding the many hundreds of options open to me as a Pizza Hut patron.

'You're kinda slow arentcha?' she observed brightly.

I was embarrassed. 'I'm sorry. I'm out of touch. I've . . . just got out of prison.'

Her eyes widened. 'Really?'

'Yes. I murdered a waitress who rushed me.'

With an uncertain smile she backed off and gave me lots and lots of time to make up my mind. In the end I had a medium-sized deep dish pepperoni pizza with extra onions and mushrooms, and I can recommend it without hesitation.

Afterwards, to round off a perfect evening, I clambered over to a nearby K-Mart and had a look around. K-Marts are a chain of discount stores and they are really depressing places. You could take Mother Theresa to a K-Mart and she would get depressed. It's not that there's anything wrong with the K-Marts themselves, it's the customers. K-Marts are always full of the sort of people who give their children names that rhyme: Lonnie, Donnie, Ronnie, Connie, Bonnie. The sort of people who would stay in to watch *The Munsters*. Every woman there has at least four children and they all look as if they have been fathered by a different man. The woman always weighs 250 pounds. She is always walloping a child and bawling; 'If you don't behave, Ronnie, I'm not gonna bring you back here no more!' As if Ronnie could give a toss about never going to a K-Mart again. It's the place you would go if you wanted to buy a stereo system for under $35 and didn't care if it sounded like the band was playing in a mailbox under water in a distant lake. If you go shopping at K-Mart you know that you've touched bottom. My dad liked K-Marts.

I went in and looked around. I picked up some disposable razors and a pocket notebook, and then, just to make an occasion of it, a bag of Reese's Peanut Butter Cups, which were attractively priced at $1·29. I paid for these and went outside. It was 7·30 in the evening. The stars were rising above the parking lot. I was alone with a small bag of pathetic treats in the most boring town in America and frankly I felt sorry for myself. I clambered over a wall and dodged across the highway to a Kwik-Krap mini supermarket, purchased a cold six-pack of Pabst Blue Ribbon beer, and returned with it to my room where I watched cable TV, drank beer, messily ate Reese's Peanut Butter Cups (wiping my hands on the sheets) and drew meagre comfort from the thought that in Carbondale, Illinois, that was about as good a time as you were ever likely to get.

FIVE

In the morning I rejoined Highway 127 south. This was marked on my map as a scenic route and for once this proved to be so. It really was attractive countryside, better than anything I knew Illinois possessed, with rolling hills of winebottle green, prosperous-looking farms and deep woods of oak and beech. Surprisingly, considering I was heading south, the foliage here was more autumnal than elsewhere – the hillsides were a mixture of mustard, dull orange and pale green, quite fetching – and the clear, sunny air had an agreeable crispness to it. I could live here, in these hills, I thought.

It took me a while to figure out what was missing. It was billboards. When I was small, billboards thirty feet wide and fifteen feet high stood in fields along every roadside. In places like Iowa and Kansas they were about the only stimulation you got. In the 1960s Lady Bird Johnson, in one of those misguided campaigns in which Presidents' wives are always engaging themselves, had most of the roadside billboards removed as part of a highway beautification programme. In the middle of the Rocky Mountains this was doubtless a good thing, but out here in the lonesome heartland billboards were practically a public service. Seeing one standing a mile off you would become interested to see what it said, and would watch with mild absorption as it advanced towards you and passed. As roadside excitements went, it was on about a par with the little windmills in Pella, but it was better than nothing.

The superior billboards would have a three-dimensional element to them – the head of a cow jutting out if it was for a dairy, or a cut-out of a bowling ball scattering pins if it was for a bowling alley. Sometimes the billboard would be for some coming attraction. There might be a figure of a ghost and the words. VISIT SPOOK CAVERNS! OKLAHOMA'S GREAT FAMILY ATTRACTION! JUST 69 MILES! A couple of miles later there would be another sign saying PLENTY OF FREE PARKING AT SPOOK CAVERNS, JUST 67 MILES! And so it would go, with sign after sign promising the most thrilling and instructive afternoon any family could ever hope to have, at least in Oklahoma. These promises would be supported by illustrations showing eerily-lit underground chambers, the size of cathedrals, in which the stalactites and stalagmites had magically fused into the shapes of witches' houses, bubbling cauldrons, flying bats and Casper the Friendly Ghost. It all looked extremely promising. So we children in the back would begin suggesting that we stop and have a look, taking it in turns to say, in a sincere and moving way, 'Oh, *please* Dad, oh, pleeeeease.'

Over the next sixty miles my father's position on the matter would proceed through a series of well-worn phases, beginning with a flat refusal on the grounds that it was bound to be expensive and anyway our behaviour since breakfast had been so disgraceful that it didn't warrant any special treats, to studiously ignoring our pleas (this phase would last for up to eleven minutes), to asking my mother privately in a low voice what she thought about the idea and receiving an equivocal answer, to ignoring us again in the evident hope that we would forget about it and stop nagging (one minute, twelve seconds), to saying that we *might* go if we started to behave and kept on behaving more or less forever, to saying that we definitely would *not* go because, just look at us, we were already squabbling again and we hadn't even gotten there, to finally announcing – sometimes in an exasperated bellow, sometimes in a death-bed whisper – that all right, we would go. You could always tell when Dad was on the brink of acceptance because his neck would turn red. It was always the same. He always said yes in the end. I never understood why he didn't just accede to our demands at the outset and save himself thirty minutes of anguish. Then he would always quickly add, 'But we're only going for half an hour – and you're not going to buy anything. Is that clear?' This seemed to restore to him a sense that he was in charge of things.

By the last two or three miles, the signs for Spook Caverns would be every couple of hundred yards, bringing us to a fever pitch of excitement. Finally there would be a billboard the size of a battleship with a huge arrow telling us to turn right here and drive eighteen miles. 'Eighteen miles!' Dad would cry shrilly, his forehead veins stirring to life in preparation for the inevitable discovery that after eighteen miles of bouncing down a dirt road with knee-deep ruts there would be no sign of Spook Caverns, that, indeed, after nineteen miles the road would end in a desolate junction without any clue to which way to turn, and that Dad would turn the wrong way. When eventually found, Spook Caverns would prove to be rather less than advertised – in fact, would give every appearance of being in the last stages of solvency. The caverns, damp and ill-lit and smelling like a long-dead horse, would be about the size of a garage and the stalactites and stalagmites wouldn't look the least bit like witches' houses and Casper the Ghost. They would look like – well, like stalactites and stalagmites. It would all be a huge let-down. The only possible way of assuaging our disappointment, we would discover, would be if Dad bought us each a rubber Bowie knife and bag of plastic dinosaurs in the adjoining gift shop. My sister and I would drop to the ground and emit mournful noises to remind him what a fearful thing unassuaged grief can be in a child.

So, as the sun sank over the brown flatness of Oklahoma and Dad, hours behind schedule, embarked on the difficult business of not being able to find a room for the night (ably assisted by my mother, who would misread the maps and mistakenly identify almost every approaching building as a possible motel), we children would pass the time in the back by having noisy and vicious knife fights, breaking off at intervals to weep, report wounds and complain of hunger, boredom and the need for toilet facilities. It was a kind of living hell. And now there appeared to be almost no billboards along the highways. What a sad loss.

I headed for Cairo, which is pronounced Kay-ro. I don't know why. They do this a lot in the South and Midwest. In Kentucky, Athens is pronounced AY-thens and Versailles is pronounced Vur-SAYLES. Bolivar, Missouri, is BAW-liv-er. Madrid, Iowa, is MAD-rid. I don't know whether the people in these towns pronounce them that way because they are backward undereducated shitkickers who don't know any better or whether they know better but don't care that everybody thinks they are backward undereducated shitkickers. It's not really the sort of question you can ask them, is it? At Cairo I stopped for gas and in fact I did ask the old guy who doddered out to fill my tank why they pronounced Cairo as they did.

'Because that's its *name*,' he explained as if I were kind of stupid.

'But the one in Egypt is pronounced Ki-ro.'

'So I've heard,' agreed the man.

'And most people, when they see the name, think Ki-ro, don't they?'

'Not in Kay-ro they don't,' he said, a little hotly.

There didn't seem to be much to be gained by pursuing the point, so I let it rest there, and I still don't know why the people call it Kay-ro. Nor do I know why any citizen of a free country would choose to live in such a dump, however you pronounce it. Cairo is at the point where the Ohio River, itself a great artery, joins the Mississippi, doubling its grandeur. You would think that at the confluence of two such mighty rivers there would be a great city, but in fact Cairo is a poor little town of 6,000 people. The road in was lined with battered houses and unpainted tenements. Aged black men sat on the porches and stoops on old sofas and rocking-chairs, waiting for death or dinner, whichever came first. This surprised me. You don't expect to see tenements and porches full of black people in the Midwest – at least not outside big cities like Chicago and Detroit. But then I realised that I was no longer really in the Midwest. The speech patterns of southern Illinois are more Southern than Midwestern. I was nearly as far south as Nashville. Mississippi was only 160 miles away. And Kentucky was just across the river. I crossed it now, on a long, high bridge. From here on down to Louisiana the Mississippi is immensely broad. It looks safe and lazy, but in fact it is full of danger. Scores of people die in it every year. Farmers out fishing stare at the water and think, 'I wonder what would happen if I just stuck my toe in there a little bit,' and the next thing you know their bodies bob up in the Gulf of Mexico, bloated but looking strangely serene. The river is deceptively fierce. In 1927, when the Mississippi overflowed, it flooded an area the size of Scotland. That is a serious river.

On the Kentucky side of the river I was greeted by huge signs everywhere saying FIREWORKS! In Illinois fireworks are illegal; in Kentucky they are not. So if you live in Illinois and want to blow your hand off, you drive across the river to Kentucky. You used to see a lot more of this sort of thing. If one state had a lower sales tax on cigarettes than a neighbouring state, all the state-line gas stations and cafés would put big signs on their roofs saying TAX-FREE CIGARETTES! 40 CENTS A PACK! NO TAX! and all the people from the next state would come and load their cars up with cut-price cigarettes. Wisconsin used to ban margarine to protect its dairy farmers, so everybody in Wisconsin, including all the dairy farmers, would drive to Iowa where there were big signs everywhere saying MARGARINE FOR SALE! All the

Iowans, in the meantime, were driving off to Illinois, where there was no sales tax on anything, or Missouri where the sales tax on gasoline was fifty per cent lower. The other thing you used to get a lot of was states going their own way in terms of daylight saving time, so in the summer Illinois might be two hours adrift from Iowa and one hour behind Indiana. It was all kind of crazy, but it made you realise to what an extent the United States is really fifty independent countries (forty-eight countries in those days). Most of that seems to have gone now, yet another sad loss.

I drove through Kentucky thinking of sad losses and was abruptly struck by the saddest loss of all – the Burma Shave sign. Burma Shave was a shaving cream that came in a tube. I don't know if it's still produced. In fact, I never knew anyone who ever used it. But the Burma Shave company used to put clever signs along the highway. They came in clusters of five, expertly spaced so that you read them as a little poem as you passed: IF HARMONY / IS WHAT YOU CRAVE / THEN GET / A TUBA / BURMA SHAVE. Or: BEN MET / ANNA / MADE A HIT / NEGLECTED BEARD / BEN-ANNA SPLIT. Great, eh? Even in the 1950s the Burma Shave signs were pretty much a thing of the past. I can only remember seeing half a dozen in all the thousands of miles of highway we covered. But as roadside diversions went they were outstanding, ten times better than billboards and Pella's little twirling windmills. The only things that surpassed them for diversion value were multiple car pile-ups with bodies strewn about the highway.

Kentucky was much like southern Illinois – hilly, sunny, attractive – but the scattered houses were less tidy and prosperous-looking than in the north. There were lots of wooded valleys and iron bridges over twisting creeks, and an abundance of dead animals pasted to the road. In every valley stood a little white Baptist church and all along the road were signs to remind me that I was now in the Bible Belt: JESUS SAVES. PRAISE THE LORD. CHRIST IS KING.

I was out of Kentucky almost before I knew it. The state tapers to a point at its western edge, and I was cutting across a chunk of it only forty miles wide. In a veritable eyeblink in terms of American travelling time I was in Tennessee. It isn't often you can dispense with a state in less than an hour, and Tennessee would not detain me much longer. It is an odd-looking state, shaped like a Dutch brick, stretching more than 500 miles from east to west, but only 100 miles from top to

bottom. Its landscape was much the same as that of Kentucky and
Illinois – indeterminate farming country laced with rivers, hills and
religious zealots – but I was surprised, when I stopped for lunch at a
Burger King in Jackson, at how warm it was. It was eighty-three
degrees, according to a sign on the drive-in bank across the street, a
good twenty degrees higher than it had been in Carbondale that
morning. I was still obviously deep in the Bible Belt. A sign in the yard
of a church next door said CHRIST IS THE ANSWER. (The question, of
course, is: What do you say when you strike your thumb with a
hammer?) I went into the Burger King. A girl at the counter said, 'Kin I
hep yew?' I had entered another country.

SIX

Just south of Grand Junction, Tennessee, I passed over the state line into Mississippi. A sign beside the highway said WELCOME TO MISSISSIPPI. WE SHOOT TO KILL. It didn't really. I just made that up. This was only the second time I had ever been to the Deep South and I entered it with a sense of foreboding. It is surely no coincidence that all those films you have ever seen about the South – *Easy Rider*, *In the Heat of the Night*, *Cool Hand Luke*, *Brubaker*, *Deliverance* – depict Southerners as murderous, incestuous, shitty-shoed rednecks. It really is another country. Years ago, in the days of Vietnam, two friends and I drove to Florida during college spring break. We all had long hair. *En route* we took a short cut across the back roads of Georgia and stopped late one afternoon for a burger at a dinette in some dreary little crudville, and when we took our seats at the counter the place fell silent. Fourteen people just stopped eating, their food resting in their mouths, and stared at us. It was so quiet in there you could have heard a fly fart. A whole roomful of good ole boys with cherry-coloured cheeks and bib overalls watched us in silence and wondered whether their shotguns were loaded. It was disconcerting. To them, out here in the middle of nowhere, we were at once a curiosity – some of them had clearly never seen no long-haired, nigger-loving, Northern, college-edjicated, commie hippies in the flesh before – and yet unspeakably loathsome. It was an odd sensation to feel so deeply hated by people who hadn't really had a proper chance to acquaint themselves with one's shortcomings. I remember thinking that our parents didn't have the first idea where we were, other than that we were somewhere in the continental vastness between Des Moines and the Florida Keys, and that if we disappeared we would never be found. I had visions of my family sitting around the living room in years to come and my mother saying, 'Well, I wonder whatever happened to Billy and his friends. You'd think we'd have had a postcard by now. Can I get anybody a sandwich?'

That sort of thing did really happen down there, you know. This was only five years after three freedom riders were murdered in Mississippi. They were a twenty-one-year-old black from Mississippi named James Chaney and two white guys from New York, Andrew Goodman, twenty, and Michael Schwerner, twenty. I give their names because they deserve to be remembered. They were arrested for speeding, taken to the Neshoba County Jail in Philadelphia, Mississippi, and never seen again – at least not until weeks later when their bodies were hauled out of a swamp. These were kids, remember. The police had released them to a waiting mob, which had taken them away and done things to them that a child wouldn't do to an insect. The sheriff in the case, a smirking, tobacco-chewing fat boy named Lawrence Rainey, was acquitted of negligent behaviour. No one was ever charged with murder. To me this was and always would be the South.

I followed Highway 7 south towards Oxford. It took me along the western edge of the Holly Springs National Forest, which seemed to be mostly swamp and scrubland. I was disappointed. I had half expected that as soon as I crossed into Mississippi there would be Spanish mosses hanging from the trees and women in billowy dresses twirling parasols and white-haired colonels with handlebar moustaches drinking mint juleps on the lawn while darkies gathered the cotton and sang sweet hymns. But this landscape was just scrubby and hot and nondescript. Occasionally there would be a shack set up on bricks, with an old black man in a rocking-chair on the porch, but precious little sign of life or movement elsewhere.

At the town of Holly Springs stood a sign for Senatobia, and I got briefly excited. Senatobia! What a great name for a Mississippi town! All the stupidity and pomposity of the Old South seemed to be encapsulated in those five golden syllables. Maybe things were picking up. Maybe now I would see chain-gangs toiling in the sun and a prisoner in heavy irons legging it across fields and sloshing through creeks while pursued by bloodhounds, and lynch mobs roaming the streets and crosses burning on lawns. The prospect enlivened me, but I had to calm down because a state trooper pulled up alongside me at a traffic light and began looking me over with that sort of casual disdain you often get when you give a dangerously stupid person a gun and a squad car. He was sweaty and overweight and sat low in his seat. I assume he was descended from the apes like all the rest of us, but clearly in his case it had been a fairly gentle slope. I stared straight ahead with a look that I hoped conveyed seriousness of purpose mingled with a warm heart and innocent demeanour. I could *feel* him looking at me. At the very least I expected him to gob a wad of tobacco juice down the side of my head. Instead, he said, 'How yew doin'?'

This so surprised me that I answered, in a cracking voice, 'Pardon?'

'I said, how yew doin'?'

'I'm fine,' I said. And then added, having lived some years in Britain, 'Thank you.'

'Y'on vacation?'

'Yup.'

'Hah doo lack Miss Hippy?'

'Pardon?'

'I say, Hah doo lack Miss Hippy?'

I was quietly distressed. The man was armed and Southern and I couldn't understand a word he was saying to me. 'I'm sorry,' I said, 'I'm kind of slow, and I don't understand what you're saying.'

'I say' – and he repeated it more carefully – 'how doo yew *lack* Mississippi?'

It dawned on me. 'Oh! I like it fine! I like it heaps! I think it's wonderful. The people are so friendly and helpful.' I wanted to add that I had been there for an hour and hadn't been shot at once, but the light changed and he was gone, and I sighed and thought, 'Thank you, Jesus.'

I drove on to Oxford, home of the University of Mississippi, or 'Ole Miss', as it's known. The people named the town after Oxford in England in the hope that this would persuade the state to build the university there, and the state did. This tells you most of what you need to know about the workings of the Southern mind. Oxford appeared to be an agreeable town. It was built around a square, in the middle of which stood the Lafayette County Courthouse, with a tall clock-tower and Doric columns, basking grandly in the Indian summer sunshine. Around the perimeter of the square were attractive stores and a tourist information office. I went into the tourist information office to get directions to Rowan Oak, William Faulkner's home. Faulkner lived in Oxford for the whole of his life, and his home is now a museum, preserved as it was on the day he died in 1962. It must be unnerving to be so famous that you know they are going to come in the moment you

croak and hang velvet cords across all the doorways and treat
everything with reverence. Think of the embarrassment if you left a
copy of *Reader's Digest Condensed Books* on the bedside table.

Behind the desk sat a large, exceptionally well-dressed black
woman. This surprised me a little, this being Mississippi. She wore a
dark two-piece suit, which must have been awfully warm in the
Mississippi heat. I asked her the way to Rowan Oak.

'You parked on the square?' she said. Actually she said, 'You
pocked on the skwaya?'

'Yes.'

'Okay, honey, you git in yo' car and you makes the skwaya. You
goes out the other end, twoads the university, goes three blocks, turns
rat at the traffic lats, goes down the hill and you there, un'stan?'

'No.'

She sighed and started again. 'You git in yo' car and you makes the
skwaya –'

'What, I drive around the square?'

'That's rat, honey. You *makes* the skwaya.' She was talking to me
the way I would talk to a French person. She gave me the rest of the
instructions and I pretended to understand, though they meant almost
nothing to me. All I kept thinking was what funny sounds they were to
be emerging from such an elegant-looking woman. As I went out the
door she called out, 'Hit doan really matter anyhow cuz hit be's closed
now.' She really said hit; she really said be's.

I said, 'Pardon?'

'Hit be's closed now. You kin look arond the grounz if you woan,
but you caint go insod.'

I wint outsod thinking that Miss Hippy was goan be hard work. I
walked around the square looking at the stores, most of them selling
materials for a country club life-style. Handsome, well-dressed
women bounded in and out. They were all tanned and rich-looking.
On one of the corners was a bookstore with a magazine stand. I went
in and looked around. At the magazine stand I picked up a *Playboy*
and browsed through it. As one does. I was distressed to see that
Playboy is now printed on that awful glossy paper that makes the
pages stick together like wet paper towels. You can't flick through it
any more. You have to prise each page apart, like peeling paper off a
stick of butter. Eventually I peeled my way to the main photo spread. It

was of a naked paraplegic. I swear to God. She was sprawled – perhaps not the best choice of words in the context – in various poses on beds and divans, looking pert and indisputably attractive, but with satiny material draped artfully over her presumably withered legs. Now is it me, or does that seem just a little bit strange?

Clearly *Playboy* had lost its way, and this made me feel old and sad and foreign, because *Playboy* had been a corner-stone of American life for as long as I could remember. Every man and boy I knew read *Playboy*. Some men, like my dad, pretended not to. He used to get embarrassed if you caught him looking at it at the supermarket, and would pretend that he was really looking for *Better Homes and Gardens* or something. But he read it. He even had a little stash of men's magazines in an old hatbox at the back of his clothes closet. Every kid I knew had a father with a little stash of men's magazines which the father thought was secret and which the kids knew all about. Once in a while we would swap our dads' magazines among ourselves and then imagine their perplexity when they went to the closet and found that instead of last month's issue of *Gent* they now possessed a two-year-old copy of *Nugget* and, as a bonus, a paperback book called *Ranchhouse Lust*. You could do this knowing that your dad would never say a word to you about it. All that would happen would be that the next time you went back the stash would be in a different place. I don't know whether women in the 1950s didn't sleep with their husbands or what, but this dedication to girlie magazines was pretty well universal. I think it may have had something to do with the war.

The magazines our fathers read had names like *Dude* and *Swell* and the women in them were unappealing, with breasts like deflated footballs and hips of abundant fleshiness. The women in *Playboy* were young and pretty. They didn't look like somebody you'd meet on shore leave. Beyond the incalculable public service *Playboy* performed by printing pictures of attractive naked women was the way it offered a whole attendant life-style. It was like a monthly manual telling you how to live, how to play the stock market and buy a hi-fi and mix sophisticated cocktails and intoxicate women with your wit and sense of style. Growing up in Iowa, you could use help with such matters. I used to read every issue from cover to cover, even the postal regulations at the bottom of the contents page. We all did. Hugh

Hefner was a hero to all of us. Looking back now, I can hardly believe it because really – let's be frank – Hugh Hefner has always struck me as a kind of an asshole. I mean honestly, if you had all that money, would you want a huge circular bed and to spend your life in a silk dressing-gown and carpet slippers? Would you want to fill a wing of your house with the sort of girls who would be happy to engage in pillow-fights in the nude and wouldn't mind you taking pictures of them while so occupied for publication in a national magazine? Would you want to come downstairs of an evening and find Buddy Hackett, Sammy Davis Jr and Joey Bishop standing around the piano in your living room? Do I hear a chorus of 'Shit, no's' out there? Yet I bought it whole. We all did.

Playboy was like an older brother to my generation. And over the years, just like an older brother, it had changed. It had had a couple of financial reversals, a little problem with gambling, and had eventually moved out to the coast. Just like real brothers do. We had lost touch. I hadn't really thought about it for years. And then here suddenly, in Oxford, Mississippi, of all places, who should I run into but *Playboy*. It was exactly like seeing an old high school hero and discovering that he was bald and boring and still wearing those lurid V-neck sweaters and shiny black shoes with gold braid that you thought were so neat in about 1961. It was a shock to realise that both *Playboy* and I were a lot older than I had thought and that we had nothing in common any more. Sadly I returned the *Playboy* to the rack and realised it would be a long time – well, thirty days anyway – before I picked up another one.

I looked at the other magazines. There were at least 200 of them, but they all had titles like *Machine-Gun Collector*, *Obese Bride*, *Christian Woodworker*, *Home Surgery Digest*. There was nothing for a normal person, so I left.

I drove out on South Lamar Street towards Rowan Oak, having first made the square, following the tourist lady's instructions as best I could, but I couldn't for the life of me find it. To tell you the truth, this didn't disturb me a whole lot because I knew it was closed and in any case I have never managed to read a William Faulkner novel beyond about page three (roughly half-way through the first sentence), so I wasn't terribly interested in what his house looked like. At any rate, in driving around I came across the campus of the University of

Mississippi and that was much more interesting. It was a handsome campus, full of fine buildings that looked like banks and courthouses. Long shadows fell across the lawns. Young people, all looking as healthy and as wholesome as a bottle of milk, walked along with books tucked under their arms or sat at tables doing homework. At one table, a black student sat with white people. Things had clearly changed. It so happened that twenty-five years ago to the very week there had been a riot on this campus when a young black named James Meredith, escorted by 500 federal marshals, enrolled as a student at Ole Miss. The people of Oxford were so inflamed at the thought of having to share their campus with a 'Niggra boy' that they wounded thirty of the marshals and killed two journalists. Many of the parents of these serene-looking students must have been among the rioters, hurling bricks and setting cars alight. Was it really possible that that kind of hate could have been extinguished in just one generation? It seemed unlikely. But then it was impossible to imagine these tranquil students ever rioting over a matter of race. Come to that, it was impossible to imagine such a well-scrubbed, straight-arrow group of young people rioting over anything – except perhaps the number of chocolate chips in the dining-hall cookies.

I decided on an impulse to drive on to Tupelo, Elvis Presley's hometown, thirty-five miles to the east. It was a pleasant drive, with the sun low and the air warm. Black woods pressed in on the road from both sides. Here and there in clearings there were shacks, usually with large numbers of black youngsters in the yard, passing footballs or riding bikes. Occasionally there were also nicer houses – white people's houses – with big station wagons standing in the driveways and a basketball hoop over the garage and large, well-mown lawns. Often these houses were remarkably close – sometimes right next door – to a shack. You would never see that in the North. It struck me as notably ironic that Southerners could despise blacks so bitterly and yet live comfortably alongside them, while in the North people by and large did not mind blacks, even respected them as humans and wished them every success, just so long as they didn't have to mingle with them too freely.

By the time I reached Tupelo it was dark. Tupelo was a bigger place than I had expected, but by now I was coming to expect things to be not like I expected them to be, if you see what I mean. It had a long, bright strip of shopping malls, motels and gas stations. Hungry and weary, I saw for the first time the virtue of these strips. Here it all was, laid out for you – a glittering array of establishments offering every possible human convenience, clean, comfortable, reliable, reasonably-priced places where you could rest, eat, relax and re-equip with the minimum of physical and mental exertion. On top of all this they give you glasses of iced water and free second cups of coffee, not to mention free matchbooks and scented toothpicks wrapped in paper to cheer you on your way. What a wonderful country, I thought, as I sank gratefully into Tupelo's welcoming bosom.

SEVEN

In the morning I went to Elvis Presley's birthplace. It was early, and I expected it to be closed, but it was open and there were already people there, taking photographs beside the house or waiting to file in at the front door. The house, tidy and white, stood in a patch of shade in a city park. It was amazingly compact, shaped like a shoe-box, with just two rooms: a front room with a bed and dresser, and a plain kitchen behind. But it looked comfortable and had a nice homey feel. It was certainly superior to most of the shacks I had seen along the highway. A pleasant lady with meaty arms sat in a chair and answered questions. She must get asked the same questions about a thousand times a day, but she didn't seem to mind. Of the dozen or so people there, I was the only one under the age of sixty. I'm not sure if this was because Elvis was so clapped-out by the end of his career that his fans were all old people, or whether it is just that old people are the only ones with the time and inclination to visit the homes of dead celebrities.

A path behind the house led to a gift shop where you could buy Elvis memorabilia – albums, badges, plates, posters. Everywhere you looked his handsome, boyish face was beaming down at you. I bought two postcards and six books of matches, which I later discovered, with a strange sense of relief, I had lost somewhere. There was a visitors' book by the door. All the visitors came from towns with nowhere names like Coleslaw, Indiana, Dead Squaw, Oklahoma, Frigid, Minnesota, Dry Heaves, New Mexico, Colostomy, Montana. The book had a column for remarks. Reading down the list they said, 'Nice', 'Real nice', 'Very nice', 'Nice'. Such eloquence. I turned back to an earlier page. One visitor had misunderstood the intention of the remarks column and had written 'Visit'. Every other visitor on that page and the facing page had written 'Visit', 'Visit', 'Re-visit', 'Visit', until someone had turned the page and they got back on the right track.

The Elvis Presley house is in Elvis Presley Park on Elvis Presley

Drive, just off the Elvis Presley Memorial Highway. You may gather from this that Tupelo is proud of its most famous native son. But it hadn't done anything tacky to exploit his fame, and you had to admire it for that. There weren't scores of gift shops and wax museums and souvenir emporia all trying to make a quick killing from Presley's fading fame, just a nice little house in a shady park. I was glad I had stopped.

From Tupelo I drove due south towards Columbus, into a hot and rising sun. I saw my first cotton fields, dark and scrubby but with fluffs of real cotton poking out from every plant. The fields were surprisingly small. In the Midwest you get used to seeing farms that sweep away to the horizon; here they were the size of a couple of vegetable patches. There were more shacks as well, a more or less continuous line of them along the highway. It was like driving through the world's roomiest slum. And these were real shacks. Some of them looked dangerously uninhabitable, with sagging roofs and walls that looked as if they had been cannon-balled. Yet as you passed you would see someone lurking in the doorway, watching you. There were many roadside stores as well, more than you would have thought such a poor and scattered populace could support, and they all had big signs announcing a motley of commodities: GAS, FIREWORKS, FRIED CHICKEN, LIVE BAIT. I wondered just how hungry I would have to be to eat fried chicken prepared by a man who also dealt in live bait. All the stores had Coke machines and gas pumps out front, and almost all of them had rusting cars and assorted scrap scattered around the yard. It was impossible to tell if they were still solvent or not by their state of dereliction.

Every once in a while I would come to a town, small and dusty, with loads of black people hanging around outside the stores and gas stations, doing nothing. That was the most arresting difference about the South – the number of black people everywhere. I shouldn't really have been surprised by it. Blacks make up thirty-five per cent of the population in Mississippi and not much less in Alabama, Georgia and South Carolina. In some counties in the South, blacks outnumber whites by four to one. Yet until as recently as twenty-five years ago, in many of those counties not a single black person was registered to vote.

With so much poverty everywhere, Columbus came as a welcome surprise. It was a splendid little city, hometown of Tennessee

Williams, with a population of 30,000. During the Civil War it was briefly the state capital, and it still had some large *ante bellum* homes lining the well-shaded road in from the highway. But the real jewel was its downtown, which seemed hardly to have changed since about 1955. Crenshaw's Barber Shop had a rotating pole out front and across the street was a genuine five and dime called McCrory's and on the corner was the Bank of Mississippi in an imposing building with a big clock hanging over the sidewalk. The county courthouse, city hall and post office were all handsome and imposing edifices but built to a small-town scale. The people looked prosperous. The first person I saw was an obviously well-educated black man in a three-piece suit carrying a *Wall Street Journal*. It was all deeply pleasing and encouraging. This was a first-rate town. Combine it with Pella's handsome square and you would almost have my long-sought Amalgam. I was beginning to realise that I was never going to find it in one place. I would have to collect it piecemeal – a courthouse here, a fire station there – and here I had found several pieces.

I went for a cup of coffee in a hotel on Main Street and bought a copy of the local daily paper, the *Commercial Dispatch* ('Mississippi's Most Progressive Newspaper'). It was an old-fashioned paper with a banner headline across eight columns on page one that said 'Taiwanese Business Group to Visit Golden Triangle Area', and beneath that a crop of related single-column subheadings all in different sizes, typefaces and degrees of coherence:

Visitors Are Looking
At Opportunities
For Investment

AS PART
OF TRADE
MISSION

Group To Arrive In
Golden Triangle
Thursday

STATE OFFICIALS

COORDINATE VISIT

All the stories inside suggested a city ruled by calmness and compassion: 'Trinity Place Home-makers Give Elderly A Helping Hand', 'Lamar Landfill Is Discussed', 'Pickens School Budget Adopted'. I read the police blotter. 'During the past twenty-four hours,' it said, 'the Columbus Police Department had a total of thirty-four activities.' What a wonderful place — the police here didn't deal with crimes, they had activities. According to the blotter the most exciting of these activities had been arresting a man for driving on a suspended licence. Elsewhere in the paper I discovered that in the past twenty-four hours six people had died — or had death activities, as the police blotter might have put it — and three births had been recorded. I developed an instant affection for the *Commercial Dispatch* (which I rechristened in my mind the *Amalgam Commercial Dispatch*) and with the town it served.

I could live here, I thought. But then the waitress came over and said, 'Yew honestly a breast menu, honey?' and I realised that it was out of the question. I couldn't understand a word these people said to me. She might as well have addressed me in Dutch. It took many moments and much gesturing with a knife and fork to establish that what she had said to me was, 'Do you want to see a breakfast menu, honey?' In fact I had been hoping to see a lunch menu, but rather than spend the afternoon trying to convey this notion, I asked for a Coca-Cola, and was enormously relieved to find that this did not elicit any subsidiary questions.

It isn't just the indistinctness with which Southerners speak that makes it so difficult to follow, it's also the slowness. This begins to get to you after a while. The average Southerner has the speech patterns of someone slipping in and out of consciousness. I can change my shoes and socks faster than most people in Mississippi can speak a sentence. Living there would drive me crazy. Slowly.

Columbus is just inside the state boundary line and I found myself, twenty minutes after leaving town, in Alabama, heading for Tuscaloosa by way of Ethelsville, Coal Fire and Reform. A sign by the highway said DON'T LITTER. KEEP ALABAMA THE BEAUTIFUL. 'OK, I the will,' I replied cheerfully.

I put the radio on. I had been listening to it a lot in the last couple of days, hoping to be entertained by backward and twangy radio stations playing songs by artists with names like Hank Wanker and Brenda

Buns. This is the way it always used to be. My brother, who was something of a scientific wizard, once built a short-wave radio from old baked bean cans and that sort of thing, and late at night when we were supposed to be asleep he would lie in bed in the dark twiddling his knob (so to speak), searching for distant stations. Often he would pick up stations from the South. They would always be manned by professional hillbillies playing twangy music. The stations were always crackly and remote, as if the broadcasts were being beamed to us from another planet. But now there were hardly any backward-sounding people. In fact, there were hardly any Southern accents at all. All the disc jockeys sounded as if they came from Ohio.

Outside Tuscaloosa I stopped for gas and was surprised that the young man who served me also sounded as if he came from Ohio. In point of fact he did. He had a girl-friend at the University of Alabama, but he hated the South because it was so slow and backward. I asked him about the voices on the radio since he seemed to be an on-the-ball sort of guy. He explained that Southerners had become so sensitive about their reputation for being shit-squishing rednecks that all the presenters on TV and radio tried to sound as if they came from the North and had never in their whole lives nibbled a hush puppy or sniffed a grit. Nowadays it was the only way to get a job. Apart from anything else, the zippier Northern cadences meant the radio stations could pack in three or four commercials in the time it would take the average Southerner to clear his throat. That was certainly very true, and I tipped the young man 35¢ for his useful insight.

From Tuscaloosa, I followed Highway 69 south into Selma. All Selma meant to me was vague memories from the civil rights campaigns in the 1960s, when Martin Luther King led hundreds of blacks on forty-mile marches from there to Montgomery, the state capital, to register to vote. It was another surprisingly attractive town – this corner of the South seemed to be awash with them. It was about the same size as Columbus, and just as shady and captivating. Trees had been planted along the streets downtown and the sidewalks had recently been repaved in brick. Benches had been set out, and the waterfront area, where the city ended in a sharp bluff overlooking the Alabama River, had been cleaned up. It all had an agreeable air of prosperity. At a tourist information office I picked up some pamphlets extolling the town, including one boasting of its black heritage. I was heartened by this. I had seen nothing even faintly praiseworthy of blacks in Mississippi. Moreover, blacks and whites here seemed to be on far better terms. I could see them chatting at bus-stops, and I saw a black nurse and white nurse travelling together in a car, looking like old friends. Altogether, it seemed a much more relaxed atmosphere than in Mississippi.

I drove on, through rolling, open countryside. There were some cotton fields still, but mostly this was dairy country, with green fields and bright sunshine. In the late afternoon, almost the early evening, I reached Tuskegee, home of the Tuskegee Institute. Founded by Booker T. Washington and developed by George Washington Carver, it is America's premier college for blacks. It is also the seat of one of the poorest counties in America. Eighty-two per cent of the county population is black. More than half the county residents live below the poverty level. Almost a third of them still don't have indoor plumbing. That is really poor. Where I come from you are poor if you can't afford a refrigerator that makes its own ice-cubes and your car doesn't have automatic windows. Not having running water in the house is something beyond the realms of the imaginable to most Americans.

The most startling thing about Tuskegee was that it was completely black. It was in every respect a typical small American city, except that it was poor, with lots of boarded shopfronts and general dereliction, and that every person in every car, every pedestrian, every storekeeper, every fireman, every postman, every last soul was black. Except me. I had never felt so self-conscious, so visible. I suddenly appreciated what a black person must feel like in North Dakota. I stopped at a Burger King for a cup of coffee. There must have been fifty people in there. I was the only person who wasn't black, but no one seemed to notice or care. It was an odd sensation – and rather a relief, I must say, to get back out on the highway.

I drove on to Auburn, twenty miles to the north-east. Auburn is also a college town and roughly the same size as Tuskegee, but the contrast could hardly have been more striking. Auburn students were white and rich. One of the first sights I saw was a blonde sweeping past in a replica Duesenberg that must have cost her daddy $25,000. It was obviously a high school graduation present. If I could have run fast enough to keep up, I would happily have urinated all down the side of it. Coming so soon after the poverty of Tuskegee, it made me feel strangely ashamed.

However, I must say that Auburn appeared to be a pleasant town. I've always liked college towns anyway. They are about the only places in America that manage to combine the benefits of a small-town pace of life with a dash of big city sophistication. They usually have nice bars and restaurants, more interesting shops, an altogether more worldly air. And there is a pleasing sense of being around 20,000 young people who are having the best years of their lives.

In my day, the principal concerns of university students were sex, smoking dope, rioting and learning. Learning was something you did only when the first three weren't available, but at least you did it. Nowadays, American students' principal concerns seem to be sex and keeping their clothes looking nice. I don't think learning comes into it very much. Just at this time, there was an outcry in America over the contagion of ignorance that appeared to be sweeping through the nation's young people. The principal focus of this nationwide hand-wringing was a study by the National Endowment for the Humanities. It had recently tested 8,000 high school seniors and found that they were as stupid as pig dribble. More than two thirds of them did not know when the US Civil War took place, couldn't identify Stalin or Churchill, and didn't know who wrote *The Canterbury Tales*. Almost half thought World War I started before 1900. A third thought that Roosevelt was President during the Vietnam war and that Columbus sailed to America after 1750. Forty-two per cent – this is my favourite – couldn't name a single country in Asia. I would scarcely have believed all this myself except that the summer before I had taken two American high school girls for a drive around Dorset – bright girls, both of them now enrolled in colleges of high repute – and neither of them had ever heard of Thomas Hardy. How can you live to be eighteen years old and never have at least *heard* of Thomas Hardy?

I don't know the answer to that, but I suspect you could spend a week in Auburn kissing the ass of every person who had ever heard of Thomas Hardy and not get chapped lips. Perhaps that is a grossly unjustified comment. For all I know, Auburn may be a hotbed of Hardy scholarship. But what I do know, from having spent only a short while there, is that it hasn't got a single decent bookstore. How can a university town not have a decent bookstore? There was *a* bookstore, but all it sold was textbooks and a decidedly unliterary assortment of sweat-shirts, stuffed animals and other paraphernalia bearing the Auburn University seal. Most American universities like Auburn have 20,000 students or more, and upwards of 800 or 1,000 professors and lecturers. How can any community with that many educated people not support a single decent bookstore? If I were the National Endowment for the Humanities, I would find that at least as compelling a question as why high school seniors do so poorly on general knowledge tests.

Incidentally, I'll tell you why they do so poorly. They answer the questions as fast as they can, at random, and then sleep. We used to do it all the time. Once a year in high school, our principal, Mr Toerag, would file the whole school into the auditorium and make us spend a tedious day answering multiple choice questions on a variety of subjects for some national examination. It didn't take you long to deduce that if you filled in the circles without bothering to look at the questions, you could complete the work in a fraction of the time, and then shut your eyes and lose yourself in erotic eyelid movies until it was time for the next test. As long as your pencil was neatly stowed and you didn't snore, Mr Toerag, whose job it was to wander up and down the rows looking for miscreants, would leave you alone. That was what Mr Toerag did for a living, wander around all day looking for people misbehaving. I always imagined him at home in the evening walking around the dining-room table and poking his wife with a ruler if she slouched. He must have been hell to live with. His name wasn't really Mr Toerag, of course. It was Mr Superdickhead.

EIGHT

I drove through bright early-morning sunshine. Here and there the road plunged into dense pine forests and led past collections of holiday cabins in the woods. Atlanta was only an hour's drive to the north and the people here-abouts were clearly trying to cash in on that proximity. I passed through a little town called Pine Mountain, which seemed to have everything you could want in an inland resort. It was attractive and had nice shops. The only thing it lacked was a mountain, which was a bit of a disappointment considering its name. I had intentionally chosen this route because Pine Mountain conjured up to my simple mind a vision of clean air, craggy precipices, scented forests and tumbling streams – the sort of place where you might bump into John-Boy Walton. Still, who could blame the locals if they stretched the truth a little in the pursuit of a dollar? You could hardly expect people to drive miles out of their way to visit something called Pine Flat-Place.

The countryside became gradually more hilly, though obstinately uncraggy, before the road made a gentle descent into Warm Springs. For years I had been harbouring an urge to go there. I'm not sure why. I knew nothing about the place except that Franklin Roosevelt had died there. In the Register and Tribune Building in Des Moines the main corridor was lined with historic front pages which I found strangely absorbing when I was small. One of them said 'President Roosevelt Dies at Warm Springs', and I thought even then that it sounded like such a nice place to pass away.

In the event, Warm Springs was a nice place. There was just a main street, with an old hotel on one side and row of shops on the other, but they had been restored as expensive boutiques and gift shops for visitors from Atlanta. It was all patently artificial – there was even outdoor Muzak, if you can stand it – but I quite liked it.

I drove out to the Little White House, about two miles outside town. The parking lot was almost empty, except for an old bus from which a load of senior citizens were disembarking. The bus was from the

Calvary Baptist Church in some place like Firecracker, Georgia, or Bareassed, Alabama. The old people were noisy and excited, like schoolchildren, and pushed in front of me at the ticket booth, little realising that I wouldn't hesitate to give an old person a shove, especially a Baptist. But I just smiled benignly and stood back, comforted by the thought that soon they would be dead.

I bought my ticket and quickly overtook the old people on the slope up to the Roosevelt compound. The path led through woods of tall pine trees that seemed to go up and up forever and sealed out the sunlight so effectively that the ground at their bases was bare, as if it had just been swept. The path was lined with large rocks from each state. Every governor had evidently been asked to contribute some hunk of native stone and here they were, lined up like a guard of honour. It's not often you see an idea that stupid brought to fruition. Many had been cut in the shape of the state, then buffed to a glossy finish and engraved. But others, clearly not catching the spirit of the enterprise, were just featureless hunks with a terse little plaque saying 'Delaware. Granite.' Iowa's contribution was, as expected, carefully middling. The stone had been cut to the shape of the state, but by someone who had clearly never attempted such a thing before. I imagine he had impulsively put in the lowest bid and was surprised to get the contract. At least the state had found a rock to send. I had half feared it might be a clump of dirt.

Beyond this unusual diversion was a white bungalow, which had formerly been a neighbouring home and was now a museum. As always with these things in America, it was well done and interesting. Photographs of Roosevelt at Warm Springs covered the walls and lots of his personal effects were on display in glass cases – his wheelchairs, crutches, leg-braces and other such implements. Some of these were surprisingly elaborate and exerted a morbid interest because F. D. R. was always careful not to let the public see him as the cripple he was. And here we were viewing him with his trousers off, so to speak. I was particularly taken with a room full of all the handmade gifts that had been given to him when he was President and then presumably stuck at the back of a very large cupboard. There were carved walking-sticks by the dozen and maps of America made of inlaid wood and portraits of F. D. R. scratched on walrus tusks and etched with acid into slate. The amazing thing was how well done they all were. Every one of them represented hundreds of hours of delicate carving and tireless polishing, and all to be given away to a stranger for whom it would be just one more item in a veritable cavalcade of personalised keepsakes. I became so absorbed in these items that I scarcely noticed when the old people barged in, a trifle breathless but none the less lively. A lady with a bluish tint to her hair pushed in front of me at one of the display cases. She gave me a brief look that said, 'I am an old person. I can go where I want,' and then she dismissed me from her mind. 'Say, Hazel,' she called in a loud voice, 'did you know you shared a birthday with Eleanor Roosevelt?'

'Is that so?' answered a grating voice from the next room.

'I share a birthday with Eisenhower myself,' the lady with the bluish hair went on, still loudly, consolidating her position in front of me with a twitch of her ample butt. 'And I've got a cousin who shares a birthday with Harry Truman.'

I toyed for a moment with the idea of grabbing the woman by both ears and driving her forehead into my knee, but instead passed into the next room where I found the entrance to a small cinema in which they showed us a crackling black and white film all about Roosevelt's struggle with polio and his long stays at Warm Springs trying to rub life into his spindly legs, as if they had merely gone to sleep. It too was excellent. Written and narrated by a correspondent from UPI, it was moving without being mawkish, and the silent home movies, with their jerky movements that made all the participants look as if someone just out of camera range was barking at them to hurry up, exerted the same sort of voyeuristic fascination as F.D.R.'s leg-braces. Afterwards we were at last released to see the Little White House itself. I fairly bounded ahead in order not to have to share the experience with the old people. It was down another path, through more pine trees and beyond a white sentry-box. I was surprised at how small it was. It was just a little white cottage in the woods, all on one floor, with five small rooms, all panelled in dark wood. You would never believe that this could be the property of a President, particularly a rich President like Roosevelt. He did, after all, own most of the surrounding countryside, including the hotel on Main Street, several cottages and the springs themselves. Yet the very compactness of the cottage made it all the more snug and appealing. Even now, it looked comfy and lived-in. You couldn't help but want it for yourself, even if it meant coming to Georgia to enjoy it. In every room there was a short taped commentary, which explained how Roosevelt worked and underwent therapy at the cottage. What it didn't tell you was that what he really came here for was a bit of rustic bonking with his secretary, Lucy Mercer. Her bedroom was on one side of the living-room and his was on the other. The taped recording made nothing of this, but it did point out that Eleanor's bedroom, tucked away at the back and decidedly inferior to the secretary's, was mostly used as a guest-room because Eleanor seldom made the trip south.

From Warm Springs I went some miles out of my way to take the scenic road into Macon, but there didn't seem to be a whole lot scenic about it. It wasn't unscenic particularly, it just wasn't scenic. I was beginning to suspect that the scenic route designations on my maps had been applied somewhat at random. I imagined some guy who had never been south of Jersey City sitting in an office in New York and saying, 'Warm Springs to Macon? Ooh, that sounds nice,' and then carefully drawing in the orange dotted line that signifies a scenic route, his tongue sticking ever so slightly out of the corner of his mouth.

Macon was nice – all the towns in the South seemed to be nice. I stopped at a bank for money and was served by a lady from Great Yarmouth, something that brought a little excitement to both of us, and then continued on my way over the Otis Redding Memorial Bridge. There is a fashion in many parts of America, particularly the South, to name things made out of concrete after some local worthy – the Sylvester C. Grubb Memorial Bridge, the Chester Ovary Levee, that sort of thing. It seems a very odd practice to me. Imagine working all your life, clawing your way to the top, putting in long hours, neglecting your family, stabbing people in the back and generally being thought a shit by everyone you came in contact with, just to have a highway bridge over the Tallapoosa River named after you. Doesn't seem right somehow. Still, at least this one was named after someone I had heard of.

I headed east for Savannah, down Interstate 16. It was a 173-mile drive of unspeakable tedium across the red-clay plain of Georgia. It took me five hot and unrewarding hours to reach Savannah. While you, lucky reader, have only to flit your eyes to the next paragraph.

I stood agog in Lafayette Square in Savannah, amid brick paths, trickling fountains and dark trees hung with Spanish moss. Before me rose up a cathedral of exquisite linen-fresh whiteness with twin Gothic spires, and around it stood 200-year-old houses of weathered brick, with hurricane shutters that were still clearly used. I did not know that such perfection existed in America. There are twenty such squares in Savannah, cool and quiet beneath a canopy of trees, and long straight side-streets equally dark and serene. It is only when you stumble out of this urban rain forest, out into the open streets of the modern city, exposed to the glare of the boiling sun, that you realise just now sweltering the South can be. This was October, a time of flannel shirts and hot toddies in Iowa, but here summer was unrelenting. It was only eight in the morning and already businessmen were loosening their ties and mopping their foreheads. What must it be like in August? Every store and restaurant is air-conditioned. You step inside and the sweat is freeze-dried on your arms. Step back outside and the air meets you as something hot and unpleasant, like a dog's breath. It is only in its squares that the climate achieves a kind of pleasing equilibrium.

Savannah is a seductive city and I found myself wandering almost involuntarily for hours. The city has more than 1,000 historic buildings, many of them still lived in as houses. This was, New York apart, the first American city I had ever been in where people actually lived downtown. What a difference it makes, how much more vibrant and alive it all seems, to see children playing ball in the street or skipping rope on the front stoops. I wandered along the cobbled sidewalk of Oglethorpe Avenue to the Colonial Park Cemetery, full of mouldering monuments and densely packed with the gravestones of people famous to the state's history – Archibald Bulloch, the first president of Georgia, James Habersham, 'a leading merchant', and Button Gwinnett, who is famous in America for being one of the signatories of the Declaration of Independence and for having the silliest first name in Colonial history. The people of Savannah, in a careless moment, appear to have lost old Button. The historical marker said that he might be buried where I was standing now or then again he might be over in the corner or possibly somewhere else altogether. You could walk around all day and never know when you were on the Button, so to speak.

The business district in Savannah was frozen in a perpetual 1959 – the Woolworth's store didn't appear to have changed its stock since about then. There was a handsome old movie-house, Weis's, but it was shut. Downtown movie-houses are pretty much a thing of the past in America, alas, alas. You are always reading how buoyant the movie industry is in America, but all the theatres now are at shopping malls in the suburbs. You go to the movies there and you get a choice of a dozen pictures, but each theatre is about the size of a large fridge-freezer and only marginally more comfortable. There are no balconies. Can you imagine that? Can you imagine movie theatres without balconies? To me, going to the movies means sitting in the front row of the balcony with your feet up, dropping empty candy boxes on to the people below (or, during the more boring love-scenes, dribbling Coke) and throwing Nibs at the screen. Nibs were a liquorice-flavoured candy, thought to be made from rubber left over from the Korean War, which had a strange popularity in the 1950s. They were practically inedible, but if you sucked on one of them for a minute and then threw it at the screen, it would stick with an interesting 'pock' sound. It was a tradition on Saturdays for everybody to take the bus downtown to the Orpheum, buy a box of Nibs and spend the afternoon bombarding the screen.

You had to be careful when you did this because the theatre manager employed vicious usherettes, drop-outs from Tech High School whose one regret in life was that they hadn't been born into Hitler's Germany, who patrolled the aisles with high-powered flashlights looking for children who were misbehaving. Two or three times during the film their darting lights would fix on some hapless youngster, half out of his seat, poised in throwing position with a moistened Nib in his hand, and they would rush to subdue him. He would be carried off squealing. This never happened to my friends or me, thank God, but we always assumed that the victims were taken away and tortured with electrical instruments before being turned over to the police for a long period of mental readjustment in a reform school. Those were the days! You cannot tell me that some suburban multiplex with shoe-box theatres and screens the size of bath towels can offer anything like the enchantment and community spirit of a cavernous downtown movie-house. Nobody seems to have noticed it yet, but ours could well be the last generation for which movie-going has anything like a sense of magic.

On this sobering thought I strolled to Water Street, on the Savannah River, where there was a new riverside walk. The river itself was dark and smelly and on the South Carolina side opposite there was nothing to look at but down-at-heel warehouses and, further downriver, factories dispensing billows of smoke. But the old cotton warehouses overlooking the river on the Savannah side were splendid. They had been restored without being over-gentrified. They contained boutiques and oyster bars on the ground floor, but the upper floors were left a tad shabby, giving them that requisite raffish air I had been looking for since Hannibal. Some of the shops were just a bit twee, I must admit. One of them was called The Cutest Little Shop in Town, which made me want to have the Quickest Little Puke in the County. A sign on the door said 'Absotively, posilutely no food or drink in shop'. I sank to my knees and thanked God that I had never had to meet the proprietor. The shop was closed so I wasn't able to go inside and see what was so cute about it.

Towards the end of the street stood a big new Hyatt Regency hotel, an instantly depressing sight. Massive and made of shaped concrete, it was from the Fuck You school of architecture so favoured by the big American hotel chains. There was nothing about it in scale or appearance even remotely sympathetic to the old buildings around it. It just said, 'Fuck you, Savannah.' The city is particularly ill-favoured in this respect. Every few blocks you come up against some discordant slab – the De Soto Hilton, the Ramada Inn, the Best Western Riverfront, all about as appealing as spittle on a johnny cake, as they say in Georgia. Actually, they don't say anything of the sort in Georgia. I just made it up. But it has a nice Southern ring to it, don't you think? I was just about at the point where I was starting to get personally offended by the hotels, and in serious danger of becoming tiresome here, when my attention was distracted by a workman in front of the city courthouse, a large building with a gold dome. He had a leaf blower, a noisy contraption with miles of flex snaking back into the building behind him. I had never seen such a thing before. It looked something like a vacuum cleaner – actually, it looked like one of the Martians in *It Came From Outer Space* – and it was very noisy. The idea, I gathered, was that you would blow all the leaves into a pile and then gather them up by hand. But every time the man assembled a little pile of leaves, a breeze would come along and unassemble it. Sometimes he would chase one leaf half a block or more with his blower, whereupon all the leaves back at base would seize the opportunity to scuttle off in all directions. It was clearly an appliance that must have looked nifty in the catalogue but would never work in the real world, and I vaguely wondered, as I strolled past, whether the people at the Zwingle Company were behind it in some way.

I left Savannah on the Herman Talmadge Memorial Bridge, a tall, iron-strutted structure that rises up and up and up and flings you, wide-eyed and quietly gasping, over the Savannah River and into South Carolina. I drove along what appeared on my map to be a meandering coast road, but was in fact a meandering inland road. This stretch of coast is littered with islands, inlets, bays, and beaches of rolling sand dunes, but I saw precious little of it. The road was narrow and slow. It must be hell in the summer when millions of vacationers from all over the eastern seaboard head for the beaches and resorts – Tybee Island, Hilton Head, Laurel Bay, Fripp Island.

It wasn't until I reached Beaufort (pronounced Bew-furt) that I got my first proper look at the sea. I rounded a bend to find myself, suddenly and breathtakingly, gazing out on a looking-glass bay full of boats and reed beds, calm and bright and blue, the same colour as the sky. According to my *Mobil Travel Guide*, the three main sources of income in the area are tourism, the military and retired people. Sounds awful, doesn't it? But in fact Beaufort is lovely, with many mansions and an old-fashioned business district. I parked on Bay Street, the main road through town, and was impressed to find that the meter fee was only 5¢. That must be just about the last thing a nickel will buy you in America – thirty minutes of peace of mind in Beaufort, South Carolina. I strolled down to a little park and marina, which had been recently built, from the look of it. This was only the fourth time I had seen the Atlantic from this side. When you come from the Midwest, the ocean is a thing rarely encountered. The park was full of signs instructing you not to enjoy yourself or do anything impertinent. They were every few yards, and said NO SWIMMING OR DIVING FROM SEAWALL. NO BIKE-RIDING IN PARK. CUTTING OR DAMAGING FLOWERS, PLANTS, TREES OR SHRUBS PROHIBITED. NO CONSUMPTION OR POSSESSION OF BEER, WINE, OR ALCOHOLIC BEVERAGES IN CITY PARKS WITHOUT SPECIAL PERMISSION OF THE CITY. VIOLATORS WILL BE PROSECUTED. I don't know what sort of mini-Stalin they have running the council in Beaufort, but I've never seen a place so officially unwelcoming. It put me off so much that I didn't want to be there any more, and abruptly I left, which was a shame really because I still had twelve minutes of unexpired time on the meter.

As a result of this, I arrived in Charleston twelve minutes earlier than planned, which was good news. I had thought that Savannah was the most becoming American city I had ever seen, but it thumped into second place soon after my arrival in Charleston. At its harbour end, the city tapers to a rounded promontory which is packed solid with beautiful old homes, lined up one after the other along straight, shady streets like oversized books on a crowded shelf. Some are of the most detailed Victorian ornateness, like fine lace, and some are plain white clapboard with black shutters, but all of them are at least three storeys high and imposing – all the more so as they loom up so near the road. Almost no one has any yard to speak of – though everywhere I looked there were Vietnamese gardeners minutely attending to patches of lawn the size of table-cloths – so children play on the street and women, all of them white, all of them young, all of them rich, gossip on the front steps. This isn't supposed to happen in America. Wealthy children in America don't play on the street; there isn't any need. They lounge beside the pool or sneak reefers in the $3,000 treehouse that daddy had built for them for their ninth birthday. And their mothers, when they wish to gossip with a neighbour, do it on the telephone or climb into their air-conditioned station wagons and drive a hundred yards. It made me realise how much cars and suburbs – and indiscriminate wealth – have spoiled American life. Charleston had the climate and ambience of a Naples, but the wealth and style of a big American city. I was enchanted. I walked away the afternoon, up and down the peaceful streets, secretly admiring all these impossibly happy and good-looking people and their wonderful homes and rich, perfect lives.

The promontory ended in a level park, where children wheeled and bounced on BMXs and young couples strolled hand in hand and Frisbees sailed through the long strips of dark and light caused by the lowering sun filtering through the magnolia trees. Every person was youthful, good-looking and well-scrubbed. It was like wandering into a Pepsi commercial. Beyond the park, a broad stone promenade overlooked the harbour, vast and shimmery and green. I went and peered over the edge. The water slapped the stone and smelled of fish.

Two miles out you could see the island of Fort Sumter where the Civil War began. The promenade was crowded with cyclists and sweating joggers, who weaved expertly among the pedestrians and shuffling tourists. I turned around and walked back to the car, the sun warm on my back, and had the sneaking feeling that after such perfection things were bound to be downhill from now on.

NINE

For the sake of haste I got on Interstate 26, which runs in a 200-mile diagonal across South Carolina, through a landscape of dormant tobacco fields and salmon-coloured soil. According to my *Mobil Travel Guide*, I was no longer in the Deep South but in the Middle Atlantic states. But it had the heat and glare of the South and the people in gas stations and cafés along the way sounded Southern. Even the radio announcers sounded Southern, in attitude as much as accent. According to one news broadcast, the police in Spartanburg were looking for two black men 'who raped a white girl'. You wouldn't hear *that* outside the South.

As I neared Columbia, the fields along the road began to fill with tall signs advertising motels and quick food places. These weren't the squat, rectangular billboards of my youth, with alluring illustrations and three-dimensional cows, but just large unfriendly signs standing atop sixty-foot-high metal poles. Their messages were terse. They didn't invite you to do anything interesting or seductive. The old signs were chatty and would say things like WHILE IN COLUMBIA, WHY NOT STAY IN THE MODERN SKYLINER MOTOR INN, WITH OUR ALL NEW SENSUMATIC VIBRATING BEDS. YOU'LL LOVE 'EM! SPECIAL RATES FOR CHILDREN. FREE TV. AIR-COOLED ROOMS. FREE ICE. PLENTY OF PARKING. PETS WELCOME. ALL-U-CAN-EAT CATFISH BUFFET EVERY TUES 5–7 P.M. DANCE NITELY TO THE VERNON STURGES GUITAR ORCHESTRA IN THE STARLITE ROOM. (PLEASE—NO NEGROES). The old signs were like oversized postcards, with helpful chunks of information. They provided something to read, a little food for thought, a snippet of insight into the local culture. Attention spans had obviously contracted since then. The signs now simply announced the name of the business and how to get there. You could read them from miles away: HOLIDAY INN, EXIT 26E, 4 MI. Sometimes these instructions were more complex and would say things like: BURGER KING—31 MILES. TAKE EXIT 17B 5 MI TO US49 SOUTH, TURN RIGHT AT LIGHTS, THEN WEST PAST AIRPORT FOR 2½ MI. Who could want a Whopper that much? But the signs are effective, no doubt about it. Driving along in a state of idle mindlessness, suffering from hunger and a grease deficiency, you see a sign that says MCDONALD'S—EXIT HERE, and it's almost instinctive to swerve onto the exit ramp and follow it. Over and over through the weeks I found myself sitting at plastic tables with little boxes of food in front of me which I didn't want or have time to eat, all because a sign had instructed me to be there.

At the North Carolina border, the dull landscape ended abruptly, as if by decree. Suddenly the countryside rose and fell in majestic undulations, full of creeping thickets of laurel, rhododendron and palmetto. At each hilltop the landscape opened out to reveal hazy views of the Blue Ridge Mountains, part of the Appalachian chain. The Appalachians stretch for 2,100 miles from Alabama to Canada and were once higher than the Himalayas (I read that on a book of matches once and have been waiting years for an opportunity to use it), though now they are smallish and rounded, fetching rather than dramatic. All along their length they go by different names – the Adirondacks, Poconos, Catskills, Alleghenies. I was headed for the Smokies, but I intended to stop *en route* at the Biltmore Estate, just outside Asheville, North Carolina. Biltmore was built by George Vanderbilt in 1895 and was one of the biggest houses ever constructed in America – a 255-room pile of stone in the style of a Loire château, in grounds of 10,000 acres. When you arrive at Biltmore you are directed to park your car and go into a building by the gate to purchase your ticket before proceeding on to the estate. I thought this was curious until I went into the building and discovered that a gay afternoon at Biltmore would involve a serious financial commitment. The signs telling you the admission fee were practically invisible, but you could see from the ashen-faced look on people as they staggered away from the ticket windows that it must be a lot. Even so I was taken aback when my turn came and the unpleasant-looking woman at the ticket window told me that the admission fee was $17.50 for adults and $13 for children. 'Seventeen dollars and fifty cents!' I croaked. 'Does that include dinner and a floor show?'

The woman was obviously used to dealing with hysteria and snide remarks. In a monotone she said, 'The admission fee includes admission to the George Vanderbilt house, of which fifty of the 250 rooms are open to the public. You should allow two to three hours for the self-guided tour. It also includes admission to the extensive gardens for which you should allow thirty minutes to one hour. It also includes admission and guided tour of the winery with audio-visual presentation and complimentary wine tasting. A guide to the house and grounds, available for a separate charge, is recommended. Afterwards you may wish to spend further large sums of money in the Deerpark Restaurant or, if you are a relatively cheap person, in the Stable Café, as well as avail yourself of the opportunity to buy expensive gifts and remembrances in the Carriage House Gift Shop.'

But by this time I was already on the highway again, heading for the Great Smoky Mountains, which, thank God, are free.

I drove ten miles out of my way in order to spend the night in Bryson City, a modest self-indulgence. It was a small, nondescript place of motels and barbecue shacks strung out along a narrow river valley on the edge of the Great Smoky Mountains National Park. There is little reason to go there unless your name happens to be Bryson, and even then, I have to tell you, the pleasure is intermittent. I got a room in the Bennett's Court Motel, a wonderful old place that appeared not to have changed a bit since 1956, apart from an occasional light dusting. It was precisely as motels always used to be, with the rooms spread out along a covered verandah overlooking a lawn with two trees and a tiny concrete swimming-pool, which at this time of year was empty but for a puddle of wet leaves and one pissed-off looking frog. Beside each door was a metal armchair with a scallop-shaped back. By the sidewalk an old neon sign thrummed with the sound of coursing neon gas and spelled out BENNETT'S COURT/VACANCY/AIR-CONDITIONED/ GUEST POOL/TV, all in green and pink beneath a tasteful blinking arrow in yellow. When I was small all motels had signs like that. Now you only see them occasionally in small forgotten towns on the edge of nowhere. Bennett's Court clearly would be the motel in Amalgam.

I took my bags inside, lowered myself experimentally on to the bed and switched on the TV. Instantly there came up a commercial for Preparation H, an unguent for haemorrhoids. The tone was urgent. I don't remember the exact words, but they were something like, 'Hey, you! Have you got haemorrhoids? Then get some Preparation H! That's an order! Remember that name, you inattentive moron! Preparation H! And even if you haven't got haemorrhoids, get some

Preparation H anyway! Just in case!' And then a voice-over quickly added, 'Now available in cherry flavour.' Having lived abroad so long, I was unused to the American hard sell and it made me uneasy. I was equally unsettled by the way television stations in America can jump back and forth between commercials and programmes without hesitation or warning. You'll be lying there watching *Kojak*, say, and in the middle of a gripping shoot-out somebody starts cleaning a toilet bowl and you sit up, thinking, 'What the —' and then you realise it is a commercial. In fact, it is several minutes of commercials. You could go out for cigarettes and a pizza during commercial breaks in America, *and* still have time to wash the toilet bowl before the programme resumed.

The Preparation H commercial vanished and a micro-instant later, before there was any possibility of the viewer reflecting on whether he might wish to turn to another channel, was replaced by a clapping audience, the perky sound of steel guitars and happy but mildly brain-damaged people in sequinned outfits. This was *Grand Ole Opry*. I watched for a couple of minutes. By degrees my chin dropped onto my shirt as I listened to their singing and jesting with a kind of numb amazement. It was like a visual lobotomy. Have you ever watched an infant at play and said to yourself, 'I wonder what goes on in his little head'? Well, watch *Grand Ole Opry* for five minutes sometime and you will begin to have an idea.

After a couple of minutes another commercial break noisily intruded and I was snapped back to my senses. I switched off the television and went out to investigate Bryson City. There was more to it than I had first thought. Beyond the Swain County Courthouse was a small business district. I was gratified to note that almost everything had a Bryson City sign on it — Bryson City Laundry, Bryson City Coal and Lumber, Bryson City Church of Christ, Bryson City Electronics, Bryson City Police Department, Bryson City Fire Department, Bryson City Post Office. I began to appreciate how George Washington might feel if he were to be brought back to life and set down in the District of Columbia. I don't know who the Bryson was whom this town was so signally honouring, but I had certainly never seen my name spread around so lavishly, and I regretted that I hadn't brought a crowbar and monkey wrench because many of the signs would have made splendid keepsakes. I particularly fancied having the Bryson City Church of

Christ sign beside my front gate in England and being able to put up different messages every week like 'Repent Now, Limeys.'

It didn't take long to exhaust the possibilities for diversion in downtown Bryson City, and almost before I realised it I found myself on the highway out of town leading towards Cherokee, the next town along the valley. I followed it for a little way but there was nothing to see except a couple of derelict gas stations and barbecue shacks, and hardly any shoulder to walk on so that cars shot past only inches away and whipped my clothes into a disconcerting little frenzy. All along the road were billboards and large hand-lettered signs in praise of Christ: 'GET A GRIP ON YOUR LIFE—PRAISE JESUS, GOD LOVES YOU, AMERICA, and the rather more enigmatic WHAT WOULD HAPPEN IF YOU DIED TOMORROW? (Well, I thought, there would be no more payments on the freezer for a start.) I turned around and went back into town. It was 5.30 in the afternoon, Bryson City was a crypt with sidewalks, and I was at a complete loss. Down a small hill, beside the rushing river, I spied an A & P supermarket, which appeared to be open, and I went down there for want of something better to do. I often used to hang out in supermarkets. Robert Swanson and I, when we were about twelve and so obnoxious that it would have been a positive mercy to inject us with something lethal, would often go to the Hinky-Dinky supermarket on Ingersoll Avenue in Des Moines during the summer because it was air-conditioned, and pass the time by doing things I am now ashamed to relate – loosening the bottom of a bag of flour and then watching it pour on to the floor when some unsuspecting woman picked it up, or putting strange items like goldfish food and emetics in people's shopping carts when their backs were turned. I didn't intend to do anything like that in the A & P now – unless of course I got *really* bored – but I thought it would be comforting, in this strange place, to look at foodstuffs from my youth. And it was. It was almost like visiting old friends – Skippy Peanut Butter, Pop Tarts, Welch's Grape Juice, Sara Lee cakes. I wandered the aisles, murmuring tiny cries of joy at each sighting of an old familiar nutrient. It cheered me up no end.

Then suddenly I remembered something. Months before, in England, I had noticed an ad for panty shields in the *New York Times Magazine*. These panty shields had dimples on them and the dimples had a name that was trade-marked. This struck me as remarkable. Can you imagine being given the job of thinking up a catchy name for dimples on a panty shield? But I couldn't remember what it was. So now, for no reason other than that I had nothing better to do, I went over and had a look at the A & P's panty shield section. There was a surprising diversity of them. I would never have guessed that the market was so buoyant or indeed that there were so many panties in Bryson City that needed shielding. I had never paid much attention to this sort of thing before and it was really kind of interesting. I don't know how long I spent poking about among the various brands and reading the instructions for use, or whether I might even have started talking to myself a little, as I sometimes do when I am happily occupied. But I suppose it must have been quite some time. In any case, at the very moment that I picked up a packet of New Freedom Thins, with Funnel-Dot Protection ⓉⓂ, and cried triumphantly, 'Aha! There you are, you little buggers!', I turned my head a fraction and noticed that at the far end of the aisle the manager and two female assistants were watching me. I blushed and clumsily wedged the packet back on the shelves. 'Just browsing!' I called in an unconvincing voice, hoping I didn't look too dangerous or insane, and made for the exit. I remembered reading some weeks before in *The Independent* (Britain's liveliest quality daily newspaper – order your copy today!) that it is still against the law in twenty US states, most of them in the Deep South, for heterosexuals to engage in oral or anal intercourse. I had nothing like that in mind just now, you understand, but I think it indicates that some of these places can be doggedly unenlightened in matters pertaining to sex and could well have ordinances with respect to the unlawful handling of panty shields. It would be just my luck to pull a five to ten stretch for some unintended perversion in a place like North Carolina. At all events, I felt fortunate to make it back to my motel without being intercepted by the authorities, and spent the rest of my short stay in Bryson City behaving with the utmost circumspection.

The Great Smoky Mountains National Park covers 500,000 acres in North Carolina and Tennessee. I didn't realise it before I went there, but it is the most popular national park in America, attracting nine million visitors a year, three times as many as any other national park, and even early on a Sunday morning in October it was crowded. The road between Bryson City and Cherokee, at the park's edge, was a straggly collection of motels, junky-looking auto repair shops, trailer courts and barbecue shacks perched on the edge of a glittering stream in a cleft in the mountains. It must have been beautiful once, with dark mountains squeezing in from both sides, but now it was just squalid. Cherokee itself was even worse. It is the biggest Indian reservation in the eastern United States and it was packed from one end to the other with souvenir stores selling tawdry Indian trinkets, all of them with big signs on their roofs and sides saying MOCCASINS! INDIAN JEWELRY! TOMAHAWKS! POLISHED GEMSTONES! CRAPPY ITEMS OF EVERY DESCRIPTION! Some of the places had a caged brown bear out front – the Cherokee mascot, I gathered – and around each of these was a knot of small boys trying to provoke the animal into a show of ferocity, encouraged from a safe distance by their fathers. At other stores you could have your photograph taken with a genuine, hung-over, flabby-titted Cherokee Indian in war dress for $5, but not many people seemed interested in this and the model Indians sat slumped in chairs looking as listless as the bears. I don't think I had ever been to a place quite so ugly, and it was jammed with tourists, almost all of them ugly also – fat people in noisy clothes with cameras dangling on their bellies. Why is it, I wondered idly as I nosed the car through the throngs, that tourists are always fat and dress like morons?

Then, abruptly, before I could give the question the consideration it deserved, I was out of Cherokee and in the national park and all the garishness ceased. People don't live in national parks in America as they do in Britain. They are areas of wilderness – often enforced wilderness. The Smoky Mountains were once full of hillbillies who lived in cabins up in the remote hollows, up among the clouds, but they were moved out and now the park is sterile as far as human activities go. Instead of trying to preserve an ancient way of life, the park authorities eradicated it. So the dispossessed hillbillies moved down to valley towns at the park's edge and turned them into junkvilles selling crappy little souvenirs. It seems a very strange approach to me. Now a few of the cabins are preserved as museum pieces. There was one at a visitors' centre just inside the park, which I dutifully stopped to have a look at. It was exactly like the cabins at the Lincoln village at New Salem in Illinois. I had not realised that it is actually possible to overdose on log cabins, but as I drew near the cabin I began to feel a sudden onset of brain-stem death and I retreated to the car after only the briefest of looks.

The Smoky Mountains themselves were a joy. It was a perfect October morning. The road led steeply up through broad-leaved forests of dappled sunshine, full of paths and streams, and then, higher up, opened out to airy vistas. All along the road through the park there were look-out points where you could pull the car over and go 'Ooh!' and 'Wow!' at the views. They were all named after mountain passes that sounded like condominium developments for yuppies – Pigeon Gap, Cherry Cove, Wolf Mountain, Bear Trap Gap. The air was clear and thin and the views were vast. The mountains rolled away to a distant horizon, gently shading from rich green to charcoal blue to hazy smoke. It was a sea of trees – like looking out over a landscape from Colombia or Brazil, so virginal was it all. In all the rolling vastness there was not a single sign of humanity, no towns, no water-towers, no plume of smoke from a solitary farmstead. It was just endless silence beneath a bright sky, empty and clear apart from one distant bluish puff of cumulus, which cast a drifting shadow over a far-off hill.

The Oconaluftee Highway across the park is only thirty miles long, but it is so steep and winding that it took me all morning to cross it. By 10 A.M. there was a steady stream of cars in both directions, and free spaces at the look-out points were hard to find. This was my first serious brush with real tourists – retired people with trailer homes heading for Florida, young families taking off-season vacations, honeymooners. There were cars and trailers, campers and motor homes from thousands of miles away – California, Wyoming, British Columbia –and at every look-out point people were clustered around their vehicles with the doors and trunks opened, feeding from ice coolers and portable fridges. Every few yards there was a Winnebago or Komfort Motor Home – massive, self-contained dwellings on wheels that took up three parking spaces and jutted out so far that cars coming in could only barely scrape past.

All morning I had been troubled by a vague sense of something being missing, and then it occurred to me what it was. There were no hikers such as you would see in England – no people in stout boots and short pants, with knee-high tasselled stockings. No little rucksacks full of Marmite sandwiches and flasks of tea. And no platoons of cyclists in şkin-tight uniforms and bakers' caps labouring breathlessly up the mountainsides, slowing up traffic. What slowed the traffic here were the massive motor homes lumbering up and down the mountain passes. Some of them, amazingly, had cars tethered to their rear bumpers, like dinghies. I got stuck behind one on the long, sinuous descent down the mountain into Tennessee. It was so wide that it could barely stay within its lane and kept threatening to nudge oncoming cars off into the picturesque void to our left. That, alas, is the way of vacationing nowadays for many people. The whole idea is not to expose yourself to a moment of discomfort or inconvenience – indeed, not to breathe fresh air if possible. When the urge to travel seizes you, you pile into your thirteen-ton tin palace and drive 400 miles across the country, hermetically sealed against the elements, and stop at a campground where you dash to plug into their water supply and electricity so that you don't have to go a single moment without air-conditioning or dishwasher and microwave facilities. These things, these 'recreational vehicles', are like life-support systems on wheels. Astronauts go to the moon with less back-up. RV people are another breed – and a largely demented one at that. They become obsessed with trying to equip their vehicles with gadgets to deal with every possible contingency. Their lives become ruled by the dread thought that one day they may find themselves in a situation in which they are not entirely self-sufficient. I once went camping for two days at Lake Darling in Iowa with a friend whose father – an RV enthusiast – kept trying to press labour-saving devices on us. 'I got a great little solar-powered can opener here,' he would say. 'You wanna take that?'

'No thanks,' we would reply. 'We're only going for two days.'

'How about this combination flashlight/carving knife? You can run it off the car cigarette-lighter if you need to, and it doubles as a flashing siren if you get lost in the wilderness.'

'No thanks.'

'Well, at least take the battery-powered microwave.'

'Really, we don't want it.'

'Then how the hell are you going to pop popcorn out there in the middle of nowhere? Have you thought about that?'

A whole industry (in which no doubt the Zwingle Company of New York is actively involved) has grown up to supply this market. You can see these people at campgrounds all over the country, standing around their vehicles comparing gadgets – methane-powered ice-cube makers, portable tennis-courts, anti-insect flame-throwers, inflatable lawns. They are strange and dangerous people and on no account should be approached.

At the foot of the mountain, the park ended and suddenly all was squalor again. I was once more struck by this strange compartmentalisation that goes on in America – a belief that no commercial activities must be allowed inside the park, but permitting unrestrained development outside, even though the landscape there may be just as outstanding. America has never quite grasped that you can live in a place without making it ugly, that beauty doesn't have to be confined behind fences, as if a national park were a sort of zoo for nature. The ugliness intensified to fever pitch as I rolled into Gatlinburg, a community that had evidently dedicated itself to the endless quest of trying to redefine the lower limits of bad taste. It is the world capital of tat. It made Cherokee look decorous. There is not much more to it than a single mile-long main street, but it was packed from end to end with the most dazzling profusion of tourist clutter – the Elvis Presley Hall of Fame, Stars Over Gatlinburg Wax Museum, two haunted houses, the National Bible Museum, Hillbilly Village, Ripley's Believe It or Not Museum, the American Historical Wax Museum, Gatlinburg Space Needle, something called Paradise Island, something else called World of Illusions, the Bonnie Lou and Buster Country Music Show, Carbo's Police Museum ('See "Walking Tall" Sheriff Buford Pusser's Death Car!'), Guinness Book of Records Exhibition Centre and, not least, the Irlene Mandrell Hall of Stars Museum and Shopping Mall. In between this galaxy of entertainments were scores of parking lots and noisy, crowded restaurants, junk food stalls, ice-cream parlours, and gift shops of the sort that sell wanted posters with YOUR NAME HERE and baseball caps with droll embellishments, like a coil of realistic-looking plastic turd on the brim. Walking in an unhurried fashion up and down the street were more crowds of overweight tourists in boisterous clothes, with cameras bouncing on their bellies, consuming ice-creams, cotton candy and corn dogs, sometimes simultaneously, and wearing baseball caps with plastic turds jauntily attached to the brim.

I loved it. When I was growing up, we never got to go to places like Gatlinburg. My father would rather have given himself brain surgery with a Black and Decker drill than spend an hour in such a place. He had just two criteria for gauging the worth of a holiday attraction: was it educational, and was it free? Gatlinburg was patently neither of these. His idea of holiday heaven was a museum without an admission charge. My dad was the most honest man I ever met, but vacations blinded him to his principles. When I had pimples scattered across my face and stubble on my chin he was still swearing at ticket booths that I was eight years old. He was so cheap on vacations that it always surprised me he didn't make us sift in litter-bins for our lunch. So Gatlinburg to me was a heady experience. I felt like a priest let loose in Las Vegas with a sockful of quarters. All the noise and glitter, and above all the possibilities for running through irresponsible sums of money in a short period, made me giddy.

I wandered through the crowds, and hesitated at the entrance to the Ripley's Believe It Or Not Museum. I could sense my father, a thousand miles away, beginning to rotate slowly in his grave as I looked at the posters. They told me that inside I would see a man who could hold three billiard balls in his mouth at once, a two-headed calf, a human unicorn with a horn protruding from his forehead and hundreds of other riveting oddities from all over the globe collected by the tireless Robert Ripley and crated back to Gatlinburg for the edification of discerning tourists such as myself. The admission fee was $5. The pace of my father's rotating quickened as I looked into my wallet, and then sped to a whirring blur as I fished out a five-dollar bill and guiltily handed it to the unsmiling woman in the ticket booth. 'What the hell,' I thought as I went inside, 'at least it will give the old man some exercise.'

Well, it was superb. I know $5 is a lot of money for a few minutes' diversion. I could just see my father and me standing outside on the sidewalk bickering. My father would say, 'No, it's a big gyp. For that kind of money, you could buy something that would give you years of value.'

'Like what – a box of carpet tiles?' I would reply with practised sarcasm. 'Oh, please, Dad, just this once don't be cheap. There's a two-headed calf in there.'

'No, son, I'm sorry.'

'I'll be good forever. I'll take out the garbage every day until I get married. Dad, there is a guy in there who can hold three billiard balls in his mouth at once. There is a *human unicorn* in there. Dad, we could be throwing away the chance of a lifetime here.'

But he would not be moved. 'I don't want to hear any more about it. Now let's all get in the car and drive 175 miles to the Molasses Point Historical Battlefield. You'll learn lots of worthwhile things about the little-known American war with Ecuador of 1802 and it won't cost me a penny.'

So I went through the Ripley's Believe It or Not Museum and I savoured every artefact and tasteless oddity. It was outstanding. I mean honestly, where else are you going to see a replica of Columbus's flagship, the *Santa Maria*, made entirely of chicken bones? And how can you possibly put a price on seeing an eight-foot-long model of the Circus Maximus constructed of sugar cubes, or the death-mask of John Dillinger, or a room made entirely of matchsticks by one Reg Polland of Manchester, England (well done, Reg; Britain is proud of you)? We are talking lasting memories here. I was pleased to note that England was further represented by, of all things, a chimney-pot, circa 1940. Believe it or not. It was all wonderful – clean, nicely presented, sometimes even believable – and I spent a happy hour there.

Afterwards, feeling highly content, I purchased an ice-cream cone the size of a baby's head and wandered with it through the crowds of people in the afternoon sunshine. I went into a series of gift shops and tried on baseball caps with plastic turds on the brim, but the cheapest one I saw was $7.99 and I decided, out of deference to my father, that that would be just too much extravagance for one afternoon. If it came to it, I could always make my own, I thought as I returned to the car and headed for the dangerous hills of Appalachia.

TEN

In 1587, a group of 115 English settlers – men, women and children – sailed from Plymouth to set up the first colony in the New World, on Roanoke Island off what is now North Carolina. Shortly after they arrived, a child named Virginia Dare was born and thus became the first white person to arrive in America head first. Two years later, a second expedition set off from England to see how the settlers were getting on and to bring them their mail and tell them that the repairman from British Telecom had finally shown up and that sort of thing. But when the relief party arrived, they found the settlement deserted. There was no message of where the settlers had gone, nor any sign of a struggle, but just one word mysteriously scratched on a wall: 'Croatoan'. This was the name of a nearby island where the Indians were known to be friendly, but a trip to the island showed that the settlers had never arrived there. So where did they go? Did they leave voluntarily or were they spirited off by Indians? This has long been one of the great mysteries of the colonial period.

I bring this up here because one theory is that the settlers pushed inland, up into the hills of Appalachia, and settled there. No one knows why they might have done this, but fifty years later, when European explorers arrived in Tennessee, the Cherokee Indians told them that there was a group of pale people living in the hills already, people who wore clothes and had long beards. These people, according to a contemporary account, 'had a bell which they rang before they ate their meals and had a strange habit of bowing their heads and saying something in a low voice before they ate.'

No one ever found this mysterious community. But in a remote and neglected corner of the Appalachians, high up in the Clinch Mountains above the town of Sneedville in north-eastern Tennessee, there still live some curious people called Melungeons who have been there for as long as anyone can remember. The Melungeons (no one knows where the name comes from) have most of the characteristics of Europeans – blue eyes, fair hair, lanky build – but a dark, almost

Negroid skin colouring that is distinctly non-European. They have English family names – Brogan, Collins, Mullins – but no one, including the Melungeons themselves, has any idea of where they come from or what their early history might have been. They are as much of a mystery as the lost settlers of Roanoke Island. Indeed, it has been suggested that they may *be* the lost settlers of Roanoke.

Peter Dunn, a colleague at *The Independent* in London, put me on to the Melungeon story when he heard that I was going to that part of the world, and kindly dug out an article he had done for the *Sunday Times Magazine* some years before. This was illustrated with remarkable photographs of Melungeons. It is impossible to describe them except to say that they were simply white people with black skin. Their appearance was, to say the least, striking. For this reason they have long been outcasts in their own county, consigned to shacks in the hills in an area called Snake Hollow. In Hancock County, 'Melungeon' is equivalent to 'Nigger'. The valley people – who are themselves generally poor and backward – regard the Melungeons as something strange and shameful, and the Melungeons as a consequence keep to themselves, coming down from the mountains only at widely-spaced intervals to buy provisions. They don't like outsiders. Neither do the valley people. Peter Dunn told me that he and the photographer who accompanied him were given a reception that ranged from mild hostility to outright intimidation. It was an uncomfortable assignment. A few months later a reporter from *Time Magazine* was actually shot near Sneedville for asking too many questions.

So you can perhaps imagine the sense of foreboding that seeped over me as I drove up Tennessee Highway 31 through a forgotten landscape of poor and scattered tobacco farms, through the valley of the twisting Clinch River, *en route* to Sneedville. This was the seventh poorest county in the nation and it looked it. Litter was adrift in the ditches and most of the farmhouses were small and unadorned. In every driveway there stood a pickup truck with a gun rack in the back window, and where there were people in the yards they stopped what they were doing to watch me as I passed. It was late afternoon, nearly dusk, when I reached Sneedville. Outside the Hancock County Courthouse a group of teenagers were perched on the fronts of pickup trucks, talking to each other, and they too stared at me as I passed. Sneedville is so far from anywhere, such an improbable destination, that a stranger's car attracts notice. There wasn't much to the town: the courthouse, a Baptist church, some box houses, a gas station. The gas station was still open, so I pulled in. I didn't particularly need gas, but I wasn't sure when I would find another station. The guy who came out to pump the gas had an abundance of fleshy warts – a veritable crop – scattered across his face like button mushrooms. He looked like a genetic experiment that had gone horribly wrong. He didn't speak except to establish what kind of gas I wanted and he didn't remark on the fact that I was from out of state. This was the first time on the trip that a gas station attendant hadn't said in an engaging manner, 'You're a long way from home, arentcha?' or, 'What brings you all the way here from I-o-way?' or something like that. (I always told them that I was on my way east to have vital heart surgery, in the hope that they would give me extra Green Stamps.) I was very probably the first person from out of state this man had seen all year, yet he appeared resolutely uninterested in what I was doing there. It was odd. I said to him – blurted really – 'Excuse me, but didn't I read somewhere that some people called Melungeons live around here somewhere?'

He didn't answer. He just watched the pump counter spin. I thought he hadn't heard me, so I said, 'I say, excuse me, but didn't I hear that some people –'

'Don't know,' he said abruptly without looking at me. Then he looked at me. 'Don't know nothin' about that. You want your oil checked?'

I hesitated, surprised by the question. 'No thank you.'

'That's eleven dollars.' He took my money without thanks and went back inside. I was fairly dumbfounded. I don't know quite why. Through the window I could see him pick up his telephone and make a call. He looked at me as he did it. Suddenly I felt alarmed. What if he was calling the police to tell them to come out and shoot me? I laid a small patch of rubber on his driveway as I departed – something you don't often see achieved with a Chevette – and made the pistons sing as I floored the accelerator and hurtled out of town at a breakneck twenty-seven miles an hour. But a mile or so later I slowed down. Partly this was because I was going up an almost vertical hill and the car wouldn't go any faster – for one breathless moment I thought it might actually start rolling backwards – and partly because I told myself not to be so jumpy. The guy was probably just calling his wife to remind her to buy more wart lotion. Even if he was calling the police to report an outsider asking impertinent questions, what could they do to me? It was a free country. I hadn't broken any laws. I had asked an innocent question, and asked it politely. How could anyone take offence at that? Clearly I was being silly to feel any sense of menace. Even so, I found myself glancing frequently into the rear-view mirror and half expecting to see the hill behind me crawling with flashing squad cars and posses of volunteer vigilantes in pickup trucks coming after me. Judiciously, I stepped up my speed from eleven to thirteen miles a hour.

High up the hill I began to encounter shacks set back in clearings in the woods, and peered at them in the hope of glimpsing a Melungeon or two. But the few people I saw were white. They stared at me with a strange look of surprise as I lumbered past, the way you might stare at a man riding an ostrich, and generally made no response to my cheerful wave, though one or two did reply with an automatic and economic wave of their own, a raised hand and a twitch of fingers.

This was real hillbilly country. Many of the shacks looked like something out of *Li'l Abner*, with sagging porches and tilting chimneys. Some were abandoned. Many appeared to have been handmade, with rambling extensions that had clearly been fashioned from scraps of plundered wood. People in these hills still made moonshine, or stump liquor as they call it. But the big business these days is marijuana, believe it or not. I read somewhere that whole mountain villages band together and can make $100,000 a month from a couple of acres planted in some remote and lofty hollow. More than the Melungeons, that is an excellent reason not to be a stranger asking questions in the area.

Although I was clearly climbing high up into the mountains, the woods all around were so dense that I had no views. But at the summit the trees parted like curtains to provide a spectacular outlook over the valley on the other side. It was like coming over the top of the earth, like the view from an aeroplane. Steep green wooded hills with alpine meadows clinging to their sides stretched away for as far as the eye could see until at last they were consumed by a distant and colourful sunset. Before me a sinuous road led steeply down to a valley of rolling farms spread out along a lazy river. It was as perfect a setting as I had ever seen. I drove through the soft light of dusk, absorbed by the beauty. And the thing was, every house along the roadside was a shack. This was the heart of Appalachia, the most notoriously impoverished region of America, and it was just inexpressibly beautiful. It was strange that the urban professionals from the cities of the eastern seaboard, only a couple of hours' drive to the east, hadn't colonized an area of such arresting beauty, filling the dales with rusticky weekend cottages, country clubs, and fancy restaurants.

It was strange, too, to see white people living in poverty. In America, to be white and impoverished really takes some doing. Of course, this was American poverty, this was white people's poverty, which isn't like poverty elsewhere. It isn't even like the poverty in Tuskegee. It has been suggested with more than a touch of cynicism that when Lyndon Johnson launched his great War on Poverty in 1964, the focus was placed on Appalachia not because it was so destitute but because it was so white. A little-publicised survey at the time showed that forty per cent of the poorest people in the region owned a car and a third of those had been bought new. In 1964, my future father-in-law in England was, like most people there, years away from owning his first car and even now he has never owned a new one, yet no one ever called him destitute or sent him a free sack of flour and some knitting wool at Christmas. Still, I can't deny that by American standards the scattered shacks around me were decidedly modest. They had no satellite dishes in the yard, no Weber barbecues, no station wagons standing in the drive. And I daresay they had no microwaves in the kitchen, poor devils, and by American standards that is pretty damn deprived.

ELEVEN

I drove through a landscape of gumdrop hills, rolling roads, neat farms. The sky was full of those big fluffy clouds you always see in nautical paintings, and the towns had curious and interesting names: Snowflake, Fancy Gap, Horse Pasture, Meadows of Dan, Charity. Virginia went on and on. It never seemed to end. The state is nearly 400 miles across, but the twisting road must have added at least a hundred miles to that. In any case, every time I looked at the map I seemed to have moved a remarkably tiny distance. From time to time I would pass a sign that said HISTORICAL MARKER AHEAD, but I didn't stop. There are thousands of historical markers all over America and they are always dull. I know this for a fact because my father stopped at every one of them. He would pull the car up to them and read them aloud to us, even when we asked him not to. They would say something like: [SINGING TREES SACRED BURIAL SITE]

For centuries this land, known as the Valley of the Singing Trees, was a sacred burial site for the Blackbutt Indians. In recognition of this the US Government gave the land to the tribe in perpetuity in 1880. However, in 1882 oil was discovered beneath the singing trees and, after a series of skirmishes in which 27,413 Blackbutts perished, the tribe was relocated to a reservation at Cyanide Springs, New Mexico.

What am I saying? They were never as good as that. Usually they would commemorate something palpably obscure and uninteresting – the site of the first Bible college in western Tennessee, the birthplace of the inventor of the moist towelette, the home of the author of the Kansas state song. You knew before you got there that they were going to be boring because if they had been even remotely interesting somebody would have set up a hamburger stand and sold souvenirs. But Dad thrived on them and would never fail to be impressed. After reading them to us he would say in an admiring tone, 'Well, I'll be darned,' and then without fail would pull back onto the highway into the path of an oncoming truck, which would honk furiously and shed part of its load as it swerved past. 'Yes, that was really very interesting,' he would add reflectively, unaware that he had just about killed us all.

I was heading for the Booker T. Washington National Monument, a restored plantation near Roanoke where Booker T. Washington grew up. He was a remarkable man. A freed slave, he taught himself to read and write, secured an education and eventually founded the Tuskegee Institute in Alabama, the first college in America for blacks. Then, as if that were not achievement enough, he finished his career as a soul musician, churning out a series of hits in the 1960s on the Stax record label with the backup group the MGs. As I say, a remarkable man. My plan was to visit his monument and then zip over to Monticello for a leisurely look around Thomas Jefferson's home. But it was not to be. Just beyond Patrick Springs, I spied a side road leading to a place called Critz, which I calculated with a glance at the map could cut thirty miles off my driving distance. Impulsively I hauled the car around the corner, making the noise of squealing tyres as I went. I had to make the noise myself because the Chevette couldn't manage it, though it did shoot out some blue smoke.

I should have known better. My first rule of travel is never to go to a place that sounds like a medical condition and Critz clearly was an incurable disease involving flaking skin. The upshot is that I got hopelessly lost. The road, once I lost sight of the highway, broke up into a network of unsignposted lanes hemmed in by tall grass. I drove for ages, with that kind of glowering, insane resolve that you get when you are lost and become convinced that if you just keep moving you will eventually end up where you want to be. I kept coming to towns that weren't on my map — Sanville, Pleasantville, Preston. These weren't two-shack places. They were proper towns, with schools, gas stations, lots of houses. I felt as if I should call the newspaper in Roanoke and inform the editor that I had found a lost county.

Eventually, as I passed through Sanville for the third time, I decided I would have to ask directions. I stopped an old guy taking his dog out to splash urine around the neighbourhood and asked him the way to Critz. Without batting an eyelid he launched into a set of instructions of the most breathtaking complexity. He must have talked for five minutes. It sounded like a description of Lewis and Clark's journey through the wilderness. I couldn't follow it at all, but when he paused and said, 'You with me so far?' I lied and said I was.

'Okay, well that takes you to Preston,' he went on. 'From there you follow the old drover's road due east out of town till you come to the McGregor place. You can tell it's the McGregor place because there's a sign out front saying: The McGregor Place. About a hundred yards further on there's a road going off to the left with a sign for Critz. But whatever you do don't go down there because the bridge is out and you'll plunge straight into Dead Man's Creek.' And on he went like that for many minutes. When at last he finished I thanked him and drove off without conviction in the general direction of his last gesture. Within 200 yards I had come to a T-junction and didn't have a clue which way to go. I went right. Ten minutes later, to the surprise of both of us, I was driving past the old guy and his ever-urinating dog again. Out of the corner of my eye I could see him gesturing excitedly, shouting at me that I had gone the wrong way, but as this was already abundantly evident to me, I ignored his hopping around and went left at the junction. This didn't get me any nearer Critz, but it did provide me with a new set of dead ends and roads to nowhere. At three o'clock in the afternoon, two hours after I set off for Critz, I blundered back onto Highway 58. I was 150 feet further down the road than I had been when I left it. Sourly I pulled back on to the highway and drove for many long hours in silence. It was too late to go to the Booker T. Washington National Monument or to Monticello, even assuming I could summon the intelligence to find them. The day had been a complete washout. I had had no lunch, no life-giving infusions of coffee. It had been a day without pleasure or reward. I got a room in a motel in Fredricksburg, ate at a pancake-house of ineffable crappiness and retired to my room in a dim frame of mind.

In the morning I drove to Colonial Williamsburg, a restored historic village near the coast. It is one of the most popular tourist attractions in the east and even though it was early on a Tuesday morning in October when I arrived, the car-parks were already filling up. I parked and joined a stream of people following the signs to the visitors' centre. Inside it was cool and dark. Near the door was a scale model of the village in a glass case. Oddly, there was no you-are-here arrow to help you get oriented. Indeed, the visitors' centre wasn't even shown. There was no way of telling where the village was in relation to where you were now. That seemed strange to me and I became suspicious. I stood back and watched the crowds. Gradually it became clear to me that the whole thing was a masterpiece of crowd management. Everything was contrived to leave you with the impression that the only way into Williamsburg was to buy a ticket, pass through a door ominously marked 'Processing' and then climb aboard a shuttle bus which would whisk you off to the historic site, presumably some distance away. Unless, like me, you pulled out of the river of people, you found yourself standing at the ticket counter making an instant decision on which of three kinds of ticket to buy – a Patriot's Pass for $24·50, a Royal Governor's Pass for $20 or a Basic Admission Ticket for $15·50, each allowing entrance to a different number of restored buildings. Most visitors found themselves parted from a lot of money and standing in the line to the processing doorway before they knew what had hit them.

I hate the way these places let you get all the way there before disclosing just how steep and confiscatory the admission price is. They should be required to put up roadside signs saying THREE MILES TO COLONIAL WILLIAMSBURG. GET YOUR CHEQUE—BOOKS READY! or ONE MILE TO COLONIAL WILLIAMSBURG. IT'S PRETTY GOOD, BUT REAL EXPENSIVE. I felt that irritation, bordering on wild hate, that I generally experience when money is being tugged out of me through my nostrils. I mean honestly, $24·50 just to walk around a restored village for a couple of hours. I gave silent thanks that I had ditched the wife and kids at Manchester Airport. A day out here with the family could cost almost $75 – and that's before paying for ice-creams and soft drinks and sweat-shirts saying 'Boy, Were We Screwed at Colonial Williamsburg'.

There was something wrong with the whole set-up, something deeply fishy about the way it worked. I had lived in America long enough to know that if the only way into Williamsburg was to buy a ticket there would be an enormous sign on the wall saying YOU MUST HAVE A TICKET. DON'T EVEN THINK ABOUT TRYING TO GET IN WITHOUT ONE. But there wasn't any such sign. I went outside, back out into the bright sunshine, and watched where the shuttle buses were going. They went down the driveway, joined a dual carriageway and disappeared around a bend. I crossed the dual carriageway, dodging the traffic, and followed a path through some woods. In a few seconds I was in the village. It was as simple as that. I didn't have to pay a penny. Nearby the shuttle buses were unloading ticket-holders. They had had a ride of roughly 200 yards and were about to discover that what their tickets entitled them to do was join long, ill-humoured lines of other ticket-holders standing outside each restored historic building, sweating in silence and shuffling forward at a rate of one step every three minutes. I don't think I had ever seen quite so many people failing to enjoy themselves. The glacial lines put me in mind of Disney World, which was not altogether inappropriate since Williamsburg is really a sort of Disney World of American history. All the ticket takers and street sweepers and information givers were dressed in period costumes, the women in big aprons and muffin hats, the men in tricornered hats and breeches. The whole idea was to give history a happy gloss and make you think that spinning your own wool and dipping your own candles must have been bags of fun. I half expected to see Goofy and Donald Duck come waddling along dressed as soldiers in the Colonial Army.

The first house I came to had a sign saying DR MCKENZIE'S APOTHECARY. The door was open, so I went inside, expecting to see eighteenth-century apothecary items. But it was just a gift shop selling twee reproductions at outrageous prices – brass candle snifters at $28, reproduction apothecary jars at $35, that sort of thing. I fled back outside, wanting to stick my head in Ye Olde Village Puking Trough. But then, slowly and strangely, the place began to grow on me. As I strolled up Duke of Gloucester Street I underwent a surprising transformation. Slowly, I found that I was becoming captivated by it all. Williamsburg is big – 173 acres – and the size of it alone is impressive. There are literally dozens of restored houses and shops. More than that, it really is quite lovely, particularly on a sunny morning in October with a mild wind wandering through the ash and beech trees. I ambled along the leafy lanes and broad greens. Every house was exquisite, every cobbled lane inviting, every tavern and vine-clad shoppe remorselessly a-drip with picturesque charm. It is impossible, even for a flinty-hearted jerk-off such as your narrator, not to be won over. However dubious Williamsburg may be as a historical document – and it is plenty dubious – it is at least a model town. It makes you realise what an immeasurably nice place much of America could be if only people possessed the same instinct for preservation as they do in Europe. You would think the millions of people who come to Williamsburg every year would say to each other, 'Gosh, Bobbi, this place is beautiful. Let's go home to Smellville and plant lots of trees and preserve all the fine old buildings.' But in fact that never occurs to them. They just go back and build more parking lots and Pizza Huts.

A lot of Williamsburg isn't as old as they like you to think it is. The town was the capital of colonial Virginia for eighty years, from 1699 to 1780. But when the capital was moved to Richmond, Williamsburg fell into decline. In the 1920s John D. Rockefeller developed a passion for the place and began pouring money into its restoration – $90 million so far. The problem now is that you never quite know what's genuine and what's fanciful. Take the Governor's Palace. It looks to be very old – and, as I say, no one discourages you from believing that it is – but in fact it was only built in 1933. The original building burned down in 1781 and by 1930 had been gone for so long that nobody knew what it had looked like. It was only because somebody found a drawing of it in the Bodleian Library at Oxford that they were able to make a reasonable stab at reproducing it. But it isn't old and it may not even be all that accurate.

Everywhere you turn you are confronted, exasperatingly, with bogus touches. At the Bruton Parish Church, the gravestones were clearly faked, or at least the engravings had been reground. Rockefeller or someone else in authority had obviously been disappointed to discover that after a couple of centuries in the open air gravestones become illegible, so now the inscriptions are as fresh and deep-grooved as if they had been cut only last week, which they may well have been. You find yourself constantly wondering whether you are looking at genuine history or some Disneyesque embellishment. Was there really a Severinus Dufray and would he have had a sign outside his house saying 'Genteel Tailoring'? Possibly. Would Dr McKenzie have a note in florid lettering outside his dispensary announcing: 'Dr McKenzie begs Leave to inform the Public he has just received a large Quantity of fine Goods, viz: Tea, Coffee, fine Soap, Tobacco, etc., to be SOLD here at his shop'? Who can say?

Thomas Jefferson, a man of some obvious sensitivity, disliked Williamsburg and thought it ugly. (This is something else they don't tell you.) He called the college and hospital 'rude, misshapen piles' and the Governor's Palace 'not handsome'. He can't have been describing the same place because the Williamsburg of today is relentlessly attractive. And for that reason I liked it.

I drove on to Mount Vernon, George Washington's home for most of his life. Washington deserves his fame. What he did in running the Colonial Army was risky and audacious, not to say skilful. People tend to forget that the Revolutionary War dragged on for eight years and that Washington often didn't get a whole lot of support. Out of a populace of 5·5 million, Washington sometimes had as few as 5,000 soldiers in his army – one soldier for every 1,100 people. When you see what a tranquil and handsome place Mt Vernon is, and what an easy and agreeable life he led there, you wonder why he bothered. But that's the appealing thing about Washington, he is such an enigma. We don't even know for sure what he looked like. Almost all the portraits of him were done by, or copied from the works of, Charles Willson Peale. Peale painted sixty portraits of Washington, but unfortunately he wasn't very hot at faces. In fact, according to Samuel Eliot Morison, Peale's pictures of Washington, Lafayette and John Paul Jones all look to be more or less the same person.

Mount Vernon was everything Williamsburg should have been and was not – genuine, interesting, instructive. For well over a century it has been maintained by the Mount Vernon Ladies' Association and what a lucky thing it is we have them. Amazingly, when the house was put up for sale in 1853, neither the federal government nor the state of Virginia was prepared to buy it for the nation. So a group of dedicated women hastily formed the Mount Vernon Ladies' Association, raised the money to buy the house and 200 acres of grounds and then set about restoring it to precisely as it was in Washington's day, right down to the correct pigments of paint and patterns of wallpaper. Thank God John D. Rockefeller didn't get hold of it. Today the Association continues to run it with a dedication and skill that should be models to preservation groups everywhere, but alas are not. Fourteen rooms are open to the public and in each a volunteer provides an interesting and well-informed commentary – and is sufficiently clued-up to answer almost any question – on how the room was used and decorated. The house was very much Washington's creation. He was involved in the daintiest questions of décor, even when he was away on military campaigns. It was strangely pleasing to imagine him at Valley Forge, with his troops dropping dead of cold and hunger, agonising over the purchase of lace ruffs and tea cosies. What a great guy. What a hero.

TWELVE

I spent the night on the outskirts of Alexandria and in the morning drove into Washington. I remembered Washington from my childhood as hot and dirty and full of the din of jackhammers. It had that special kind of grimy summer heat you used to get in big cities in America before air-conditioning came along. People spent every waking moment trying to alleviate it – wiping their necks with capacious handkerchiefs, swallowing cold glasses of lemonade, lingering by open refrigerators, sitting listlessly before electric fans. Even at night there was no relief. It was tolerable enough outside where you might catch a puff of breeze, but indoors the heat never dissipated. It just sat, thick and stifling. It was like being inside a vacuum cleaner bag. I can remember lying awake in a hotel in downtown Washington listening to the sounds of an August night wash in through the open window: sirens, car horns, the thrum of neon from the hotel sign, the swish of traffic, people laughing, people yelling, people being shot.

We once saw a guy who had been shot, one sultry August night when we were out for a late snack after watching the Washington Senators beat the New York Yankees 4–3 at Griffith Stadium. He was a black man and he was lying among a crowd of legs in what appeared to me at the time to be a pool of oil, but which was of course the blood that was draining out of the hole in his head. My parents hustled us past and told us not to look, but we did, of course. Things like that didn't happen in Des Moines, so we gaped extensively. I had only ever seen murders on TV on programmes like *Gunsmoke* and *Dragnet*. I thought it was something they did just to keep the story moving. It had never occurred to me that shooting someone was an option available in the real world. It seemed such a strange thing to do, to stop someone's life just because you found him in some way disagreeable. I imagined my fourth grade teacher, Miss Bietlebaum, who had hair on her upper lip and evil in her heart, lying on the floor beside her desk, stilled forever, while I stood over her with a smoking gun in my hand. It was an interesting concept. It made you think.

At the diner where we went for our snack, there was yet another curious thing that made me think. White people like us would come in and take seats at the counter, but black people would place an order and then stand against the wall. When their food was ready, it would be handed to them in a paper bag and they would take it home or out to their car. My father explained to us that Negroes weren't allowed to sit at luncheon counters in Washington. It wasn't against the law exactly, but they didn't do it because Washington was enough of a Southern city that they just didn't dare. That seemed strange too and it made me even more reflective.

Afterwards, lying awake in the hot hotel room, listening to the restless city, I tried to understand the adult world and could not. I had always thought that once you grew up you could do anything you wanted – stay up all night or eat ice-cream straight out of the container. But now, on this one important evening of my life, I had discovered that if you didn't measure up in some critical way, people might shoot you in the head or make you take your food out to the car. I sat up on one elbow and asked my dad if there were places where Negroes ran lunch counters and made white people stand against the wall.

My dad regarded me over the top of a book and said he didn't think so. I asked him what would happen if a Negro tried to sit at a luncheon counter, even though he wasn't supposed to. What would they do to him? My dad said he didn't know and told me I should go to sleep and not worry about such things. I lay down and thought about it for a while and supposed that they would shoot him in the head. Then I rolled over and tried to sleep, but I couldn't, partly because it was so hot and I was confused and partly because earlier in the evening my brother had told me that he was going to come over to my bed when I was asleep and wipe boogers on my face because I hadn't given him a bite of my frosted malt at the ball game, and I was frankly unsettled by this prospect, even though he seemed to be sleeping soundly now.

The world has changed a lot since those days, of course. Now if you lie awake in a hotel room at night, you don't hear the city any more. All you hear is the white sound of your air conditioner. You could be in a jet over the Pacific or in a bathysphere beneath the sea for all you hear. Everywhere you go is air-conditioned, so the air is always as cool and clean as a freshly-laundered shirt. People don't wipe their necks much any more or drink sweating glasses of lemonade, or lay their bare arms gratefully on cool marble soda-fountains, because nowadays summer heat is something out there, something experienced only briefly when you sprint from your parking lot to your office or from your office to the luncheon counter down the block. Nowadays, black people sit at luncheon counters, so it's not as easy to get a seat, but it's more fair. And no one goes to Washington Senators games any more because the Washington Senators no longer exist. In 1972 the owner moved the team to Texas because he could make more money there. Alas. But perhaps the most important change, at least as far as I am concerned, is that my brother no longer threatens to wipe boogers on me when I annoy him.

Washington feels like a small city. Its metropolitan population is three million, which makes it the seventh largest in America. And if you add Baltimore, right next door, it rises to over five million. But the city itself is quite small, with a population of just 637,000, less than Indianapolis or San Antonio. You feel as if you are in some agreeable provincial city, but then you turn a corner and come up against the headquarters of the FBI or the World Bank or the IMF and you realise what an immensely important place it is. The most startling of all these surprises is the White House. There you are, shuffling along down-town, looking in department store windows, browsing at cravats and négligés, and you turn a corner and there it is – the White House – right in the middle of the downtown. So handy for shopping, I thought. It's smaller than you expect. Everybody says that.

Across the street there is a permanent settlement of disaffected people and crazies, living in cardboard boxes, protesting at the Central Intelligence Agency controlling their thoughts from outer space. (Well, wouldn't you?) There was also a guy panhandling for quarters. Can you believe that? Right there in our nation's capital, right where Nancy Reagan could see him from her bedroom window.

Washington's most fetching feature is the Mall, a broad, grassy strip of parkland which stretches for a mile or so from the Capitol building at the eastern end to the Lincoln Memorial at the western side, overlooking the Potomac. The dominant landmark is the Washington Monument. Slender and white, shaped like a pencil, it rises 555 feet above the park. It is one of the simplest and yet handsomest structures I know, and all the more impressive when you consider that its massive stones had to be brought from the Nile delta on wooden rollers by

Sumerian slaves. I'm sorry, I'm thinking of the Great Pyramids at Giza. Anyway, it is a real feat of engineering and very pleasing to look at. I had hoped to go up it, but there was a long line of people, mostly restive schoolchildren, snaked around the base and some distance into the park, all waiting to squeeze into an elevator about the size of a telephone booth, so I headed east in the direction of Capitol Hill, which isn't really much of a hill at all.

Scattered around the Mall's eastern end are the various museums of the Smithsonian Institution – the Museum of American History, the Museum of Natural History, the Air and Space Museum, and so on. The Smithsonian – which, incidentally, was donated to America by an Englishman who had never been there – used to be all in one building, but they keep splitting off sections of it and putting them in new buildings all over town. Now there are fourteen Smithsonian museums. The biggest ones are arrayed around the Mall, the others are mostly scattered around the city. Partly they had to do this because they get so much stuff every year – about a million items. In 1986, just to give you some idea, the Smithsonian's acquisitions included 10,000 moths and butterflies from Scandinavia, the entire archives of the Panama Canal Zone postal service, part of the old Brooklyn Bridge and a MiG-25 jet fighter. All of this used to be kept in a wonderful old Gothic brick building on the Mall called the Castle, but now the Castle is just used for administration and to show an introductory film.

I strolled down towards the Castle now. The park was full of joggers. I found this a little worrying. I kept thinking, 'Shouldn't they be running the country, or at least destabilising some Central American government?' I mean to say, don't you usually have something more important to do at 10·30 on a Wednesday morning than pull on a pair of Reeboks and go sprinting around for forty-five minutes?

At the Castle I found the entrance area blocked with wooden trestles and lengths of rope. American and Japanese security men in dark suits were standing around. They all looked as if they spent a lot of time jogging. Some of them had headphones on and were talking into radios. Others had dogs on long leashes or mirrors on poles and were checking out cars parked along Jefferson Drive in front of the building. I went up to one of the American security men and asked him who was coming, but he said he wasn't allowed to tell me. I thought this was bizarre. Here I was in a country where, thanks to the Freedom of Information Act, I could find out how many suppositories Ronald Reagan's doctor had prescribed for him in 1986*, but I couldn't be told which foreign dignitary would shortly be making a public appearance on the steps of a national institution. The lady next to me said, 'It's Nakasone. President of Japan.'

'Oh, really,' I replied, always ready to see a celebrity. I asked the security man when he would be arriving. 'I'm not allowed to tell you that either, sir,' he said and passed on.

I stood with the crowd for a while and waited for Mr Nakasone to come along. And then I thought, 'Why am I standing here?' I tried to think of anyone I knew who would be impressed to hear that I had seen with my own eyes the Prime Minister of Japan. I imagined myself saying to my children, 'Hey, kids, guess who I saw in Washington – Yasuhiro Nakasone!' and being met with silence. So I walked on to the National Air and Space Museum, which was more interesting.

But not nearly as interesting as it ought to be, if you ask me. Back in the 1950s and 60s, the Smithsonian *was* the Castle. Everything was crammed into this one wonderfully dark and musty old building. It was like the nation's attic and, like an attic, it was gloriously random. Over here was the shirt Lincoln was wearing when he was shot, with a brown blood-stain above the heart. Over there was a diorama showing a Navajo family fixing dinner. Up above you, hanging from the gloomy rafters, were the Spirit of St Louis and the Wright Brothers' first plane. You didn't know where to look next or what you would find around each corner. Now it is as if everything has been sorted out by a fussy spinster, folded neatly and put in its proper place. You go to the Air and Space Museum and you see the Spirit of St Louis and the Wright Brothers' plane and lots of other famous planes and rocket ships and it's all highly impressive, but it is also clinical and uninspired. There is no sense of discovery. If your brother came running up to you and said, 'Hey, you'll never guess what I found in this room over here!' you would in fact guess, more or less, because it would have to be either an aeroplane or a rocket ship. At the old Smithsonian it could have been absolutely anything – a petrified dog, Custer's scalp, human heads adrift in bottles. There's no element of surprise any more. So I spent the day trudging around the various

* 1,472.

museums dutifully and respectfully, with interest but not excitement. Still, there was so much to see that a whole day passed and I had seen only a part of it.

In the evening I came to the Mall, and walked across it to the Jefferson Memorial. I had hoped to see it at dusk, but I arrived late and the darkness fell like a blanket. Before I was very far into the park it was pitch dark. I expected to be mugged – indeed, I took it as my due, wandering into a city park like this on a dark night – but evidently the muggers couldn't see me. The only physical risk I ran was being bowled over by one of the many joggers who sprinted invisibly along the dark paths. The Jefferson Memorial was beautiful. There's not much to it, just a large marble rotunda in the shape of Monticello, with a gigantic statue of Jefferson inside and his favourite sayings engraved on the walls ('Have a nice day,' 'Keep your shirt on,' 'You could have knocked me over with a feather' etc.), but when it is lit up at night it is entrancing, with the lights of the memorial smeared across the pool of water called the Tidal Basin. I must have sat for an hour or more just listening to the rhythmic swish of the distant traffic, the sirens and car horns, the far-off sounds of people shouting, people singing, people being shot.

I lingered so long that it was too late to go to the Lincoln Memorial and I had to come back in the morning. The Lincoln Memorial is exactly as you expect it to be. He sits there in his big high chair looking grand and yet kindly. There was a pigeon on his head. There is always a pigeon on his head. I wondered idly if the pigeon thought that all the people who came every day were there to look at him. Afterwards, as I strolled across the Mall, I spied yet more trestles and draped ropes, with security men hanging about. They had closed off a road across the park and had brought in two helicopters with the presidential seal on their sides and seven cannons and the Marine Corps Band. It was quite early in the morning and there were no crowds, so I went and stood beside the roped enclosure, the only spectator, and none of the security men bothered me or even seemed to notice me.

After a couple of minutes, a wailing of sirens filled the air and a cavalcade of limousines and police motor cycles drew up. Out stepped Nakasone and some other Japanese men, all in dark suits, escorted by some junior-looking Aryans from the State Department. They all stood politely while the Marine Corps Band blared a lively tune which

I didn't recognise. Then there was a twenty-one-gun salute, but the cannons didn't go BOOM! as you would expect. They went puff. They were filled with some kind of noiseless powder, presumably so as not to waken the President in the White House across the way, so when the battery commander shouted, 'Ready, steady, go!' or whatever it was he shouted, there followed seven quick puff sounds and then a dense cloud of smoke drifted over us and went on a long slow waft across the park. This was done three times because there were only seven cannons. Then Nakasone gave a friendly wave to the crowd – which is to say, to me – and sprinted with his party to the presidential helicopters, whose blades were already whirring to life. After a moment they rose up, tilted past the Washington Monument and were gone, and everyone back on the ground relaxed and had a smoke.

Weeks afterwards, back in London, I told people about my private encounter with Nakasone and the Marine Corps Band and the noiseless cannons and how the Prime Minister of Japan had waved to me alone. Most of them would listen politely, then allow a small pause and say, 'Did I tell you that Mavis has to go back into hospital next week to have her feet done?' or something like that. The English can be so crushing sometimes.

From Washington I took US 301 out past Annapolis and the US Naval Academy and over a long, low bridge across the Chesapeake Bay into eastern Maryland. Before 1952, when the bridge was built, the eastern side of the bay had enjoyed centuries of isolation. Ever since then, people have been saying that outsiders will flood in and ruin the peninsula, but it still looked pretty unspoiled to me, and my guess is that it's the outsiders who have kept it that way. It's always the outsiders who are the most fiercely opposed to shopping malls and bowling alleys, which the locals in their simple, trusting way tend to think might be kind of handy.

Chestertown, the first town of any size I came to, confirmed this. The first thing I saw was a woman in a bright pink track suit zipping past on a bicycle with a wicker basket on the front. Only an urban *émigré* would have a bicycle with a wicker basket. A local person would have a Subaru pickup truck. There seemed to be a lot of these bike ladies about, and between them they had clearly made Chestertown into a model community. The whole place was as neat as a pin. The sidewalks were paved with brick and lined with trees, and there was a well-tended park in the middle of the business district. The library was busy. The movie theatre was still in business and not showing a *Death Wish* movie. Everything about the place was tranquil and appealing. This was as nice a town as I had seen. This was almost Amalgam.

I drove on through the low, marshy flatlands, much taken with the simple beauty of the Chesapeake peninsula, with its high skies and scattered farms and forgotten little towns. Late in the morning I crossed into Delaware, *en route* to Philadelphia. Delaware may well be the most obscure of all the American states. I once met a girl from Delaware and couldn't think of a single thing to say to her. I said, 'So you come from Delaware? Gosh. Wow.' And she moved quickly onto someone more verbally dextrous, and also better looking. For a while it troubled me that I could live in America for twenty years, have the benefit of an expensive education and not know anything at all about one of the fifty states. I went around asking people if they had ever heard Delaware mentioned on television or seen a story pertaining to it in the newspaper or read a novel set there and they'd say, 'You know, I don't think I ever have,' and then they'd look kind of troubled too.

I determined that I would read up on Delaware so that the next time I met a girl from there I could say something droll and apposite and she might go to bed with me. But I could find almost nothing written about Delaware anywhere. Even the entry in the *Encyclopaedia Britannica* was only about two paragraphs long and finished in the middle of a sentence, as I recall. And the funny thing was that as I drove across Delaware now I could feel it vanishing from my memory as I went, like those children's drawing slates on which you erase the picture by lifting the transparent sheet. It was as if a giant sheet were being lifted up behind me as I drove, expunging the experience as it unfolded. Looking back now, I can just vaguely recall some semi-industrial landscape and some signs for Wilmington.

And then I was in the outskirts of Philadelphia, the city that gave the world Sylvester Stallone and Legionnaire's disease, among other things, and was too preoccupied with the disturbing thoughts that this called up to give Delaware any further consideration.

THIRTEEN

When I was a child, Philadelphia was the third biggest city in America. What I remembered of it was driving through endless miles of ghettos, one battered block after another, on a hot July Sunday, with black children playing in the spray of fire hydrants and older people lounging around on the street corners or sitting on the front stoops. It was the poorest place I had ever seen. Trash lay in the gutters and doorways, and whole buildings were derelict. It was like a foreign country, like Haiti or Panama. My dad whistled tunelessly through his teeth the whole time, as he always did when he was uneasy, and told us to keep the windows rolled up even though it was boiling in the car. At stop lights people would stare stonily at us and Dad would whistle in double time and drum the steering wheel with his fingers and smile apologetically at anyone who looked at him, as if to say, 'Sorry, we're from out of state.'

Things have changed now, naturally. Philadelphia is no longer the third biggest city in America. Los Angeles pushed it into fourth place in the 1960s, and now there are freeways to whisk you into the heart of town without soiling your tyres in the ghettos. Even so, I managed a brief, inadvertent visit to one of the poorer neighbourhoods when I wandered off the freeway in search of a gas station. Before I could do anything about it, I found myself sucked into a vortex of one-way streets that carried me into the most squalid and dangerous-looking neighbourhood I had ever seen. It may have been, for all I know, the very ghetto we passed through all those years before – the brownstone buildings looked much the same – but it was many times worse than the one I remembered. The ghetto of my childhood, for all its poorness, had the air of a street carnival. People wore colourful clothes and seemed to be having a good time. This place was just bleak and dangerous, like a war zone. Abandoned cars, old refrigerators, burnt-out sofas littered every vacant lot. Garbage cans looked as if they had been thrown to the street from the roof-tops. There were no gas stations – I wouldn't have stopped anyway, not in a place like this, not for a million dollars – and most of the storefronts were boarded with plywood. Every standing object had been spray-painted with graffiti. There were still a few young people on the stoops and corners, but they looked listless and cold – it was a chilly day – and they seemed not to notice me. Thank God. This was a neighbourhood where clearly you could be murdered for a pack of cigarettes – a fact that was not lost on me as I searched nervously for a way back onto the freeway. By the time I found it, I wasn't whistling through my teeth so much as singing through my sphincter.

It really was the most uncomfortable experience I had had in many years. God, what it must be like to live there and to walk those streets daily. Do you know that if you are a black man in urban America you now stand a one in nineteen chance of being murdered? In World War II, the odds of being killed were one in fifty. In New York City there is one murder every four hours. Murder there has become the most common cause of death for people under thirty-five – and yet New York isn't even the most murderous city in America. At least eight other cities have a higher murder rate. In Los Angeles there are more murders each year on schoolgrounds alone than there are in the whole of London. So perhaps it is little wonder that people in American cities take violence as routine. I don't know how they do it.

On my way to Des Moines to start this trip, I passed through O'Hare Airport in Chicago where I ran into a friend who worked for the *St Louis Post Dispatch*. He told me he had been working extra hard lately because of something that had happened to his boss. The boss had been driving home from work late one Saturday night when he had stopped at some traffic lights. As he waited for the lights to change, the passenger door opened and a man with a gun got in. The gunman made the boss drive down to the riverfront, where he shot him in the head and took his money. The boss had been in a coma for three weeks and they weren't sure whether he was going to live.

My friend was telling me this not because it was such an incredible story, but simply by way of elucidating why he was having to work so damned hard lately. As for his boss, his attitude seemed to be that if you forget to lock your car doors when you're driving through St Louis late at night, well, you've got to expect to take a bullet in the head from time to time. It was very odd, his deadpan attitude, but it seems to be more and more the way in America now. It made me feel like a stranger.

*

I drove downtown and parked near City Hall. On top of the building is a statue of William Penn. It's the main landmark downtown, visible from all around the city, but it was covered in scaffolding. In 1985, after decades of neglect, the city fathers decided to refurbish the statue before it fell down. So they covered it in scaffolding. However, this cost so much that there was no money left to do the repairs. Now, two years later, the scaffolding was still there and not a lick of work had been done. A city engineer had recently announced with a straight face that before long the scaffolding itself would need to be refurbished. This is more or less how Philadelphia works, which is to say, not very well. No other city in America pursues the twin ideals of corruption and incompetence with quite the same enthusiasm. When it comes to asinine administration, Philadelphia is in a league of its own.

Consider: in 1985, a bizarre sect called Move barricaded itself into a tenement house on the west side of town. The police chief and mayor considered the options open to them and decided that the most intelligent use of their resources would be to blow up the house – but of course! – even though they knew there were children inside and it was in the middle of a densely-populated part of the city. So they dropped a bomb on the house from a helicopter. This started a fire that quickly grew out of control and burned down most of the neighbour- hood – sixty-one houses in all – and killed eleven people, including all the children in the barricaded home.

When they aren't being incompetent, city officials like to relax with a little corruption. Just as I was driving into town I heard on the radio that a former city councillor had been sentenced to ten years in jail and his aide to eight years for attempted extortion. The judge called it a gross breach of public trust. He should know. Across town a state review board was calling for the dismissal of nine of the judge's colleagues for taking cash gifts from members of the Roofers Union. Two of those judges were already awaiting trial on extortion charges. This sort of thing is routine in Philadelphia. A few months earlier, when a state official named Bud Dwyer was similarly accused of corruption, he called a press conference, pulled out a gun and, as cameras rolled, blew his brains out. This led to an excellent local joke.

Q: What is the difference between Bud Dwyer and Bud Lite?

A: Bud Lite has a head on it.

Yet for all its incompetence and criminality, Philadelphia is a likeable place. For one thing, unlike Washington, it feels like a big city. It had skyscrapers and there was steam rising through vents in the sidewalk and on every corner stood a stainless steel hot dog stand, with a chilly-looking guy in a stocking cap bobbing around behind it. I wandered over to Independence Square – actually it's now called Independence National Historical Park – and looked respectfully at all the historic buildings. The main building is Independence Hall, where the Declaration of Independence was drawn up and the Constitution ratified. When I was first there in 1960, there was a long line stretching out of the building. There still was – in fact, it seemed not to have moved in twenty-seven years. Deep though my respect is for both the Constitution and the Declaration of Independence, I was disinclined to spend my afternoon in such a long and immobile queue. I went instead to the visitors' centre. National park visitors' centres are always the same. They have some displays in glass cases that manage to be both boring and uninformative, a locked auditorium with a board out front saying that the next showing of the free twelve-minute introductory film will be at 4 p.m. (just before 4 p.m. somebody comes and changes it to 10 a.m.), some racks of books and brochures with titles like *Pewter in History* and *Vegetables of Old Philadelphia*, which are too dull even to browse through, much less buy, and a drinking fountain and rest-rooms, which everyone makes use of because there's not much else to do. Every visitor to every national park goes into the visitors' centre, stands around kind of stupidly for a while, then has a pee and a drink of water and wanders back outside. That is what I did now.

From the visitors' centre I ambled along Independence Mall to Franklin Square, which was full of winos, many of whom had the comical idea that I might be prepared to give them twenty-five cents of my own money without their providing any product or service in return. According to my guidebook, Franklin Square had 'lots of interesting things' to see – a museum, a working book bindery, an archaeological exhibit and 'the only post office in the United States which does not fly the American flag' (don't ask me why) – but my heart wasn't in it, especially with piteous and unwashed winos tugging at my sleeves all the while, and I fled back to the real world of downtown Philadelphia.

Late in the afternoon, I found my way to the offices of the
Philadelphia Inquirer, where an old friend from Des Moines, Lucia
Herndon, was life-style editor. The *Inquirer* offices were like newspaper offices everywhere – grubby, full of junk, littered with
coffee-cups in which cigarette butts floated like dead fish in a polluted
lake – and Lucia's desk, I was impressed to note, was one of the
messiest in the room. This may have accounted in part for her
impressive rise at the *Inquirer*. I only ever knew one journalist with a
truly tidy desk, and he was eventually arrested for molesting small
boys. Make of that what you will; but just bear it in mind the next time
somebody with a tidy desk invites you camping.

We drove in my car out to the district of Mt Airy, where,
conveniently for me – and for her too, come to that – Lucia lived with
another old friend of mine from Des Moines, her husband, Hal. All
day long I had been wondering, vaguely and intermittently, why Hal
and Lucia liked Philadelphia so much – they had moved there about a
year before – but now I understood. The road to Mt Airy led through
the most beautiful city park I had ever been in. Called Fairmount Park
and covering almost 9,000 rolling acres, it is the largest municipal
park in America and it is full of trees and fragrant shrubs and bosky
glades of infinite charm. It stretches for miles along the banks of the
Schuylkill River. We drove through a dreamy twilight. Boats sculled
along the water. It was perfection.

Mt Airy was out in the Germantown section of the city. It had a nice
settled feeling to it, as if people had lived there for generations – which
is in fact the case in Philadelphia, Lucia told me. The city was still full
of the sort of neighbourhoods where everybody knew everybody else.
Many people scarcely ever ventured more than a few hundred yards
from their homes. It was not uncommon to get lost and find that
hardly anybody could reliably direct you to a neighbourhood three
miles away. Philadelphia also had its own vocabulary – downtown
was called centre city, sidewalks were called pavements, as in Britain
–and peculiarities of pronunciation.

In the evening I sat in Hal and Lucia's house, eating their food,
drinking their wine, admiring their children and their house and
furniture and possessions, their easy wealth and comfort, and felt a sap
for ever having left America. Life was so abundant here, so easy, so
convenient. Suddenly I wanted a refrigerator that made its own ice-

cubes and a waterproof radio for the shower. I wanted an electric orange juicer and a room ioniser and a wristwatch that would keep me in touch with my biorhythms. I wanted it all. Once in the evening I went upstairs to go to the bathroom and walked past one of the children's bedrooms. The door was open and a bedside light was on. There were toys everywhere – on the floor, on shelves, tumbling out of a wooden trunk. It looked like Santa's workshop. But there was nothing extraordinary about this; it was just a typical middle-class American bedroom.

And you should see American closets. They are always full of yesterday's enthusiasms: golf-clubs, scuba diving equipment, tennis-rackets, exercise machines, tape recorders, dark-room equipment, objects that once excited their owner and then were replaced by other objects even more shiny and exciting. That is the great, seductive thing about America – the people always get what they want, right now, whether it is good for them or not. There is something deeply worrying, and awesomely irresponsible, about this endless self-gratification, this constant appeal to the baser instincts.

Do you want zillions off your state taxes even at the risk of crippling education?

'Oh, yes!' the people cry.

Do you want TV that would make an imbecile weep?

'Yes, please!'

Shall we indulge ourselves with the greatest orgy of consumer spending that the world has ever known?

'Sounds neat! Let's go for it!'

The whole of the global economy is based on supplying the cravings of two per cent of the world's population. If Americans suddenly stopped indulging themselves, or ran out of closet space, the world would fall apart. If you ask me, that's crazy.

I should point out that I am not talking about Hal and Lucia in all this. They are good people and lead modest and responsible lives. Their closets aren't full of scuba diving equipment and seldom-used tennis-rackets. They are full of mundane items like buckets and galoshes, ear-muffs and scouring powders. I know this for a fact because late in the night when everyone was asleep I crept out of bed and had a good look.

*

In the morning, I dropped Hal at his office downtown – correction, centre city – and the drive through Fairmount Park was as enchanting in the morning sunshine as it had been at dusk. All cities should have parks like this, I thought. He told me some more interesting things about Philadelphia: that it spent more money on public art than any other city in America – one per cent of the total city budget – and yet it had an illiteracy rate of forty per cent. He pointed out to me, in the middle of Fairmount Park, the palatial Philadelphia Museum of Art, which had become the city's top tourist attraction, not because of its collection of 500,000 paintings, but because its front steps were the ones Sylvester Stallone sprinted up in *Rocky*. People were actually coming to the museum in buses, looking at the steps and leaving without ever going inside to see the pictures. And he introduced me to a radio talk show hosted by a man named Howard Stern, of which Hal was a devotee. Howard Stern had a keen interest in sex and was engagingly direct with his callers. 'Good morning, Marilyn,' he would say to a caller, 'are you wearing panties?' This, we agreed, beat most early-morning talk shows hands down. Howard queried his callers with arresting candour and a measure of prurience I had not before encountered on American radio.

Unfortunately, I lost the station soon after dropping Hal off and spent the rest of the morning searching for it without success, and eventually ended up listening to a competing phone-in programme, which featured a woman who was an expert on dealing with intestinal worms in dogs. As this principally consisted of giving the dogs a tablet to make the worms die, it was not long before I felt as if I were something of an expert myself. And so the morning passed.

I drove to Gettysburg, where the decisive battle of the American Civil War was fought over three days in July 1863. There were over 50,000 casualties. I parked at the visitors' centre and went inside. It contained a small, ill-lit museum with glass cases containing bullets, brass buttons, belt buckles and that sort of thing, each with a yellowed typed caption beside it saying 'Buckle from uniform of 13th Tennessee Mountaineers. Found by Festus T. Scrubbins, local farmer, and donated by his daughter, Mrs Marienetta Stumpy.' There was precious little to give you any sense of the battle itself. It was more like the gleanings of a treasure hunt.

One interesting thing was a case devoted to the Gettysburg Address, where I learned that Lincoln was invited to speak only as an afterthought and that everyone was taken aback when he accepted. It was only ten sentences long and took just two minutes to deliver. I was further informed that he gave the address many months after the battle. I had always imagined him making it more or less immediately afterwards, while there were still bodies lying around and wraiths of smoke rising from the ruins of distant houses and people like Festus T. Scrubbins poking around among the twitching casualties to see what useful souvenirs they could extract. The truth, as so often in this life, was disappointing.

I went outside and had a look at the battlefield, which sprawls over 3,500 acres of mostly flat countryside, fringed by the town of Gettysburg with its gas stations and motels. The battlefield had the great deficiency common to all historic battlefields. It was just countryside. There was nothing much to distinguish this stretch of empty fields from that one. You had to take their word for it that a great battle was fought there. There were a lot of cannons scattered about, I'll give them that. And along the road leading to the site of Pickett's charge, the attack by Confederate troops that turned the tide of battle in the Union's favour, many of the regiments had erected obelisks and monuments to their own glory, some of them very grand. I strolled down there now. Through my dad's old binoculars I could clearly see how Pickett's troops had advanced from the direction of the town, a mile or so to the north, sweeping across the Burger King parking lot, skirting the Tastee Delite Drive-In and regrouping just outside the Crap-o-Rama Wax Museum and Gift Shop. It's all very sad. Ten thousand soldiers fell there in an hour; two out of every three Confederate soldiers didn't make it back to base. It is a pity, verging on the criminal, that so much of the town of Gettysburg has been spoiled with tourist tat and that it is so visible from the battlefield.

When I was little, my dad bought me a Union cap and a toy rifle and let me loose on the battlefield. I was in heaven. I dashed about the whole day crouching behind trees, charging over to Devil's Den and Little Round Top, blowing up parties of overweight tourists with cameras around their necks. My dad was in heaven too because the park was free and there were literally hundreds of historical plaques for him to read. Now, however, I found it difficult to summon any real excitement for the place.

I was about to depart, feeling guilty that I had come so far without getting anything much out of the experience, when I saw a sign at the visitors' centre for tours to the Eisenhower home. I had forgotten that Ike and Mamie Eisenhower lived on a farm just outside Gettysburg. Their old home was now a national historical monument and could be toured for $2·50. Impulsively I bought a ticket and went outside where a bus was just about to depart to take half a dozen of us to the farm four or five miles away down a country lane.

Well, it was great. I can't remember the last time I had such a good time in a Republican household. You are greeted at the door by a fragrant woman with a chrysanthemum on her bosom, who tells you a little about the house, about how much Ike and Mamie loved to sit around and watch TV and play canasta, and then gives you a leaflet describing each room and lets you wander off on your own so that you can linger or stride on as it pleases you. Each doorway was blocked off with a sheet of perspex, but you could lean against it and gaze into the interior. The house has been preserved precisely as it was when the Eisenhowers lived there. It was as if they had simply wandered off and never come back (something that either of them was quite capable of doing towards the end). The décor was quintessentially early 1960s Republican. When I was growing up we had some neighbours who were rich Republicans and this was practically a duplicate of their house. There was a big TV console in a mahogany cabinet, table-lamps made out of pieces of driftwood, a padded leather cocktail bar, French-style telephones in every room, bookshelves containing about twelve books (usually in matching sets of three) and otherwise filled with large pieces of flowery gilt-edged porcelain of the sort favoured by homosexual French aristocrats.

When the Eisenhowers bought the place in 1950, a 200-year-old farmhouse stood on the site, but it was draughty and creaked on stormy nights, so they had it torn down and replaced with the present building, which *looks* like a 200-year-old farmhouse. Isn't that great? Isn't that just so Republican? I was enchanted. Every room contained things I hadn't seen for years – 1960s kitchen appliances, old copies of *Life Magazine*, boxy black and white portable TVs, metal alarm clocks. Upstairs the bedrooms were just as Ike and Mamie had left them. Mamie's personal effects were on her bedside table – her diary, reading glasses, sleeping-pills – and I dare say that if you knelt down and looked under the bed you would find all her old gin bottles.

In Ike's room his bathrobe and slippers were laid out and the book he had been reading on the day he died was left open on the chair beside the bed. The book was – and I ask you to remember for a moment that this was one of the most important men of this century, a man who held the world's destiny in his hands throughout much of World War II and the Cold War, a man chosen by Columbia University to be its president, a man venerated by Republicans for two generations, a man who throughout the whole of my childhood had his finger on The Button – the book was *West of the Pecos* by Zane Grey.

From Gettysburg, I headed north up US 15 towards Bloomsburg, where my brother and his family had recently moved. For years they had lived in Hawaii, in a house with a swimming-pool, near balmy beaches, beneath tropical skies and whispering palms, and now, just when I had landed a trip to America and could go anywhere I wanted, they had moved to the Rust Belt. Bloomsburg, as it turned out, was actually very nice – a bit short on balmy beaches and hula girls with swaying hips, but still nice for all that.

It's a college town, with a decidedly sleepy air. You feel at first as if you should be wearing slippers and a bathrobe. Main Street was prosperous and tidy and the surrounding streets were mostly filled with large old houses sitting on ample lawns. Here and there church spires poked out from among the many trees. It was pretty well an ideal town – one of those rare American places where you wouldn't need a car. From almost any house in town it would be a short and pleasant stroll to the library and post office and stores. My brother and his wife told me that a developer was about to build a big shopping mall outside town and most of the bigger merchants were going to move out there. People, it appeared, didn't want to stroll to do their shopping. They actually wanted to get in their cars and drive to the edge of town, where they could then park and walk a similar distance across a flat, treeless parking lot. That is how America goes shopping and they wanted to be part of it. So now downtown Bloomsburg is likely to become semi-derelict and another nice little town will be lost. So the world progresses.

Anyway, it was a pleasure to see my brother and his family, as you can imagine. I did all the things you do when you visit relatives – ate their food, used their bathtub, washing-machine and telephone, stood around uselessly while they searched for spare blankets and grappled with a truculent sofa bed, and of course late at night when everyone was asleep I crept out of my room and had a good look in their closets.

As it was the weekend and as they had some spare time, my brother and his wife decided to take me down to Lancaster County to show me the Amish country. It was a two-hour drive. *En route*, my brother pointed out the Three Mile Island nuclear reactor at Harrisburg, where a few years before some careless employees had very nearly irradiated the whole of the eastern seaboard, and then forty-five miles further on we passed the Peach Bottom nuclear power station, where seventeen employees had recently been dismissed after it had been revealed that they spent their working hours sleeping, taking drugs, having rubber band fights and playing video games. At some times every person in the plant was dozing, according to investigators. Allowing state utilities in Pennsylvania to run nuclear power stations is a bit like letting Prince Philip fly through London airspace. In any case, I made a mental note to bring an anti-radiation suit with me next time I came to Pennsylvania.

Lancaster County is the home of the Pennsylvania Dutch, the Amish and Mennonites. The Mennonites are named after a well-known brand of speed-stick deodorant. They aren't really. I just made that up. They are named after Menno Simons, one of their early leaders. In Europe they were called Anabaptists. They came to Lancaster County 250 years ago. Today there are 12,500 Amish people in the county, almost all of them descended from thirty original couples. The Amish split from the Mennonites in 1693, and there have been countless subdivisions since then, but the thing that they all have in common is that they wear simple clothes and shun modern contrivances. The problem is that since about 1860 they've been squabbling endlessly over just how rigorous they should be in their shunning. Every time anybody invents something they argue about whether it is ungodly or not, and the ones who don't like it go off and form a new sect. First, they argued over whether they should have steel rims or rubber rims on their buggies, then whether they should have tractors, then electricity and television. Now presumably they argue over whether they should have a frost-free refrigerator and whether their instant coffee should be powdered or freeze-dried.

The most splendid thing about the Amish is the names they give their towns. Everywhere else in America towns are named either after the first white person to get there or the last Indian to leave. But the Amish obviously gave the matter of town names some thought and graced their communities with intriguing, not to say provocative, appellations: Blue Ball, Bird in Hand, and Intercourse, to name but three. Intercourse makes a good living by attracting passers-by such as me who think it the height of hilarity to send their friends and colleagues postcards with an Intercourse postal mark and some droll sentiment scribbled on the back.

Many people are so fascinated by the Amish way of life, by the idea of people living 200 years in the past, that they come quite literally by the millions to gawk. There were hundreds and hundreds of tourists thronging Intercourse when we arrived, and cars and buses choking the roads into town. Everyone hoped to see and photograph some genuine Amish. Up to five million people a year visit the county and non-Amish businessmen have erected vast souvenir palaces, replica farms, wax museums, cafeterias and gift shops to soak up the $350 million that the visitors are happy to spend each year. Now there is almost nothing left in these towns for the Amish themselves to buy, so they don't come in and the tourists have nothing to do but take pictures of each other.

Travel articles and movies like *Witness* generally gloss over this side of things, but the fact is that Lancaster County is now one of the most awful places in America, especially at weekends when traffic jams sometimes stretch for miles. Many of the Amish themselves have given up and moved to places like Iowa and upper Michigan where they are left alone. Out in the countryside, particularly on the back roads, you can still sometimes see the people in their dark clothes working in the fields or driving their distinctive black buggies down the highway, with a long line of tourist cars creeping along behind, pissed off because they can't get by and they really want to be in Bird in Hand so they can get some more funnel cakes and Sno-cones and perhaps buy a wrought-iron wine rack or combination mailbox/weather-vane to take back home to Fartville with them. I wouldn't be surprised if a decade from now there isn't a real Amish person left in the county. It is an unspeakable shame. They should be left in peace.

In the evening, we went to one of the many barn-like family-style

Pennsylvania Dutch restaurants that are scattered across the county. The parking lot was packed with buses and cars and there were people waiting everywhere, inside the building and out. We went in and were given a ticket with the number 621 on it and went with it to a tiny patch of floorspace just vacated by another party. Every few minutes a man would step to the door and call out a series of numbers ridiculously lower than ours – 220, 221, 222 – and a dozen or so people would follow him into the dining-room. We debated leaving, but a party of fat people beside us told us not to give up because it was worth the wait, even if we had to stay there until eleven o'clock. The food was that good, they said, and where food was concerned these people clearly had some experience. Well, they were right. Eventually our number was called and we were ushered into the dining-room with nine strangers and all seated together at one big trestle-table.

There must have been fifty other such tables in the room, all with a dozen or so people at them. The din and bustle were intense. Waitresses hurried back and forth with outsized trays and everywhere you looked people were shovelling food into their mouths, elbows flapping, as if they hadn't eaten for a week. Our waitress made us introduce ourselves to each other, which everybody thought was kind of dopey, and then she started bringing food, great platters and bowls of it – thick slabs of ham, mountains of fried chicken, buckets of mashed potatoes and all kinds of vegetables, rolls, soups and salads. It was incredible. You helped yourself and with two hands heaved the platter on to the next person. You could have as much of anything as you wanted – and when a bowl was empty the waitress brought back another and practically ordered you to clear it.

I've never seen so much food. I couldn't see over the top of my plate. It was all delicious and pretty soon everybody knew everybody else and was having a great time. I ate so much my armpits bulged. But still the food kept coming. Just when I thought I would have to summon a wheelchair to get me to the car, the waitress took away all the platters and bowls, and started bringing desserts – apple pies, chocolate cakes, bowls of homemade ice-cream, pastries, flans and God knows what else.

I kept eating. It was too delicious to pass up. Buttons popped off my shirt. My trousers burst open. I barely had the strength to lift my spoon, but I kept shovelling the stuff in. It was grotesque. Food began to leak from my ears. And still I ate. I ate the gross national product of Lesotho that night. Eventually, mercifully, the waitress prised the spoons from our hands and took the dessert stuff away, and we were able to stumble zombie-like into the night.

We got in the car, too full to speak, and headed towards the distant greenish glow of Three Mile Island. I lay on the back seat, my feet in the air, and moaned softly. I vowed that never again in my life would I eat a single morsel of food, and I meant it. But two hours later, when we arrived back at my brother's house, the agony had abated and my brother and I were able to begin a new cycle of gross overconsumption, beginning with a twelve-pack of beer and bucket of pretzels from his kitchen and concluding, in the early hours of the morning, with a plate of onion rings and two-foot-long submarine sandwiches, full of goo and spices, at an all-night eaterie out on Highway 11.

What a great country.

FOURTEEN

It was ten minutes to seven in the morning and it was cold. Standing outside the Bloomsburg bus station, I could see my breath. The few cars out this early trailed clouds of vapour. I was hung-over and in a few minutes I was going to climb on to a bus for a five-hour ride into New York. I would sooner have eaten cat food.

My brother had suggested that I take the bus because it would save having to find a place to park in Manhattan. I could leave the car with him and come back for it in a day or two. At two in the morning, after many beers, this had seemed a good plan. But now, standing in the early morning chill, I realised I was making a serious mistake. You only go on a long-distance bus in the United States because either you cannot afford to fly or — and this is really licking the bottom of the barrel in America — you cannot afford a car. Being unable to afford a car in America is the last step before living out of a plastic sack. As a result, most of the people on long-distance buses are one of the following: actively schizoid, armed and dangerous, in a drugged stupor, just released from prison, or nuns. Occasionally you will also see a pair of Norwegian students. You can tell they are Norwegian students because they are so pink-faced and healthy-looking and they wear little blue ankle socks with their sandals. But by and large a ride on a long-distance bus in America combines most of the shortcomings of prison life with those of an ocean crossing in a troop-ship.

So when the bus pulled up before me, heaving a pneumatic sigh, and its doors flapped open, I boarded it with some misgivings. The driver himself didn't appear any too stable. He had the sort of hair that made him look as if he'd been playing with live wires. There were about half a dozen other passengers, though only two of them looked seriously insane and just one was talking to himself. I took a seat near the back and settled down to get some sleep. I had drunk far too many beers with my brother the night before, and the hot spices from the submarine sandwich were now expanding ominously inside my abdomen and drifting around like the stuff they put in lava lamps. Soon, from one end or the other, it would begin to seep out.

I felt a hand on my shoulder from behind. Through the gap in the seat I could see it was an Indian man – by that I mean a man from India, not an American Indian. 'Can I smoke on this bus?' he asked me.

'I don't know,' I said. 'I don't smoke any more, so I don't pay much attention to these things.'

'But do you *think* I can smoke on this bus?'

'I really don't know.'

He was quiet for a few minutes, then his hand was on my shoulder again, not tapping it but resting there. 'I can't find an ashtray,' he said.

'No fooling,' I responded wittily, without opening my eyes.

'Do you think that means we're not allowed to smoke?'

'I don't know. I don't care.'

'But do you *think* it means we're not allowed to smoke?'

'If you don't take your hand off my shoulder I am going to dribble vomit on it,' I said.

He removed his hand quickly and was silent for perhaps a minute. Then he said, 'Would you help me look for an ashtray?'

It was seven in the morning and I was deeply unwell. 'WILL YOU PLEASE JUST LEAVE ME ALONE!' I snapped at him, just a trifle wildly. Two seats back a pair of Norwegian students looked shocked. I gave them a look as if to say, 'And don't you try anything either, you wholesome little shits!' and sank back into my seat. It was going to be a long day.

I slept fitfully, that dissatisfying, semi-conscious sleep in which you incorporate into your dreams the things going on around you – the grinding of gears, the crying of babies, the mad swervings of the bus back and forth across the highway as the driver gropes for a dropped cigarette or lapses into a psychotic episode. Mostly I dreamt of the bus plunging over a cliff-face, sailing into a void; in my dream, we fell for miles, tumbling through the clouds, peacefully, with just the sound of air whisking past outside, and then the Indian saying to me: 'Do you think it would be all right if I smoked *now*?'

When I awoke there was drool on my shoulder and a new passenger opposite me, a haggard woman with lank grey hair who was chain-smoking cigarettes and burping prodigiously. They were the sort of burps children make to amuse themselves – rich, resonant, basso profundo burps. The woman was completely unselfconscious about it.

She would look at me and open her mouth and out would roll a burp.
It was amazing. Then she would take a drag on her cigarette and burp
a large puff of smoke. That was amazing too. I glanced behind me. The
Indian man was still there, looking miserable. Seeing me, he started to
lean forward to ask a supplementary question, but I stopped him with
a raised finger and he sank back. I stared out the window, feeling ill,
and passed the time by trying to imagine circumstances less congenial
than this. But apart from being dead or at a Bee Gees concert I couldn't
think of a single thing.

We reached New York in the afternoon. I got a room in a hotel near
Times Square. The room cost $110 a night and was so small I had to go
out into the corridor to turn around. I had never been in a room where
I could touch all four walls at once. I did all the things you do in hotel
rooms – played with the lights and TV, looked in the drawers, put all
the towels and ashtrays in my suitcase – and then wandered out to
have a look at the city.

   The last time I had been in New York was when I was sixteen and
my friend Stan and I came out to visit my brother and his wife, who
were then living in a strange, Kafkaesque community in Queens called
Lefrak City. It consisted of about a dozen tall apartment buildings
clustered around a series of lonesome quadrangles, the sort of
quadrangles where rain-puddles stand for weeks and the flower-beds
are littered with supermarket trolleys. Something like 50,000 people
lived there. I had never conceived of so many people gathered in one
place. I couldn't understand why in such a big, open country as
America people would choose to live like that. But for all these people
this was it. This was home. They would live out their lives never having
their own back yard, never having a barbecue, never stepping out the
back door at midnight to have a pee in the bushes and check out the
stars. Their children would grow up thinking that supermarket
trolleys grew wild, like weeds.

   In the evenings, when my brother and his wife went out, Stan and I
would sit with binoculars and scan the windows of the neighbouring
buildings. There were hundreds of windows to choose from, each
containing a ghostly glow of television. What we were looking for, of
course, were naked women – and to our amazement we did actually
see some, though usually this resulted in such fervent grappling for

control of the binoculars that the women had dressed and gone out for the evening by the time we got their windows back in view. Mostly what we saw, however, were other men with binoculars scanning the windows of our building.

What I particularly remember was the sense of menace whenever we left the building. Groups of leather-jacketed teenagers with no place to go would sit on the walls around the complex watching anyone who passed. I always expected them to fall in behind us as we went by and to take our money and stick us with knives they had made in the prison workshop, but they never bothered us. They just stared. Even so it was frightening because we were just skinny kids from Iowa.

New York still frightened me. I felt the same sense of menace now as I walked down to Times Square. I had read so much for so long about murders and street crime that I felt a personal gratitude to everyone who left me alone. I wanted to hand out cards that said 'Thank you for not killing me'.

But the only people who assaulted me were panhandlers. There are 36,000 vagrants in New York and in two days of walking around every one of them asked me for money. Some of them asked twice. People in New York go to Calcutta to get some relief from begging. I began to regret that I didn't live in an age when a gentleman could hit such people with his cane. One guy, my favourite, came up and asked if he could borrow a dollar. That knocked me out. I wanted to say, 'Borrow a dollar? Certainly. Shall we say interest at one per cent above prime and we'll meet back here on Thursday to settle?' I wouldn't give him a dollar, of course – I wouldn't give my closest friend a dollar – but I pressed a dime into his grubby mitt and gave him a wink for his guile.

Times Square is incredible. You've never seen such lights, such hustle. Whole sides of buildings are given over to advertisements that blink and ripple and wave. It's like a storm on an electronic sea. There are perhaps forty of these massive inducements to spend and consume, and all but two of them were for Japanese companies: Mita Copiers, Canon, Panasonic, Sony. My mighty homeland was represented by just Kodak and Pepsi Cola. The war is over, Yankee dog, I thought bleakly.

The most riveting thing about New York is that anything can happen there. Only the week before, a woman had been eaten by an escalator. Can you beat that? She had been on her way to work, minding her own business, when suddenly the stair beneath her gave way and she was plummeted into the interior mechanism, into all the whirring cogs and gears, with the sort of consequences you can well imagine. How would you like to be the cleaner in *that* building? ('Bernie, can you come in early tonight? And listen, you'd better bring along a wire brush and a *lot* of Ajax.') New York is always full of amazing and unpredictable things. A front page story in the *New York Post* was about a pervert with AIDS who had been jailed that day for raping little boys. Can you believe that? 'What a city!' I thought. 'Such a madhouse!' For two days I walked and stared and mumbled in amazement. A large black man on Eighth Avenue reeled out of a doorway, looking dangerously disordered, and said to me, 'I been smoking ice! Big bowls of ice!' I gave him a quarter real fast, even though he hadn't asked for anything, and moved off quickly. On Fifth Avenue I went into the Trump Tower, a new skyscraper. A guy named Donald Trump, a developer, is slowly taking over New York, building skyscrapers all over town with his name on them, so I went in and had a look around. The building had the most tasteless lobby I had ever seen – all brass and chrome and blotchy red and white marble that looked like the sort of thing that you would walk around if you saw it on the sidewalk. Here it was everywhere – on the floors, up the walls, on the ceiling. It was like being inside somebody's stomach after he'd eaten pizza. 'Incredible,' I muttered, and walked on. Next door a store sold pornographic videos, right there on Fifth Avenue. My favourite was *Yiddish Erotica, Volume 2*. What could this possibly consist of – rabbis with their trousers down, tarty women lying spread-eagled and saying, 'You wanna fuck already?' 'Superb, incredible,' I mumbled, and plodded on.

In the evening, as I strolled back along Times Square, my eye was caught by a strip-tease club with a photograph of the strippers in the window. They were nice-looking girls. One of the photos was of Samantha Fox. Since Ms Fox was at this time being paid something like £250,000 a year to show off her comely udders to readers of British newspapers such as the *Sun*, it seemed to me improbable, to say the least, that she would be peeling off for strangers in a smoky basement room on Times Square. In fact, I would go so far as to suggest that there was a little fraud at work here. It's a mean trick to play on a horny person.

They always used to do this to you at the Iowa State Fair. The strippers' tents behind the rides would be covered with wildly erotic paintings of the most beautiful, silky-haired, full-breasted, lithe-bodied women you ever saw – women whose moist and pouty lips seemed to be saying, 'I want you – yes, you there, with the zits and glasses. Come and fulfil me, little man.' Aged fourteen and delirious with lust, you would believe these pictures with all your heart and many of the neighbouring organs. You would hand over a crumpled dollar and go inside, into a dusty tent that smelt of horse manure and rubbing alcohol and find on stage a weary stripper looking not unlike your own mother. It was the sort of disappointment from which you never really recover, and my heart went out now to the lonely sailors and Japanese photocopier salesmen who were down there drinking sweet, warm cocktails and having a night of overpriced disappoint-ment. 'We learn from our mistakes,' I remarked sagely to myself with a rueful smile and told a panhandler to piss off.

I went back to my room, pleased not to have been mugged, more pleased not to have been murdered. On top of my television was a card saying that for $6·50 I could have an in-room movie. There was, as I recall, a choice of four – *Friday the Thirteenth Part 19*, in which a man with a personality disorder uses knives, hatchets, Magimixes and a snow blower to kill a succession of young women just as they are about to climb in the shower; *Death Wish 11*, in which Charles Bronson tracks down and kills Michael Winner; *Bimbo*, in which Sylvester Stallone as Rambo has a sex-change operation and then blows up a lot of Oriental people; and, on the adult channel, *My Panties Are Dripping*, a sensitive study of interpersonal relationships and social conflict in post-modern Denmark, with a lot of vigorous bonking thrown in for good measure. I toyed for a moment with the idea of watching a bit of the last one – just to help me relax, as they say in evangelical circles – but I was too cheap to spend $6·50 and anyway I've always suspected that if I did punch the requisite button (which was worn to a nubbin, I can tell you), the next day a bellboy would confront me with a computer print-out and tell me that if I didn't give him $50 he would send a copy of the room receipt to my mother with 'Miscellaneous charges: Deviant Porno Movie, $6·50' circled in red. So instead I lay on the bed and watched a rerun on normal television of a 1960s comedy programme called *Mr Ed*, which was about a talking horse. Judging by the quality of the jokes, I would guess that Mr Ed wrote his own material. But at least there was nothing in it that would get me blackmailed.

And thus ended my day in New York, the most exciting and stimulating city in the world. I couldn't help but reflect that I had no reason to feel superior to my fellow lonely hearts in the strip-tease club twenty floors below. I was just as lonesome as they were. Indeed, all over this big, heartless city there were no doubt tens of thousands of people just as solitary and friendless as me. What a melancholy thought.

'But I wonder how many of them can do this?' I remarked to myself and with both hands and both feet reached out and touched all four walls at once.

FIFTEEN

It was the Columbus Day weekend and the roads were busy. Columbus has always seemed to me an odd choice of hero for a country that celebrates success as America does, because he was such a dismal failure. Consider the facts: he made four long voyages to the Americas, but never once realised that he wasn't in Asia and never found anything worthwhile. Every other explorer was coming back with exciting new products like potatoes and tobacco and nylon stockings, and all Columbus found to bring home were some puzzled-looking Indians – and he thought they were Japanese. ('Come on, you guys, let's see a little sumo.')

But perhaps Columbus's most remarkable shortcoming was that he never actually saw the land that was to become the United States. This surprises a lot of people. They imagine him trampling over Florida, saying, 'You know, this would make a nice resort.' But in fact his voyages were all spent in the Caribbean and bouncing around the swampy, bug-infested coasts of Central America. If you ask me, the Vikings would make far more worthy heroes for America. For one thing, they did actually discover it. On top of that, the Vikings were manly and drank out of skulls and didn't take any crap from anybody. Now *that's* the American way.

When I lived in America Columbus Day was one of those semi-bogus holidays that existed only for the benefit of public workers with strong unions. There was no mail on Columbus Day and if you innocently drove all the way over to the east side of town to the Iowa State Vehicle Licensing Center to renew your driver's licence you would find the door locked and a notice hanging in the window saying 'Closed for Columbus Day Holiday. So Tough Shit To You'. But otherwise life was no different than on any other day. Now, however, it appeared that the Columbus Day holiday had spread. There were lots of cars and recreational vehicles on the highway and the radio announcers kept talking about things like the number of fatalities that were expected 'this Columbus Day weekend'. (How do they know these things anyway? Is there some kind of a secret quota?) I had been looking forward to reaching New England because I wanted to see the autumn colour. In addition, the states would be small and varied and there wouldn't be that awful rolling tedium that comes with all the other American states, even the attractive ones. But I was wrong. Of course. New England states are indubitably tiny – Connecticut is only eighty miles across; Rhode Island is smaller than London – but they are crowded with cars, people and cities. Connecticut appeared to be just one suburb. I drove up US 202 towards Litchfield, which was marked on my map as a scenic route, and it was, to be sure, more scenic than a suburb, but it wasn't exactly spectacular.

Perhaps I was expecting too much. In the movies in the 1940s people were always going to Connecticut for the weekend, and it always looked wonderfully green and rustic. It was always full of empty roads and stone cottages in leafy glades. But this was just semi-suburban: ranch-houses with three-car garages and lawns with twirling sprinklers and shopping centres every six blocks. Litchfield itself was very handsome, the quintessential New England town, with an old courthouse and a long sloping green with a cannon and a memorial to the war dead. On one side of the green stood pleasant shops and on the other was a tall, white steepled church, dazzling in the October sunshine. And there was colour – the trees around the green were a rich gold and lemon. This was more like it.

I parked in front of MacDonald Drug and crossed the green through a scuffle of fallen leaves. I strolled along residential streets where big houses squatted on wide lawns. Each was a variation on the same theme: rambling clapboard with black shutters. Many had wooden plaques on them pertaining to their history – 'Oliver Boardman 1785'; '1830 Col. Webb'. I spent over an hour just poking around. It was a pleasant town for poking.

Afterwards I drove east, sticking to back highways. Soon I was in the suburbs of Hartford, and then in Hartford itself, and then in the suburbs on the other side of Hartford. And then I was in Rhode Island. I stopped beside a sign saying WELCOME TO RHODE ISLAND and stared at the map. Was that really all there was to Connecticut? I considered turning back and having another sweep across the state – there had to be more to it than that – but it was getting late, so I pressed on, venturing into a deep and rather more promising pine forest.

Considering Rhode Island's microscopic size it seemed to take me ages to find my way out of the forest. By the time I hit Narragansett Bay, a heavily-islanded inlet which consumes almost a quarter of the state's modest square mileage, it was almost dark, and there were lights winking from the villages scattered along the shoreline.

At Plum Point a long bridge crossed the sound to Conanicut Island, which rode low and dark on the water, like a corpse. I crossed the bridge and drove around the island a little, but by now it was too dark to see much. At one place where the shore came in near the road, I parked and walked to the beach. It was a moonless night and I could hear the sea before I could see it, coming in with a slow, rhythmic whoosh-whoosh. I went and stood at the water's edge. The waves fell on to the beach like exhausted swimmers. The wind played at my jacket. I stared for a long time out across the moody sea, the black vastness of the Atlantic, the fearsome, primordial, storm-tossed depths from which all of life has crawled and will no doubt one day return, and I thought, 'I could murder a hamburger.'

In the morning I drove into Newport, America's premier yachting community, home of the America's Cup races. The old part of town had been fixed up in recent years, by the look of it. Shops with hanging wooden signs out front lined the streets. They all had jauntily nautical names like 'The Flying Ship' and 'Shore Thing'. The harbour was almost too picturesque, with its crowds of white yachts and bare masts undulating beneath a sky in which gulls danced and reeled. But all around the fringe of the downtown there were unsightly parking lots, and a busy four-lane road, more freeway than city street, divided the waterfront from the town. Spindly trees stood along it like scrawny afterthoughts. The city had also built a little park, Perrott Park, but it was unkempt and full of graffiti. I had not encountered this kind of neglect before. Most American towns are spotless and this really surprised me, especially considering the importance of tourism to Newport. I walked up Thames Street, where some fine old sea captains' homes were fighting a losing battle with litter and dog shit and the encroachment of gas stations and car transmission places. It was all very sad. This was a place where the people didn't seem to care, or perhaps just didn't notice, how shabby they had let things grow. It reminded me of London.

I drove out to Fort Adams State Park across the bay. From there
Newport looked another town altogether – a charming cut-out of
needle-shaped church spires and Victorian roof-tops protruding from
a parkland of trees. The bay glittered in the sunshine and its scores of
sail-boats bobbed on the gentle waves. It was captivating. I drove on
along the shore road, past Brenton Point, and then down Bellevue
Avenue, where the most fabulous summer homes ever built line the
road on both sides and spill over on to many of the streets beyond.

Between about 1890 and 1905, America's richest families – the
Vanderbilts, the Astors, the Belmonts, dozens of others – tried to
outdo each other by building magnificent homes, which they insisted
on calling cottages, all along this half-mile strip of imposing cliffs.
Most were loosely modelled on French châteaux and filled with
furniture, marble and tapestries shipped at huge expense from Europe.
Hostesses routinely spent $300,000 or more on entertainment for a
season that lasted only six or eight weeks. For forty years or so this was
the world headquarters of conspicuous consumption.

Most of the houses are now run as museums. They charge an arm
and a leg to get in and in any case the queues outside most of them were
enormous (this was the Columbus Day weekend, remember). You
can't see much from the street – the owners didn't want common
people staring at them as they sat on the lawn counting their money, so
they put up dense hedges and high walls – but I discovered quite by
chance that the city had built an asphalt footpath all along the cliff-
edge, from which I could see the backs of the grander mansions, as well
as enjoy giddying views of the ocean breaking onto the rocks far
below. I had the path almost to myself and walked along it in a state of
quiet amazement, with my mouth open. I had never seen such a
succession of vast houses, such an excess of architecture. Every house
looked like a cross between a wedding-cake and a state capitol
building. I knew that the grandest of all the houses was The Breakers,
built by the Vanderbilts, and I kept thinking, 'Well, *this* must be it' and
'Now surely *this* must be it,' but then the next house along would be
even more awesome. When at last I reached The Breakers, it was
absolutely enormous, a mountain with windows. You can't look at it
without thinking that nobody, with the possible exception of oneself,
deserves to be that rich.

On the other side of the fence, the lawns and terraces were full of

pudgy tourists in Bermuda shorts and silly hats, wandering in and out
of the house, taking pictures of each other and trampling the begonias,
and I wondered what Cornelius Vanderbilt would make of that, the
dog-faced old prick.

I drove on to Cape Cod, another place I had never been and for which I
had high expectations. It was very picturesque, with its old saltbox
homes, its antique shops and wooden inns, its pretty villages with
quaint names: Sagamore, Sandwich, Barnstable, Rock Harbor. But it
was jam-packed with tourists in overloaded cars and rumbling motor
homes. Boy, do I hate motor homes! Especially on crowded peninsulas
like Cape Cod where they clog the streets and block the views – and all
so that some guy and his dumpy wife can eat lunch and empty their
bladders without stopping.

The traffic was so dense and slow-moving that I almost ran out of
gas and just managed to limp into a two-pump station outside West
Barnstable. It was run by a man who was at least ninety-seven years
old. He was tall and rangy and very spry. I've never seen anybody
pump gas with such abandon. First he slopped a quantity of it down
the side of the car and then he got so engaged in talking about where I
came from – 'Ioway, eh? We don't get many from Ioway. I think
you're the first this year. What's the weather like in Ioway this time of
year?' – that he let the pump run over and I had to point out to him that
gasoline was cascading down the side of the car and gathering in a pool
at our feet. He withdrew the nozzle, sloshing another half-gallon over
the car and down his trousers and shoes, and kind of threw it back at
the pump, where it dribbled carelessly.

He had a cigarette butt plugged into the side of his mouth and I was
terrified he would try to light it. And he did. He pulled out a crumpled
book of matches and started to fidget one of them to life. I was too
stunned to move. All I could think of was a television newsreader
saying, 'And in West Barnstable today a tourist from Iowa suffered
third degree burns over ninety-eight per cent of his body in an
explosion at a gas station. Fire officials said he looked like a piece of
toast that had been left under the grill too long. The owner of the
gas station has still not been found.' But we didn't explode. The little
stub of cigarette sprouted smoke, which the man puffed up into a
good-sized billow, and then he pinched out the match with his fingers.

I suppose after all these decades of pumping gas he had become more or less incombustible, like those snake handlers who grow immune to snake venom. But I wasn't inclined to test this theory too closely. I paid him hastily and pulled straight back onto the highway, much to the annoyance of a man in a forty-foot motor home who dripped mustard on his lap in braking to avoid me. 'That'll teach you to take a building on vacation,' I muttered uncharitably, and hoped that something heavy had fallen on his wife in the back.

Cape Cod is a long, thin peninsula that sprouts out of the base of Massachusetts, runs out to sea for twenty miles or so and then curls back in on itself. It looks like an arm flexed to make a muscle – in fact, it looks remarkably like my arm because there's almost no muscle in it. There are three roads along the lower part of the peninsula – one along the north shore, one along the south shore and one up the middle – but at the peninsula's elbow at Rock Harbor, where it narrows and abruptly turns north, the three roads come together and there is just one long slow highway up the forearm to Provincetown at the fingertips. Provincetown was swarming with tourists. The town has just one route in and one route out. Only a few hundred people live there, but they get as many as 50,000 visitors a day during the summer and at holiday weekends such as this one. Parking was not allowed in the town itself – there were mean-spirited tow-away warnings everywhere – so I paid a couple of bucks to leave my car with several hundred others out in the middle of nowhere and trudged a long way into town.

Provincetown is built on sand. All around it stand rolling dunes broken only by occasional clumps of straw-coloured grass. The names of the businesses – Windy Ridge Motel, Gale Force Gift Shop – suggested that wind might be something of a local feature, and indeed there was sand drifted across the roads and piled in the doorways, and with every whipping breeze it flew in your eyes and face and dusted whatever food you happened to be eating. It must be an awful place to live. I might have disliked it less if Provincetown had tried just a little harder to be charming. I had seldom seen a place so singularly devoted to sucking money out of tourists. It was filled with ice-cream parlours and gift shops and places selling T-shirts, kites and beach para-phernalia.

I walked around for a while and had a hot dog with mustard and sand and a cup of coffee with cream and sand and had a look in a window of a real estate agency, where I noticed that a basic two-bedroom house by the beach was on offer at $190,000, though it did include a fireplace and all the sand you could eat. The beaches looked nice enough, but apart from that I couldn't see a single real attraction in the place.

Provincetown is where the pilgrim fathers first touched American soil in 1620. There's a big campanile-type tower in the middle of the town to commemorate the event. The pilgrims, curiously enough, didn't mean to land on Cape Cod at all. They were aiming for Jamestown in Virginia, but missed their target by a mere 600 miles. I think that is a considerable achievement. Here's another curious thing: they didn't bring with them a single plough or horse or cow or even a fishing line. Does that strike you as just a little bit foolish? I mean to say, if you were going to start a new life in a land far, far away, don't you think you would give some thought to how you were going to fend for yourself once you got there? Still, for all their shortcomings as planners, the pilgrim fathers were sufficiently on the ball not to linger in the Provincetown area and at the first opportunity they pushed on to mainland Massachusetts. So did I.

I had hoped to go to Hyannis Port, where the Kennedys had their summer home, but the traffic was so slow, especially around Woods Hole, where the ferry to Martha's Vineyard departs, that I dared not. Every motel I passed – and there were hundreds – said No Vacancy. I got on Interstate 93, thinking I would follow it for a few miles just to get away from Cape Cod, and start looking for a room, but before I knew it I was in Boston, caught in the evening rush-hour. Boston's freeway system is insane. It was clearly designed by a person who had spent his childhood crashing toy trains. Every few hundred yards I would find my lane vanishing beneath me and other lanes merging with it from the right or left, or sometimes both. This wasn't a road system, it was mobile hysteria. Everybody looked worried. I had never seen people working so hard to keep from crashing into each other. And this was a Saturday – God knows what it must be like on a weekday.

Boston is a big city and its outer suburbs dribble on and on all the way up to New Hampshire. So, late in the evening, without having any clear idea of how I got there, I found myself in one of those placeless

places that sprout up along the junctions of interstate highways –
purplishly-lit islands of motels, gas stations, shopping centres and fast
food places – so brightly lit they must be visible from outer space. This
one was somewhere in the region of Haverhill. I got a room in a Motel
6 and dined on greasy fried chicken and limp French fries at a Denny's
Restaurant across the way. It had been a bad day, but I refused to get
depressed. Just a couple of miles down the road was New Hampshire
and the start of the real New England. Things could only get better.

SIXTEEN

I had always thought that New England was nothing but maple trees and white churches and old guys in checked shirts sitting around iron stoves in country general stores swapping tall tales and spitting in the cracker barrel. But if lower New Hampshire was anything to go by, clearly I had been misinformed. There was just modern commercial squalor – shopping centres, gas stations, motels. Every once in a while there would be a white church or clapboard inn standing incongruously in the midst of Burger Kings and Texacos. But far from mollifying the ugliness, it only intensified it, reminding you what had been thrown away for the sake of drive-thru burgers and cheap gasoline.

At Salisbury, I joined old Route 1, intending to follow it up the coast through Maine. Route 1, as the name suggests, is the patriarch of American roads, the first federal highway. It stretches for 2,500 miles from the Canadian border to the Florida Keys. For forty years it was the main highway along the eastern seaboard, connecting all the big cities of the North – Boston, New York, Philadelphia, Baltimore, Washington – with the beaches and citrus groves of the South. It must have been wonderful in the 1930s and 1940s to drive from Maine to Florida on vacation, going through all those big marvellous cities and then passing on to the hills of Virginia and the green mountains of the Carolinas, getting warmer with the passing miles. But by the 1960s Route 1 had become too congested to be practical – a third of all Americans live within twenty miles of it – and Interstate 95 was built to zip traffic up and down the coast with only the most fleeting sense of a changing landscape. Today Route 1 is still there, but you would need weeks to drive its entire length. Now it is just a local road, an endless city street, an epic stretch of shopping malls.

I had hoped that here in rural New England it would retain something of its former charm, but it seemed not to. I drove through a chill morning drizzle and wondered if ever I would find the real New England. At Portsmouth, an instantly forgettable little town, I crossed over into Maine on an iron bridge over the grey Piscataqua River. Seen through the rhythmic swish of windscreen wipers, Maine too looked ominously unpromising, a further sprawl of shopping centres and muddy new housing developments.

Beyond Kennebunkport the suburbs at last gave way to forest. Here and there massive brown boulders emerged eerily from the earth, like subterranean creatures coming up for air, and occasionally I caught glimpses of the sea – a grey plain, cold and bleak. I drove and drove, thinking that any moment now I would encounter the fabled Maine of lobster-pots and surf-battered shores and lonely lighthouses standing on rocks of granite, but the towns I passed through were just messy and drear, and the countryside was wooded and unmemorable. Once, outside Falmouth, the road ran for a mile or so along a silvery bay with a long, low bridge leading over it to a landscape of snug farms nestled in a fold of hills, and I got briefly excited. But it was a false alarm and the landscape quickly grew dull again. The rest of the time the real Maine eluded me. It was always just over there, like the amusement parks my dad used to miss.

At Wiscasset, a third of the way up the coast to New Brunswick, I lost heart altogether. Wiscasset bills itself on the signboard at the edge of town as the prettiest village in Maine, which doesn't say a whole lot for the rest of the state. I don't mean to suggest that Wiscasset was awful, because it wasn't. It had a steep main street lined with craft shops and other yuppie emporia sloping down to a placid inlet of the Atlantic. Two old wooden ships sat rotting on the bank. It was OK. It just wasn't worth driving four hours to get there.

Abruptly I decided to abandon Route 1 and plunge northward, into the dense pine forests of central Maine, heading in an irregular line for the White Mountains, on a road that went up and down, up and down, like a rucked carpet. After a few miles I began to sense a change of atmosphere. The clouds were low and shapeless, the daylight meagre. Winter clearly was closing in. I was only seventy miles or so from Canada and it was evident that winters here were long and severe. It was written in the crumbling roads and in the huge stacks of firewood that stood outside each lonely cabin. Many chimneys were already sprouting a wintry wisp of smoke. It was barely October, but already the land had the cold and lifeless feel of winter. It was the kind of atmosphere that makes you want to turn up your collar and head for home.

Just beyond Gilead I passed into New Hampshire and the landscape became more interesting. The White Mountains rose up before me, big and round, the colour of wood-ash. Presumably they take their name from the birch trees that cover them. I drove on an empty highway through a forest of trembling leaves. The skies were still flat and low, the weather cold, but at least I was out of the monotony of the Maine woods. The road rose and fell and swept along the edge of a boulder-strewn creek. The scenery was infinitely better – but still there was no colour, none of the brilliant golds and reds of autumn that I had been led to expect. Everything from the ground to the sky was a dull, cadaverous grey.

I drove past Mt Washington, the highest peak in the north-eastern US (6,288 feet, for those of you who are keeping notes). But its real claim to fame is as the windiest place in America. It's something to do with . . . well, with the way the wind blows, of course. Anyway, the highest wind speed ever recorded anywhere on earth was logged on the top of Mt Washington in April 1934 when a gust of – pencils ready? – 231 miles an hour whistled through. That must have been an experience and a half for the meteorologists who worked up there. Can you imagine trying to describe a wind like that to somebody? 'Well, it was, you know, real . . . *windy*. I mean, *really* windy. Do you know what I'm saying?' It must be very frustrating to have a truly unique experience.

Just beyond it, I came to Bretton Woods, which I had always pictured as a quaint little town. But in fact there was no town at all, just a hotel and a ski lift. The hotel was huge and looked like a medieval fortress, but with a bright red roof. It looked like a cross between Monte Cassino and a Pizza Hut. It was here in 1944 that economists and politicians from twenty-eight nations got together and agreed to set up the International Monetary Fund and the World Bank. It certainly looked a nice place to make economic history. As John Maynard Keynes remarked at the time in a letter to his brother, Milton: 'It has been a most satisfactory week. The negotiations have been cordial, the food here is superb and the waiters are ever so pretty.'

I stopped for the night at Littleton, which, as the name suggests, was a little town near the Vermont border. I pulled into the Littleton Motel on the main street. On the office door was a sign that said 'If you want ice or advice, come before 6·30. I'm taking the wife to dinner. ("And about time too!" – wife).' Inside was an old guy on crutches who told me I was very lucky because he had just one room left. It would be $42 plus tax. When he saw me start to froth and back off, he hastily added, 'It's a real nice room. Got a brand new TV. Nice carpets. Beautiful little shower. We've got the cleanest rooms in town. We're famous for that.' He swept an arm over a selection of testimonials from satisfied customers which he displayed under glass on the counter-top. 'Our room must have been the cleanest room in town!' – A. K., Aardvark Falls, Ky. 'Boy, was our room ever clean! And such nice carpets!' – Mr and Mrs J. F., Spotweld, Ohio. That sort of thing.

Somehow I doubted the veracity of these claims, but I was too weary to return to the road, so with a sigh I said all right and signed in. I took my key and a bucket of ice (at $42 plus tax I intended to have everything that was going) and went with them to my room. And by golly it *was* the cleanest room in town. The TV was brand new and the carpet was plush. The bed was comfortable and the shower really was a beauty. I felt instantly ashamed of myself and retracted all my bad thoughts about the proprietor. ('I was a pompous little shit to have doubted you.' – Mr B. B., Des Moines, Iowa.)

I ate fourteen ice-cubes and watched the early evening news. This was followed by an old episode of *Gilligan's Island*, which the TV station had thoughtfully put on as an inducement to its non-brain-damaged viewers to get up immediately and go do something more useful. This I did. I went out and had a look around the town. The reason I had chosen to stop for the night at Littleton was that a book I had with me referred to it as picturesque. In point of fact, if Littleton was characterised by anything it was a singular lack of picturesqueness. The town consisted principally of one long street of mostly undistinguished buildings, with a supermarket parking lot in the middle and the shell of a disused gas station a couple of doors away. This, I think we can agree, does not constitute picturesqueness. Happily, the town had other virtues. For one thing, it was the friendliest little place I had ever seen. I went into the Topic of the Town restaurant. The other customers smiled at me, the lady at the cash register showed me where to put my jacket, and the waitress, a plump and dimpled little lady, couldn't do enough for me. It was as if they had all been given some kind of marvellous tranquilliser.

The waitress brought me a menu and I made the mistake of saying thank you. 'You're welcome,' she said. Once you start this there's no stopping. She came and wiped the table with a damp cloth. 'Thank you,' I said. 'You're welcome,' she said. She brought me some cutlery wrapped in a paper napkin. I hesitated, but I couldn't stop myself. 'Thank you,' I said. 'You're welcome,' she said. Then came a place-mat with Topic of the Town written on it, and then a glass of water and then a clean ashtray, and then a little basket of Saltine crackers wrapped in cellophane, and at each we had our polite exchange. I ordered the fried chicken special. As I waited I became uncomfortably aware that the people at the next table were watching me and smiling at me in a deranged fashion. The waitress was watching me too, from a position by the kitchen doorway. It was all rather unnerving. Every few moments she would come over and top up my iced water and tell me that my food would only be a minute.

'Thank you,' I'd say.

'You're welcome,' she'd say.

Eventually the waitress came out of the kitchen with a tray the size of a table-top and started setting down plates of food in front of me – soup, salad, a platter of chicken, a basket of steaming rolls. It all looked delicious. Suddenly I realised that I was starving.

'Can I get you anything else?' she said.

'No, this is just fine, thank you,' I answered, knife and fork plugged in my fists, ready to lunge at the food.

'Would you like some ketchup?'

'No thank you.'

'Would you like a little more dressing for your salad?'

'No thank you.'

'Have you got enough gravy?'

There was enough gravy to drown a horse. 'Yes, plenty of gravy, thank you.'

'How about a cup of coffee?'

'Really, I'm fine.'

'You sure there's nothing I can do for you?'

'Well, you might just piss off and let me eat my dinner,' I wanted to say, but I didn't, of course. I just smiled sweetly and said no thank you and after a while she withdrew. But she stood with a pitcher of iced water and watched me closely the whole meal. Every time I took a sip of water, she would come forward and top up my glass. Once when I reached for the pepper, she misread my intentions and started forward with the water pitcher, but then had to retreat. After that, whenever my hands left the cutlery for any reason, I would semi-mime an explanation to her of what I was about to do – 'I'm just going to butter my roll now' – so that she wouldn't rush over to give me more water. And all the while the people at the next table watched me eat and smiled encouragingly. I couldn't wait to get out of there.

When at last I finished the waitress came over and offered me dessert. 'How about a piece of pie? We've got blueberry, blackberry, raspberry, boysenberry, huckleberry, whortleberry, cherry berry, hairy berry, chuckberry and berry-berry.'

'Gosh, no thanks, I'm too full,' I said placing my hands on my stomach. I looked as if I had stuffed a pillow under my shirt.

'Well, how about some ice-cream? We've got chocolate chip, chocolate fudge, chocolate ripple, chocolate-vanilla fudge, chocolate nut fudge, chocolate marshmallow swirl, chocolate mint with fudge chips, and fudge nut with or without chocolate chips.'

'Have you got just plain chocolate?'

'No, I'm afraid there's not much call for that.'

'I don't think I'll have anything then.'

'Well, how about a piece of cake. We've got –'

'Really, no thank you.'

'A cup of coffee?'

'No thank you.'

'You sure now?'

'Yes, thank you.'

'Well, I'll just get you a little more water then,' and she was off for the water jug before I could get her to give me my bill. The people at the next table watched this with interest and smiled a smile that said 'We are completely off our heads. How are you?'

Afterwards, I had a walk around the town – that is to say, I walked up one side of the street and down the other. For the size of place it was a nice town. It had two bookstores, a picture gallery, a gift shop, a movie-house. People on the sidewalk smiled at me as I passed. This was beginning to worry me. Nobody, even in America, is *that* friendly. What did they want from me? Up at the far end of the street there was a BP service station, the first one I had seen in America. Feeling vaguely homesick for Blighty, I walked up to have a look at it and was disappointed to see that there wasn't anything particularly British about it. The guy behind the counter wasn't even wearing a turban. When he saw me looking in the window he smiled at me with the same strange, unsettling smile. Suddenly I realised what it was – it was the look of someone from outer space, that odd, curiously malevolent B-movie smile of a race of interplanetary creatures who have taken over a small town in the middle of nowhere as their first step towards becoming . . . *Earth Masters*. I know this sounds improbable, but crazier things have happened – look who was in the White House, for Christ's sake. As I strolled back to the motel, I gave everyone I passed that same eerie smile, thinking I ought to keep on their good side, just in case. 'And you never know,' I remarked to myself in a low voice, 'if they do take over the planet, there might be some openings for a guy of your talents.'

In the morning I got up very early to a day that promised splendour. I peered out of my motel window. A pink dawn was spilled across the sky. I dressed quickly and hit the road before Littleton had even begun to stir. A few miles out of town I crossed the state line. Vermont presented an altogether greener, tidier prospect than New Hampshire. The hills were fat and soft, like a sleeping animal. The scattered farms looked more prosperous and the meadows climbed high up the rolling hillsides, giving the valleys an alpine air. The sun was soon high and warm. On a ridge overlooking an expanse of hazy foothills, I passed a sign that said PEACHAM, SETTLED 1776 and beyond that stood a village. I parked beside a red general store and got out to have a look around. There was no one about. Presumably the people of Littleton had come in the night and taken them off to the planet Zog.

I walked past the Peacham Inn – white clapboard, green shutters, no sign of life – and wandered up a hill, past a white Congregational church and pleasant, dozing houses. At the crest of the hill stood a broad green, with an obelisk and flagpole, and beside it an old cemetery. A zephyr wind teased the flag. Down the hill, across a broad valley, a series of pale green and brown hills rolled away to the horizon, like the swells of a sea. Below me the church bell tolled the hour, but otherwise there was not a sound. This was as perfect a spot as I had ever seen. I had a look at the obelisk. COMMEMORATING PEACHAM SOLDIERS 1869, it said, and had names carved in it, good

New England names like Elijah W. Sargent, Lowell Sterns, Horace
Rowe. There were forty-five names in all, too many surely for a mere
hamlet in the hills. But then the cemetery beside the green also looked
far too large for the size of town. It covered the hillside and the
grandeur of many of the monuments suggested that this had once been
a place of wealth.

I went through the gate and had a look around. My eye was caught
by one particularly handsome stone, an octagonal marble column
surmounted by a granite sphere. The column logged the copious
deaths of Hurds and their near relatives from Capt. Nathan Hurd in
1818 to Frances H. Bement in 1889. A small panel on the back said:

> Nathan H. died July 24 1852 AE. 4 Y's 1 M'o.
> Joshua F. died July 31 1852 AE. 1 YR 11 M's.
> Children of J. & C. Pitkin.

What could it have been, I wondered, that carried off these two little
brothers just a week apart? A fever? It seemed unlikely in July. An
accident in which one died and the other lingered? Two unrelated
events? I pictured the parents crouched at Joshua F.'s bedside,
watching his life ebb, praying to God not to take him as well, and
having their hopes crushed. Isn't life shitty? Everywhere I looked there
was disappointment and heartbreak recorded in the stones: 'Joseph,
son of Ephraim and Sarah Carter, died March 18 1846, aged 18 yrs',
'Alma Foster, daut. of Zadock and Hannah Richardson, d. May 22,
1847, AE. 17 yrs'. So many were so young. I became infected with an
inexpressible melancholy as I wandered alone among these hundreds
of stilled souls, the emptied lives, the row upon row of ended dreams.
Such a sad place! I stood there in the mild October sunshine, feeling so
sorry for all these luckless people and their lost lives, reflecting bleakly
on mortality and on my own dear, cherished family so far away in
England, and I thought, 'Well, fuck this,' and walked back down the
hill to the car.

I drove west across Vermont, into the Green Mountains. The
mountains were dark and round and the valleys looked rich. Here the
light seemed softer, sleepier, more autumnal. There was colour
everywhere – trees the colour of mustard and rust, meadows of gold
and green, colossal white barns, blue lakes. Here and there along the

roadside, produce stands brimmed with pumpkins and squash and other autumn fruits. It was like a day trip to heaven. I wandered around on back roads. There was a surprising lot of small houses, some little better than shacks. I supposed there couldn't be much work in a place like Vermont. The state has hardly any towns or industry. The biggest city, Burlington, has a population of just 37,000. Outside Groton I stopped at a roadside café for coffee and listened along with the other three customers to a fat young woman with a pair of ill-kempt children moaning in a loud voice about her financial problems to the woman behind the counter. 'I still only get four dollars an hour,' she was saying. 'Harvey, he's been at Fibberts for three years and he's only just got his first raise. You know what he gets now? Four dollars and sixty-five cents an hour. Isn't that pathetic? I told him, I said, "Harvey, they're just walkin' all over you." But he won't do nothin' about it.' She broke off here to rearrange the features on one of her children's faces with the back of her hand. 'HOW MANY TIMES HAVE I TOLD YOU NOT TO INNARUP ME WHEN I'M *TALKING*?' she inquired rhetorically of the little fellow, and then in a calmer voice turned back to the café lady and launched into a candid list of Harvey's other shortcomings, which were manifold.

Only the day before in Maine I had seen a sign in a McDonald's offering a starting wage of $5 an hour. Harvey must have been immensely moronic and unskilled – doubtless both – not to be able to keep pace with a sixteen-year-old burger jockey at McDonald's. Poor guy! And on top of that here he was married to a woman who was slovenly, indiscreet, and had a butt like a barn door. I hoped old Harvey had sense enough to appreciate all the incredible natural beauty with which God had blessed his native state because it didn't sound as if He had blessed Harvey very much. Even his kids were ugly as sin. I was half tempted to give one of them a clout myself as I went out of the door. There was just something about his nasty little face that made you itch to smack him.

I drove on, thinking what an ironic thing it was that the really beautiful places in America – the Smoky Mountains, Appalachia, and now Vermont – were always inhabited by the poorest, most under-educated people. And then I hit Stowe and realized that when it comes to making shrewd generalisations, I am a cretin. Stowe was anything but poor. It was a rich little town, full of chichi boutiques and expensive ski lodges. In fact, for most of the rest of the day, as I wandered around and through the Green Mountain ski resorts, I saw almost nothing but wealth and beauty – rich people, rich houses, rich cars, rich resorts, beautiful scenery. I drove around quite struck by it all, wandered over to Lake Champlain – also immensely beautiful – and idled down the western side of the state, just over the border from New York State.

Below Lake Champlain the landscape became more open, more rolling, as if the hills had been flattened out from the edges, like someone pulling a crease out of a bedspread. Some of the towns and villages were staggeringly pretty. Dorset, for instance, was an exquisite little place, standing around an oval green, full of beautiful white clapboard houses, with a summer playhouse and an old church and an enormous inn. And yet. And yet there was something about these places. They were too perfect, too rich, too yuppified. At Dorset there was a picture shop called the Dorset Framery. At Bennington, just down the road, I passed a place called the Publyk House Restaurant. Every inn and lodge had a quaint and picturesque name – the Black Locust Inn, the Hob Knob, the Blueberry Inn, the Old Cutter Inn – and a hanging wooden sign out front. There was always this air of twee artifice pushing in on everything. After a while I began to find it oddly oppressive. I longed to see a bit of neon and a restaurant with a good old family name – Ernie's Chop House, Zweiker's New York Grille – with a couple of blinking beer signs in the front window. A bowling alley or drive-in movie theatre would have been most welcome. It would have made it all seem real. But this looked as if it had been designed in Manhattan and brought in by truck.

One village I went through had about four stores and one of them was a Ralph Lauren Polo Shop. I couldn't think of anything worse than living in a place where you could buy a $200 sweater but not a can of baked beans. Actually, I could think of a lot of worse things – cancer of the brain, watching every episode of a TV mini-series starring Joan Collins, having to eat at a Burger Chef more than twice in one year, reaching for a glass of water in the middle of the night and finding that you've just taken a drink from your grandmother's denture cup, and so on. But I think you get my point.

SEVENTEEN

I spent the night in Cobleskill, New York, on the northern fringes of the Catskills, and in the morning drove to Cooperstown, a small resort on Lake Otsego. Cooperstown was the home of James Fenimore Cooper, from whose family the town takes its name. It was a handsome town, as handsome as any I had seen in New England, and more replete with autumn colour, with a main street of square-topped brick buildings, old banks, a movie theatre, family stores. The Cooperstown Diner, where I went for breakfast, was busy, friendly and cheap – all that a diner should be. Afterwards I went for a stroll around the residential streets, shuffling hands-in-pockets through the dry leaves, and down to the lakeside. Every house in town was old and pretty; many of the larger ones had been converted into inns and expensive B & Bs. The morning sunlight filtered through the trees and threw shadows across the lawns and sidewalks. This was as nice a little town as I had seen on the trip; it was almost Amalgam.

The only shortcoming with Cooperstown is that it is full of tourists, drawn to the town by its most famous institution, the Baseball Hall of Fame, which stands by a shady park at the far end of Main Street. I went there now, paid $8·50 admission and walked into its cathedral-like calm. For those of us who are baseball fans and agnostics, the Hall of Fame is as close to a religious experience as we may ever get. I walked serenely through its quiet and softly-lit halls, looking at the sacred vestments and venerated relics from America's national pastime. Here, beautifully preserved in a glass case, was 'the shirt worn by Warren Spahn when registering win N° 305, which tied him with Eddie Plank for most by a left-hander.' Across the aisle was 'the glove used by Sal Maglie on September 25, 1958, no-hitter vs Phillies.' At each case people gazed reverently or spoke in whispers.

One room contained a gallery of paintings commemorating great moments in baseball history, including one depicting the first professional night game under artificial lighting played in Des Moines, Iowa, on May 2, 1930. This was exciting news to me. I had no idea that Des

Moines had played a pivotal role in the history of both baseball and luminescence. I looked closely to see if the artist had depicted my father in the press-box, but then I realised that my father was only fifteen years old in 1930 and still in Winfield. This seemed kind of a pity.

In an upstairs room I suppressed a whoop of joy at the discovery of whole cases full of the baseball cards that my brother and I had so scrupulously collected and catalogued, and which my parents, in an early flirtation with senility, had taken to the dump during an attic spring-cleaning in 1981. We had the complete set for 1959 in mint condition; it is now worth something like $1,500. We had Mickey Mantle and Yogi Berra as rookies, Ted Williams from the last year he hit .400, the complete New York Yankees teams for every year between 1956 and 1962. The whole collection must have been worth something like $8,000 – enough, at any rate, to have sent Mom and Dad for a short course of treatment at a dementia clinic. But never mind! We all make mistakes. It's only because everyone throws these things out that they grow so valuable for the lucky few whose parents don't spend their retirements getting rid of all the stuff they spent their working lives accumulating. Anyway it was a pleasure to see all the old cards again. It was like visiting a friend in hospital.

The Hall of Fame is surprisingly large, much larger than it looks from the road, and extremely well presented. I wandered through it in a state of complete contentment, reading every label, lingering at every display, reliving my youth, cocooned in a happy nostalgia, and when I stepped back out on to Main Street and glanced at my watch I was astonished to discover that three hours had elapsed.

Next door to the Hall of Fame was a shop selling the most wonderful baseball souvenirs. In my day all we could get were pennants and baseball cards and crummy little pens in the shape of baseball bats that stopped working about the second time you tried to sign your name with them. But now little boys could get everything with their team's logo on it – lamps, towels, clocks, throw rugs, mugs, bedspreads and even Christmas tree ornaments, plus of course pennants, baseball cards and pens that stop working about the second time you use them. I don't think I have ever felt such a pang of longing to be a child again. Apart from anything else, it would mean I'd get my baseball cards back and I could put them somewhere safe where my parents couldn't get at them; then when I got to my age I could buy a Porsche.

I was so taken with all the souvenirs that I began to fill my arms with stuff, but then I noticed that the store was full of Do Not Touch signs and on the counter by the cash register had been taped a notice that said 'Do Not Lean on Glass – If You Break, Cost to You Is $50.' What a jerky thing to say on a sign. How could you expect kids to come into a place full of wonderful things like this and not touch them? This so elevated my hackles that I deposited my intended purchases on the counter and told the girl I didn't want them after all. This was perhaps just as well because I'm not altogether sure that my wife would have wanted St Louis Cardinals pillowcases.

My ticket to the Hall of Fame included admission to a place on the edge of town called the Farmers Museum, where a couple of dozen old buildings – a schoolhouse, a tavern, a church and the like – have been preserved on a big site. It was about as exciting as it sounds, but having bought the ticket I felt obliged to go and have a look at it. If nothing else, the walk through the afternoon sunshine was pleasant. But I was relieved to get back in the car and hit the road again. It was after four by the time I left town. I drove on across New York State for several hours, through the Susquehanna Valley, which was very fetching, especially at this time of day and year in the soft light of an autumn afternoon: watermelon-shaped hills, golden trees, slumbering towns. To make up for my long day in Cooperstown, I drove later than usual, and it was after nine by the time I stopped at a motel on the outskirts of Elmira.

I went straight out for dinner, but almost every place I approached was closed, and I ended up eating in a restaurant attached to a bowling alley – in clear violation of Bryson's third rule of dining in a strange town. Generally, I don't believe in doing things on principle – it's kind of a principle of mine – but I do have six rules of public dining to which I try to adhere. They are:

1. Never eat in a restaurant that displays photographs of the food it serves. (But if you do, never believe the photographs.)
2. Never eat in a restaurant with flock wallpaper.
3. Never eat in a restaurant attached to a bowling-alley.
4. Never eat in a restaurant where you can hear what they are saying in the kitchen.

5. Never eat in a restaurant that has live entertainers with any of the following words in their titles: Hank, Rhythm, Swinger, Trio, Combo, Hawaiian, Polka.
6. Never eat in a restaurant that has blood-stains on the walls.

In the event, the bowling-alley restaurant proved quite acceptable. Through the wall I could hear the muffled rumblings of falling bowling-pins and the sounds of Elmira's hairdressers and grease monkeys having a happy night out. I was the only customer in the restaurant. In fact, I was quite clearly the only thing standing between the waitresses and their going home. As I waited for my food, they cleared away the other tables, removed the ashtrays, sugar-bowls and table-cloths, so that after a while I found myself dining alone in a large room, with a white table-cloth and flickering candle in a little red bowl, amid a sea of barren formica table-tops.

The waitresses stood against the wall and watched me chew my food. After a while they started whispering and tittering, still watching me as they did so, which frankly I found a trifle unsettling. I may only have imagined it, but I also had the distinct impression that someone was little by little turning a dimmer switch so that the light in the room was gradually disappearing. By the end of my meal I was finding my food more or less by touch and occasionally by lowering my head to the plate and sniffing. Before I was quite finished, when I just paused for a moment to grope for my glass of iced water somewhere in the gloom beyond the flickering candle, my waitress whipped the plate away and put down my bill.

'You want anything else?' she said in a tone that suggested I had better not. 'No thank you,' I answered politely. I wiped my mouth with the table-cloth, having lost my napkin in the gloom, and added a seventh rule to my list: never go into a restauraunt ten minutes before closing time. Still, I never really mind bad service in a restaurant. It makes me feel better about not leaving a tip.

In the morning I woke early and experienced that sinking sensation that overcomes you when you first open your eyes and realise that instead of a normal day ahead of you, with its scatterings of simple gratifications, you are going to have a day without even the tiniest of pleasures; you are going to drive across Ohio.

I sighed and got up. I shuffled around the room in my old man posture, gathered up my things, washed, dressed and without enthusiasm hit the highway. I drove west through the Alleghenies and then into a small, odd corner of Pennsylvania. For 200 miles the border between New York and Pennsylvania is a straight line, but at its north-western corner, where I was now, it abruptly juts north, as if the draughtsman's arm had been jogged. The reason for this small cartographical irregularity was to let Pennsylvania have its own outlet on to Lake Erie so that it wouldn't have to cross New York State, and it remains today a 200-year-old reminder of how the early states weren't at all confident that the union was going to work. That it did was far more of an achievement than is often appreciated nowadays.

Just inside the Pennsylvania state line, the highway merged with Interstate 90. This is the main northern route across America, stretching 3,016 miles from Boston to Seattle, and there were lots of long-distance travellers on it. You can always tell long-distance travellers because they look as if they haven't been out of the car for weeks. You only glimpse them when they pass, but you can see that they have already started to set up home inside – there are pieces of washing hanging in the back, remnants of takeaway meals on the window-sill, and books, magazines and pillows scattered around. There's always a fat woman asleep in the front passenger seat, her mouth hugely agape, and a quantity of children going crazy in the back. You and the father exchange dull but not unsympathetic looks as the two cars slide past. You glance at each other's licence plates and feel envy or sympathy in proportion to your comparative distances from home. One car I saw had Alaska plates on it. This was unbelievable. I had never seen Alaska licence plates before. The man must have driven over 4,500 miles, the equivalent of going from London to Zambia. He was the most forlorn looking character I had ever seen. There was no sign of a wife and children. I expect by now he had killed them and put their bodies in the trunk.

A drizzly rain hung in the air. I drove along in that state of semi-mindlessness that settles over you on interstate highways. After a while Lake Erie appeared on the right. Like all the Great Lakes, it is enormous, more an inland sea than a lake, stretching 200 miles from west to east and about forty miles across. Twenty-five years ago Lake Erie was declared dead. Driving along its southern shore, gazing out at its flat grey immensity, this appeared to be a remarkable achievement.

It hardly seemed possible that something as small as man could kill something as large as a Great Lake. But just in the space of a century or so we managed it. Thanks to lax factory laws and the triumph of greed over nature in places like Cleveland, Buffalo, Toledo, Sandusky and other bustling centres of soot and grit, Lake Erie was transformed in just three generations from a bowl of blue water into a large toilet. Cleveland was the worst offender. Cleveland was so vile that its river, a slow-moving sludge of chemicals and half-digested solids called the Cuyahoga, once actually caught fire and burned out of control for four days. This also was a remarkable achievement, I feel. Things are said to be better now. According to a story in the *Cleveland Free Press*, which I read during a stop for coffee near Ashtabula, an official panel with the ponderous title of the International Joint Commission's Great Lakes Water Quality Board had just released a survey of chemical substances in the lake, and it had found only 362 types of chemical compared with more than a thousand the last time they had counted. That still seemed an awful lot to me and I was surprised to see a pair of fishermen standing on the shore, hunched down in the drizzle, hurling lines out on to the greenish murk with long poles. Maybe they were fishing for chemicals.

Through dull rain I drove through the outer suburbs of Cleveland, past signs for places that were all called Something Heights: Richmond Heights, Maple Heights, Garfield Heights, Shaker Heights, University Heights, Warrensville Heights, Parma Heights. Curiously the one outstanding characteristic of the surrounding landscape was its singular lack of eminences. Clearly what Cleveland was prepared to consider the heights was what others would regard as distinctly middling. Somehow this did not altogether surprise me. After a time Interstate 90 became the Cleveland Memorial Shoreway, and followed the sweep of the bay. The windscreen wipers of the Chevette flicked hypnotically and other cars threw up spray as they swished past. Outside my window the lake sprawled dark and vast until it was consumed by a distant mist. Ahead of me the tall buildings of downtown Cleveland appeared and slid towards me, like shopping on a supermarket conveyor belt.

Cleveland has always had a reputation for being a dirty, ugly, boring city, though now they say it is much better. By 'they' I mean reporters from serious publications like the *Wall Street Journal*,

Fortune and the *New York Times Sunday Magazine*, who visit the city at five-yearly intervals and produce long stories with titles like 'Cleveland Bounces Back' and 'Renaissance in Cleveland'. No one ever reads these articles, least of all me, so I couldn't say whether the improbable and highly relative assertion that Cleveland is better now than it used to be is wrong or right. What I can say is that the view up the Cuyahoga as I crossed it on the freeway was of a stew of smoking factories that didn't look any too clean or handsome. And I can't say that the rest of the town looked such a knock-out either. It may be improved, but all this talk of a renaissance is clearly exaggerated. I somehow doubt that if the Duc d'Urbino were brought back to life and deposited in downtown Cleveland he would say, 'Goodness, I am put in mind of fifteenth-century Florence and the many treasures therein.'

And then, quite suddenly, I was out of Cleveland and on the James W. Shocknessy Ohio Turnpike in the rolling rural emptiness between Cleveland and Toledo, and highway mindlessness once more seeped in. To relieve the tedium I switched on the radio. In fact, I had been switching it on and off all day, listening for a while but then giving up in despair. Unless you have lived through it, you cannot conceive of the sense of hopelessness that comes with hearing *Hotel California* by the Eagles for the fourteenth time in three hours. You can feel your brain cells disappearing with little popping sounds. But it's the disc jockeys that make it intolerable. Can there anywhere be a breed of people more irritating and imbecilic than disc jockeys? In South America there is a tribe of Indians called the Janamanos, who are so backward they cannot even count to three. Their counting system goes: 'One, two . . . oh, gosh, a whole bunch.' Obviously disc jockeys have a better dress sense and possess a little more in the way of social skills, but I think we are looking at a similar level of mental acuity.

Over and over I searched the airwaves for something to listen to, but I could find nothing. It wasn't as if I was asking for all that much. All I wanted was a station that didn't play endless songs by bouncy pre-pubescent girls, didn't employ disc jockeys who said 'H-e-y-y-y-y' more than once every six seconds and didn't keep telling me how much Jesus loved me. But no such station existed. Even when I did find something half-way decent, the sound would begin to fade after ten or twelve miles, and the old Beatles song that I was listening to with quiet pleasure would gradually be replaced by a semi-demented man talking about the word of God and telling me that I had a friend in the Lord.

Many American radio stations, particularly out in the hinterland, are ridiculously small and cheap. I know this for a fact because when I was a teenager I used to help out at KCBC in Des Moines. KCBC had the contract to broadcast the Iowa Oaks professional baseball games, but it was too cheap to send its sportscaster, a nice young guy named Steve Shannon, on the road with the team. So whenever the Oaks were in Denver or Oklahoma City or wherever, Shannon and I would go out to the KCBC studio – really just a tin hut standing beside a tall transmitter tower in a farmer's field somewhere south-east of Des Moines – and he would broadcast from there as if he were in Omaha. It was bizarre. Every couple of innings someone at the ballpark would call me on the phone and give me a bare summary of the game, which I would scribble into a scorebook and pass to Shannon, and on the basis of this he would give a two-hour broadcast.

It was a remarkable experience to sit there in a windowless hut on a steaming August night listening to the crickets outside and watching a man talking into a microphone and saying things like, 'Well, it's a cool evening here in Omaha, with a light breeze blowing in off the Missouri River. There's a special guest in the crowd tonight, Governor Warren T. Legless, who I can see sitting with his pretty young wife, Bobbie Rae, in a box seat just below us here in the press-box.' Shannon was a genius at this sort of thing. I remember one time the phone call from the ballpark didn't come through – the guy at the other end had gotten locked in a toilet or something – and Shannon didn't have anything to tell the listeners. So he delayed the game with a sudden downpour, having only a moment before said it was a beautiful cloudless evening, and played music while he called the ballpark and begged somebody there to let him know what was going on. Funnily enough, I later read that the exact same thing had happened to Ronald Reagan when he was a young sportscaster in Des Moines. Reagan responded by having the batter do a highly improbable thing – hit foul balls one after the other for over half an hour – while pretending that there was nothing implausible about it, which when you think about it is kind of how he ran the country as President.

Late in the afternoon, I happened on to a news broadcast by some station in Crudbucket, Ohio, or some such place. American radio news broadcasts usually last about thirty seconds. It went like this: 'A young Crudbucket couple, Dwayne and Wanda Dreary, and their seven children, Ronnie, Lonnie, Connie, Donnie, Bonnie, Johnny and Tammy-Wynette, were killed in a fire after a light airplane crashed into their house and burst into flames. Fire Chief Walter Embers said he could not at this stage rule out arson. On Wall Street, shares had their biggest one-day fall in history, losing 508 points. And the weather outlook for greater Crudbucket: clear skies with a two per cent chance of precipitation. You're listening to radio station K-R-U-D where you get more rock and less talk.' There then followed *Hotel California* by the Eagles.

I stared at the radio, wondering whether I had heard that second item right. The biggest one-day fall in shares in history? The collapse of the American economy? I twirled the dial and found another news broadcast: '. . . but Senator Poontang denied that the use of the four Cadillacs and the trips to Hawaii were in any way connected with the $120 million contract to build the new airport. On Wall Street, shares suffered their biggest one-day fall in history, losing 508 points in just under three hours. And the weather outlook here in Crudbucket is for cloudy skies and a ninety-eight per cent chance of precipitation. We'll have more music from the Eagles after this word.'

The American economy was coming apart in shreds and all I could get were songs by the Eagles. I twirled and twirled the dial, thinking that surely somebody somewhere must be giving the dawn of a new Great Depression more than a passing mention – and someone was, thank goodness. It was CBC, the Canadian network, with an excellent and thoughtful programme called *As It Happens*, which was entirely devoted that evening to the crash of Wall Street. I will leave you, reader, to consider the irony in an American citizen, travelling across his own country, having to tune in to a foreign radio network to find out the details of one of the biggest domestic news stories of the year. To be scrupulously fair, I was later told that the public service network in America – possibly the most underfunded broadcast organisation in the developed world – also devoted a long report to the crash. I expect it was given by a man sitting in a tin hut in a field somewhere, reading scribbled notes off a sheet of paper.

At Toledo, I joined Interstate 75, and drove north into Michigan, heading for Dearborn, a suburb of Detroit, where I intended spending the night. Almost immediately I found myself in a wilderness of warehouses and railroad tracks and enormous parking lots leading to distant car factories. The parking lots were so vast and full of cars that I half wondered if the factories were there just to produce sufficient cars to keep the parking lots full, thus eliminating any need for consumers. Interlacing all this were towering electricity pylons. If you have ever wondered what becomes of all those pylons you see marching off to the horizon in every country in the world, like an army of invading aliens, the answer is that they all join up in a field just north of Toledo, where they discharge their loads into a vast estate of electrical transformers, diodes and other contraptions that look for all the world like the inside of a television set, only on a rather grander scale, of course. The ground fairly thrummed as I drove past and I fancied I felt a crackle of blue static sweep through the car, briefly enlivening the hair on the back of my neck and leaving a strangely satisfying sensation in my armpits. I was half inclined to turn around at the next intersection and go back for another dose. But it was late and I pressed on. For some minutes I thought I smelled smouldering flesh and kept touching my head tentatively. But this may only have been a consequence of having spent too many lonely hours in a car.

At Monroe, a town halfway between Toledo and Detroit, a big sign beside the highway said WELCOME TO MONROE—HOME OF GENERAL CUSTER. A mile or so later there was another sign, even larger, saying MONROE, MICHIGAN—HOME OF LA-Z-BOY FURNITURE. Goodness, I thought, will the excitement never stop? But it did, and the rest of the journey was completed without drama.

EIGHTEEN

I spent the night in Dearborn for two reasons. First, it would mean not having to spend the night in Detroit, the city with the highest murder rate in the country. In 1987, there were 635 homicides in Detroit, a rate of 58·2 per 100,000 people, or eight times the national average. Just among children, there were 365 shootings in which both the victims and gunmen were under sixteen. We are talking about a tough city – and yet it is still a rich one. What it will become like as the American car industry collapses in upon itself doesn't bear thinking about. People will have to start carrying bazookas for protection.

My second and more compelling reason for going to Dearborn was to see the Henry Ford Museum, a place my father had taken us when I was small and which I remembered fondly. After breakfast in the morning, I went straight there. Henry Ford spent his later years buying up important Americana by the truckload and crating it to his museum, beside the big Ford Motor Company Rouge Assembly Plant. The car-park outside the museum was enormous – on a scale to rival the factory car-parks I had passed the day before – but at this time of year there were few cars in it. Most of them were Japanese.

I went inside and discovered without surprise that the entrance charge was steep: $15 for adults and $7·50 for children. Americans are clearly prepared to fork out large sums for their pleasures. Grudgingly I paid the admission charge and went in. But almost from the moment I passed through the portals I was enthralled. For one thing, the scale of it is almost breathtaking. You find yourself in a great hangar of a building covering twelve acres of ground and filled with the most indescribable assortment of stuff – machinery, railway trains, refrigerators, Abraham Lincoln's rocking-chair, the limousine in which John F. Kennedy was killed (nope, no bits of brains on the floor), George Washington's campaign chest, General Tom Thumb's ornate miniature billiard-table, a bottle containing Thomas Edison's last breath. I found this last item particularly captivating. Apart from being ridiculously morbid and sentimental, how did they know which breath was going to be Edison's last one? I pictured Henry Ford standing at the death-bed shoving a bottle in his face over and over and saying, 'Is that it?'

This was the way the Smithsonian once was and still should be – a cross between an attic and a junk shop. It was as if some scavenging genius had sifted through all the nation's collective memories and brought to this one place everything from American life that was splendid and fine and deserving fondness. It was possible here to find every single item from my youth – old comic books, lunch pails, bubble gum cards, *Dick and Jane* reading books, a Hotpoint stove just like the one my mom used to have, a soda pop dispenser like the one that used to stand in front of the pool hall in Winfield.

There was even a collection of milk bottles exactly like those that Mr Morrisey, the deaf milkman, used to bring to our house every morning. Mr Morrisey was the noisiest milkman in America. He was about sixty years old and wore a large hearing-aid. He always travelled with his faithful dog Skipper. They would arrive like clockwork just before dawn. Milk had to be delivered early, you see, because in the Midwest it spoiled quickly once the sun came up. You always knew when it was 5.30 because Mr Morrisey would arrive, whistling for all he was worth, waking all the dogs for blocks around, which would get Skipper very excited and set him to barking. Being deaf, Mr Morrisey tended not to notice his own voice and you could hear him clinking around on your back porch with his rack of milk bottles and saying to Skipper, 'WELL, I WONDER WHAT THE BRYSONS WANT TODAY! LET'S SEE . . . FOUR QUARTS OF SKIMMED AND SOME COTTAGE CHEESE. WELL, SKIPPER, WOULD YOU FUCKING BELIEVE IT, I LEFT THE COTTAGE CHEESE ON THE GOD DAMN TRUCK!' And then you would look out the window to see Skipper urinating on your bicycle and lights coming on in houses all over the neighbourhood. Nobody wanted to get Mr Morrisey fired, on account of his unfortunate disability, but when Flynn Dairies discontinued home deliveries in about 1960 on economic grounds ours was one of the few neighbourhoods in the city from which there was no outcry.

I walked through the museum in a state of sudden, deep admiration for Henry Ford and his acquisitive instincts. He may have been a bully and an anti-Semite, but he sure could build a nifty museum. I could happily have spent hours picking around among the memorabilia. But the hangar is only a fractional part of it. Outside there is a whole village – a little town – containing eighty homes of famous Americans. These are the actual homes, not replicas. Ford criss-crossed the country acquiring the residences and workshops of the people he most admired – Thomas Edison, Harvey Firestone, Luther Burbank, the Wright brothers and of course himself. All these he crated up and shipped back to Dearborn where he used them to build this 250-acre fantasy land – the quintessential American small town, a picturesque and timeless community where every structure houses a man of genius (almost invariably a white, Christian man of genius from the Middle West). Here in this perfect place, with its broad greens and pleasing shops and churches, the lucky resident could call on Orville and Wilbur Wright for a bicycle inner tube, go to the Firestone farm for milk and eggs (but not for rubber yet – Harvey's still working on it!), borrow a book from Noah Webster and call on Abraham Lincoln for legal advice, always assuming he's not too busy with patent applications for Charles Steinmetz or emancipating George Washington Carver, who lives in a tiny cabin just across the street.

It is really quite entrancing. For a start, places like Edison's workshop and the boarding-house where his employees lodged have been scrupulously preserved. You can really see how these people worked and lived. And there is a certain undeniable convenience in having the houses all brought together. Who in a million years would go to Columbiana, Ohio, to see the Harvey Firestone birthplace, or to Dayton to see where the Wright brothers lived? Not me, brother. Above all, bringing these places together makes you realise just how incredibly inventive America has been in its time, what a genius it has had for practical commercial innovation, often leading to unspeakable wealth, and how many of the comforts and pleasures of modern life have their roots in the small towns of the American Middle West. It made me feel proud.

I drove north and west across Michigan, lost in a warm afterglow of pleasure from the museum. I was past Lansing and Grand Rapids and entering the Manistee National Forest, 100 miles away, almost before I knew it. Michigan is shaped like an oven mitt and is often about as exciting. The Manistee forest was dense and dull – endless groves of uniform pine trees – and the highway through it was straight and flat. Occasionally I would see a cabin or little lake in the woods, both just glimpsable through the trees, but mostly there was nothing of note. Towns were rare and mostly squalid – scattered dwellings and ugly prefab buildings where they made and sold ugly prefab cabins, so that people could buy their own little bit of ugliness and take it out into the woods.

After Baldwin, the road became wider and emptier and the commercialism grew sparser. At Manistee, the highway ran down to Lake Michigan, and then followed the shoreline off and on for miles, going through rather more pleasant little communities of mostly boarded-up summer homes – Pierport, Arcadia, Elberta ('A Peach of A Place'), Frankfort. At Empire I stopped to look at the lake. The weather was surprisingly cold. A blustery wind blew in from Wisconsin, seventy miles away across the steely grey water, raising white caps and wavelets. I tried to go for a stroll, but I was only out for about five minutes before the wind blew me back to the car.

I went on to Traverse City, where the weather was milder, perhaps because it was more sheltered. Traverse City looked to be a wonderful old town that seemed not to have changed since about 1948. It still had a Woolworth's, a J. C. Penney, an old-fashioned movie theatre called The State and a wonderful old restaurant, the Sydney, with black booths and a long soda-fountain. You just don't see places like that any more. I had coffee and felt very pleased to be there. Afterwards I drove on north on a road running up one side of Grand Traverse Bay and down the other, so that you could always see where you were going or where you had been, sometimes veering inland past farms and cherry orchards for a couple of miles and then sweeping back down to the water's edge. As the afternoon progressed, the wind settled and the sun came out, tentatively at first, like a shy guest, and then stayed on, giving the lake bright patches of silver and blue. Far out over the water, perhaps twenty miles away, dark clouds dumped rain on the lake. It fell in a pale grey curtain. And high above a faint rainbow reached across the sky. It was inexpressibly beautiful. I drove transfixed.

In the early evening I reached Mackinaw City, on the tip of the oven mitt, the point where the shorelines of southern and northern

Michigan pinch together to form the Straits of Mackinac, which separate Lake Michigan from Lake Huron. A suspension bridge, five miles long, spans the gap. Mackinaw City – they are fairly casual about how they spell the word up this way – was a scattered and unsightly little town, full of gift shops, motels, ice-cream parlours, pizzerias, car-parks, and firms operating ferries to Mackinac Island. Almost every place of business, including the motels, was boarded up for the winter. The Holiday Motel, on the shore of Lake Huron, seemed to be open so I went inside and rang the desk bell. The young guy who came out looked surprised to have a customer. 'We were just about to close up for the season,' he said. 'In fact, everybody's gone out to dinner to celebrate. But we've got rooms if you want one.'

'How much?' I asked.

He seemed to snatch a figure from the air. 'Twenty dollars?' he said.

'Sounds good to me,' I said and signed in. The room was small but nice and it had heating, which was a good thing. I went out and had a walk around, to look for something to eat. It was only a little after seven, but it was dark already and the chill air felt more like December than October. I could see my breath. It was odd to be in a place so full of buildings and yet so dead. Even the McDonald's was closed, with a sign in the window telling me to have a good winter.

I walked down to the Shepler's Ferry terminal – really just a big parking lot with a shed – to see what time the ferry to Mackinac Island would depart in the morning. That was my reason for being here. There was one at eleven. I stood beside the pier, facing into the wind, and gazed for a long time out across Lake Huron. Mackinac Island was berthed a couple of miles out in the lake like a glittering cruise ship. Nearby, even larger but with no lights, was Bois Blanc Island, dark and round. Off to the left, Mackinac Bridge, lit up like a Christmas decoration, spanned the strait. Everywhere the lights shimmered on the water. It was odd that such a nothing little town could have such a wonderful view.

I ate dinner in a practically empty restaurant and then had some beers in a practically empty bar. Both places had turned on the heating. It felt good, cosy. Outside the wind beat against the plate glass windows, making a woppa-woppa sound. I liked the quiet bar. Most bars in America are dark and full of moody characters – people drinking alone and staring ahead. There's none of that agreeable coffee-house atmosphere that you find in bars in Europe. American bars are, by and large, just dark places to get drunk in. I don't like them much, but this one was OK. It was snug and quiet and well lit, so I could sit and read. Before too long I was fairly well lit myself. This was also OK.

In the morning I woke early and gave the steamy window a wipe with my hand to see what kind of day it was. The answer was: not a good one. The world was full of sleety snow, dancing about in the wind like a plague of white insects. I switched on the TV and crept back into the warm bed. The local PBS station came on. PBS is the Public Broadcasting System, what we used to call educational TV. It is supposed to show quality stuff, though because it is always strapped for funds this consists mostly of BBC melodramas starring Susan Hampshire and domestically-produced programmes that cost about $12 to make – cookery programmes, religious discussions, local high school wrestling matches. It's pretty well unwatchable most of the time, and it's getting worse. In fact, the station I was watching was holding a telethon to raise funds for itself. Two middle-aged men in casual clothes were sitting in swivel chairs, with a pair of phones on a table between them, asking for money. They were trying to look perky and cheerful, but there was a kind of desperation in their eyes.

'Wouldn't it be tragic for your children if they didn't have Sesame Street any more?' one of them was saying to the camera. 'So come on, moms and dads, give us a call and make a pledge now.' But nobody was calling. So the two talked to each other about all the wonderful programmes on PBS. They had clearly been having this conversation for some time. After a while one of them had a phone call. 'I've had my first caller,' he said as he put the phone down. 'It was from Melanie Bitowski of Traverse City and it's her fourth birthday today. So happy birthday, honey. But next time you or any of you other kids call in, why don't you get your mom or dad to pledge some money, sweetheart?' These guys were clearly begging for their jobs, and the whole of northern Michigan was turning a blind eye to their pleadings.

I showered and dressed and packed up my bag, all the while keeping an eye on the TV to see if anyone made a pledge and no one ever did. When I switched off, one of them was saying, with just a hint of peevishness, 'Now come on, I can't believe that *nobody* out there is watching us. Somebody must be awake out there. Somebody must want to preserve quality public television for themselves and their children.' But he was wrong.

I had a large breakfast in the same place I had eaten the night before and then, because there was absolutely nothing else to do, I went and stood on the quayside, waiting for the ferry. The wind had died. The last sleet melted as it hit the ground and then stopped falling altogether. Everywhere there was the tip-tip-tip sound of dripping, off the roofs, off branches, off me. It was only ten o'clock and nothing was happening at the quayside – the Chevette, dressed with sleety snow, stood alone and forlorn in the big car-park – so I went and walked around, down to the site of the original Fort Mackinac and then along residential streets full of treeless lawns and one-storey ranch-houses. When I returned to the ferry site, about forty minutes later, the Chevette had gained some company and there was a fair crowd of people – twenty or thirty at least – already boarding the boat.

We all sat on rows of seats in one small room. The hydroplane started up with a noise like a vacuum cleaner, then turned and slid out onto the green bleakness of Lake Huron. The lake was choppy, like a pan of water simmering on a low heat, but the ride was smooth. The people around me were strangely excited. They kept standing up to take pictures and point things out to each other. It occurred to me that many of them had never been on a ferry before, perhaps had never even seen an island, not one big enough to be inhabited anyway. No wonder they were excited. I was excited too, though for a different reason.

I had been to Mackinac Island before. My dad took us there when I was about four and I remembered it fondly. In fact, it was probably my oldest clear memory. I remembered that it had a big white hotel with a long porch and banks of flowers, positively dazzling in the July sunshine, and I could remember a big fort on a hill, and that the island had no cars, but just horse-drawn carriages, and that there was horse manure everywhere, and that I stepped in some, warm and squishy, and that my mother cleaned my shoe with a twig and a Kleenex, gagging delicately, and that as soon as she put the shoe back on my foot, I stepped backwards into some more with my other shoe, and that she didn't get cross. My mother never got cross. She didn't exactly do cartwheels, you understand, but she didn't shout or snap or look as if she were suppressing apoplexy, as I do with my children when they step in something warm and squishy, as they always do. She just looked kind of tired for a moment, and then she grinned at me and said it was a good thing she loved me, which was very true. She's a saint, my mother, especially where horse shit is concerned.

Mackinac Island is only small – about five miles long, a couple of miles wide – but like most islands it seems bigger when you are on it. Since 1901, no cars or motorised vehicles of any type have been allowed on the island, so when you step off the boat on to Main Street you find a line-up of horse-drawn carriages waiting at the kerb – a fancy one to take customers to the Grand Hotel, open phaetons to take people on expensive tours of the island, and a kind of sledge to deal with luggage and freight. Mackinac village was just as perfect as I remembered it, a string of white Victorian buildings along a sloping Main Street, snug cottages climbing up the steep hill to old Fort Mackinac, built in 1780 to defend the strait and still standing guard over the town.

I wandered off through the town, picking my way around little piles of horse manure. Without cars, the silence was almost complete. The whole island appeared to be on the brink of a six-month coma. Almost all the stores and restaurants along Main Street were shut for the season. I expect it's awful there in the summer with all the thousands of day trippers. A brochure that I picked up by the harbour listed sixty gift shops alone and more than thirty restaurants, ice-cream parlours, pizzerias and cookie stalls. But now at this time of year it all looked quaint and restful and incredibly pretty.

For a while, Mackinac Island was the biggest trading post in the New World – John Jacob Astor's fur trading company was based here – but its real glory dates from the late nineteenth century when wealthy people from Chicago and Detroit came to escape the city heat and enjoy the pollen-free air. The Grand Hotel, the biggest and oldest resort hotel in America, was built and the country's wealthiest industrialists constructed ornate summer houses on the bluffs over-looking Mackinac village and Lake Huron. I walked up there now. The views across the lake were fantastic, but the houses were simply breathtaking. They are some of the grandest, most elaborate houses ever built of wood, twenty-bedroomed places with every embellish-ment known to the Victorian mind – cupolas, towers, domes, gables, turrets, and front porches you could ride a bike around. Some of the cupolas had cupolas. They are just incredibly splendid and there are scores of them, standing side by side on the bluffs flanking Fort Mackinac. What it must be to be a child and play hide-and-seek in those houses, to have a bedroom in a tower and be able to lie in bed and gaze out on such a lake, to go bicycling on carless roads to little beaches and hidden coves, and above all to explore the woodland of beech and birch that cover the back three quarters of the island.

I wandered into them now, along one of the many paved paths that run through the dark woods, and felt like a seven-year-old on a grand adventure. Every turn in the path brought up some exotic surprise – Skull Cave, where, according to a sign beside it, an English fur trader hid from the Indians in 1763; Fort Holmes, an old British redoubt on the highest point on the island, 325 feet above Lake Huron; and two mossy old cemeteries out in the middle of nowhere, one Catholic and one Protestant. Both seemed impossibly big for such a small island, and they consisted mostly of the same few names going back generations – the Truscotts, Gables, Sawyers. I happily wandered for three hours without seeing a soul or hearing a sound made by man, and only barely sampled the island. I could easily have stayed for days. I returned to the village by way of the Grand Hotel, quite the most splendid and obnoxiously hoity-toity such institution I have ever come across. A rambling white wooden building with the biggest porch in the world (660 feet), it is indubitably swish and expensive. A single room at the time I was there cost $135 a night. A sign in the street leading down to the hotel said GRAND HOTEL—PROPER DRESS REQUIRED AT THE HOTEL AND HOTEL-OWNED STREET. GENTLEMEN AFTER 6 P.M. MUST BE ATTIRED IN A COAT AND TIE. LADIES MAY NOT BE ATTIRED IN SLACKS. This is possibly the only place in the world where you are told how to dress just to walk down the street. Another sign said a charge would be levied on anyone coming in to the hotel just to gawp. Honestly. I suppose they have a lot of trouble with day trippers. I walked stealthily down the road towards the hotel, half expecting to see a sign saying 'Anyone Passing Beyond This Point Wearing Plaid Trousers or White Shoes Will Be Arrested.' But there wasn't anything. I had it in my mind to put my head in the front door, just to see what life is like for really rich people, but there was a liveried doorman standing guard, so I had to beat a retreat.

I caught the afternoon ferry back to the mainland, and drove over the Mackinac Bridge to the chunk of land Michigan people call the upper peninsula. Before the bridge was built in 1957, this bit of Michigan was pretty well cut off from its own state, and even now it has an overwhelming sense of remoteness. It is mostly just a bleak and sandy peninsula, 150 miles long, squeezed between three of the Great Lakes, Superior, Huron and Michigan. Once again, I was almost in Canada. Sault Sainte Marie was just to the north. Its great locks connect Lake Huron and Lake Superior and are the busiest in the world, carrying a greater volume of tonnage than the Suez and Panama canals combined, believe it or not.

I was on Route 2, which follows the northern shoreline of Lake Michigan for most of its length. It is impossible to exaggerate the immensity of the Great Lakes. There are five of them, Erie, Huron, Michigan, Superior and Ontario, and they stretch 700 miles from top to bottom, 900 miles from east to west. They cover 94,500 square miles, making them almost precisely the size of the United Kingdom. Together they form the largest expanse of fresh water on earth.

More squally storms were at work far out on the lake, though where I was it was dry. About twenty miles offshore was a group of islands – Beaver Island, High Island, Whiskey Island, Hog Island and several others. High Island was once owned by a religious sect called the House of David, whose members all had beards and specialised, if you can believe it, in playing baseball. In the 1920s and 30s they toured the country taking on local teams wherever they went and I guess they were just about unbeatable. High Island was reputedly a kind of penal colony for members of the sect who committed serious infractions – struck out too often or something. It was said that people were sent there and never heard from again. Now, like all the other islands in the group except Beaver, it is uninhabited. I felt a strange pang of regret that I couldn't go over and explore them. In fact, the whole of the Great Lakes was exerting a strange hold on me, which I couldn't begin to understand. There was something alluring about the idea of a great inland sea, about the thought that if you had a boat you could spend years just bouncing around from one Great Lake to another, chugging from Chicago to Buffalo, Milwaukee to Montreal, pausing *en route* to investigate islands, bays and towns with curious names like Deadman's Point, Egg Harbor, Summer

Island. A lot of people do just that, I guess – buy a boat and disappear. I can see why.

All over the peninsula I kept encountering roadside food stands with big signs on them saying PASTIES. Most of them were closed and boarded up, but at Menominee, the last town before I crossed into Wisconsin, I passed one that was open and impulsively I turned the car around and went back to it. I had to see if they were real Cornish pasties or something else altogether but with the same name. The guy who ran the place was excited to have a real Englishman in his store. He had been making pasties for thirty years but he had never seen a real Cornish pasty or a real Englishman, come to that. I didn't have the heart to tell him that actually I came from Iowa, the next state over. Nobody ever gets excited at meeting an Iowan. The pasties were the real thing, brought to this isolated corner of Michigan by nineteenth-century Cornishmen who came to work in the local mines. 'Everybody eats them up here in the upper peninsula,' the man told me. 'But nobody's ever heard of them anywhere else. You cross the state line into Wisconsin, just over the river, and people don't know what they are. It's kind of strange.'

The man handed me the pasty in a paper bag and I went with it out to the car. It did seem to be a genuine Cornish pasty except that it was about the size of a rugby ball. It came on a styrofoam platter with a plastic fork and some sachets of ketchup. Eagerly I tucked into it. Apart from anything else I was starving.

It was awful. There wasn't anything wrong with it exactly – it was a genuine pasty, accurate in every detail – it was just that after more than a month of eating American junk food it tasted indescribably bland and insipid, like warmed cardboard. 'Where's the grease?' I thought. 'Where's the melted cheese patty and pan-fried chicken gravy? Where, above all, is the chocolate fudge frosting?' This was just meat and potatoes, just natural unenhanced flavour. 'No wonder it's never caught on over here,' I grumbled and pushed it back into the bag.

I started the car and drove on into Wisconsin, looking for a motel and a restaurant where I could get some real food – something that would squirt when I bit into it and run down my chin. That, of course, is the way food should be.

NINETEEN

'At Northern Wisconsin General Hospital, we'll help you to achieve your birthing goals,' said a voice on the radio. Oh, God, I thought. This was yet another new development since I had left America – the advent of hospital advertising. Everywhere you go you now encounter hospital ads. Who are they for? A guy gets hit by a bus, does he say, 'Quick, take me to Michigan General. They've got a magnetic resonance imager there.' I don't understand it. But then I don't understand anything to do with American health care.

Just before I left on this trip, I learned that a friend was in Mercy Hospital in Des Moines. So I looked up the number in the phone book and under Mercy Hospital there were ninety-four telephone numbers listed. The phone numbers started with Admitting and proceeded alphabetically through Biofeedback, Cancer Hotline, Impotency Program, Infant Apnea Hotline, Osteoporosis Program, Public Relations, Sleep Referral Services, something called Share Care Ltd, Smoke Stoppers and on and on. Health care in America is now a monolithic industry and it is completely out of control.

The person I was visiting, an old family friend, had just learned that she had ovarian cancer. As a complication arising from this, she also had pneumonia. As you might imagine, she looked a trifle under the weather. While I was with her, a social worker came in and gently explained to her some of the costings involved in her treatment. My friend could, for instance, have Medicine A, which would cost $5 a dose, but which she would have to take four times a day, or she could have Medicine B, which would cost $18 a dose, but which she would have to take only once a day. That was the social worker's job, to act as a liaison between the doctor, the patient and the insurance company, and to try to see to it that the patient wasn't hit with a lot of bills that the insurance company wouldn't pay. My friend would, of course, be billed for this service. It seemed so crazy, so unreal, to be watching an old friend sucking air from an oxygen mask, all but dead, and giving weak yes-or-no nods to questions concerning the continuance of her own life based on her ability to pay.

Contrary to popular belief abroad, it is possible, indeed quite easy, to get free treatment in America by going to a county hospital. They aren't very cheery places, in fact they are generally pretty grim, but they are no worse than any NHS hospital. There has to be free treatment because there are 40 million people in America without hospital insurance. God help you, however, if you try to sneak into a county hospital for a little free health care if you've got money in the bank. I worked for a year at the county hospital in Des Moines and I can tell you that they have batteries of lawyers and debt collectors whose sole job is to dig into the backgrounds of the people who use their facilities and make sure they really are as destitute as they claim to be.

Despite the manifest insanities of private health care in America, there is no denying that the quality of treatment is the best in the world. My friend received superb and unstinting care (and, not incidentally, they cured both her cancer and her pneumonia). She had a private room with a private bath, a remote control television and video recorder, her own telephone. The whole hospital was carpeted and full of exotic palms and cheerful paintings. In government hospitals in Britain, the only piece of carpet or colour TV you find is in the nursing officers' lounge. I worked in an NHS hospital years ago and once late at night I sneaked into the nursing officers' lounge just to see what it was like. Well, it was like the Queen's sitting-room. It was all velvety furniture and half-eaten boxes of Milk Tray chocolates.

The patients, in the meantime, slept beneath bare light bulbs in cold and echoing barrack halls, and spent their days working on jigsaw puzzles that had at least a fifth of the pieces missing, awaiting a fortnightly twenty-second visit by a swift-moving retinue of doctors and students. Those were, of course, the good old days of the NHS. Things aren't nearly so splendid now.

Forgive me. I seem to have gone off on a little tangent there. I was supposed to be guiding you across Wisconsin, telling you interesting facts about America's premier dairy state, and instead I go off and make unconstructive remarks about British and American health care. This was unwarranted.

Anyway, Wisconsin is America's premier dairy state, producing seventeen per cent of the nation's cheese and milk products, by golly, though as I drove across its rolling pleasantness I wasn't particularly struck by an abundance of dairy cows. I drove for long hours, south past Green Bay, Appleton and Oshkosh and then west towards Iowa. This was quintessential Midwestern farming country, a study in browns, a landscape of low wooded hills, bare trees, faded pastures, tumbledown corn. It all had a kind of muted beauty. The farms were large, scattered and prosperous-looking. Every half mile or so I would pass a snug-looking farmhouse, with a porch swing and a yard full of trees. Standing nearby would be a red barn with a rounded roof and a tall grain silo. Everywhere corn cribs were packed to bursting. Migrating birds filled the pale sky. The corn in the fields looked dead and brittle, but often I passed large harvesters chewing up rows and spitting out bright yellow ears.

I drove through the thin light of afternoon along back highways. It seemed to take forever to cross the state, but I didn't mind because it was so fetching and restful. There was something uncommonly alluring about the day, about the season, the sense that winter was drawing in. By four o'clock the daylight was going. By five the sun had dropped out of the clouds and was slotting into the distant hills, like a coin going into a piggy bank. At a place called Ferryville, I came suddenly up against the Mississippi River. It fairly took my breath away, it was so broad and beautiful and graceful lying there all flat and calm. In the setting sun it looked like liquid stainless steel.

On the far bank, about a mile away, was Iowa. Home. I felt a strange squeeze of excitement that made me hunch up closer to the wheel. I drove for twenty miles down the eastern side of the river, gazing across to the high dark bluffs on the Iowa side. At Prairie du Chien I crossed the river on an iron bridge full of struts and crossbars. And then I was in Iowa. I actually felt my heart quicken. I was home. This was my state. My licence plate matched everyone else's. No one would look at me as if to say, 'What are you doing here?' I belonged.

In the fading light, I drove almost randomly around north-east Iowa. Every couple of miles I would pass a farmer on a tractor juddering along the highway, heading home to dinner on one of the sprawling farms up in these sheltered hills above the Mississippi. It was Friday, one of the big days of the farmer's week. He would wash his arms and neck and sit down with his family to a table covered with great bowls of food. They would say grace together. After dinner the family would drive into Hooterville and sit out in the cold October air and through their steamy breath watch the Hooterville High Blue Devils beat Kraut City 28–7 at football. The farmer's son, Merle Jr, would score three of the touchdowns. Afterwards Merle senior would go to Ed's Tavern to celebrate (two beers, never more) and receive the admiration of the community for his son's prowess. Then it would be home to bed and up early in the frosty dawn to go out hunting for deer with his best friends, Ed and Art and Wally, trudging across the fallow fields, savouring the clean air and the companionship. I was seized with a huge envy for these people and their unassuming lives. It must be wonderful to live in a safe and timeless place, where you know everyone and everyone knows you, and you can all count on each other. I envied them their sense of community, their football games, their bring-and-bake sales, their church socials. And I felt guilty for mocking them. They were good people.

I drove through the seamless blackness, past Millville, New Vienna, Cascade, Scotch Grove. Every once in a while I would pass a distant farmhouse whose windows were pools of yellow light, warm and inviting. Occasionally there would be a larger town, with a much larger pool of light scooped out of the darkness – the high school football field, where the week's game was in progress. These football fields lit up the night; they were visible from miles off. As I drove through each town, it was clear that everybody was out at the game. There was nobody on the streets. Apart from one forlorn teenaged girl standing behind the counter in the local Dairy Queen, waiting for the post-game rush, everyone in town was at the football game. You could drive in with a fleet of trucks and strip the town during a high school football game in Iowa. You could blow open the bank with explosives and take the money out in wheelbarrows and no one would be there to see it. But of course nobody would think of such a thing because crime doesn't exist in rural Iowa. Their idea of a crime in these places would be to miss the Friday football game. Anything worse than that only exists on television and in the newspapers, in a semi-mythic distant land called the Big City.

I had intended to drive on to Des Moines, but on an impulse I stopped at Iowa City. It's a college town, the home of the University of Iowa, and I still had a couple of friends living there – people who had gone to college there and then never quite found any reason to move on. It was nearly ten o'clock when I arrived, but the streets were packed with students out carousing. I called my old friend John Horner from a street corner phone and he told me to meet him in Fitzpatrick's Bar. I stopped a passing student and asked him the way to Fitzpatrick's Bar, but he was so drunk that he had lost the power of speech. He just gazed numbly at me. He looked to be about fourteen years old. I stopped a group of girls, similarly intoxicated, and asked them if they knew the way to the bar. They all said they did and pointed in different directions, and then became so convulsed with giggles that it was all they could do to stand up. They moved around in front of me like passengers on a ship in heavy seas. They looked about fourteen years old too.

'Are you girls always this happy?' I asked.

'Only at homecoming,' one of them said.

Ah, that explained it. Homecoming. The big social event of the college year. There are three ritual stages attached to homecoming celebrations at American universities: (1) get grossly intoxicated; (2) throw up in a public place; (3) wake up not knowing where you are or how you got there and with your underpants on backwards. I appeared to have arrived in town somewhere between stages one and two, though in fact a few of the more committed revellers were already engaged in gutter serenades. I picked my way through the weaving throngs in downtown Iowa City asking people at random if they knew the way to Fitzpatrick's Bar. No one seemed to have heard of it – but then many of the people I encountered probably could not have identified themselves in a roomful of mirrors. Eventually I stumbled on the bar myself. Like all bars in Iowa City on a Friday night, it was packed to the rafters. Everybody looked to be fourteen years old, except one person – my friend John Horner, who was standing at the bar looking all of his thirty-five years. There is nothing like a college town to make you feel old before your time. I joined Horner at the bar. He hadn't changed a lot. He was now a pharmacist and a respectable member of the community, though there was still a semi-wild glint in his eye. In his day, he had been one of the most committed drug-takers in the community. Indeed, although he always strenuously denied it, everyone knew that his motive for studying pharmacology was to be able to create a more exotic blend of hallucinogenic drugs. We had been friends almost forever, since first grade at least. We exchanged broad smiles and warm handshakes and tried to talk, but there was so much noise and throbbing music that we were just two men watching each other's mouths move. So we gave up trying to talk and instead had a beer and stood smiling inanely at each other, the way you do with someone you haven't seen for years, and watching the people around us. I couldn't get over how young and fresh-looking they all seemed. Everything about them looked brand new and unused – their clothes, their faces, their bodies. When we had drained our beer bottles, Horner and I stepped out on to the street and walked to his car. The fresh air felt wonderful. People were leaning against buildings everywhere and puking. 'Have you ever seen so many twerpy little assholes in all your life?' Horner asked me rhetorically.

'And they're all just fourteen years old,' I added.

'Physically they are fourteen years old,' he corrected me, 'but emotionally and intellectually they are still somewhere shy of their eighth birthday.'

'Were we like that at their age?'

'I used to wonder that, but I don't think so. I may have been that stupid once, but I was never that shallow. These kids wear button-down collar shirts and penny loafers. They look like they're on their way to an Osmonds concert. And they don't know *anything*. You talk to them in a bar and they don't even know who's running for President. They've never heard of Nicaragua. It's scary.'

We walked along thinking about the scariness of it all. 'But there's something even worse,' Horner added. We were at his car. I looked at him across the top of it. 'What's that?' I asked.

'They don't smoke dope. Can you believe that?'

Well, I couldn't. The idea of students at the University of Iowa not smoking dope is . . . well, simply inconceivable. On any list of reasons for going to the University of Iowa, smoking dope took up at least two of the first five places. 'Then what are they here for?'

'They're getting an *education*.' Horner said in a tone of wonder. 'Can you believe that? They *want* to be insurance salesmen and computer programmers. That's their dream in life. They want to make a lot of money so they can go out and buy more penny loafers and Madonna albums. It terrifies me sometimes.'

We got in his car and drove through dark streets to his house. Horner explained to me how the world had changed. When I left America for England, Iowa City was full of hippies. Difficult as it may be to believe, out here amid all these cornfields, the University of Iowa was for many years one of the most radical colleges in the country, at its peak exceeded in radicalness only by Berkeley and Columbia. Everybody there was a hippie, the professors as much as the students. It wasn't just that they smoked dope and frequently rioted; they were also open-minded and intellectual. People cared about things like politics and the environment and where the world was going. Now, from what Horner was telling me, it was as if all the people in Iowa City had had their brains laundered at the Ronald McDonald Institute of Mental Readjustment.

'So what happened?' I asked Horner when we were settled at his house with a beer. 'What made everyone change?'

'I don't know exactly,' he said. 'The main thing, I guess, is that the Reagan Administration has this obsession with drugs. And they don't distinguish between hard drugs and soft drugs. If you're a dealer and you're caught with pot, you get sent away for just as long as if it were heroin. So now nobody sells pot. All the people who used to sell it have moved on to crack and heroin because the risk is no worse and the profits are a lot better.'

'Sounds crazy,' I said.

'Of course it's crazy!' Horner answered, a little hotly. Then he calmed down. 'Actually a lot of people just stopped dealing in pot altogether. Do you remember Frank Dortmeier?'

Frank Dortmeier was a guy who used to ingest drugs by the sackful. He would snort coke through a garden hose given half a chance. 'Yeah, sure,' I said.

'I used to get my pot from him. Then they brought in this law that if you are caught selling dope within a thousand yards of a public school they put you in jail for ever. It doesn't matter that you may only be selling one little reefer to your own mother, they still put you away for eternity just as if you were standing on the school steps shoving it down the throats of every snivelling little kid who passed by. Well, when they brought this law in, Dortmeier started to get worried because there was a school up the street from him. So one night under cover of darkness, he goes out with a hundred-foot tape measure and measures the distance from his house to the school and damn me but it's 997 yards. So he just stops selling dope, just like that.' Horner drank his beer sadly. 'It's really frustrating. I mean, have you ever tried to watch American TV without dope?'

'It must be tough,' I agreed.

'Dortmeier gave me the name of his supplier so I could go and get some myself. Well, this guy was in Kansas City. I had no idea. So I drove all the way down there, just to buy a couple of ounces of pot, and it was crazy. The house was full of guns. The guy kept looking out the window like he was expecting the police to tell him to come out with his hands up. He was half convinced that I was an undercover narcotics officer. I mean here I am, a thirty-five-year-old family man, with a college education and a respectable job, I'm 180 miles from home and I'm wondering if I'm going to get blown away, and all so that I can just have a little something to help me get through *Love Boat* reruns on TV. It was too crazy for me. You need somebody like Dortmeier for a situation like that – somebody with a lust for drugs and no brain.' Horner shook the beer can by his ear to confirm that it was empty and then looked at me. 'You wouldn't by any wild chance have any dope with you?' he asked.

'I'm sorry, John,' I said.

'Shame,' said Horner and went out to the kitchen to get us more beers.

I spent the night in Horner's spare room and in the morning stood with him and his pleasant wife in the kitchen drinking coffee and chatting while small children swirled about our legs. Life is odd, I thought. It seemed so strange for Horner to have a wife and children and a paunch and a mortgage and to be, like me, approaching the cliff-face of middle age. We had been boys for so long together that I suppose I had thought the condition was permanent. I realised with a sense of dread that the next time we met we would probably talk about gallstone operations and the relative merits of different brands of storm windows. It put me in a melancholy mood and kept me there as I reclaimed my car from its parking space downtown and returned to the highway.

I drove along old Route 6, which used to be the main highway to Chicago, but now, with Interstate 80 just three miles to the south, it is all but forgotten, and I hardly saw a soul along its length. I drove for an hour and a half without much of a thought in my head, just a weary eagerness to get home, to see my mom, to have a shower, and not to touch a steering wheel for a long, long time.

Des Moines looked wonderful in the morning sunshine. The dome on the state capitol building gleamed. The trees were still full of colour. They've changed the city completely – downtown now is all modern buildings and bubbling fountains and whenever I'm there now I have to keep looking up at the street signs to get my bearings – but it felt like home. I suppose it always will. I hope so. I drove through the city, happy to be there, proud to be part of it.

On Grand Avenue, near the governor's mansion, I realised I was driving along behind my mother, who had evidently borrowed my sister's car. I recognised her because the right turn signal was blinking pointlessly as she proceeded up the street. My mother generally puts the turn signal on soon after pulling out of the garage and then leaves it on for pretty much the rest of the day. I used to point this out to her, but then I realised it is actually a good thing because it alerts other motorists that they are approaching a driver who may not be entirely on top of matters. I followed along behind her. At Thirty-First Street the blinking turn signal jumped from the right side of the car to the left – I had forgotten that she likes to move it around from time to time – as we turned the corner for home, but then it stayed cheerily blinking on the left for the last mile, down Thirty-First Street and up Elmwood Drive.

I had to park a fair distance from the house and then, despite a boyish eagerness to see my mother, I took a minute to log the final details of the trip in a notebook I had been carrying with me. It always made me feel oddly important and professional, like a jumbo jet pilot at the end of a transatlantic flight. It was 10.38 a.m., and I had driven 6,842 miles since leaving home thirty-four days earlier. I circled this figure, then got out, grabbed my bags from the trunk, and walked briskly to the house. My mother was already inside. I could see her through the back window, moving around in the kitchen, putting away groceries and humming. She is always humming. I opened the back door, dropped my bags and called out those four most all-American words: 'Hi, Mom, I'm home!'

She looked real pleased to see me. 'Hello, dear!' she said brightly and gave me a hug. 'I was just wondering when I'd be seeing you again. Can I get you a sandwich?'

'That would be great,' I said even though I wasn't really hungry.

It was good to be home.

PART TWO

West

TWENTY

I was headed for Nebraska. Now there's a sentence you don't want to have to say too often if you can possibly help it. Nebraska must be the most unexciting of all the states. Compared with it, Iowa is paradise. Iowa at least is fertile and green and has a hill. Nebraska is like a 75,000-square-mile bare patch. In the middle of the state is a river called the Platte, which at some times of the year is two or three miles wide. It looks impressive until you realise that it is only about four inches deep. You could cross it in a wheelchair. On a landscape without any contours or depressions to shape it, the Platte just lies there, like a drink spilled across a table-top. It is the most exciting thing in the state.

When I was growing up, I used to wonder how Nebraska came to be lived in. I mean to say, the original settlers, creaking across America in their covered wagons, must have passed through Iowa, which is green and fertile and has, as I say, a hill, but stopped short of Colorado, which is green and fertile and has a mountain range, and settled instead for a place that is flat and brown and full of stubble and prairie-dogs. Doesn't make a lot of sense, does it? Do you know what the original settlers made their houses of? Dried mud. And do you know what happened to all those mud houses when the rainy season came every year? That's correct, they slid straight into the Platte River.

For a long time I couldn't decide whether the original settlers in Nebraska were insane or just stupid, and then I saw a stadium full of University of Nebraska football fans in action on a Saturday and realised that they must have been both. I may be a decade or so out of touch here but when I left America, the University of Nebraska didn't so much play football as engage in weekly ritual slaughters. They were always racking up scores of 58–3 against hapless opponents. Most schools, when they get a decent lead, will send in a squad of skinny freshmen in unsoiled uniforms to let them run around a bit and get dirty and, above all, to give the losers a sporting chance to make the score respectable. It's called fair play.

Not Nebraska. The University of Nebraska would send in flame-throwers if it were allowed. Watching Nebraska play football every week was like watching hyenas tearing open a gazelle. It was unseemly. It was unsporting. And of course the fans could never get enough of it. To sit among them with the score 66–0 and watch them bray for more blood is a distinctly unnerving experience, particularly when you consider that a lot of these people must work at Strategic Air Command in Omaha. If Iowa State ever upset Nebraska, I wouldn't be at all surprised if they nuked Ames. All of these thoughts percolated through my mind on this particular morning and frankly left me troubled.

I was on the road again. It was a little after 7.30 a.m. on a bright but still wintry Monday morning in April. I drove west out of Des Moines on Interstate 80, intending to zip across the western half of Iowa and plunge deep into Nebraska. But I couldn't face Nebraska just yet, not this early in the morning, and abruptly at De Soto, just fifteen miles west of Des Moines, I pulled off the interstate and started wandering around on back roads. Within a couple of minutes I was lost. This didn't altogether surprise me. Getting lost is a family trait.

My father, when behind the wheel, was more or less permanently lost. Most of the time he was just kind of lost, but whenever we got near something we were intent on seeing he would become seriously lost. Generally it would take him about an hour to realise that he had gone from the first stage to the second. All during that time, as he blundered through some unfamiliar city, making sudden and unpredictable turns, getting honked at for going the wrong way down one-way streets or for hesitating in the middle of busy intersections, my mother would mildly suggest that perhaps we should pull over and ask directions. But my father would pretend not to hear her and would press on in that semi-obsessional state that tends to overcome fathers when things aren't going well.

Eventually, after driving the wrong way down the same one-way street so many times that merchants were beginning to come and watch from their doorways, Dad would stop the car and gravely announce, 'Well, I think we should ask directions', in a tone suggesting that this had been his desire all along.

This was always a welcome development, but seldom more than a partial breakthrough. Either my mom would get out and stop a patently unqualified person – a nun on an exchange visit from Costa Rica, usually – and come back with directions that were hopelessly muddled, or my father would go off to find somebody and then not come back. The problem with my dad was that he was a great talker. This is always a dangerous thing in a person who gets lost a lot. He would go into a café to ask the way to Giant Fungus State Park and the next thing you knew he would be sitting down having a cup of coffee and a chat with the proprietor or the proprietor would be taking him out back to show him his new septic tank or something. In the meantime the rest of us would have to sit in a quietly baking car, with nothing to do but sweat and wait and listlessly watch a pair of flies copulate on the dashboard.

After a very long time my father would reappear, wiping crumbs from around his mouth and looking real perky. 'Darnedest thing,' he would say, leaning over to talk to my mom through the window. 'Guy in there collects false teeth. He's got over 700 sets down in his basement. He was so pleased to have someone to show them to that I just couldn't say no. And then his wife insisted that I have a piece of blueberry pie and see the photographs from their daughter's wedding. They'd never heard of Giant Fungus State Park, I'm afraid, but the guy said his brother at the Conoco station by the traffic lights would know. *He* collects fanbelts, of all things, and apparently has the largest collection of pre-war fanbelts in the upper Midwest. I'm just going down there now.' And then, before anybody could stop him, he'd be gone again. By the time he finally returned my father would know most of the people in town and the flies on the dashboard would have a litter of infants.

Eventually I found what I was looking for: Winterset, birthplace of John Wayne. I drove around the town until I found his house – Winterset is so small that this only took a minute – and slowed down to look at it from the car. The house was tiny and the paint was peeling off it. Wayne, or Marion Morrison as he then was, only lived there for a year or so before his family moved to California. The house is run as a museum now, but it was shut. This didn't surprise me, as pretty much everything in the town was shut, quite a lot of it permanently from the look of things. The Iowa Movie Theater on the square was clearly out of business, its marquee board blank, and many of the other stores were gone or just hanging on. It was a depressing sight

because Winterset was really quite a nice-looking little town with its
county courthouse and square and long streets of big Victorian
houses. I bet, like Winfield, it was a different place altogether fifteen or
twenty years ago. I drove back out to the highway past the Gold Buffet
('Dancing Nitely') feeling an odd sense of emptiness.

Every town I came to was much the same – peeling paint, closed
businesses, a deathly air. South-west Iowa has always been the poorest
part of the state and it showed. I didn't stop because there was nothing
worth stopping for. I couldn't even find a place to get a cup of coffee.
Eventually, much to my surprise, I blundered on to a bridge over the
Missouri River and then I was in Nebraska City, in Nebraska. And it
wasn't at all bad. In fact, it was really quite pleasant – better than Iowa
by a long chalk, I was embarrassed to admit. The towns were more
prosperous-looking and better maintained, and the roadsides everywhere were full of bushes from which sprang a profusion of creamy
flowers. It was all quite pretty, though in a rather monotonous way.
That is the problem with Nebraska. It just goes on and on, and even
the good bits soon grow tedious. I drove for hours along an
undemanding highway, past Auburn, Tecumseh, Beatrice (a town of
barely 10,000 people but which produced two Hollywood stars, Harold
Lloyd and Robert Taylor), Fairbury, Hebron, Deshler, Ruskin.

At Deshler I stopped for coffee and was surprised at how cold it was.
Where the weather is concerned, the Midwest has the worst of both
worlds. In the winter the wind is razor-sharp. It skims down from the
Arctic and slices through you. It howls and swirls and buffets the
house. It brings piles of snow and bone-cracking cold. From
November to March you walk leaning forward at a twenty-degree
angle, even indoors, and spend your life waiting for your car to warm
up, or digging it out of drifts or scraping futilely at ice that seems to
have been applied to the windows with Superglue. And then one day
spring comes. The snow melts, you stride about in shirt-sleeves, you
incline your face to the sun. And then, just like that, spring is over and
it's summer. It is as if God has pulled a lever in the great celestial
powerhouse. Now the weather rolls in from the opposite direction,
from the tropics far to the south, and it hits you like a wall of heat. For
six months, the heat pours over you. You sweat oil. Your pores gape.
The grass goes brown. Dogs look as if they could die. When you walk
downtown you can feel the heat of the pavement rising through the

soles of your shoes. Just when you think you might very well go crazy, autumn comes and for two or three weeks the air is mild and nature is friendly. And then it's winter and the cycle starts again. And you think, 'As soon as I'm big enough, I'm going to move far, far away from here.'

At Red Cloud, home of Willa Cather, I joined US 281 and headed south toward Kansas. Just over the border is Smith Center, home of Dr Brewster M. Higley, who wrote the words to *Home on the Range*. Wouldn't you just know that *Home on the Range* would be written by somebody with a name like Brewster M. Higley? You can see the log cabin where he wrote the words. But I was headed for something far more exciting – the geographical centre of the United States. You reach it by turning off the highway just outside the little town of Lebanon and following a side road for about a mile through the wheat fields. Then you come to a forlorn little park with picnic tables and a stone monument with a wind-whipped flag atop it and a plaque saying that this is the centremost point in the continental United States, by golly. Beside the park, adding to the sense of forlornness, was a closed-down motel, which had been built in the evident hope that people would want to spend the night in this lonely place and send postcards to their friends saying, 'You'll never guess where we are.' Clearly the owner had misread the market.

I climbed onto a picnic table and could instantly see for miles across the waving fields. The wind came at me like a freight train. I felt as if I were the first person to come there for years. It was a strange feeling to think that of all the 230 million people in the United States I was the most geographically distinctive. If America were invaded, I would be the last person captured. This was it, the last stand, and as I climbed down off the table and returned to the car I felt an uneasy sense of guilt for leaving the place undefended.

I drove into the gathering evening gloom. The clouds were low and swift. The landscape was a sea of white grass, fine as a child's hair. It was strangely beautiful. By the time I reached Russell, it was dark and rain was falling. The headlights swept over a sign that said WELCOME TO BOB DOLE COUNTRY. Russell is the home town of Bob Dole, who was at this time running for the Republican nomination for President. I stopped and got a room for the night, figuring that if Dole were elected President, I could tell my children that I had once spent the night in his home town and perhaps thereby deepen their respect for me. Also, every time Russell was shown on TV over the next four years I could say, 'Hey, I was there!' and make everybody in the room stop talking while I pointed out things I had seen. In the event, Dole dropped out of the race two days later, primarily because nobody could stand him, apart from his family and some other people around Russell, and the town, alas, lost its chance at fame.

I awoke to a more promising day. The sun was bright and the air was clear. Bugs exploded colourfully against the windscreen, a sure sign of spring in the Midwest. In the sunshine Kansas seemed an altogether more agreeable place, which surprised me a little. I had always thought one of the worst things anyone could say to you was, 'We're transferring you to Kansas, son.' Kansas calls itself 'the Wheat State'. That kind of says it all, don't you think? It really makes you want to cancel that Barbados trip, doesn't it? But in fact Kansas was OK. The towns I went through all looked trim and prosperous and quintessen-tially American. But then Kansas is the most quintessential of American states. It is, after all, where Superman and Dorothy from the Wizard of Oz grew up, and all the towns I went through had a cosy, leafy, timeless air to them. They looked like the sort of places where you could still have your groceries delivered by a boy on a bike and people would still say things like 'By golly' and 'Gee willickers'. At Great Bend, I stopped on the square beside the Barton County Courthouse and had a look around. It was like passing through a time warp. The place appeared not to have changed a fraction since 1965. The Crest Movie Theater was still in business. Nearby stood the *Great Bend Daily Tribune* and the Brass Buckle Clothing Store, with a big sign on it that said FOR GUYS AND GALS. Gee willickers. A man and his wife passed me on the sidewalk and said good morning like old friends. The man even tipped his hat. From a passing car came the sound of the Everly Brothers. This was almost too eerie. I half expected Rod Serling to step out from behind a tree and say, 'Bill Bryson doesn't know it, but he's just driven into a community that doesn't exist in time or space. He's just embarked on a one-way trip into . . . The Twilight Zone.'

I had a look in the window of the Family Pharmacy and Gift Shop, which had an interesting and unusual display that included a wheelchair, a packet of disposable absorbent underpants (it isn't often you find a store catering for the incontinent impulse shopper), teddy bears, coffee-mugs bearing wholesome sentiments like World's Best Grandma, mother's day cards and a variety of porcelain animals. In one corner of the window was a poster for a concert by – you are never going to believe this – Paul Revere and the Raiders. Can you beat that? There they were, still dressed up like Continental soldiers, prancing about and grinning, just like when I was in junior high school. They would be performing at the Civic Auditorium in Dodge City in two weeks. Tickets started at $10.75. This was all becoming too much for me. I was glad to get in the car and drive on to Dodge City, which at least is intentionally unreal.

Somewhere during the seventy miles between Great Bend and Dodge City you leave the Midwest and enter the West. The people in the towns along the way stop wearing baseball caps and shuffling along with that amiable dopeyness characteristic of the Midwest and instead start wearing cowboy hats and cowboy boots, walking with a lope and looking vaguely suspicious and squinty, as if they think they might have to shoot you in a minute. People in the West like to shoot things. When they first got to the West they shot buffalo.* Once there were 70 million buffalo on the plains and then the people of the West started blasting away at them. Buffalo are just cows with big heads. If you've ever looked a cow in the face and seen the unutterable depths of trust and stupidity that lie within, you will be able to guess how difficult it must have been for people in the West to track down buffalo and shoot them to pieces. By 1895, there were only 800 buffalo left, mostly in zoos and touring Wild West shows. With no buffalo left to kill, Westerners started shooting Indians. Between 1850 and 1890 they reduced the number of Indians in America from 2 million to 90,000.

Nowadays, thank goodness, both have made a recovery. Today there are 30,000 buffalo and 300,000 Indians, and of course you are not allowed to shoot either, so all the Westerners have left to shoot at are road signs and each other, both of which they do rather a lot. There you have a capsule history of the West.

---

* Many people will tell you that you mustn't call them buffalo, that they are really bison. Buffalo, these people will tell you, actually live in China or some other distant country and are a different breed of animal altogether. These are the same people who tell you that you must call geraniums pelargoniums. Ignore them.

When they weren't shooting things, the people of the West went into towns like Dodge City for a little social and sexual intercourse. At its peak, Dodge City was the biggest cow town and semen sink in the West, full of drifters, drovers, buffalo hunters and the sort of women that only a cowboy could find attractive. But it was never as tough and dangerous as you were led to believe on *Gunsmoke* and all those movies about Bat Masterson and Wyatt Earp. For ten years it was the biggest cattle market in the world; that's all.

In all those years, there were only thirty-four people buried in Boot Hill Cemetery and most of those were just vagrants found dead in snowdrifts or of natural causes. I know this for a fact because I paid $2·75 to go and see Boot Hill and the neighbouring 'Historic Front Street', which has been rebuilt to look like it did when Dodge City was a frontier town and Bat Masterson and Wyatt Earp were the sheriffs. Matt Dillon never existed, I was distressed to learn, though Bat Masterson and Wyatt Earp were both real enough. Bat Masterson ended his life as sports editor of the *New York Morning Telegraph*. Isn't that interesting? And here's another interesting fact, which I didn't tell you about earlier because I've been saving it: Wyatt Earp was from Pella, the little Iowa town with the windmills. Isn't that great?

Fifty miles beyond Dodge City is Holcomb, Kansas, which gained a small notoriety as the scene of the murders described with lavish detail in the Truman Capote book *In Cold Blood*. In 1959, two small-time crooks broke into the house of a wealthy Holcomb rancher named Herb Clutter because they had heard he had a safe full of money. In fact he didn't. So, chagrined, they tied Clutter's wife and two teenaged children to their beds and took Clutter down to the basement and killed them all. They slit Clutter's throat (Capote described his gurglings with a disturbing relish) and shot the others in the head at point-blank range. Because Clutter had been prominent in state politics, the *New York Times* ran a small story about the murders. Capote saw the story, became intrigued and spent five years interviewing all the main participants – friends, neighbours, relatives, police investigators and the murderers themselves. The book, when it came out in 1965, was considered an instant classic, largely because Capote told everyone it was. In any case, it was sufficiently seminal, as we used to say in college, to have made a lasting impact and it occurred to me that I could profitably re-read it and then go to Holcomb and make a lot of trenchant observations about crime and violence in America.

I was wrong. I quickly realised there was nothing typical about the Clutter murders: they would be as shocking today as they were then. And there was nothing particularly seminal about Capote's book. It was essentially just a grisly and sensational murder story that pandered, in a deviously respectable way, to the reader's baser instincts. All that a trip to Holcomb would achieve would be to provide me with the morbid thrill of gawping at a house in which a family had long before been senselessly slaughtered. Still, that's about all I ask out of life, and it was bound, at the very least, to be more interesting than Historic Front Street in Dodge City.

In Capote's book, Holcomb was a tranquil, dusty hamlet, full of intensely decent people, a place whose citizens didn't smoke, drink, lie, swear or miss church, a place in which sex outside marriage was unforgivable and sex before marriage unthinkable, in which teenagers were home at eleven on a Saturday night, in which Catholics and Methodists didn't mingle if they could possibly help it, in which doors were never locked, and children of eleven or twelve were allowed to drive cars. For some reason I found the idea of children driving cars particularly astonishing. In Capote's book, the nearest town was Garden City, five miles down the highway. Things had clearly changed. Now Holcomb and Garden City had more or less grown together, connected by an umbilicus of gas stations and fast food places. Holcomb was still dusty, but no longer a hamlet. On the edge of town was a huge high school, obviously new, and all around were cheap little houses, also new, with barefooted Mexican children running around in the front yards. I found the Clutter house without too much trouble. In the book it stood apart from the town, down a shady lane. Now the lane was lined with houses. There was no sign of occupancy at the Clutter house. The curtains were drawn. I hesitated for a long time and then went and knocked at the front door, and frankly was relieved that no one answered. What could I have said? Hello, I'm a stranger passing through town with a morbid interest in sensational murders and I just wondered if you could tell me what it's like living in a house in which several people have had their brains spattered on to the walls? Do you ever think about it at mealtimes, for instance?

I got back in the car and drove around, looking for anything that
was familiar from the book, but the shops and cafés all seemed to have
gone or been renamed. I stopped at the high school. The main doors
were locked – it was four in the afternoon – but some students from
the track team were drifting about on the playing fields. I accosted two
of them standing along the perimeter and asked them if I could talk to
them for a minute about the Clutter murders. It was clear that they
didn't know what I was talking about.

'You know,' I prompted. '*In Cold Blood*. The book by Truman
Capote.'

They looked at me blankly.

'You've never heard of *In Cold Blood*? Truman Capote?' They
hadn't. I could scarcely believe it. 'Have you ever heard of the Clutter
murders – a whole family killed in a house over there beyond that
water-tower?'

One of them brightened. 'Oh, yeah,' he said. 'Whole family just
wiped out. It was, you know, weird.'

'Does anybody live in the house now?'

'Dunno,' said the student. 'Somebody used to live there, I think. But
now I think maybe they don't. Dunno really.' Talking was clearly not
his strongest social skill, though compared with the second student he
was a veritable Cicero. I thought I had never met two such remarkably
ignorant young men, but then I stopped three others and none of them
had heard of *In Cold Blood* either. Over by the pole-vaulting pit I
found the coach, an amiable young social sciences teacher named Stan
Kennedy. He was supervising three young athletes as they took turns
sprinting down a runway with a long pole and then crashing with their
heads and shoulders into a horizontal bar about five feet off the
ground. If knocking the hell out of a horizontal bar was a sport in
Kansas, these guys could be state champions. I asked Kennedy if he
thought it odd that so many of the students had never heard of *In Cold
Blood*.

'I was surprised at that myself when I first came here eight years
ago,' he said. 'After all, it was the biggest thing that ever happened in
the town. But you have to realise that the people here hated the book.
They banned it from the public library and a lot of them even now
won't talk about it.'

This surprised me. A few weeks before I had read an article in an old

Life magazine about how the townspeople had taken Truman Capote to their hearts even though he was a mincing little poof who talked with a lisp and wore funny caps. In fact, it turns out, they disdained him not only as a mincing little poof, but as a meddler from the big city who had exploited their private grief for his own gain. Most people wanted to forget the whole business and discouraged their children from developing an interest in it. Kennedy had once asked his brightest class how many of the students had read the book, and three quarters of them had never even looked at it.

I said I thought that was surprising. If I had grown up in a place where something famous had happened I would want to read about it. 'So would I,' Kennedy said. 'So would most people from our generation. But kids these days are different. A lot of them can barely read. And you just can't teach them anything. There's no spark of enthusiasm there. It's as if years of watching TV have hypnotised them. Some of them can hardly speak a coherent sentence.'

We agreed that this was, you know, weird.

There is nothing much to be said for the far west of Kansas except that the towns are small and scattered and the highways mostly empty. Every ten miles or so there is a side road, and at every side road there is an old pickup truck stopped at a stop sign. You can see them from a long way off – in Kansas you can see everything from a long way off – glinting in the sunshine. At first you think the truck must be broken down or abandoned, but just as you get within thirty or forty feet of it, it pulls out onto the highway in front of you, causing you to make an immediate downward adjustment in your speed from sixty miles an hour to about twelve miles an hour and to test the resilience of the steering wheel with your forehead. This happens to you over and over. Curious to see what sort of person could inconvenience you in this way in the middle of nowhere, you speed up to overtake it and see that sitting at the wheel is a little old man of eighty-seven, wearing a cowboy hat three sizes too large for him, staring fixedly at the empty road as if piloting a light aircraft through a thunderstorm. He is of course quite oblivious of you. Kansas has more drivers like this than any other state in the nation, more than can be accounted for by simple demographics. Other states must send them their old people, perhaps by promising them a free cowboy hat when they get there.

TWENTY-ONE

I should have known better, but I had it in my mind that Colorado was nothing but mountains. Somehow I thought that the moment I left Kansas I would find myself amid the snow-tipped Rockies, in lofty meadows of waving buttercups, where the skies were blue and the air was as crisp as fresh celery. But it was nothing like that at all. It was just flat and brown and full of remote little towns with charmless names: Swink, Ordway, Manzanola. They in turn were all full of poor-looking people and mean-looking dogs nosing around on the margins of liquor stores and gas stations. Broken bottles glittered among the stubble in the roadside ditches and the signs along the way were pocked from shotgun blasts. This sure wasn't the Colorado John Denver was forever yodelling on about.

I was imperceptibly climbing. Every town along the highway announced its elevation, and each was several hundred feet higher than the previous one, but it wasn't until I had nearly reached Pueblo, 150 miles into the interior, that I at last saw mountains. Suddenly there they were, blue and craggy and heavy with snow.

My plan was to take State Highway 67 north up to Victor and Cripple Creek, two old gold-mining towns. The road was marked on my map as scenic. What I didn't realise was that it was unpaved and that it led through a mountain pass ominously called Phantom Canyon. It was the most desolate and bone-shaking road I have ever been on, full of ruts and rocks – the kind of road that makes everything in the car dance about and doors fly open. The problem was that there was no way to turn around. One side of the road hugged a wall of rock, rising up and up, like the side of a skyscraper; the other fell sharply away to a creek of excited water. Meekly I pressed on, driving at a creeping pace and hoping that things would improve in a while. But of course they didn't. The road grew ever steeper and more perilous. Here and there the two sides of the canyon would narrow and I would be hemmed in for a while by walls of fractured stone that looked as if they had been struck with a hammer, and then suddenly it would open out again to reveal hair-raising views down to the twisting canyon floor far, far below.

Everywhere above me house-sized boulders teetered on pin-heads of rock, just waiting to tumble down the mountainside and make a doormat of me. Rockslides were evidently common. The valley floor was a graveyard of boulders. I prayed that I would not meet another vehicle coming down the hill and have to reverse all the way to the valley floor. But I needn't have worried because of course not a single other person in the whole of North America was sufficiently moronic to drive through Phantom Valley at this time of year, when a sudden storm could turn the road to mud and bog the car down for months, or send it slipping and sliding over the void. I wasn't used to dealing with landscapes that can kill you. Cautiously I pressed on.

High up in the mountains I crossed a wooden bridge of laughable ricketyness over a deep chasm. It was the sort of bridge on which, in the movies, a slat always breaks, causing the heroine to plunge through up to her armpits with her pert legs wiggling helplessly above the chasm, until the hero dashes back to save her, spears falling all around them. When I was twelve years old, I could never understand why the hero, operating from this position of superiority, didn't say to the lady, 'OK, I'll save your life, but later you have to let me see you naked. Agreed?'

Beyond the bridge wet snow began to fly about. It mixed with the hundreds of insects that had been flinging themselves into the windscreen since Nebraska (what a senseless waste of life!) and turned it into a brown sludge. I attacked it with window washer solution, but this just converted it from a brown sludge to a creamy sludge and I still couldn't see. I stopped and jumped out to wipe at the window with my sleeve, certain that at any moment a bobcat, seeing the chance of a lifetime, would drop onto my shoulders and rip off my scalp with a sound like two strips of Velcro being parted. I imagined myself, scalpless, stumbling down the mountainside with the bobcat nipping at my heels. This formed such a vivid image in my mind that I jumped back into the car, even though I had only created a small rectangle of visibility about the size of an envelope. It was like looking out of a tank turret.

The car wouldn't start. Of course. Drily I said, 'Oh, thank you, God.' Up here in the thin air, the Chevette just gasped and wheezed and quickly became flooded. While I waited for the flooding to subside, I looked at the map and was dismayed to discover that I still had twenty miles to go. I had only done eight miles so far and I had been at it for well over an hour. The possibility that the Chevette might not make it to Victor and Cripple Creek took root in my skull. For the first time it occurred to me that perhaps no one ever came along this road. If I died out here, I reflected bleakly, it could be years before anyone found me or the Chevette, which would obviously be a tragedy. Apart from anything else the battery was still under warranty.

But of course I didn't die out there. In fact, to tell you the truth, I don't intend ever to die. The car started up; I crept up over the last of the high passes and thence into Victor without further incident. Victor was a wonderful sight, a town of Western-style buildings perched incongruously in a high green valley of the most incredible beauty. Once it and Cripple Creek, six miles down the road, were boom towns to beat all boom towns. At their peak, in 1908, they had 500 gold mines between them and a population of 100,000. Miners were paid in gold. In twenty-five years or so the mines produced $800 million worth of gold and made a lot of people rich. Jack Dempsey lived in Victor and started his career there.

Today only a couple of working mines are left and the population is barely a thousand. Victor had the air of a ghost town, though at least the streets were paved. Chipmunks darted among the buildings and grass was growing through cracks in the sidewalk. The town was full of antique stores and craft shops, but almost all of them were closed, evidently waiting for the summer season. Quite a few were empty and one, the Amber Inn, had been seized for non-payment of taxes. A big sign in the window said so. But the post office was open and one café, which was full of old men in bib overalls and younger men with beards and pony tails. All the men wore baseball caps, though here they advertised brands of beer – Coors, Bud Lite, Olympia – rather than brands of fertiliser.

I decided to drive on to Cripple Creek for lunch, and then wished I hadn't. Cripple Creek stands in the shadows of Mt Pisgah and Pikes Peak and was far more touristy than Victor. Most of the stores were open, though they weren't doing much business. I parked on the main street in front of the Sarsaparilla Saloon and had a look around. Architecturally, Cripple Creek was much the same as Victor, but here the businesses were almost all geared to tourists: gift shops, snack bars, ice-cream parlours, a place where children could pan for gold in an artificial creek, a miniature golf-course. It was pretty awful, and made worse by the bleakening weather. Flurries of snow were still swirling about. It was cold and the air was thin. Cripple Creek is nearly two miles up. At that altitude, if you're not used to it, you feel uncomfortably breathless a lot of the time and vaguely unwell all of the time. Certainly the last thing I wanted was an ice-cream or a game of miniature golf, so I returned to the car and pressed on.

At the junction of US 24, I turned left and headed west. Here the weather was superb. The sun shone, the sky was blue. Out of the west, a flotilla of clouds sailed in, fluffy and benign, skimming the peaks. The highway was of pink asphalt; it was like driving along a strip of bubble gum. The road led up and over the Wilkerson Pass and then down into a long valley of rolling meadows with glittering streams and log cabins set against a backdrop of muscular mountains. It looked like a scene out of a deodorant commercial. It was glorious, and I had it almost all to myself. Near Buena Vista the land dramatically dropped away to reveal a plain and beyond it the majestic Collegiate Peaks, the highest range in the United States, with sixteen peaks of over 14,000 feet along a thirty-mile stretch. I fell with the highway down the mountainside and crossed the plain towards the Collegiate range, tall and blue and snow-peaked. It was like driving into the opening credits of a Paramount movie.

I had intended to make for Aspen, but at the turning at Twin Lakes I found a white barrier barring the way and a sign saying that the highway to Aspen over Independence Pass was closed because of snow. Aspen was just twenty miles away down the closed road, but to reach it by the alternative northern route would have required a detour of 150 miles. Disappointed, I looked for some place else to go for the night and drove on to Leadville, a place about which I knew nothing and indeed had never even heard.

Leadville was outstanding. The outskirts of the town were ragged and shabby – there's a surprising amount of poverty in Colorado – but the main street was broad and lined with sturdy Victorian buildings, many of them with turrets and towers. Leadville was another gold and silver mining town; it was here that the Unsinkable Molly Brown got her start, as did Meyer Guggenheim. Like Cripple Creek and Victor, it

now catered to tourists – every place in the Rockies caters to tourists –
but it had a much more genuine feel to it. Its population was 4,000,
enough to give it an independent life apart from what the tourists
brought it.

I got a room in the Timberline Motel, had a stroll around the town
and a creditable meal at the Golden Burro Café – not the greatest food
in the world, or even possibly in Leadville, but at $6 for soup, salad,
chicken fried steak, mashed potatoes, green beans, coffee and pie,
who's bitching? – followed by a moonlight stroll back to the motel, a
hot shower and a little TV. If only life could always be so simple and
serene. I was asleep by ten, dreaming happy dreams in which I
manfully dealt with pouncing bobcats, swaying wooden bridges and
windscreens full of sticky insects. The heroine even let me see her with
her clothes off. It was a night to remember.

TWENTY-TWO

In the morning, the weatherman on the TV said that a 'frunnal system' was about to dump many inches of snow on the Rockies. This seemed to please him a lot. You could see it in his twinkling eyes. His map showed a band of unpleasantness sitting like a curse over almost the whole of the West. Roads would be shut, he said, a hint of grin tugging at the corners of his mouth, and travel advisories would be issued. Why are television weathermen always so malicious? Even when they are trying to be sincere, you can see that it's a front – that just under the surface there lurks a person who spent his childhood pulling the wings off insects and snickering whenever another child fell under the wheels of a passing vehicle.

Abruptly, I decided to head south for the arid mountains of New Mexico, over which the weather-map showed nothing much in particular happening. I had a niece at a small, exclusive college in Santa Fe whom I hadn't seen for a long time and I was sure she would be delighted for all her friends on campus to witness a slobby, overweight man pull up in a cheap, dusty car, leap out and embrace her, so I decided to drive straight there.

I headed south on US 285, which runs along the line of the continental divide. All around me was the most incredible natural beauty, but the landscape was constantly blemished by human intrusions – ugly trailer parks, untidy homesteads, even junk yards. Every town was mostly a collection of fast food places and gas stations, and all along the road for many miles stood signs the size of barns saying CAMPGROUND, MOTEL, RAFTING.

The further south I went the more barren the landscape grew, and after a while the signs disappeared. Beyond Saguache the wide plain between the mountains became a sweep of purple sage, interspersed with dead brown earth. Here and there a field of green had been snatched from the scrub with the aid of massive wheeled water-sprinklers. In the middle of these oases would stand a neat farmhouse. But otherwise the landscape between the distant mountain ranges was as featureless as a dried seabed. Between Saguache and Monte Vista lies one of the ten or twelve longest stretches of straight road in America: almost forty miles without a single bend or kink. That may not sound such a lot on paper, but it feels endless on the road. There is nothing like a highway stretching off to an ever-receding vanishing-point to make you feel as if you are going nowhere. At Monte Vista, the road takes a left turn – this makes you perk up and grip the wheel – and then there is another twenty-mile stretch as straight as a ruler's edge. And so it goes. Two or three times in an hour you zip through a dusty little town – a gas station, three houses, one tree, a dog – or encounter a fractional bend in the road which requires you to move the steering wheel three centimetres to the right or left for two seconds, and that's your excitement for the hour. The rest of the time you don't move a muscle. Your buttocks grow numb and begin to feel as if they belong to another person.

In the early afternoon I crossed over into New Mexico – one of the high points of the day – and sighed at the discovery that it was just as unstimulating as Colorado had been. I switched on the radio. I was so far from anywhere that I could only pick up scattered stations, and those were all Spanish-speaking ones playing that kind of aye-yi-yi Mexican music that's always sung by strolling musicians with droopy moustaches and big sombreros in the sort of restaurants where high school teachers take their wives for their thirtieth wedding anniversaries – the sort of places where they like to set your food alight to impress you. It had never once occurred to me in thirty-six years of living that anyone listened to Mexican music for pleasure. Yet here there were a dozen stations blaring it out. After each song, a disc jockey would come on and jabber for a minute or two in Spanish in the tone of a man who has just had his nuts slammed in a drawer. There would then be a break for an advertisement, read by a man who sounded even more urgent and excited – he clearly was having his nuts repeatedly slammed in a drawer – and then there would be another song. Or rather, it would be the same song again, as far as I could tell. That is the unfortunate thing about Mexican musicians. They only seem to know one tune. This may explain why they have difficulty finding work anywhere other than at second-rate restaurants.

At a hamlet called Tres Piedras – almost every place in New Mexico has a Spanish name – I took Highway 64 to Taos, and things began to improve. The hills grew darker and the sage became denser and lusher. Everyone always talks about the sky around Taos, and it is astonishing. I had never seen a sky so vivid and blue, so liquid. The air in this part of the desert is so clear you can sometimes see for 180 miles, or so my guidebook said. In any case, you can certainly see why Taos has always attracted artists and writers – or at least you can until you get to Taos itself. I had expected it to be a sweet little artists' colony, full of people with smocks and easels, and it was just a tourist trap, with slow-moving traffic and stores selling ugly Indian pottery and big silver belt buckles and postcards. There were a couple of interesting galleries, but mostly it was hot and dusty and full of silver-haired hippies. It was mildly amusing to see that hippies still existed – indeed were now grandparents – but it was scarcely worth the bother of getting there. So I drove on to Santa Fe, fearful that it would be much the same. But it was not. In fact, it was quite beautiful, and I was instantly charmed.

The first nice thing about Santa Fe is that it has trees. It has trees and grass and shade and cool plazas full of flowers and plants and the soothing burble of running water. After days of driving across the barren wastes of the West this is a treat beyond dimension. The air is warm and clean and the reddish Sangre de Cristo mountains at the city's back are just sensational, especially at sunset when they simply glow, as if lit from within, like jack-o'-lanterns. The town itself is just too rich and pretty for words. It is the oldest continuously inhabited city in America – it was founded in 1610, a decade before the pilgrims set off from Plymouth – and takes great pride in its age. Everything in Santa Fe, and I mean everything, is made out of adobe. There's an adobe Woolworth's, an adobe multi-storey parking lot, an adobe six-storey hotel. When you pass your first adobe gas station and adobe supermarket, you think, 'Hey, let's get out of here,' but then you realise that it isn't something laid on for the tourists. Adobe is simply the indigenous building material, and using it everywhere gives the town a uniformity of appearance few other places achieve. Besides, Santa Fe is filthy rich, so everything is done tastefully and well.

I drove up into the hills looking for St John's College, where my niece was a student. It was four in the afternoon and the streets were full of long shadows. The sun was settling onto the mountains and the adobe houses on every hillside were lit with a rich orange-brown glow.

St John's is a small college perched high up in the hills, with the finest view in town, looking down over Santa Fe and the rolling mountains beyond. It has only 300 students on its sleepy campus, but my niece, on this fine spring afternoon, was not among them. No one knew where she was, but everyone promised to let her know that a slobby, overweight person with dusty shoes and tropical armpits had come looking for her and would call back in the morning.

I went back into town, got a room, had a deep, hot bath, changed into clean clothes and spent the evening shambling happily around the tranquil streets of downtown Santa Fe, gazing admiringly at the window displays in the expensive galleries and boutiques, savouring the warm evening air, and disconcerting people in the more exclusive restaurants by pressing my face up against the windows and looking critically at their food. The heart of Santa Fe is the Plaza, a Spanish-style square with white benches and a tall obelisk commemorating the battle of Valverde, whatever that was. On the base was an engraved inscription in which February had been misspelled as Febuary; this pleased me very much. Another pleasing thing about the Plaza was a place on the corner called the Ore House. Downstairs it is a restaurant, but upstairs there is a bar with an open porch where you can sit – where indeed I did sit – for many tranquil hours drinking beers brought to your table by a pleasant waitress with a nice bottom, enjoying the mild evening and watching the stars fill the pale blue desert sky. Through the open door into the bar I could also watch the pianist, a well-groomed young man who played a seemingly endless series of chords and tinkling arpeggios that never really developed into anything you could call a song. But he cruised suavely up and down the keyboard and he had a winning smile and excellent teeth, which I suppose is the main thing in a cocktail bar pianist. Anyway, the ladies clearly liked him.

I don't know how many beers I had, but – I will be frank here – it was too many. I had not allowed for the fact that in the thin mountain air of Santa Fe you get drunk much faster. In any case, I was surprised to discover as I stood up a couple of hours after entering that the relationship between my mind and legs, which was normally quite a good one, had broken down. More than that, my legs now didn't seem to be getting on at all well with each other. One of them started for the stairs, as instructed, but the other, in a burst of petulance, decided to make for the rest-room. The result was that I lurched through the bar like a man on stilts, grinning inanely as if to say, 'Yes, I know I look like an asshole. Isn't this amusing?'

En route, I bumped into the table of a party of middle-aged rich people, slopping their drinks, and could only broaden my brainless smile and burble that I was ever so sorry. I patted one of the ladies affectionately on the shoulder with that easy familiarity that overcomes me when I am drunk and used her as a kind of springboard to propel myself towards the stairs, where I smiled a farewell to the room – everyone was by now watching me with interest – and descended the stairs in one fluid motion. I didn't exactly fall, but then again I didn't exactly walk down. It was more like surfing on the soles of my shoes, and was, I believe, not unimpressive. But then I often perform my best stunts while intoxicated. Once, many years ago during a party at John Horner's house, I fell backwards out of an upstairs window and bounced to my feet with an *élan* that is still widely talked about south of Grand Avenue.

In the morning, chastened with a hangover, I drove back to the campus of St John's, found my niece and embarrassed her – possibly even grossed her out – with a hug. We went to breakfast in a fancy restaurant downtown and she told me all about St John's and Santa Fe and afterwards showed me the sights of the town: St Francis's Cathedral (very beautiful), the Palace of the Governors (very boring, full of documents about territorial governors) and the famous staircase at the Loretto Chapel. This is a wooden staircase that rises twenty-one and a half feet in a double spiral up to a choir loft. The remarkable thing about it is that it is not supported by anything except its own weight. It looks as if it ought to fall down. The story is that the nuns of the chapel prayed for someone to build them a staircase and an anonymous carpenter turned up, worked on the staircase for six months and then disappeared without payment as mysteriously as he had arrived. For a hundred years the nuns milked this story for all it was worth, and then one day a few years ago they abruptly sold the chapel to a private company, which now runs it for a profit and charges you 50¢ to get in. This kind of soured me on the place, and it didn't do a whole lot for my respect for nuns.

Generally speaking – which is of course always a dangerous thing to do, generally speaking – Americans revere the past only as long as there is some money in it somewhere and it doesn't mean going without air-conditioning, free parking and other essential conveniences. Preserving the past for its own sake doesn't come into it much. There is little room for sentiment. When somebody comes along and offers a group of nuns good money for their staircase, they don't say, 'Certainly not, it is a hallowed shrine, built for us by a mysterious and rather hunky-looking courier of Jesus.' They say, 'How much?' And if the offer is good enough they sell it and use the money to build a new convent on a bigger site, with air-conditioning, lots of parking space and a games room. I don't mean to suggest for a moment that nuns are worse than other Americans in this regard. They are simply behaving in the customary American way. I find that very sad. It is no wonder that so few things last for more than a generation in America.

I left Santa Fe and drove west along Interstate 40. This used to be Route 66. Everybody loved Route 66. People used to write songs about it. But it was only two lanes wide, not at all suitable for the space age, hopelessly inadequate for people in motor homes, and every fifty miles or so it would pass through a little town where you might encounter a stop sign or a traffic light – what a drag! – so they buried it under the desert and built a new superhighway that shoots across the landscape like a four-lane laser and doesn't stop for anything, even mountains. So something else that was nice and pleasant is gone forever because it wasn't practical – like passenger trains and milk in bottles and corner shops and Burma Shave signs. And now it's happening in Britain, too. They are taking away all the nice things there because they are impractical, as if that were reason enough – the red phone-boxes, the pound note, those open London buses that you can leap on and off. There is almost no experience in life that makes you look and feel more suave than jumping on or off a moving London bus. But they aren't practical. They require two men (one to drive and one to stop thugs from kicking the crap out of the Pakistani gentleman at the back) and that is uneconomical, so they have to go. And before long there will be no more milk in bottles delivered to the doorstep or sleepy rural pubs and the countryside will be mostly shopping centres and theme parks. Forgive me. I don't mean to get upset. But you are taking my world away from me, piece by little piece, and sometimes it just pisses me off. Sorry.

I drove west along Interstate 40, through an impoverished landscape. Habitations were few. Such towns as existed were mostly just scatterings of trailer homes dumped along the roadside, as if dropped from a great height. They had no yards, no fences, nothing to separate them from the desert. Much of the land was given over to Indian reservations. Every twenty or thirty miles I would pass a lone hitch-hiker, sometimes an Indian but usually a white person, alone and with bags. I had seen hardly any hitch-hikers before now, but here there were many, the men looking dangerous, the women looking crazy. I was entering a land of drifters: dreamers, losers, vagrants, crazy people — they all always go west in America. They all have this hopeless idea that they will get to the coast and make a fortune as a movie star or rock musician or game show contestant or something. And if things don't work out they can always become a serial murderer. It's strange that no one ever goes east, that you never encounter anyone hitch-hiking to New York in pursuit of some wild and crazy dream to be a certified public accountant or make a killing in leveraged buy-outs.

The weather worsened. Dust began to blow across the road. I was driving into the storm that the weatherman had spoken of on television the morning before. Beyond Albuquerque the skies darkened and a sleety rain began to dart about. Tumbleweeds bounced across the desert and over the highway, and the car was knocked sharply sideways with each gust of wind.

I had always thought that deserts were hot and dry the year around. I can tell you now that they are not. I suppose because we always took our vacations between June and August it implanted in me the idea that everywhere in America outside the Midwest was hot the year around. Wherever you went in the summer in America it was murder. It was always ninety degrees. If you closed the windows you baked, but if you left them open everything blew everywhere – comic books, maps, loose articles of clothing. If you wore shorts, as we always did, the bare skin on your legs became part of the seat, like cheese melted onto toast, and when it was time to get up, there was a ripping sound and a screaming sensation of agony as the two parted. If in your sun-baked delirium you carelessly leaned your arm against the metal part of the door on to which the sun had been shining, the skin where it made contact would shrivel and disappear, like a plastic bag in a flame. This would always leave you speechless. It was a truly amazing, and curiously painless, spectacle to watch part of your body just vanish. You didn't know whether to shriek at your mother as if you had been gravely wounded, or do it again, in a spirit of scientific inquiry. In the end, usually, you would do nothing, but just sit listlessly, too hot to do anything else.

So I was surprised to find myself in wintry weather, in a landscape as cold as it was bleak. The darting sleet thickened as the highway climbed up and into the Zuni Mountains. Beyond Gallup it turned to snow. Wet and heavy, it fell from the sky like scattered feathers, and the afternoon became like night.

Twenty miles beyond Gallup, I entered Arizona and the further I drove into that state the more evident it became that I was entering a storm of long standing. The snow along the roadside became ankle-deep and then knee-deep. It was odd to think that only a couple of hours before I had been strolling around Santa Fe in bright sunshine and shirtsleeves. Now the radio was full of news of closed roads and atrocious weather – snow in the mountains, torrential rain elsewhere. It was the worst spring storm in decades, the weatherman said with ill-disguised glee. The Los Angeles Dodgers had been rained out at home for the third day in a row – the first time this had happened since they moved to the coast from Brooklyn thirty years before. There was nowhere I could turn to escape this storm. Bleakly, I pushed on towards Flagstaff, 100 miles to the west.

'And there's fourteen inches of snow on the ground at Flagstaff – with more expected,' the weatherman said, sounding very pleased.

TWENTY-THREE

Nothing prepares you for the Grand Canyon. No matter how many times you read about it or see it pictured, it still takes your breath away. Your mind, unable to deal with anything on this scale, just shuts down and for many long moments you are a human vacuum, without speech or breath, but just a deep, inexpressible awe that anything on this earth could be so vast, so beautiful, so silent.

Even children are stilled by it. I was a particularly talkative and obnoxious child, but it stopped me cold. I can remember rounding a corner and standing there agog while a mouthful of half-formed jabber just rolled backwards down my throat, forever unuttered. I was seven years old and I'm told it was only the second occasion in all that time that I had stopped talking, apart from short breaks for sleeping and television. The one other thing to silence me was the sight of my grandfather dead in an open coffin. It was such an unexpected sight – no one had told me that he would be on display – and it just took my breath away. There he was all still and silent, dusted with powder and dressed in a suit. I particularly remember that he had his glasses on (what did they think he was going to do with those where he was going?) and that they were crooked. I think my grandmother had knocked them askew during her last blubbery embrace and then everyone else had been too squeamish to push them back into place. It was a shock to me to realise that never again in the whole of eternity would he laugh over *I Love Lucy* or repair his car or talk with his mouth full (something for which he was widely noted in the family). It was awesome.

But not nearly as awesome as the Grand Canyon. Since, obviously, I could never hope to relive my grandfather's funeral, the Grand Canyon was the one vivid experience from my childhood that I could hope to recapture, and I had been looking forward to it for many days. I had spent the night at Winslow, Arizona, fifty miles short of Flagstaff, because the roads were becoming impassable. In the evening the snow had eased to a scattering of flakes and by morning it had stopped altogether, though the skies still looked dark and pregnant. I drove through a snow-whitened landscape towards the Grand Canyon. It was hard to believe that this was the last week of April. Mists and fog swirled about the road. I could see nothing at the sides and ahead of me except the occasional white smear of oncoming headlights. By the time I reached the entrance to Grand Canyon National Park, and paid the $5 admission, snow was dropping heavily again, thick white flakes so big that their undersides carried shadows.

The road through the park followed the southern lip of the canyon for thirty miles. Two or three times I stopped in lay-bys and went to the edge to peer hopefully into the silent murk, knowing that the canyon was out there, just beyond my nose, but I couldn't see anything. The fog was everywhere – threaded among the trees, adrift on the roadsides, rising steamily off the pavement. It was so thick I could kick holes in it. Glumly I drove on to the Grand Canyon village, where there was a visitors' centre and a rustic hotel and a scattering of administrative buildings. There were lots of tour buses and recreational vehicles in the parking lots and people hanging around in entranceways or picking their way through the slushy snow, going from one building to another. I went and had an overpriced cup of coffee in the hotel cafeteria and felt damp and dispirited. I had really been looking forward to the Grand Canyon. I sat by the window and bleakly watched the snow pile up.

Afterwards, I trudged towards the visitors' centre, perhaps 200 yards away, but before I got there I came across a snow-spattered sign announcing a look-out point half a mile away along a trail through the woods, and impulsively I went down it, mostly just to get some air. The path was slippery and took a long time to traverse, but on the way the snow stopped falling and the air felt clean and refreshing. Eventually I came to a platform of rocks, marking the edge of the canyon. There was no fence to keep you back from the edge, so I shuffled cautiously over and looked down, but could see nothing but grey soup. A middle-aged couple came along and as we stood chatting about what a dispiriting experience this was, a miraculous thing happened. The fog parted. It just silently drew back, like a set of theatre curtains being opened, and suddenly we saw that we were on the edge of a sheer, giddying drop of at least a thousand feet. 'Jesus!' we said and jumped back, and all along the canyon edge you could hear people saying 'Jesus!', like a message being passed down a long line. And then for many moments all was silence, except for the tiny fretful shiftings of the snow, because out there in front of us was the most awesome, most silencing sight that exists on earth.

The scale of the Grand Canyon is almost beyond comprehension. It is ten miles across, a mile deep, 180 miles long. You could set the Empire State Building down in it and still be thousands of feet above it. Indeed you could set the whole of Manhattan down inside it and you would still be so high above it that buses would be like ants and people would be invisible, and not a sound would reach you. The thing that gets you — that gets everyone — is the silence. The Grand Canyon just swallows sound. The sense of space and emptiness is overwhelming. Nothing happens out there. Down below you on the canyon floor, far, far away, is the thing that carved it: the Colorado River. It is 300 feet wide, but from the canyon's lip it looks thin and insignificant. It looks like an old shoelace. Everything is dwarfed by this mighty hole.

And then, just as swiftly, just as silently as the fog had parted, it closed again and the Grand Canyon was a secret once more. I had seen it for no more than twenty or thirty seconds, but at least I had seen it. Feeling semi-satisfied, I turned around and walked back towards the car, content now to move on. On the way, I encountered a young couple coming towards the edge. They asked me if I'd had any luck and I told them all about how the fog had parted for a few seconds. They looked crushed. They said they had come all the way from Ontario. It was their honeymoon. All their lives they had wanted to see the Grand Canyon. Three times every day for the past week they had put on their moonboots and honeymoon winterwear and walked hand in hand to the canyon's edge, but all they had seen so far was an unshifting wall of fog.

'Still,' I said, trying to help them look on the bright side, 'I bet you've gotten in a lot of good shagging.' I didn't really say that. Even *I* wouldn't say that. I just made sympathetic noises and said what a shame it was about the weather and wished them luck. I walked on in a reflective mood to the car, thinking about the poor honeymooners. As my father always used to tell me, 'You see, son, there's always someone in the world worse off than you.'

And I always used to think, 'So?'

*

I headed north on Highway 89 towards Utah. The radio was full of more news of bad weather in the Rockies and Sierra Nevadas, and of roads closed by rockslides and heavy snow, though here in northern Arizona there was no snow at all. Absolutely none. Ten miles beyond the Grand Canyon it just disappeared and a few miles after that it was like spring. The sun came out. The world was warm. I rolled the window down a little.

I drove and drove. That is what you do in the West. You drive and you drive and you drive, advancing from one scattered town to the next, creeping across a landscape like Neptune. For long, empty hours your one goal in life is to get to Dry Gulch or Cactus City or wherever. You sit there watching the highway endlessly unfurl and the odometer advancing with the speed of centuries and all you think about is getting to Dry Gulch and hoping by some miracle it will have a McDonald's or at least a coffee shop. And when at last you get there, all there is is a two-pump gas station and a stall with an old Indian woman selling Navajo trinkets and you realise that you have to start the process all over again with another impossibly isolated hamlet with a depressingly unpromising name: Coma, Doldrum, Dry Well, Sunstroke.

The distances are almost inconceivable. There is often thirty miles between houses and a hundred miles or more between towns. What would it take to make you live in a place where you had to drive seventy-five miles just to buy a pair of shoes – and even then they would look as if they came from a funeral home?

The answer to my question, of course, is that not many people do want to live in such a place, except for Indians, who were never given much choice. I was now driving across the largest Indian reservation in America – a Navajo reservation stretching for 150 miles from north to south and 200 miles from east to west – and most of the few cars along the highway were driven by Indians. Almost without exception these were big old Detroit cars in dreadful condition, with all the trim gone or flopping loosely, and with at least one mismatched door and important-looking pieces hanging from the undercarriage, clattering on the highway, shooting out sparks or dense smoke. They never seemed to be able to get over about forty miles an hour, but they were always difficult to pass because of the way they drifted around on the highway.

Occasionally they would drift far off to the right, sometimes even kicking up desert dust, and I would shoot past. Always it was the same sight: a car packed with Indian men and boys and a driver drunk beyond repair, sitting there with a wet-dream look on his face – the look of a man who is only barely conscious but having a splendid time none the less.

At Page, Arizona, home of the Glen Canyon Dam, I passed into Utah and almost immediately the landscape improved. The hills grew purplish and red and the desert took on a blush of colour. After a few miles, the sage-brush thickened and the hills became darker and more angular. It all looked oddly familiar. Then I consulted my Mobil guidebook and discovered that this was where all the Hollywood westerns were made. More than a hundred film and television companies had used Kanab, the next town down the road, as their headquarters for location shooting.

This excited me, and when I got to Kanab, I stopped and went into a café to see if I could find out more. A voice from the back called out that she would be just a minute, so I had a look at the menu on the wall. It was the strangest menu I had ever seen. It was full of foods I had never heard of: potato logs ('small, medium and family size'), cheese sticks for 89¢, pizza pockets for $1·39, Oreo shakes for $1·25. The special offer was '8oz log, roll and slaw, $7·49'. I decided I would have coffee. After a moment the woman who ran the café came out wiping her hands on a towel. She told me some of the films and TV shows that had been shot around Kanab: *Duel at Diablo*, *Butch Cassidy and the Sundance Kid*, *My Friend Flicka*, *The Rifleman*, some Clint Eastwood movies. I asked her whether any Hollywood stars ever came in for some potato logs or cheese sticks. She shook her head wistfully and said no. Somehow this didn't altogether surprise me.

I spent the night at Cedar City and in the morning drove to Bryce Canyon National Park, which was invisible on account of fog and snow, and then, in a surly mood, to Zion National Park, where it was like summer. This was very odd because the two parks are only about forty miles apart, and yet they seemed to inhabit different continents as far as the weather went. If I live forever I will not begin to understand the weather of the West.

Zion was incredibly beautiful. Whereas at the Grand Canyon you are on the top looking down, at Zion you are at the bottom looking up.

It is just a long, lush canyon, dense with cottonwood trees along the valley floor, hemmed in by towering copper-coloured walls of rock – the sort of dark, forbidding valley you would expect to pass through in a hunt for the lost city of gold. Here and there long, thin waterfalls emerged from the rock face and fell a thousand feet or more down to the valley, where the water collected in pools or tumbled onward into the swirling Virgin River. At the far end of the valley the high walls squeezed together until they were only yards apart. In the damp shade, plants grew out of cracks in the rock, giving the whole the appearance of hanging gardens. It was very picturesque and exotic.

The sheer walls on either side looked as if they might rain boulders at any moment – and indeed they sometimes do. Half-way along the path the little river was suddenly littered with rocks, some of them the size of houses. A sign said that on July 16, 1981, more than 15,000 tons of rock fell 1,000 feet into the river here, but it didn't say whether there were any people squashed beneath them. I dare say there were. Even now in April there were scores of people all along the path; in July there must have been hundreds. At least a couple of them must have got caught. When the rocks came tumbling down, there would be no place to run.

I was standing there reflecting on this melancholy thought when I became aware of a vaguely irritating whirring noise beside me. It was a man with a video camera, taking footage of the rocks. It was one of the early, primitive models, so he had all kinds of power packs and auxiliary paraphernalia strapped to his body, and the camera itself was enormous. It must be like going on vacation with your vacuum cleaner. Anyway, it served him right. My first rule of consumerism is never to buy anything you can't make your children carry. The man looked exhausted, but, having spent a ridiculously inflated sum to buy the camera, he was now determined to film everything that passed before his eyes, even at the risk of acquiring a hernia (and when that happened he would of course get his wife to film the operation).

I can never understand these people who rush to buy new gadgets; surely they must see that they are going to look like idiots in about a year when the manufacturers come up with tiny lightweight versions of the same thing at half the price? Like the people who paid £200 for the first pocket calculators and then a few months later they were giving them away at gas stations. Or the people who bought the first colour televisions.

One of our neighbours, Mr Sheitelbaum, bought a colour TV in 1958 when there were only about two colour programmes a month. We used to peek through his window when we knew one was coming on, and it was always the same – people with orange faces and clothes that kept changing hue. Mr Sheitelbaum kept bobbing up to fiddle with the many little knobs with which the thing was equipped while his wife shouted encouragement from across the room.

For a few moments the colour would be pretty fair – not accurate exactly, but not too disturbing – and then just as Mr Sheitelbaum placed his butt back on the sofa it would all go haywire and we would have green horses and red clouds, and he'd be back at the control panel again. It was hopeless. But having spent such a huge amount of money on this thing, Mr Sheitelbaum would never give up on it, and for the next fifteen years whenever you walked past his living-room window you would see him fiddling with the controls and muttering.

In the late afternoon, I drove on to St George, a small city not far from the state line. I got a room in the Oasis Motel and dined at Dick's Café. Afterwards, I went for a stroll. St George had a nice old-town feel about it, though in fact most of the buildings were new except for the Gaiety Movie Theater ('All Seats $2') and Dixie Drugstore next door. The drugstore was closed, but I was brought up short by the sight of a soda-fountain inside, a real marble-topped soda-fountain with twirly stools and straws in paper wrappers – the sort in which you tear off one end and then blow, sending the wrapper on a graceful trajectory into the cosmetics department.

I was crushed. This must be just about the last genuine drugstore soda-fountain in America and the place was closed. I would have given whole dollars to go in and order a green river or a chocolate soda and send a few straw wrappers wafting about and then challenge the next person along to a stool-twirling contest. My personal best is four full revolutions. I know that doesn't sound much, but it's a lot harder than it looks. Bobby Wintermeyer did five once and then threw up. It's a pretty hairy sport, believe me.

On the corner was a big brick Mormon church, or temple or tabernacle or whatever they call them. It was dated 1871 and looked big enough to hold the whole town – and indeed it probably often does since absolutely everybody in Utah is a Mormon. This sounds kind of alarming until you realise that it means Utah is the one place on the planet where you never have to worry about young men coming up to you and trying to convert you to Mormonism. They assume you are one of them already. As long as you keep your hair cut fairly short and don't say, 'Oh, shit!' in public when something goes wrong, you may escape detection for years. It makes you feel a little like Kevin McCarthy in *Invasion of the Body Snatchers*, but it is also strangely liberating.

Beyond the Mormon church things became mostly residential. Everything was green and fresh after the recent rains. The town smelled of spring, of lilacs and fresh-mown grass. The evening was creeping in. It was that relaxed time of day when people have finished their dinners and are just pootling about in the yard or garage, not doing much of anything in preparation for shortly doing even less.

The streets were the widest I've ever seen in any town, even out here in the residential neighbourhoods. Mormons sure do love wide streets. I don't know why. Wide streets and lots of wives for bonking, those are the foundation stones of Mormonism. When Brigham Young founded Salt Lake City one of the first things he did was decree that the streets be 100 feet wide, and he must have said something similar to the people of St George. Young knew the town well – he had his winter home there – so if the townspeople ever tried anything slack with the streets he'd have been on to them right away.

TWENTY-FOUR

Here's a riddle for you. What is the difference between Nevada and a toilet? Answer: You can flush a toilet.

Nevada has the highest crime rate of any state, the highest rape rate, the second highest violent crime rate (it's just pipped by New York), the highest highway fatality rate, the second highest rate of gonorrhoea (Alaska is the trophy-holder), and the highest proportion of transients – almost eighty per cent of the state's residents were born elsewhere. It has more prostitutes than any other state in America. It has a long history of corruption and strong links with organised crime. And its most popular entertainer is Wayne Newton. So you may understand why I crossed the border from Utah with a certain sense of disquiet.

But then I got to Las Vegas and my unease vanished. I was dazzled. It's impossible not to be. It was late afternoon, the sun was low, the temperature was in the high eighties, and the Strip was already thronged with happy vacationers in nice clean clothes, their pockets visibly bulging with money, strolling along in front of casinos the size of airport terminals. It all looked fun and oddly wholesome. I had expected it to be nothing but hookers and high rollers in stretched Cadillacs, the sort of people who wear white leather shoes and drape their jackets over their shoulders, but these were just ordinary folks like you and me, people who wear a lot of nylon and Velcro.

I got a room in a motel at the cheaper end of the Strip, showered lavishly, danced through a dust storm of talcum powder, pulled on my cleanest T-shirt, and went straight back out, tingling with clean skin and child-like excitement. After days of driving across the desert you are ready for a little stimulation, and Las Vegas certainly provides it. Now, in the oven-dry air of early evening, the casino lights were coming on – millions and millions of them, erupting into walls of bilious colour and movement, flashing, darting, rippling, bursting, all of them competing for my attention, for the coins in my pocket. I had never seen such a sight. It is an ocular orgasm, a three-dimensional hallucination, an electrician's wet dream. It was just as I had expected it to be but multiplied by ten.

The names on the hotels and casinos were eerily familiar: Caesar's Palace, the Dunes, the Sands, the Desert Inn. What most surprised me – what most surprises most people – is how many vacant lots there were. Here and there among the throbbing monoliths there were quarter-mile squares of silent desert, little pockets of dark calm, just waiting to be developed. When you have been to one or two casinos and seen how the money just pours into them, like gravel off a dump truck, it is hard to believe that there could be enough spare cash in the world to feed still more of them, yet more are being built all the time. The greed of mankind is practically insatiable, mine included.

I went into Caesar's Palace. It is set well back from the street, but I was conveyed in on a moving sidewalk, which rather impressed me. Inside the air was thick with unreality. The décor was supposed to be like a Roman temple or something. Statues of Roman gladiators and statesmen were scattered around the place and all the cigarette girls and ladies who gave change were dressed in skimpy togas, even if they were old and overweight, which most of them were, so their thighs wobbled as they walked. It was like watching moving Jell-O. I wandered through halls full of people intent on losing money – endlessly, single-mindedly feeding coins into slot machines or watching the clattering dance of a steel ball on a roulette wheel or playing games of blackjack that had no start or finish but were just continuous, like time. It all had a monotonous, yet anxious rhythm. There was no sense of pleasure or fun. I never saw anyone talking to anyone else, except to order a drink or cash some money. The noise was intense –the crank of one-armed bandits, the spinning of thousands of wheels, the din of clattering coins when a machine paid out.

A change lady Jell-O'd past and I got $10 worth of quarters from her. I put one in a one-armed bandit – I had never done this before; I'm from Iowa – pulled the handle and watched the wheels spin and thunk into place one by one. There was a tiny pause and then the machine spat six quarters into the pay-out bucket. I was hooked. I fed in more quarters. Sometimes I would lose and I would put in more quarters. Sometimes the machine would spit me back some quarters and I would put those in as well. After about five minutes I had no quarters left. I flagged down another ample-hipped vestal virgin and got $10 more. This time I won $12 worth of quarters straight off. It made a lot of noise. I looked around proudly, but no one paid any attention to me. Then I won $5 more. Hey, this is all right, I thought. I put all my quarters in a little plastic bucket that said Caesar's Palace on it. There seemed to be an awful lot of them, gleaming up at me, but in about twenty minutes the bucket was empty. I went and got another $10 worth of quarters, and started feeding them in. I won some and lost some. I was beginning to realise that there was a certain pattern to it: for every four quarters I put in, I would on average get three back, sometimes in a bunch, sometimes in dribbles. My right arm began to ache a little. It was boring really, pulling the handle over and over, watching the wheels spin and thunk, thunk, thunk, spin and thunk, thunk, thunk. With my last quarter I won $3 worth of quarters, and was mildly disappointed because I had been hoping to go for dinner and now here I had a mittful of quarters again. So I dutifully fed the quarters into the machine and won some more money. This really was getting tiresome. Finally, after about thirty minutes I got rid of the last quarter and was able to go and look for a restaurant.

On the way out my attention was caught by a machine making a lot of noise. A woman had just won $600. For ninety seconds the machine just poured out money, a waterfall of silver. When it stopped, the woman regarded the pile without pleasure and began feeding it back into the machine. I felt sorry for her. It was going to take her all night to get rid of that kind of money.

I wandered through room after room trying to find my way out, but the place was clearly designed to leave you disoriented. There were no windows, no exit signs, just endless rooms, all with subdued lighting and with carpet that looked as if some executive had barked into a telephone, 'Gimme 20,000 yards of the ugliest carpet you got.' It was like woven vomit. I wandered for ages without knowing whether I was getting closer to or further from an exit. I passed a little shopping centre, restaurants, a buffet, cabarets, dark and silent bars where people brooded, bars with live music and astonishingly untalented entertainers ('And gimme some astonishingly untalented entertainers while you're at it'), and one large room in which the walls were covered with giant TV screens showing live sporting events – major league baseball, NBA basketball, boxing matches, a horse race. A whole wallful of athletes were silently playing their hearts out for the benefit of the room's lone spectator, and he was asleep.

I don't know how many gaming rooms there were, but there were many. It was often hard to tell whether I was seeing a new room or an old room from another angle. In each one it was the same – long ranks of people dully, mechanically losing money. It was as if they had been hypnotised. None of them seemed to see that everything was stacked against them. It is all such an incredible con. Some of the casinos make profits of $100 million a year – that's the kind of money many large corporations make – and without having to do anything but open their doors. It takes almost no skills, no intelligence, no class to run a casino. I read in *Newsweek* that the guy who owns the Horseshoe casino downtown has never learned how to read and write. Can you believe that? That gives you some idea of the sort of level of intellectual attainment you need to be a success in Vegas. Suddenly, I hated the place. I was annoyed with myself for having been taken in by it all, the noise and sparkle, for having so quickly and mindlessly lost thirty dollars. For that kind of money I could have bought a baseball cap with a plastic turd on the brim *and* an ashtray in the shape of a toilet saying 'Place Your Butt Here. Souvenir of Las Vegas, Nevada.' This made me deeply gloomy.

I went and ate in the Caesar's Palace buffet, hoping that some food would improve my outlook. The buffet cost $8, but you could eat all you wanted, so I took a huge amount of everything, determined to recoup some of my loss. The resultant plate was such a mixture of foods, gravies, barbecue sauces and salad creams that it was really just a heap of tasteless goo. But I shovelled it all down and then had an outsized platter of chocolate goo for dessert. And then I felt very ill. I felt as if I had eaten a roll of loft insulation. Clutching my distended abdomen, I found my way to an exit. There was no moving sidewalk to return me to the street – there's no place in Las Vegas for losers or quitters – so I had to make a long weaving walk down the floodlit driveway to the Strip. The fresh air helped a little, but only a little. I limped through the crowds along the Strip, looking like a man doing a poor imitation of Quasimodo, and went into a couple of other casinos, hoping they would re-excite my greed and make me forget my swollen belly. But they were practically identical to Caesar's Palace – the same noise, the same stupid people losing all their money, the same hideous carpets. It all just gave me a headache. After a while, I gave up altogether. I plodded back to my motel and fell heavily on the bed and watched TV with that kind of glazed immobility that overcomes you when your stomach is grossly overloaded and there's no remote control device and you can't quite reach the channel switch with your big toe.

So I watched the local news. Principally this consisted of a run-down of the day's murders in Las Vegas accompanied by film from the various murder scenes. These always showed a house with the front door open, some police detectives shuffling around, a group of neighbourhood children standing on the fringes, waving happily at the camera and saying hi to their moms. In between each report the anchorman and anchorwoman would trade witless quips and then say in a breezy tone something like, 'A mother and her three young children were hacked to death by a crazed axeman at Boulder City today. We'll have a filmed report after these words.' Then there would be many long minutes of commercials, mostly for products to keep one's bowels sleek, followed by filmed reports on regional murders, house fires, light airplane crashes, multiple car pile-ups on the Boulder Highway and other bits of local carnage, always with film of mangled vehicles, charred houses, bodies under blankets, and a group of children standing on the fringes, waving happily at the cameras and saying hi to their moms. It may only have been my imagination, but I would almost swear that it was the same children in every report. Perhaps American violence had bred a new kind of person – the serial witness.

Finally there was a special report about a man awaiting release from prison who ten years before had raped a young woman and then, for reasons of obscure gratification, had sawn off her arms at the elbows. No kidding. This was so shocking even to the hardened sensibilities of Nevadans that a mob was expected to be waiting for the man when he was released at 6 a.m. the next day, according to the TV reporter, who then gave all the details necessary to enable viewers to go down and join in. The police, the reporter added with a discernible trace of pleasure, were refusing to guarantee the man's safety. The report concluded with a shot of the reporter talking to camera in front of the prison gate. Behind her a group of children were jumping up and down and waving hi to their moms. This was all becoming too bizarre for me. I got up heavily and switched the TV to *Mr Ed*. At least you know where you are with *Mr Ed*.

In the morning I took Interstate 15 south out of Las Vegas, a long, straight drive through the desert. It's the main route between Las Vegas and Los Angeles, 272 miles away, and it's like driving across an oven hob. After about an hour I passed over into California, into a shimmering landscape of bleached earth and patchy creosote bushes called the Devils Playground. The sunlight glared. The far-off Soda Mountains quivered and distant cars coming towards me looked like balls of fire, so brilliant was their reflection, and always ahead on the road there was a slick smear of mirage that disappeared as I drew near and reappeared further on. Along the shoulder of the road, sometimes out on the desert itself, were cars that had failed to complete the journey. Some of them looked to have been there for a long time. What an awful place to break down. In the summer, this was one of the hottest spots on earth. Off to the right, over the parched Avawatz Mountains, was Death Valley, where the highest temperature ever recorded in America, 134 degrees Fahrenheit, was logged in 1913 (the world record, in 1922 in Libya, is just two degrees higher). But that was the shade temperature. A thermometer lying on the ground in the sun has gone over 200 degrees. Even now in April the temperature was nudging ninety and it was very unpleasant. It was impossible to imagine it almost half as hot again. And yet people live out there, in awful little towns like Baker and Barstow, where the temperature often stays over ninety degrees for 100 days in a row and where they can go ten years without a drop of rain. I pressed on, longing for clear water and green hills.

One good thing about California is that it doesn't take long to find a complete contrast. The state has the strangest geography. At Death Valley you have the lowest point in America – 282 feet below sea level – and yet practically overlooking it is the highest point in the country (not counting Alaska) – Mt Whitney, at 14,494 feet. You could, if you wished, fry an egg on the roof of your car in Death Valley, then drive thirty miles into the mountains and quick-freeze it in a snowbank. My original intention was to cross the Sierra Nevadas by way of Death Valley (breaking off from time to time to perform experiments with eggs), but a weather lady on the radio informed me that the mountain passes were all still closed on account of the recent nasty weather. So I had to make a long and unrewarding detour across the Mojave Desert, on old Highway 58. This took me past Edwards Air Force Base, which runs for almost forty miles along the highway behind a seemingly endless stretch of chain-link fence. It was at Edwards that the Space Shuttle used to land and that Chuck Yeager broke the sound barrier, so it's really quite a hotshot place, but from the highway I couldn't see anything at all – no planes, no hangars, just mile after mile of tall chain-link fence.

Beyond the little town of Mojave, the desert ended and the landscape erupted in smooth hills and citrus groves. I crossed the Los Angeles Aqueduct, which carries water from northern California to Los Angeles, fifty miles to the south. Even out here the city's smog was threaded through the hills. Visibility was no more than a mile. Beyond that there was just a wall of brownish-grey haze. On the other side of it the sun was a bleary disc of light. Everything seemed to be bled of colour. Even the hills looked jaundiced. They were round and covered with boulders and low-growing trees. There was something strangely familiar about them – and then I realised what it was. These were the hills that the Lone Ranger and Zorro and Roy Rogers and the Cisco Kid used to ride around on in the TV shows of the 1950s. I had never noticed until now that the West of the movies and the West of television were two quite different places. Movie crews had obviously gone out into the real West – the West of buttes and bluffs and red river valleys – while television companies, being cheap, had only just driven a few miles into the hills north of Hollywood and filmed on the edges of orange groves.

Here clearly were the very boulders that Tonto, the Lone Ranger's faithful sidekick, used to creep around on. Every week the Lone Ranger would send Tonto off to creep around on some boulders in order to spy on an encampment of bad guys and every week Tonto would get captured. He was hopeless. Every week the Lone Ranger would have to ride in and save Tonto, but he didn't mind doing that because he and Tonto were very close. You could see it in the way they looked at each other.

Those were the days all right. Now children sit and watch people having their vitals sprayed around the room with a chain-saw and think nothing of it. I know that makes me sound very old and crotchety to all you youngsters out there, but I think it's a pity that we can't have some good wholesome entertainment like we had when I was a boy, when the heroes wore masks and capes, and carried whips, and liked other men a whole bunch. Seriously, have you ever stopped to think what strange role models we were given when we were children? Like Superman. Here's a guy who changes his clothes in public. Or Davy Crockett, a man who conquered the frontier, fought valiantly at the Alamo and yet never noticed that he had a dead squirrel on his head. It's no wonder people my age grew up confused and got heavily involved with drugs. My favourite hero of all was Zorro, who whenever he was peeved with someone would whip out his sword and with three deft strokes carve a Z in the offending party's shirt. Wouldn't you just love to be able to do that?

'Waiter, I specifically asked for this steak rare.'

Slash, slash, slash!

'Excuse me, but I believe I was here before you.'

Slash, slash, slash!

'What do you mean, you don't have it in my size?'

Slash, slash, slash!

For weeks, my friend Robert Swanson and I tried to master this useful trick by practising with his mother's kitchen knives, but all we had to show for it were some torn shirts and ragged wounds across our chests, and after a time we gave it up as both painful and impossible, a decision that even now I rue from time to time.

As I was close to Los Angeles, I toyed with the idea of driving on in, but I was put off by the smog and the traffic and above all by the thought that in Los Angeles someone might come up to me and carve a Z in my chest for real. I think it's only right that crazy people should have their own city, but I cannot for the life of me see why a sane person would want to go there. Besides, Los Angeles is *passé*. It has no surprises. My plan was to drive up through the hidden heart of California, through the fertile San Joaquin Valley. Nobody ever goes there. There is a simple reason for this, as I was about to discover. It is really boring.

TWENTY-FIVE

I woke up quietly excited. It was a bright clear morning and in an hour or two I was going to go to Sequoia National Park and drive through a tree. This excited me, in a calm, unshowy sort of way. When I was five, my Uncle Frank and Aunt Fern from Winfield went to California on vacation – this was, of course, before it turned out that Frank was a homo, the old devil, and ran off to Key West with his barber, which rather shocked and upset a lot of people in Winfield, especially when they realised that from now on they would have to drive all the way to Mount Pleasant to get their hair cut – and they sent us a postcard showing a redwood tree of such enormous girth that a road had been cut right through the base of it. The postcard pictured a handsome young couple in a green Studebaker convertible driving through the tree and looking as if they were having something approximating a wholesome orgasm. It made an immediate impression on me. I went to my dad and asked him if we could go to California on our next vacation and drive through a tree and he looked at the card and said, 'Well . . . maybe one day,' and I knew then that I had about as much chance of seeing the road through a tree as I had of sprouting pubic hair.

Every year my father would call a family powwow (can you believe this?) to discuss where we were going on vacation and every year I would push for going to California and the tree with a road through it, and my brother and sister would sneer cruelly and say that that was a really mega-dumb idea. My brother always wanted to go to the Rocky Mountains, my sister to Florida and my mother said she didn't care where we went as long as we were all together. And then my dad would pull out some brochures with titles like 'Arkansas – Land of Several Lakes' and 'Arkansas—the Sho' Nuff State' and 'Important Vacation Facts about Arkansas' (with a foreword by Governor Luther T. Smiley), and suddenly it would seem altogether possible that we might be going to Arkansas that year, whatever our collective views on the matter might be.

When I was eleven, we went to California, the very state that housed my dream tree, but we only went to places like Disneyland and Hollywood Boulevard and Beverly Hills. (Dad was too cheap to buy a map showing the homes of the movie stars, so we just drove around and speculated.) A couple of times at breakfast I asked if we could drive up and see the tree with a road through it, but everybody was so dismissive – it was too far away, it would be too stupendously boring for words, it would probably cost a lot of money – that I lost heart and stopped asking. And in fact I never asked again. But it stayed at the back of my mind, one of my five great unfulfilled dreams from childhood. (The others, it goes without saying, were the ability to stop time, to possess the gift of X-ray vision, to be able to hypnotise my brother and make him be my slave, and to see Sally Ann Summerfield without a stitch of clothing on.)

Not surprisingly, none of these dreams came true. (Which is perhaps just as well. Sally Ann Summerfield is a blimp now. She turned up at my high school reunion two years ago and looked like a shipping hazard.) But now here at last I was about to fulfil one of them. Hence the tingle of excitement as I slung my suitcase in the trunk and headed up Highway 63 for Sequoia National Park.

I had spent the night in the little city of Tulare, in the heart of the San Joaquin Valley. This is the richest and most fertile farming country in the world. They grow over 200 kinds of crop in the San Joaquin Valley. That very morning, on the local news on TV, they reported that the farming income for Tulare County for the previous year was $1·6 billion – that's the sort of money Austin Rover turns over – and yet it was only the second highest figure for the state. Fresno County, just up the road, was richer still. Even so, the landscape didn't look all that brilliant. The valley was as flat as a tennis-court. It stretched for miles in every direction, dull and brown and dusty, and a permanent haze hung on the horizon, like a dirty window. Perhaps it was the time of year, or perhaps it was the drought that was just beginning to choke central California, but it didn't look rich or fruitful. And the towns that speckled the plain were equally dull. They looked like towns from anywhere. They didn't look rich or modern or interesting. Except that there were oranges the size of grapefruits growing on trees in the front yards, I could have been in Indiana or Illinois or anywhere. That surprised me. On our family trip to California it had been like driving into the next decade. It had all looked sleek and modern. Things that were still novelties in Iowa — shopping centres, drive-in banks, McDonald's restaurants, miniature golf-courses, kids on skate-boards — were old and long-established in California. Now they just looked older. The rest of the country had caught up. The California of 1988 had nothing that Iowa didn't have. Except smog. And beaches. And oranges growing in front yards. And trees you could drive through.

I joined Highway 198 at Visalia and followed it as it shot through fragrant lemon groves, ran along the handsome shoreline of Lake Kaweah and climbed up into the foothills of the Sierra Nevada mountains. Just beyond Three Rivers I entered the park, where a ranger in a wooden booth charged me a $5 entrance fee and gave me a brochure detailing the sights beyond. I looked quickly through it for a photograph of a road through a tree, but there weren't any pictures, just words and a map bearing colourful and alluring names: Avalanche Pass, Mist Falls, Farewell Gap, Onion Valley, Giant Forest. I made for Giant Forest.

Sequoia National Park and Kings Canyon National Park are contiguous. Effectively they are one national park and, like all national parks in the West, it is a good-sized one — seventy miles from top to bottom, thirty miles across. Because of the twisting roads as I climbed up into the mountains, progress was slow, though splendidly scenic.

I drove for two hours on lofty roads through boulder-strewn mountains. Snow was still lying about in broad patches. At last I entered the dark and mysterious groves of the giant sequoia (Sequoiadendron giganteum, according to my brochure). The trees were tall, no doubt about it, and fat around the base, though not fat enough to take a highway. Presumably they would get fatter as I moved deeper into the forest. Sequoias are ugly trees. They soar up and up and up, but their branches are sparse and stubby, so they look silly, like the sort of trees three-year-olds draw. In the middle of the Giant Forest stands the General Sherman Tree — the biggest living thing on Earth. Surely the General Sherman was the one I was looking for.

'Oh boy, Chevette, have I got a treat for you'! I called out and patted the steering wheel fondly. When at last I neared the General Sherman, I found a small parking lot and a path leading to the tree through the woods. Evidently it was no longer possible to drive through the tree.

This was a disappointment – name me something in life that isn't – but never mind, I thought. I'll walk through it; the pleasure will last longer. Indeed, I'll walk through it severally. I will stroll and saunter and glide, and if there aren't too many people about, I might well dance around it in the light-footed manner of Gene Kelly splashing through puddles in *Singin' in the Rain*.

So I banged the car door shut and walked up the trail to the tree and there it was, with a little fence around it to keep people from getting too close. It was big all right – tall and fat – but not *that* tall, not *that* fat. And there was no hole through its base. You might just about have managed to cut a modest road through it, but – and here's the important thing – no one ever had. Beside the tree was a large wooden board with an educational message on it. It said 'The giant General Sherman is not only the biggest tree in the world, but also the biggest living thing. It is at least 2,500 years old, and thus also one of the oldest living things. Even so, it is surprisingly boring, isn't it? That is because it isn't all that tall and all that fat. What sets it apart from other redwoods is that it doesn't taper very much. It stays pretty fat all the way up. Hence it has a greater bulk than any other tree. If you want to see really impressive redwoods – ones with roads driven through their bases – you have to go to Redwood National Park, way up near the Oregon border. Incidentally, we've erected a fence around the base of the tree to keep you well back from it and intensify your disappointment. As if that were not enough, there is a party of noisy young Germans coming up the path behind you. Isn't life shitty?'

As you will appreciate, this is somewhat paraphrased, but that was the gist of it. The Germans came and were obnoxious and unthoughtful, as adolescents tend to be, and stole the tree from me. They perched on the fence and started taking pictures. I derived some small pleasure from wandering in front of the cameraman whenever he was about to click the shutter, but this is an activity from which it is difficult to extract sustained amusement, even with Germans, and after a minute or two I left them there jabbering away about *die Pop Musik* and *das Drugs Scene* and their other adolescent preoccupations.

In the car I looked at the map and was disheartened to discover that Redwood National Park was almost 500 miles away. I could hardly believe it. Here I was 300 miles north of Los Angeles and yet I could drive another 500 miles and *still* be in California. It is 850 miles from top to bottom – about the distance between London and Milan. It would take me a day and a half to get to Redwood National Park, plus a day and a half to get back to where I was now. I didn't have that kind of time. Gloomily, I started the car and drove on to Yosemite National Park, seventy miles up the highway.

And what a disappointment that proved to be. I'm sorry to moan, I truly am, but Yosemite was a let-down of monumental proportions. It is incredibly, mouth-gawpingly beautiful. Your first view of the El Capitan valley, with its towering mountains and white waterfalls spilling hundreds of feet down to the meadows of the valley floor, makes you think that surely you have expired and gone to heaven. But then you drive on down into Yosemite village and realise that if this is heaven you are going to spend the rest of eternity with an awful lot of fat people in Bermuda shorts.

Yosemite is a mess. The National Parks Service in America – let's be candid here – does a pretty half-assed job of running many of the national parks. This is surprising because in America most leisure-time activities are about a million times better than anywhere else. But not national parks. The visitors' centres are usually dull, the catering is always crappy and expensive, and you generally come away having learned almost nothing about the wildlife, geology and history of the places you've driven hundreds of miles to see. The national parks are supposed to be there to preserve a chunk of America's wilderness, but in many of them the number of animals has actually fallen. Yellowstone has lost all its wolves, mountain lions and white-tailed deer, and the numbers of beaver and bighorn sheep are greatly depleted. These animals are thriving outside Yellowstone, but as far as the Parks Service itself is concerned they are extinct.

I don't know why it should be, but the National Parks Service has a long history of incompetence. In the 1960s, if you can believe it, the Parks Service invited the Walt Disney Corporation to build a development in Sequoia National Park. Mercifully, that plan was quashed. But others have succeeded, most notably in 1923 when, after a long fight between conservationists and businessmen, the Hetch Hetchey Valley in the northern part of Yosemite – which was said to be even more spectacularly beautiful than Yosemite Valley itself – was flooded to create a reservoir to provide drinking water for San Francisco, 150 miles to the west. So for the last sixty years one of the half-dozen or so most breathtaking stretches of landscape on the planet has lain under water for commercial reasons. God help us if they ever find oil there.

The great problem at Yosemite today is simply finding your way around. I've never seen a place so badly signposted. It's as if they are trying to hide the park from you. At most parks the first thing you want to do is go to the visitors' centre and have a look at the big map to get your bearings and decide what you want to see. But at Yosemite the visitors' centre is almost impossible to find. I drove around Yosemite village for twenty-five minutes before I discovered a parking lot and then it took me a further twenty minutes, and a long walk in the wrong direction, to find the visitors' centre. By the time I found it I knew my way around and didn't need it any more.

And everything is just hopelessly, depressingly crowded – the cafeterias, the post office, the stores. This was in April; what it must be like in August doesn't bear guessing at. I have never been anywhere that was simultaneously so beautiful and so awful. In the end, I had a nice long walk and a look at the waterfalls and the scenery and it was outstanding. But I cannot believe that it can't be better run.

In the evening I drove on to Sonora, through a tranquil sunset, along sinuous mountain roads. I reached the town after dark and had difficulty finding a room. It was only the middle of the week, but most places were full. The motel I finally found was grossly overpriced and the TV reception was terrible. It was like watching people moving around in front of fun-house mirrors. Their bodies would proceed across the screen and their heads would follow a moment later, as if connected by elastic. I was paying $42 for this. The bed was like a pool table with sheets. And the toilet seat didn't have a 'Sanitized For Your Protection' wrapper on it, denying me my daily ritual of cutting it with my scissors and saying, 'I now declare this toilet open.' These things become important to you when you have been alone on the road for a while. In a sour mood I drove into town and went to a cheap restaurant for dinner. The waitress made me wait a long time before she came and took my order. She looked tarty and had an irritating habit of repeating everything I said to her.

'I'd like the chicken fried steak,' I said.

'You'd like the chicken fried steak?'

'Yes. And I would like French fries with it.'

'You want French fries with it?'

'Yes. And I would like a salad with Thousand Island dressing.'

'You want a salad with Thousand Island dressing?'

'Yes, and a Coke to drink.'

'You want a Coke to drink?'

'Excuse me, miss, but I've had a bad day and if you don't stop repeating everything I say, I'm going to take this ketchup bottle and squirt it all down the front of your blouse.'

'You're going to take that ketchup bottle and squirt it all down the front of my blouse?'

I didn't really threaten her with ketchup – she might have had a large boy-friend who would come and pummel me; also, I once knew a waitress who told me that whenever a customer was rude to her she went out to the kitchen and spat in his food, and since then I have never spoken sharply to a waitress or sent undercooked food back to the kitchen (because then the cook spits in it, you see) – but I was in such a disagreeable mood that I put my chewing-gum straight into the ashtray without wrapping it in a piece of tissue first, as my mother always taught me to do, and pressed it down with my thumb so that it wouldn't fall out when the ashtray was turned over, but would have to be prised out with a fork. And what's more – God help me – it gave me a tingle of satisfaction.

In the morning I drove north from Sonora along Highway 49, wondering what the day would bring. I wanted to head east over the Sierra Nevadas, but many of the passes were still closed. Highway 49, as it turned out, took me on an agreeably winding journey through hilly country. Groves of trees and horse pastures overlooked the road, and occasionally I passed an old farmhouse, but there was little sign that the land was used for anything productive. The towns I passed through – Tuttletown, Melones, Angel's Camp – were the places where the California Gold Rush took place. In 1848, a man named James Marshall found a lump of gold at Sutter Creek, just up the road, and people went crazy. Almost overnight, 40,000 prospectors poured into the state and in a little over a decade, between 1847 and 1860, California's population went from 15,000 to nearly 400,000. Some of the towns have been preserved as they were at the time – Sonora is not too bad in this regard – but mostly there's not much to show that this was once the scene of the greatest gold rush in history. I suppose this is largely because most of the people lived in tents and when the gold ran out so did they. Now most of the little towns offered the customary stretch of gas stations, motels and hamburger emporia. It was Anywhere, USA.

At Jackson, I found that Highway 88 was open through the mountains – the first open passage through the Sierras in almost 300 miles – and I took it. I had expected that I would have to take the next but one pass along, the infamous Donner Pass, where in 1846 a party of settlers became trapped by a blizzard for several weeks and survived by eating each other, an incident that caused a great sensation at the time. The leader of the group was named Donner. I don't know what became of him, but I bet he took some ribbing whenever he went into a restaurant after that. At any rate, it got his name on the map. The Donner Pass was also the route taken by the first transcontinental railroad, the Southern Pacific, and first transcontinental highway, old Route 40, the Lincoln Highway, on their 3,000-mile journey from New York to San Francisco. As with Route 66 further south, Route 40 had been callously dug up and converted into a dull interstate highway, so I was pleased to find a back road open through the mountains.

And it was very pleasant. I drove through pine-forested scenery, with occasional long views across unpeopled valleys, up and over Mokelumne Peak (9,332 feet), heading in the general direction of Lake Tahoe and Carson City. The road was steep and slow and it took me much of the afternoon to drive the hundred or so miles to the Nevada border. Near Woodfords I entered the Toiyabe National Forest, or at least what once had been the Toiyabe National Forest. For miles and miles there was nothing but charred land, mountainsides of dead earth and stumps of trees. Occasionally I passed an undamaged house around which a fire-break had been dug. It was an odd sight, a house with swings and a paddling-pool in the middle of an ocean of blackened stumps. A year or so before the owners must have thought they were the luckiest people on the planet, to live in the woods and mountains, amid the cool and fragrant pines. And now they lived on the surface of the moon. Soon the forest would be replanted and for the rest of their lives they could watch it grow again, inch by annual inch.

I had never seen such devastation – miles and miles of it – and yet I had no recollection of having read about it. That's the thing about America. It's so big that it just absorbs disasters, muffles them with its vastness. Time and again on this trip I had seen news stories that would elsewhere have been treated as colossal tragedies – a dozen people killed by floods in the South, ten crushed when a store roof collapsed in Texas, twenty-two dead in a snowstorm in the east – and each of them treated as a brief and not terribly consequential diversion between ads for haemorrhoid unguents and cottage cheese. Partly it is a consequence of that inane breeziness common to local TV news-readers in America, but mostly it is just the scale of the country. A disaster in Florida is regarded in California in the same way that a disaster in Italy is regarded in Britain – as something briefly and morbidly diverting, but too far away to be tragic in any personal sense.

I entered Nevada about ten miles south of Lake Tahoe. Las Vegas had so put me off that I had no desire to go to another sink of iniquity, though I was later told that Tahoe is a really nice place and not at all like Las Vegas. Now I shall never know. I can tell you, however, that Carson City was just about the most nothing little city you could ever hope to zip through. It's the state capital, but mostly it was just Pizza Huts and gas stations and cheap-looking casinos.

I headed out of town on US 50, past Virginia City and towards Silver Springs. This was more or less the spot where the map used to burst into flames on *Bonanza*. Remember that? It has been many years since I've seen the programme, but I recall Pa and Hoss and Little Joe and the surly-looking one whose name I forget all living in a landscape that was fruitful and lush, in a Western, high chaparral sort of way. But out here there was nothing but cement-coloured plains and barren hills and almost no habitations at all. Everything was grey, from the sky to the ground. This was to remain the pattern for the next two days.

It would be difficult to conceive of a more remote and cheerless state than Nevada. It has a population of just 800,000 in an area about the size of Britain and Ireland combined. Almost half of that population is accounted for by Las Vegas and Reno, so most of the rest of the state is effectively just empty. There are only seventy towns in the entire state – the British Isles have 40,000, just to give you some comparison – and some of them are indescribably remote. For instance, Eureka, a town of 1,200 in the middle of the state, is 100 miles in any direction from the nearest town. Indeed, the whole of Eureka County has just three towns and a total population of under 2,500 – and this in an area of a couple of thousand square miles.

I drove for a while across this fearsome emptiness, taking a back highway between Fallon and a spot on the map called Humboldt Sink, where I gratefully joined Interstate 80. This was a cowardly thing to do, but the car had been making odd noises off and on for the past couple of days – a sort of faint clonk clonk oh god help me clonk I'm dying oh god oh god clonk noise – which wasn't covered in the trouble-shooting section of the owner's manual. I couldn't face the prospect of breaking down and being stranded for days in some God-forsaken dust-hole while waiting for an anti-clonk device to be shipped in from Reno on the weekly Greyhound. In any case, Highway 50, the nearest alternative road, would have taken me 150 miles out of my way and into Utah. I wanted to go a more northerly route across Montana and Wyoming – the 'Big Sky' country. So it was with some relief that I joined the interstate, though even this was remarkably empty – usually I could see one car in the distance far ahead and one in the distance far behind – considering it was the main artery across the country. Indeed, with a sufficiently capacious fuel tank and bladder, you could drive the whole way between New York and San Francisco without stopping.

At Winnemucca I pulled off for gas and coffee and called my mother to let her know that I hadn't been killed yet and was doing all right for underwear – a matter of perennial concern to my mother. I was able to reassure her on this score and she reassured me that she hadn't willed her money to the International Guppy Institute or anything similarly rash (I just like to check!), so we were able to continue our respective days with light hearts.

In the phone booth was a poster with a photograph of a young woman on it under the caption 'Have you seen this girl?' She was attractive and looked youthful and happy. The poster said she was nineteen years old and had been driving from Boston to San Francisco on her way home for Christmas when she disappeared. She had called her parents from Winnemucca to tell them to expect her the next afternoon and that was the last anyone had heard of her. Now she was almost certainly dead, somewhere out there in that big empty desert.

Murder is terrifyingly easy in America. You can kill a stranger, dump the body in a place where it will never be found and be 2,000 miles away before the murdered person is even missed. At any given time there are an estimated twelve to fifteen serial murderers at large in the country, just drifting around, snatching random victims and then moving on, leaving behind few clues and no motives. A couple of years earlier in Des Moines, some teenaged boys were cleaning out an office downtown for one of their fathers on a Sunday afternoon when a stranger came in, took them into a back room and shot each of them once in the back of the head. For no reason. That guy was caught, as it happens, but he could as easily have gone off to another state and done the same thing again. Every year in America 5,000 murders go unsolved. That is an incredible number.

I spent the night in Wells, Nevada, the sorriest, seediest, most raggedy-assed town I've ever seen. Most of the streets were unpaved and lined with battered-looking trailer homes. Everyone in town seemed to collect old cars. They sat rusting and windowless in every yard. Almost everything in town appeared to exist on the edge of dereliction. Such economic life as Wells could muster came from the passing traffic of Interstate 80. A number of truck stops and motels were scattered around, though many of these were closed down and those that remained were evidently struggling. Most of the motel signs had letters missing or burnt out, so that they said 'Lone St r Mot l— V can y'. I had a walk around the business district before dinner. This consisted mostly of closed-down stores, though a few places appeared still to be in business: a drugstore, a gas station, a Trailways Bus depot, the Overland Hotel – sorry, H tel – and a movie-house called The Nevada, though this proved upon closer inspection also to be deceased. There were dogs everywhere, sniffing in doorways and peeing on pretty much everything. It was cold, too. The sun was setting behind the rough, distant peaks of the Jackson Mountains and there was a decided chill in the air. I turned up my collar and trudged the half-mile from the town proper to the interstate junction with US 93, where the most prosperous-looking truck stops were gathered, forming an oasis of brightness in the pinkish dusk.

I went into what looked to be the best of them, a large café, consisting of a gift shop, restaurant, casino and bar. The casino

was small, just a room with a couple of dozen slot-machines, mostly
nickel ones, and the gift shop was about the size of a closet. The café
was crowded and dense with smoke and chatter. Steel-guitar music
drifted out of the juke-box. I was the only person in the room who
didn't have a cowboy hat on, apart from a couple of the women.

I sat in a booth and ordered fried chicken. The waitress was real
friendly, but she had little open sores all over her hands and arms and
only about three teeth, and her apron looked as if she had spent the
afternoon butchering piglets. This put me off my dinner a bit, to tell
you the truth, and then she brought my dinner and that put me off
eating altogether.

It was absolutely the worst food I have ever had in America, at any
time, under any circumstances, and that includes hospital food, gas
station food and airport coffee shop food. It even includes Greyhound
Bus Station food and Woolworth's luncheon counter food. It was even
worse than the pastries they used to put in the food-dispensing
machines at the Register and Tribune Building in Des Moines and
those tasted like somebody had been sick on them. This food was just
plain terrible, and yet everybody in the room was shovelling it away as
if there were no tomorrow. I picked at it for a while – bristly fried
chicken, lettuce with blackened veins, French fries that had the
appearance and appeal of albino slugs – and gave up, despondent. I
pushed the plate away and wished that I still smoked. The waitress,
seeing how much I had left, asked me if I wanted a doggie bag.

'No thank you,' I said through a thin smile, 'I don't believe I could
find a dog that would eat it.'

On reflection, I can think of one eating experience even more
dispiriting than dining at that café and that was the lunch-room
at Callanan Junior High School in Des Moines. The lunch-room at
Callanan was like something out of a prison movie. You would shuffle
forward in a long, silent line and have lumpen, shapeless food
dolloped on to your tray by lumpen, shapeless women – women who
looked as if they were on day release from a mental institution,
possibly for having poisoned food in public places. The food wasn't
merely unappealing, it was unidentifiable. Adding to the displeasure
was the presence of the deputy principal, Mr Snoyd, who was always
stalking around behind you, ready to grab you by the neck and march

you off to his office if you made gagging noises or were overheard inquiring of the person across from you, 'Say, what is this shit?' Eating at Callanan was like having your stomach pumped in reverse.

I went back to the motel feeling deeply hungry and unsatisfied. I watched some TV and read a book, and then slept that fitful sleep you get when all of your body is still and resting except your stomach, which is saying, 'WHERE THE FUCK IS MY DINNER? HEY, BILL, ARE YOU LISTENING TO ME? WHERE THE F-U-C-K IS MY EVENING SUSTENANCE?'

TWENTY-SIX

Here, apropos of nothing at all, is a true story. In 1958, my grandmother got cancer of the colon and came to our house to die. At this time my mother employed a cleaning lady named Mrs Goodman, who didn't have a whole lot upstairs but was possessed of a good Catholic heart. After my grandmother's arrival, Mrs Goodman grew uncharacteristically sullen. Then one afternoon at finishing time she told my mother that she would have to quit because she didn't want to catch cancer from my grandmother. My mother soothingly reassured Mrs Goodman that you cannot 'catch cancer', and gave her a small pay increase to compensate for the extra work occasioned by my grandmother's clammy and simpering presence. So with ill-disguised reluctance Mrs Goodman stayed on. And about three months later she caught cancer and with alarming swiftness died.

Well, as you can imagine, since it was my family that killed the poor woman, I've always wanted to commemorate her in some small way and I thought that here would be as good a place as any, especially as I had nothing of interest to tell you about the drive from Wells, Nevada, to Twin Falls, Idaho.

So, goodbye, Mrs Goodman, it was nice knowing you. And we're all very, very sorry.

Twin Falls was a nice enough place – Mrs Goodman, I've no doubt, would have liked it; but then when you think about it a dead person would probably appreciate any change of scenery – and the landscape in southern Idaho was greener and more fertile than anything Nevada had to offer. Idaho is known for its potatoes, though in fact Maine, just a third its size, produces more. Its real wealth comes from mining and timber, particularly in the higher reaches of the Rockies, up towards Canada, over 500 miles north of where I was now. I was headed for Sun Valley, the famous resort up in the Sawtooth Mountains, and the neighbouring town of Ketchum, where Ernest Hemingway spent the last year of his life and blew his brains out. This has always seemed to me (not that it's any of my business, mind you) a particularly thoughtless and selfish way to kill oneself. I mean to say, your family is going to be upset enough that you are dead without your having to spoil the furniture and gross everyone out on top of that.

In any case, Ketchum was touristy, though Sun Valley itself proved to be most agreeable. It was purpose-built as a ski resort in the 1930s by the Union Pacific Railroad as a way of enticing people to travel to the region during the winter. It certainly has a beautiful setting, in a bowl of jagged mountains, and is supposed to have some of the best skiing in the country. People like Clint Eastwood and Barbra Streisand have houses there. I looked in a window in a real estate office and didn't see anything for sale for less than $250,000.

The town part of Sun Valley – it's really just a little shopping centre – is built to look like a Bavarian village. I found it oddly charming. As so often with these things in America, it was superior to a real Bavarian village. There were two reasons for this: (1) it was better built and more picturesque, and (2) the inhabitants of Sun Valley have never adopted Adolf Hitler as their leader or sent their neighbours off for gassing. Were I a skier and rich, I would on these grounds alone unhesitatingly choose it over Garmisch-Partenkirchen, say. In the meantime, being poor and skiless, there was nothing much for me to do but poke around in the shops. For the most part these sold swish skiing outfits and expensive gifts – things like large pewter elk for $200 and lead crystal paperweights at $150 – and the people who ran them were those snooty types who watch you as if they think you might do a poo in the corner given half a chance. Understandably, this soured me on the place and I declined to make any purchases. 'Your loss, not mine,' I murmured sniffily as I left.

Idaho is another big state – 550 miles from top to bottom, 300 miles across at the base – and it took me the rest of the day just to drive to Idaho Falls, near the border with Wyoming. *En route* I passed the little town of Arco, which on December 20, 1951, became the first town in the world to be lit with nuclear-powered electricity, supplied by the world's first peacetime nuclear reactor at a site ten miles south-west of town at the Idaho National Engineering Laboratory. The name is misleading because the so-called laboratory covers several hundred square miles of scrubby chaparral and is actually the biggest nuclear dump in the country. The highway between Arco and Idaho Falls runs for forty miles alongside the complex, but it is lined by high fences interspersed with military-style check-points. In the far distance stand large buildings where, presumably, workers in white space suits wander around in rooms that look like something out of a James Bond film.

I didn't realise it at the time, but the US government had recently admitted that plutonium had been found to be leaking from one of the storage facilities on the site and was working its way downward through the ground to a giant subterranean reservoir, which supplies the water for tens of thousands of people in southern Idaho. Plutonium is the most lethal substance known to man – a spoonful of it could wipe out a city. Once you make some plutonium, you have to keep it safe for 250,000 years. The United States government had managed to keep its plutonium safe for rather less than thirty-six years. This, it seems to me, is a convincing argument for not allowing your government to mess with plutonium.

And this was only one leak out of many. At a similar facility in the state of Washington, 500,000 gallons of highly radioactive substances drained away before anyone thought to put a dipstick in the tank and see how things were doing. How do you lose 500,000 gallons of anything? I don't know the answer to that question, but I do know that I would not like to be a real estate agent trying to sell houses in Pocatello or Idaho Falls five years from now when the ground starts to glow and women are giving birth to human flies.

For the time being, however, Idaho Falls remains an agreeable little city. The downtown was attractive and still evidently prospering. Trees and benches had been set out. A big banner was draped across one of the streets saying 'Idaho Falls Says NO to drugs'. That's really going to keep the kids off the hard stuff, I thought. Small-town America is obsessed with drugs, yet I suspect that if you strip-searched every teenager in Idaho Falls you would come up with nothing more illicit than some dirty magazines, a packet of condoms and a half-empty bottle of Jack Daniels. Personally, I think the young people of Idaho Falls ought to be encouraged to take drugs. It will help them to cope when they find out there's plutonium in their drinking water.

I had an excellent dinner at Happy's Chinese Restaurant. The room was empty except for one other party consisting of a middle-aged couple, their teen-aged daughter and a Swedish exchange student who was simply radiant – blonde, tanned, soft-spoken, hypnotically beautiful. I stared at her helplessly. I had never seen anyone so beautiful in a Chinese restaurant in Idaho before. After a while a man came in who was evidently a passing acquaintance of the family and stopped at their table to chat. He was introduced to the Swedish girl and asked her about her stay in Idaho Falls and if she had been to the local sights – the lava caves and hot springs. (She had. Zey were vairy nice.) Then he asked The Big Question. He said, 'Well, Greta, which do you like better, the United States or Sweden?'

The girl blushed. She obviously had not been in the country long enough to expect this question. Suddenly she looked more child than woman. With an embarrassed flutter of hands she said, 'Oh, I sink Sweden,' and a pall fell over the table. Everyone looked uncomfortable. 'Oh,' said the man in a flat, disappointed tone, and the conversation turned to potato prices.

People in middle America always ask that question. When you grow up in America you are inculcated from the earliest age with the belief – no, the *understanding* – that America is the richest and most powerful nation on earth because God likes us best. It has the most perfect form of government, the most exciting sporting events, the tastiest food and amplest portions, the largest cars, the cheapest gasoline, the most abundant natural resources, the most productive farms, the most devastating nuclear arsenal and the friendliest, most decent and most patriotic folks on Earth. Countries just don't come any better. So why anyone would want to live anywhere else is practically incomprehensible. In a foreigner it is puzzling; in a native it is seditious. I used to feel this way myself. In high school I shared a locker with a Dutch exchange student and I remember him asking me one day in a peevish tone why everybody, absolutely everybody, wanted him to like America better than The Netherlands. 'Holland is my home,' he said. 'Why can't people understand that it's where I want to live?'

I considered his point. 'Yes,' I said, 'but deep down, Anton, wouldn't you really rather live here?' And funnily enough, in the end, he decided he did. The last I heard he was a successful realtor in Florida, driving a Porsche, wearing wraparound sunglasses and saying, 'Hey, what's happening?' which of course is a considerable improvement on wearing wooden shoes, carrying pails of milk on a yoke over your shoulder and being invaded by Germany every couple of generations.

In the morning I drove to Wyoming, through scenery that looked like an illustration from some marvellous children's book of Western tales – snowy peaks, pine forests, snug farms, a twisting river, a mountain vale with a comely name: Swan Valley. That is the one thing that must be said for the men and women who carved out the West. They certainly knew how to name a place. Just on this corner of the map I could see Soda Springs, Massacre Rocks, Steamboat Mountain, Wind River, Flaming Gorge, Calamity Falls – places whose very names promised adventure and excitement, even if in reality all they contained were a DX gas station and a Tastee-Freez drive-in.

Most of the early settlers in America were oddly inept at devising place-names. They either chose unimaginative, semi-recycled names – New York, New Hampshire, New Jersey, New England – or toadying, kiss-ass names like Virginia, Georgia, Maryland and Jamestown in a generally pitiable attempt to secure favour with some monarch or powdered aristocrat back home. Or else they just accepted the names the Indians told them, not knowing whether Squashan-insect meant 'land of the twinkling lakes' or 'place where Big Chief Thunderclap paused to pass water'.

The Spanish were even worse because they gave everything religious names, so that every place in the south-west is called San this or Santa that. Driving across the south-west is like an 800-mile religious procession. The worst name on the whole continent is the Sangre de Cristo mountains in New Mexico, which means the 'Blood of Christ Mountains'. Have you ever heard of a more inane name for any geographical feature? It was only here in the real West, the land of beaver trappers and mountain men, that a dollop of romance and colour was brought to the business of giving names. And here I was about to enter one of the most beautiful and understatedly romantic of them all: Jackson Hole.

Jackson Hole isn't really a hole at all; it's just the name for a scenic valley that runs from north to south through the Grand Tetons, very probably the most majestic range in the Rockies. With their high white peaks and bluish-grey bases they look like some kind of exotic confection, like blueberry *frappés*. At the southern edge of Jackson

Hole is the small town of Jackson, where I stopped now for lunch. It was a strange place, with an odd combination of bow-legged Yosemite Sams and upmarket stores like Benetton and Ralph Lauren, which are there for the benefit of the many well-heeled tenderfeet who come for the skiing in the winter and to dude ranches in the summer. Every place in town had a Wild West motif – the Antler Motel, the Silver Dollar Saloon, the Hitching Post Lodge. Even the Bank of Jackson, where I went to cash a traveller's cheque, had a stuffed buffalo head on the wall. Yet it all seemed quite natural. Wyoming is the most fiercely Western of all the Western states. It's still a land of cowboys and horses and wide open spaces, a place where a man's gotta do what a man's gotta do, which on the face of it primarily consists of driving around in a pickup truck and being kind of slow. I had never seen so many people in cowboy apparel, and almost everybody owns a gun. Only a couple of weeks before, the state legislature in Cheyenne had introduced a rule that all legislators would henceforth have to check their handguns at the front desk before being allowed into the Statehouse. That's the sort of state Wyoming is.

I drove on to Grand Teton National Park. And there's another arresting name for you. '*Tétons*' means 'tits' in French. That's an interesting fact – a topographical titbit, so to speak – that Miss Mucus, my junior high school geography teacher, failed to share with us in the eighth grade. Why do they always keep the most interesting stuff from you in school? If I'd known in high school that Thomas Jefferson kept a black slave to help him deal with sexual tension or that Ulysses S. Grant was a hopeless drunk who couldn't button his own flies without falling over, I would have shown a livelier interest in my lessons, I can assure you.

At any rate, the first French explorers who passed through north-western Wyoming took one look at the mountains and said, '*Zut alors!* Hey, Jacques, clock those mountains. They look just like my wife's *tétons*.' Isn't it typical of the French to reduce everything to a level of sexual vulgarity? Thank goodness they didn't discover the Grand Canyon, that's all I can say. And the remarkable thing is that the Tetons look about as much like tits as . . . well, as a frying-pan or a pair of hiking boots. In a word, they don't look like tits at all, except perhaps to desperately lonely men who have been away from home for a very long time. They looked a little bit like tits to me.

Grand Teton National Park and Yellowstone National Park run
together to form one enormous area of wilderness stretching over a
hundred miles from north to south. The road connecting them, Route
191, had only just been reopened for the year, and the Teton visitors'
centres were still closed. There were hardly any other people or cars
around and for forty miles I drove in splendid isolation along the wild
meadows of the Snake River, where herds of elk grazed against the
backdrop of the tall and jagged Tetons. As I climbed into Yellowstone
the clouds grew moody and looked heavy with snow. The road I was
on is closed for six months of the year, which gives you some idea of
the sort of winters they have there. Even now the snow along the
roadside was five or six feet deep in places.

Yellowstone is the oldest national park in the world (it was created
in 1872) and it is enormous, about the size of Connecticut. I drove for
over an hour without seeing anyone, except for a park warden in a
wooden hut who charged me $10 to get in. That must be an exciting
job for a college graduate, to sit in a hut in the middle of nowhere and
take $10 off a tourist every two or three hours. Eventually I came to a
turn-off for Grant Village, and I followed it for a mile through the
snowy woods. The village was good-sized, with a visitors' centre,
motel, stores, post office and campgrounds, but everything was shut
and every window was boarded. Snowdrifts rose almost to the
rooftops of some of the buildings. I had now driven seventy miles
without seeing an open place of business, and gave silent thanks that I
had filled up with gasoline at Jackson.

Grant·Village and the neighbouring village of West Thumb are on the
banks of Yellowstone Lake, which the highway runs alongside. Steam
was rising from fumaroles in the lake and bubbling up through the mud
by the roadside. I was in the area of the park called the caldera. Once
there was a great mountain here. But 600,000 years ago it blew up in a
colossal volcanic eruption that sent 240 cubic miles of débris into the
atmosphere. The geysers, fumaroles and steaming mudpots for which
Yellowtone is famous are the spluttering relics of that cataclysm.

Just beyond West Thumb the highway split in two. One branch
went to Old Faithful, the most famous of all the geysers, but a chain
had been strung across the road with a red sign hanging from it saying
'Road Closed'. Old Faithful was seventeen miles away down the

closed road, but eighty miles away down the alternative road. I drove on to Hayden Valley, where you can stop the car at frequent lay-bys and look out upon the plain of the Yellowstone River. This is where the grizzly bears roam and buffalo graze.

When you enter the park you are given a set of stern instructions telling you not to approach the animals as they are likely to kill or maim you, though I read later that more people have been killed in the park by other people than by animals. Even so, grizzlies are still a real threat to campers, one or two of whom get carried off every year. If you camp in the park you are instructed to change your clothes after eating or cooking and put them and all your food in a bag suspended from a branch ten feet above the ground, 100 yards from your tent. Stories abound of peckish campers who eat a bar of chocolate at bedtime and five minutes later a grizzly bear puts his head in the tent and says, 'Hey, have you guys got some chocolate in here?' According to the park literature, there is even evidence that sexual intercourse and menstruation attract grizzlies. This seemed a bit rough to me.

I peered through my dad's binoculars but I didn't see any bears, possibly because they were still hibernating, and possibly because there aren't very many left in the park. Most of them have been driven out by the crush of visitors in the summer, even though large tracts of Yellowstone have been closed to people to encourage the bears to stay. There were, however, herds of buffalo everywhere. They are quite an extraordinary animal, with such big heads and shoulders on tiny legs. It must have been something to see when herds numbering in the millions filled the plains.

I drove on to Geyser Basin. This is the most volatile and unstable landscape in the world. A few miles to the east the land is rising by almost an inch a year, suggesting that another big blow-out is on the way. Geyser Basin presented the most fantastic and eerie prospect, a lunar landscape of steam vents, hissing geysers and shallow pools of the deepest blue aquamarine. You can wander all over along wooden sidewalks built above the ground. If you were to step off them, according to the signs, you would sink in the crusty soil and be scalded to death by the water just below the surface. The whole place stank of sulphur.

I walked down to Steamboat Geyser, the biggest in the world. According to the sign, it shoots water up to 400 feet into the air, though only at widely-spaced intervals. The last big eruption was three and a half years earlier, on September 26, 1984. As I was watching it erupted — suddenly I understood the expression to jump out of one's skin. The steamy mudpack before me made a flapping sound like a colossal palpitating sphincter (my own sphincter, I can tell you, began to beat a modest counterpoint) and then with a whoosh like a whale coming up for air shot out a great, steaming plume of white water. It went up only about twenty or thirty feet, but it poured forth for many seconds. Then it died and came again, and it repeated this four times, filling the cool air with blankets of steam, before it went dormant. When it finished, I shut my mouth with my hand and walked back to the car, knowing that I had seen one of the more arresting sights of my life.

There was no need to drive on to Old Faithful, still forty miles down the road. I headed instead up the steep road over Roaring Mountain, past Nymph Lake, Grizzly Lake and Sheepeater Cliff – oh, how I love those names – and on down into Mammoth Hot Springs, home of the park headquarters. Here there was a visitors' centre open, so I had a look around, and a pee and a drink of water, before driving on. When I emerged from the park at its northern end, by the little town of Gardiner, I was in a new state, Montana. I drove the sixty miles or so to Livingston through a landscape that was less wild but more beautiful than anything Yellowstone had offered. Partly this was because the sun came out and filled the late afternoon with a sudden spring-like warmth. Long, flat shadows lay across the valley. There was no snow here, though the first infusion of green was just beginning to seep into the grassy and still yellow pastures along the highway. It was almost the first of May and winter was only just now with-drawing.

I got a room in the Del Mar Motel in Livingston, had some dinner and went for a walk out along the highway at the edge of town. With the sun sinking behind the nearby mountains, the evening quickly grew cold. A bleak wind came whipping down from the emptiness of Canada, 300 miles to the north, the kind of wind that slips up the back of your jacket and humiliates your hair. It resonated down the telephone lines, like a man whistling through his teeth, and made the tall grass seethe. Somewhere a gate creaked and banged, creaked and banged. The highway stretched out flat and straight ahead of me until it narrowed to a vanishing-point some miles away. Every so often a car would come at me down the highway from behind, sounding eerily like a jet taking off. As it came nearer and nearer I would half wonder for one moment if it was going to hit me – it sounded that close – and then it would flash past and I would watch its tail-lights disappear into the gathering gloom.

A freight train came along on some tracks that ran parallel to the highway. At first it was a distant light and short bursts of horn, and then it was rolling past me, slow and stately, on its nightly procession through Livingston. It was enormous – American trains are twice the size of European ones – and at least a mile long. I counted sixty freight cars on it before I lost track, all of them with names on them like Burlington & Northern, Rock Island, Santa Fe. It struck me as curious that train lines were so often named after towns that never amounted to much. I wondered how many people a century ago lost their shirts buying property in places like Atchison and Topeka on the assumption that one day they would be as big as Chicago and San Francisco. Towards the end of the train one car went by with its door open and I could see three shadowy figures inside: hoboes. I was amazed to find that such people still existed, that it was still possible to ride the rails. In the dusk it looked a very romantic way to spend your life. It was all I could do to keep from sprinting along and climbing aboard and just disappearing with them into the night. There is nothing like an evening train rolling past to make you take leave of your senses. But instead I just turned around and trudged back along the tracks into town, feeling oddly content.

TWENTY-SEVEN

The next day I was torn between driving back into Wyoming further east along Interstate 90 and going to the little town of Cody, or staying in Montana and visiting the Custer National Battlefield. Cody takes its name from Buffalo Bill Cody, who agreed to be buried there if they named the town after him. There were presumably two further stipulations: (1) that they waited until he was dead before they buried him, and (2) that they filled the town with as much tourist tat as they could possibly manage. Seeing the chance to collect a little lucre, the townspeople happily acceded and they have been cashing in on Cody's fame ever since. Today the town offers half a dozen cowboy museums and other diversions and of course many opportunities to purchase small crappy trinkets to take back home with you.

The people of Cody like you to think that Buffalo Bill was a native son. In fact, I'm awfully proud to tell you, he was an Iowa native, born in the little town of Le Claire in 1846. The people of Cody, in one of the more desperate commercial acts of this century, bought Buffalo Bill's birthplace and re-erected it in their town, but they are lying through their teeth when they hint that he was a local. And the thing is, they have a talented native son of their own. Jackson Pollock, the artist, was born in Cody. But they don't make anything of that because, I suppose, Pollock was a complete wanker when it came to shooting buffalo.

So that was option one. Alternatively, as I say, I had the choice of driving on across Montana to Little Bighorn, where Custer came a cropper. To be perfectly frank, neither one of them seemed terribly exciting – I would have preferred something more in the way of a tall drink on a terrace overlooking the sea – but in Wyoming and Montana you don't get a lot to choose from. In the end, I opted for Custer's last stand. This rather surprised me because as a rule I don't like battlefields. I fail to see the appeal in them once they have carted off the bodies and swept up. My father used to love battlefields. He would go striding off with a guidebook and map, enthusiastically retracing the ebb and flow of the Battle of Lickspittle Ridge, or whatever.

Once I had the choice of going with my mother to a museum and looking at dresses of the Presidents' wives or staying with my dad, and I rashly chose the latter. I spent a long afternoon trailing behind him, certain that he had lost his mind. 'Now this must be the spot where General Goober accidentally shot himself in the armpit and had to be relieved of command by Lt-Col. Bowlingalley,' he would say as we hauled ourselves to the top of a steep summit. 'So that means Pillock's forces must have been regrouping over there at those trees' – and he would point to a grove of trees three hills away and stride off with his documents fluttering in the wind and I would think, 'Where's he going *now*?' Afterwards, to my great disgust, I discovered that the museum of First Ladies' dresses had only taken twenty minutes to see and my mother, brother and sister had spent the rest of the afternoon in a Howard Johnson's restaurant eating hot fudge sundaes.

So the Custer Battlefield National Monument came as a pleasant surprise. There's not much to it, but then there wasn't much to the battle. The visitors' centre contained a small but absorbing museum with relics from both the Indians and soldiers, and a topographical model of the battlefield, which employed tiny light bulbs to show you how the battle progressed. Mostly this consisted of a string of blue lights moving down the hill in a confident fashion and then scurrying back up the hill pursued by a much larger number of red lights. The blue lights formed into a cluster at the top of the hill where they blinked furiously for a while, but then one by one they winked out as the red lights swarmed over them. On the model the whole thing was over in a couple of minutes; in real life it didn't take much longer. Custer was an idiot and a brute and he deserved his fate. His plan was to slaughter the men, women and children of the Cheyenne and Sioux nations as they camped out beside the Little Bighorn River and it was just his bad luck that they were much more numerous and better armed than he had reckoned. Custer and his men fled back up the hill on which the visitors' centre now stands, but there was no place to hide and they were quickly overrun. I went outside and up a short slope to the spot where Custer made his last stand and had a look around.

It occupies a bleak and treeless hill, a place where the wind never stops blowing. From the hilltop I could see for perhaps fifty or sixty miles and there was not a tree in sight, just an unbroken sweep of yellowish grassland rolling away to a white horizon. It was a place so remote and lonely that I could see the wind coming before I felt it. The grass further down the hill would begin to ripple and a moment later a gust would swirl around me and be gone.

The site of Custer's last stand is enclosed by a black cast-iron fence. Inside this little compound, about fifty yards across, are scattered white stones to mark the spots where each soldier fell. Behind me, fifty yards or so down the far side of the hill, two white stones stood together where a pair of soldiers had obviously made a run for it and had been cut down. No one knows where or how many Indians fell because they took their dead and injured away with them. In fact, nobody really knows what happened there that day in June 1876 because the Indians gave such conflicting accounts and none of the white participants lived to tell the tale. All that is known for sure is that Custer screwed up in a mighty big way and got himself and 260 other men killed.

Scattered as they are around such a desolate and windy bluff, the marker stones are surprisingly, almost disturbingly, poignant. It's impossible to look at them and not imagine what a strange and scary death it must have been for the soldiers who dropped there, and it left me yet again in a reflective frame of mind as I walked back down the hill to the car and returned to the endless American highway.

I drove to Buffalo, Wyoming, through a landscape of mossy brown hills. Montana is enormously vast and empty. It is even bigger and emptier than Nevada, largely because there are no population centres to speak of. Helena, the state capital, has a population of just 24,000. In the whole state there are fewer than 800,000 people – this in an area of 145,000 square miles. Yet it has a kind of haunting beauty with its endless empty plains and towering skies. Montana is called the Big Sky country and it really is true. I had always thought of the sky as something fixed and invariable, but here it seemed to have grown by a factor of at least ten. The Chevette was a tiny particle beneath a colossal white dome. Everything was dwarfed by that stupendous sky.

The highway led through a big Crow Indian reservation, but I saw no sign of Indians either on the road or off it. Beyond Lodge Grass and Wyola I passed back into Wyoming. The landscape stayed the same, though here there were more signs of ranching and the map once again filled up with diverting names: Spotted Horse, Recluse, Crazy Woman Creek, Thunder Basin.

I drove into Buffalo. In 1892 it was the scene of the famous Johnson County War, the incident that inspired the movie *Heaven's Gate*, though in fact the term 'war' is a gross over-exaggeration of events. All that happened was that the local ranchers, in the guise of the Wyoming Stock Growers' Association, hired a bunch of thugs to come to Johnson County and rough up some of the homesteaders who had recently, and quite legally, begun moving in. When the thugs killed a man, the homesteaders rose up and chased them to a ranch outside town, where they laid siege until the cavalry rode in and gave the humbled bullies safe passage out of town. And that was it: just one man killed and hardly any shots fired. That was the way the West really was, by and large. It was just farmers. That's all.

I reached Buffalo a little after four in the afternoon. The town has a museum dedicated to the Johnson County War, which I was hoping to see, but I discovered when I got there that it is only open from June to September. I drove around the business district, toying with the idea of stopping for the night, but it was such a dumpy little town that I decided to press on to Gillette, seventy miles down the road. Gillette was even worse. I drove around it for a few minutes, but I couldn't face the prospect of spending a Saturday night there, so I decided to press on once again.

Thus it was that I ended up in Sundance, thirty miles further down the road. Sundance is the town from which the Sundance Kid took his name, and from all appearances that was the only thing in town worth taking. He wasn't born in Sundance; he just spent some time in jail there. It was a small, charmless place, with just one road in and one road out. I got a room in the Bear Lodge Motel on Main Street and it was pleasant in a basic sort of way. The bed was soft, the television was hooked up to HBO, the cable movie network, and the toilet had a 'Sanitized For Your Protection' banner across the seat. On the far side of the street was a restaurant that looked acceptable. Clearly I was not about to have the Saturday night of a lifetime here, but things could have been worse. And indeed very soon they were.

I had a shower and afterwards as I dressed I switched on the television and watched the Reverend Jimmy Swaggart, a TV evangelist who had recently been caught dallying with a prostitute, the old rascal. Naturally this had put a certain strain on his credibility and he had taken to the airwaves, more or less continuously as far as I could tell, to beg for mercy. Here he was once again appealing for money and forgiveness, in that order. Tears rolled from his eyes and glistened on his cheeks. He told me he was a miserable sinner. 'No argument there, Jimbo,' I said, and switched off.

I stepped out on to Main Street. It was ten of seven, as they say in this part of the world. The evening was warm and in the still air the aroma of charbroiled steaks floated over from the restaurant across the street and berthed in my nostrils. I hadn't eaten all day and the whiff of sirloin made me realise just how hungry I was. I smoothed down my wet hair, needlessly looked both ways before stepping off the sidewalk – there was nothing moving on the road for at least 100 miles in either direction – and went over. I opened the door and was taken aback to discover that the place was packed with Shriners.

The Shriners, if you are not familiar with them, are a social organisation composed of middle-aged men of a certain disposition and mentality – the sort of men who like to engage in practical jokes and pinch the bottoms of passing waitresses. They get drunk a lot and drop water balloons out of hotel windows. Their idea of advanced wit is to stick a cupped hand under their armpit and make farting noises. You can always tell a Shriner because he's wearing a red fez and his socks don't match. Ostensibly, Shriners get together to raise money for charities. This is what they tell their wives. However, here's an interesting fact that may help you to put this claim into perspective. In 1984, according to *Harper's Magazine*, the amount of money raised by the Shriners was $17·5 million; of this sum, the amount they donated to charities was $182,000. In short, what Shriners do is get together and be assholes. So you can perhaps conceive of my disquiet at the prospect of eating dinner amid a group of fifty bald-headed men who are throwing pats of butter around the room and setting fire to one another's menus.

The hostess came over. She was chewing gum and didn't look over-friendly. 'Help you?' she said.

'I'd like a table for one, please.'

She clicked her chewing gum in an unattractive fashion. 'We're closed.'

I was taken aback once more. 'You look pretty open to me.'

'It's a private party. They've reserved the restaurant for the evening.'

I sighed. 'I'm a stranger in town. Can you tell me where else I can get something to eat?'

She grinned, clearly pleased to be able to give me some bad news. 'We're the only restaurant in Sundance,' she said. Some beaming Shriners at a nearby table watched my unfolding discomfort with simple-minded merriment. 'You might try the gas station down the street,' the lady added.

'The gas station serves food?' I responded in a tone of quiet amazement.

'No, but they've got potato chips and candy bars.'

'I don't believe this is happening,' I muttered.

'Or else you can go about a mile out of town on Highway 24 and you'll come to a Tastee-Freez drive-in.'

This was great. This was just too outstanding for words. The woman was telling me that on a Saturday night in Sundance, Wyoming, all I could have for dinner was potato chips and ice-cream.

'What about another town?' I asked.

'You can try Spearfish. That's thirty-one miles down Route 14 over the state line in South Dakota. But you won't find much there either.' She grinned again, and clicked her gum, as if proud to be living in such a turdy place.

'Well, thank you *so* much for your help,' I said with elaborate insincerity and departed.

And there you have the difference between the Midwest and the West, ladies and gentlemen. People in the Midwest are nice. In the Midwest the hostess would have felt bad about my going hungry. She would have found me a table at the back of the room or at least fixed me up with a couple of roast beef sandwiches and a slab of apple pie to take back to the motel. And the Shriners, sub-imbecilic assholes that they may be, would have been happy to make room for me at one of their tables, and probably would even have given me some pats of butter to throw. People in the Midwest are good and they are kind to strangers. But here in Sundance the milk of human kindness was exceeded in tininess only by the size of the Shriners' brains.

I trudged up the road in the direction of the Tastee-Freez. I walked for some way, out past the last of the houses and on to an empty highway that appeared to stretch off into the distance for miles, but there was no sign of a Tastee-Freez, so I turned around and trudged back into town. I intended to get the car, but then I couldn't be bothered. There was something about the way they can't even spell 'freeze' right that's always put me off these places. How much faith can you place in a company that can't even spell a monosyllable? So instead I went to the gas station and bought about six dollars' worth of potato chips and candy bars, which I took back to my room and dumped on the bed. I lay there and pushed candy bars into my face, like logs into a sawmill, and watched some plotless piece of violent Hollywood excrescence on HBO, and then slept another fitful night, lying in the dark, full and yet unsatisfied, staring at the ceiling and listening to the Shriners across the street and to the ceaseless bleating of my stomach.

And so the night passed.

I woke early and peeked shivering through a gap in the curtains. It was a drizzly Sunday dawn. Not a soul was about. This would be an excellent time to fire-bomb the restaurant. I made a mental note to pack gelignite the next time I came to Wyoming. And sandwiches. Switching on the TV, I slipped back into bed and pulled the covers up to just below my eyeballs. Jimmy Swaggart was still appealing for forgiveness. Goodness me but that man can cry. He is a human waterfall. I watched for a while, but then got up and changed the channel. On all the other channels it was just more evangelists, usually with their dumpy wives sitting at their sides. You could see why they all went out for sex. Generally, the programme would also feature the evangelist's son-in-law, a graduate of the Pat Boone school of grooming, who would sing a song with a title like 'You've Got A Friend in Jesus And Please Send Us Lots of Money'. There can be few experiences more dispiriting than to lie alone in a darkened motel room in a place like Wyoming and watch TV early on a Sunday morning.

I can remember when we didn't even have TV on Sunday mornings; that's how old I am. You would turn on WOI and all you would get was a test pattern and you would sit there and watch that because there was nothing else. Then after a while they would take off the test pattern and show *Sky King*, which was an interesting and exciting programme, at least compared to a test pattern. Nowadays they don't show test patterns at all on American TV, which is a shame because given a choice between test patterns and TV evangelists, I would unhesitatingly choose the test patterns. They were soothing in an odd way and of course they didn't ask you for money or make you listen to their son-in-law sing.

It was just after eight when I left the motel. I drove through the drizzle to Devils Tower, about twenty-five miles away. Devils Tower was the mountain used by Steven Spielberg in *Close Encounters of the Third Kind*, the one on which the aliens landed. It is so singular and extraordinary that you cannot imagine what Spielberg would have used as an alternative if it hadn't been available. You can see it long before you get to it, but as you draw nearer the scale of it becomes really quite awesome. It is a flat-topped cone of rock 850 feet high, soaring out of an otherwise featureless plain. The scientific explanation is that it was a volcanic fluke – an outsized lump of warm rock that shot out of the earth and then cooled into its present arresting shape. In the moonlight it is said to glow, though even now on a wet Sunday morning with smoky clouds brushing across its summit it looked decidedly supernatural, as if it were placed there aeons ago for the eventual use of aliens. I only hope that when they do come they don't expect to eat out.

I stopped at a lay-by near the tower and got out to look at it, squinting through the drizzle. A wooden sign beside the road said that the tower was considered sacred by the Indians and that in 1906 it became the first designated national monument in America. I stared at the tower for a long time, hypnotised both by its majesty and by a dull need for coffee, and then realised that I was getting very wet, so I returned to the car and drove on. Having gone without dinner the night before, I intended to indulge myself in that greatest of all American gustatory pleasures – going out for Sunday breakfast.

Everybody in America goes out for Sunday breakfast. It is such a popular pastime that you generally have to queue for a table, but it's always worth the wait. Indeed, the inability to achieve instant oral gratification is such an unusual experience in America that queuing actually intensifies the pleasure. You wouldn't want to do it all the time, of course, you wouldn't want to get British about it or anything, but once a week for twenty minutes is kinda neat, as they say. One reason you have to queue is that it takes the waitress about thirty minutes just to take each order. First you have to tell her whether you want your eggs sunny side up, over easy, scrambled, poached, parboiled or in an omelette, and if in an omelette whether you want it to be a plain, cheese, vegetable, hot 'n' spicy or chocolate nut 'n' fudge omelette, and then you have to decide whether you want your toast to be white, rye, whole wheat, sourdough, or pumpernickel bread and whether you want whipped butter, pat butter, or low-cholesterol butter substitute, and then there's a complicated period of negotiation in which you ask if you can have cornflakes instead of the cinnamon roll and link sausages instead of patties. So the waitress, who is only sixteen years old and not real smart, has to go off to the manager and ask him whether that's possible, and she comes back and tells you that you can't have cornflakes instead of the cinnamon roll, but you can have Idaho fries instead of the short stack of pancakes or you can have an English muffin and bacon instead of whole wheat toast, but only if you order a side of hashed browns and a large orange juice. This is unacceptable to you, and you decide that you will have waffles instead, so the waitress has to rub everything out with her nubby little eraser and start all over again. And across the room the queue on the other side of the 'Please Wait to Be Seated' board grows longer and longer, but the people don't mind because the food smells so good and anyway all this waiting is, as I say, kinda neat.

I drove along Highway 24 through a landscape of low hills, in a state of tingly anticipation. There were three little towns over the next twenty miles and I felt certain that one of them would have a roadside restaurant. I was nearly at the South Dakota state line. I was leaving the ranching country and entering more conventional farmland. Farmers cannot exist without a roadside restaurant every couple of miles, so I had no doubt that I would find one just around the next bend. One by one I passed through the little towns – Hulett, Alva, Aladdin – but there was nothing to them, just sleeping houses. No one was awake. What kind of place was this? Even on Sundays farmers are up at dawn. Beyond Beulah I passed the larger community of Belle Fourche and then St Onge and Sturgis, but still there was nothing. I couldn't even get a cup of coffee.

At last I came to Deadwood, a town that, if nothing else, lived up to its first syllable. For a few years in the 1870s, after gold was discovered in the Black Hills, Deadwood was one of the liveliest and most famous towns in the West. It was the home of Calamity Jane. Wild Bill Hickock was shot dead while playing cards in a local saloon. Today the town makes a living by taking large sums of money off tourists and giving them in return some crappy little trinket to take home and put on their mantelpiece. Almost all the stores along the main street were souvenir emporia, and several of them were open even though it was a Sunday morning. There were even a couple of coffee shops, but they were closed.

I went into the Gold Nugget Trading Post and had a look around. It was a large room selling nothing but souvenirs – moccasins, beaded Indian bags, arrowheads, nuggets of fool's gold, Indian dolls. I was the only customer. I didn't see anything to buy, so I left and went into another store a couple of doors away, The World Famous Prospectors Gift Shop, and found exactly the same stuff at identical prices and again I was the only customer. At neither place did the people running things say hello or ask me how I was doing. They would have in the Midwest. I went back out into the miserable drizzle and walked around the town looking for a place to eat, but there was nothing. So I got back in the car and drove on to Mount Rushmore, forty miles down the road.

Mount Rushmore is just outside the little town of Keystone, which is even more touristy than Deadwood, but at least there were some restaurants open. I went in one and was seated immediately, which rather threw me. The waitress gave me a menu and went off. The menu had about forty breakfasts on it. I had only read to number 17 ('Pigs in a Blanket') when the waitress returned with a pencil ready, but I was so hungry that I just decided, more or less arbitrarily, that I would have breakfast number 3. 'But can I have link sausages instead of hashed browns?' I added. She tapped her pencil against a notice on the menu. It said NO SUBSTITUTIONS. What a drag. That was the most fun part. No wonder the place was half-empty. I started to make a protest, but I fancied I could see her forming a bolus of saliva at the back of her mouth and I broke off. I just smiled and said, 'OK, never mind, thank you!' in a bright tone. 'And please don't spit in my food!' I wanted to add as she went off, but somehow I felt this would only encourage her.

Afterwards I drove to Mount Rushmore, a couple of miles outside town up a steep road. I had always wanted to see Mount Rushmore, especially after watching Cary Grant clamber over Thomas Jefferson's nose in *North by Northwest* (a film that also left me with a strange urge to strafe someone in a cornfield from a low-flying aeroplane). I was delighted to discover that Mount Rushmore was free. There was a huge terraced parking lot, though hardly any cars in it. I parked and walked up to the visitors' centre. One whole wall was glass, so that you could gaze out at the monument, high up on the neighbouring mountainside. It was shrouded in fog. I couldn't believe my bad luck. It was like peering into a steam bath. I thought I could just make out Washington, but I wasn't sure. I waited for a long time, but nothing happened. And then, just as I was about to give up and depart, the fog mercifully drifted away and there they were – Washington, Jefferson, Lincoln and Teddy Roosevelt, staring glassily out over the Black Hills.

The monument looked smaller than I had expected. Everybody says that. It's just that, positioned as you are well below and looking at it from a distance of perhaps a quarter of a mile, it looks more modest than it is. In fact, Mount Rushmore is enormous. Washington's face is sixty feet high, his eyes eleven feet wide. If they had bodies, according to a sign on the wall, the Rushmore figures would be 465 feet tall.

In an adjoining room there was an excellent and more or less continuous movie presentation giving the history of Mount Rushmore, with lots of impressive statistics about the amount of rock that was shifted, and terrific silent film footage showing the work in progress. Mostly this consisted of smiling workmen packing dynamite into the rockface, followed by a big explosion and then the dust would clear and what had been rock before was now revealed to be Abraham Lincoln. It was remarkable. The whole thing is an extraordinary achievement, one of America's glories, and surely one of the great monuments of this century.

The project took from 1927 to 1941 to complete. Just before it was finished, Gutzon Borglum, the man behind it all, died. Isn't that tragic? He did all that work for all those years and then just when they were about to crack open the champagne and put out the little sausages on toothpicks, he keeled over and expired. On a bad luck scale of 0 to 10, I would call that an 11.

I drove east across South Dakota, past Rapid City. I had intended to stop off and see Badlands National Park, but the fog and drizzle were so dense that it seemed pointless. More than that, according to the radio I was just half a step ahead of another perilous frunnal system. Snow was expected on the higher reaches of the Black Hills. Already many roads in Colorado, Wyoming and Montana were shut by fresh snowfalls, including the highway between Jackson and Yellowstone. If I had gone to Yellowstone a day later, I would now be stranded, and if I didn't keep moving, I could well be stranded for a couple of days in South Dakota. On a bad luck scale of 0 to 10 I would call that a 12.

Fifty miles beyond Rapid City is the little town of Wall, home of the most famous drugstore in the West, Wall Drug. You know it's coming because every 100 yards or so along the whole of that fifty miles you pass a big billboard telling you so: STEAKS AND CAKES—WALL DRUG, 47 MILES, HOT BEEF SANDWICHES—WALL DRUG, 36 MILES, FIVE CENT COFFEE—WALL DRUG, 25 MILES, and so on. It is the advertising equivalent of the Chinese water torture. After a while the endless drip drip drip of billboards so unstabilises your judgement that you have no choice but to leave the interstate and have a look at it.

It's an awful place, one of the world's biggest tourist traps, but I loved it and I won't have a word said against it. In 1931, a guy named Ted Hustead bought Wall Drug. Buying a drugstore in a town in South Dakota with a population of 300 people at the height of a great depression must be about as stupid a business decision as you can make. But Hustead realised that people driving across places like South Dakota were so delirious with boredom that they would stop and look at almost anything. So he put up a lot of gimmicks like a life-sized dinosaur, a 1908 Hupmobile, a stuffed buffalo, and a big pole with arrows giving the distances and directions from Wall Drug to places all over the world, like Paris and Hong Kong and Timbuctoo. Above all, he erected hundreds of billboards all along the highway between Sioux Falls and the Black Hills, and filled the store with the most exotic and comprehensive assortment of tourist crap human eyes have ever seen, and pretty soon people were pouring in. Now Wall Drug takes up most of the town and is surrounded by parking lots so enormous that you could land a jumbo jet on them. In the summer they get up to 20,000 visitors a day, though when I arrived things were decidedly more quiet and I was able to park right out front on Main Street.

I was hugely disappointed to discover that Wall Drug wasn't just an overgrown drugstore as I had always imagined. It was more a mini shopping mall, with about forty little stores selling all kinds of different things – postcards, film, Western wear, jewellery, cowboy boots, food, paintings and endless souvenirs. I bought a very nice kerosene lamp in the shape of Mount Rushmore. The wick and the glass jar that encloses it sprout directly out of George Washington's head. It was made in Japan and the four Presidents have a distinctly oriental slant to their eyes. There were many other gifts and keepsakes of this type, though none quite as beautiful or charming. Sadly, there were no baseball caps with plastic turds on the brim. Wall Drug is a family store, so that sort of thing is right out. It was a pity because this was the last souvenir place I was likely to encounter on the trip. Another dream would have to go unfulfilled.

TWENTY-EIGHT

I drove on and on across South Dakota. God, what a flat and empty state. You can't believe how remote and lonely it feels out in the endless fields of yellow grass. It is like the world's first drive-through sensory deprivation chamber. The car was still making ominous clonking noises, and the thought of breaking down out here filled me with disquiet. I was in a part of the world where you could drive hundreds of miles in any direction before you found civilisation, or at least met another person who didn't like accordion music. In a forlorn attempt to pass the time, I thumbed through my Mobil guides, leaning them against the steering wheel while drifting just a trifle wildly in and out of my lane, and added up the populations and sizes of the four states of the high plains: North and South Dakota, Montana and Wyoming. Altogether they take up 385,000 square miles – an area about the size of France, Germany, Switzerland and the Low Countries combined – but they have a total population of just 2·6 million. There are almost four times as many people in Paris alone. Isn't that interesting? Here's another interesting fact for you. The population density of Wyoming is 1·9 people per square kilometre; in South Dakota it is a little over two people per square kilometre. In Britain, there are 236·2 people per square kilometre. The number of people airborne in the United States at any given time (136,000) is greater than the combined populations of the largest cities in each of these four states. And finally, here's a really interesting fact. According to a survey by *Current Health Magazine*, the percentage of salad bar customers in the United States seen 'touching or spilling food or otherwise being unsanitary' is sixty per cent. I am of course aware that this has nothing to do with the population of the northern plains states, but I thought a brief excursion into irrelevancy was a small price to pay for information that could change your life. It certainly has changed mine.

I stopped for the night in a nothing little town called Murdo, got a room in a Motel 6 overlooking Interstate 90 and went for dinner in a

big truck stop across the highway. A highway patrol car was parked by
the restaurant door. There is always a highway patrol car parked by
the restaurant door. As you walk past it you can hear muffled
squawking on the radio. 'Attention, attention! Zero Tango Charlie! A
Boeing 747 has just crashed into the nuclear power plant on Highway
69. People are wandering around with their hair on fire. Do you read
me?' Inside, oblivious of all this, are the two highway patrolmen,
sitting at the counter eating apple pie with ice-cream and shooting the
breeze with the waitress. Every once in a great while – perhaps twice in
a day – the two patrolmen will get up from the counter and drive out to
the highway to ticket some random motorists for trying to cross the
state at seven miles an hour above the permitted limit. Then they will
go and have some more pie. That is what it is to be a highway
patrolman.

In the morning I continued on across South Dakota. It was like driving
over an infinite sheet of sandpaper. The skies were low and dark. The
radio said there was a tornado-watch in effect for the region. This
always freaks out visitors from abroad – chambermaids in hotels in
the Midwest are forever going into rooms and finding members of
Japanese trade delegations cowering under the bed because they've
heard a tornado siren – but locals pay no attention to these warnings
because after years of living in the tornado belt you just take it as part
of life. Besides, the chances of being hit by a tornado are about one in a
million.

The only person I ever knew who came close was my grandfather.
He and my grandmother (this is an absolutely true story, by the way)
were sleeping one night when they were awakened by a roaring noise
like the sound of a thousand chain-saws. The whole house shook.
Pictures fell off the walls. A clock toppled off the mantelpiece in the
living-room. My grandfather plodded over to the window and peered
out, but he couldn't see a thing, just pitch blackness, so he climbed
back into bed, remarking to my grandmother that it seemed a bit
stormy out there, and went back to sleep. What he didn't realise was
that a tornado, the most violent force in nature, had passed just
beyond his nose. He could literally have reached out and touched it –
though of course had he done so he would very probably have been
sucked up and hurled into the next county.

In the morning, he and Grandma woke up to a fine clear day. They were surprised to see trees lying everywhere. They went outside and discovered, with little murmurings of astonishment, a swath of destruction stretching across the landscape in two directions and skirting the very edge of their house. Their garage was gone, but their old Chevy was standing on the concrete base without a scratch on it. They never saw a single splinter of the garage again, though later in the day a farmer brought them their mailbox, which he had found in a field two miles away. It just had a tiny dent in it. That's the sort of thing tornadoes do. All those stories you've ever read about tornadoes driving pieces of straw through telegraph poles or picking up cows and depositing them unharmed in a field four miles away are entirely true. In south-west Iowa there is a cow that has actually had this happen to it twice. People come from miles around to see it. This alone tells you a lot about the mysteries of tornadoes. It also tells you a little something about what there is to do for fun in south-west Iowa.

In mid afternoon, just beyond Sioux Falls, I at last left South Dakota and passed into Minnesota. This was the thirty-eighth state of my trip and the last new one I would visit, though really it hardly counted because I was just skimming along its southern edge for a while. Off to the right, only a couple of miles away over the fields, was Iowa. It was wonderful to be back in the Midwest, with its rolling fields and rich black earth. After weeks in the empty west, the sudden lushness of the countryside was almost giddying. Just beyond Worthington, Minnesota, I passed back into Iowa. As if on cue, the sun emerged from the clouds. A swift band of golden light swept over the fields and made everything instantly warm and spring-like. Every farm looked tidy and fruitful. Every little town looked clean and friendly. I drove on spellbound, unable to get over how striking the landscape was. There was nothing much to it, just rolling fields, but every colour was deep and vivid: the blue sky, the white clouds, the red barns, the chocolate soil. I felt as if I had never seen it before. I had no idea Iowa could be so beautiful.

I drove to Storm Lake. Somebody once told me that Storm Lake was a nice little town, so I decided to drive in and have a look. And by golly, it was wonderful. Built around the blue lake from which it takes its name, it is a college town of 8,000 people. Maybe it was the time of year, the mild spring air, the fresh breeze, I don't know, but it seemed

just perfect. The little downtown was solid and unpretentious, full of
old brick buildings and family-owned stores. Beyond it a whole series
of broad, leafy streets, all of them lined with fine Victorian homes, ran
down to the lakefront where a park stood along the water's edge. I
stopped and parked and walked around. There were lots of churches.
The whole town was spotless. Across the street, a boy on a bike slung
newspapers on to front porches and I would almost swear that in the
distance I saw two guys in 1940s suits cross the street without
breaking stride. And somewhere at an open window, Deanna Durbin
sang.

Suddenly I didn't want the trip to be over. I couldn't stand the
thought that I would go to the car now and in an hour or two I would
crest my last hill, drive around my last bend, and be finished with
looking at America, possibly for ever. I pulled my wallet out and
peered into it. I still had almost $75. It occurred to me to drive up to
Minneapolis and take in a Minnesota Twins baseball game. Suddenly
this seemed an excellent idea. If I drove just a little bit maniacally, I
could be there in three hours – easily in time for a night game. I bought
a copy of *USA Today* from a street-corner machine and went with it
into a coffee shop. I slid into a booth and eagerly opened it to the sports
pages to see if the Twins were at home. They were not. They were in
Baltimore, a thousand miles away. I was desolate. I couldn't believe I
had been in America all this time and it hadn't occurred to me before
now, the last day of the trip, to go to a ball game. What an incredibly
stupid oversight.

My father always took us to ball games. Every summer he and my
brother and I would get in the car and drive to Chicago or Milwaukee
or St Louis for three or four days and go to movies in the afternoon and
to ball games in the evening. It was heaven. We would always go to the
ballpark hours before the game started. Because dad was a sports
writer of some standing – no, to hell with the modesty, my dad was one
of the finest sports writers in the country and widely recognised as such
– he could go into the press-box and on to the field before the game and
to his eternal credit he always took us with him. We got to stand beside
him at the batting cage while he interviewed people like Willie Mays
and Stan Musial. If you're British this means nothing to you, I know,
but believe me it was a real privilege. We got to sit in the dug-outs (they
always smelled of tobacco juice and urine; I don't know what those

guys got up to down there) and we got to go in the dressing-room and watch the players dress for the games. I've seen Ernie Banks naked. Not a lot of people can say that, even in Chicago.

The best feeling was to walk around the field knowing that kids in the stands were watching us enviously. Wearing my Little League baseball cap with its meticulously-creased brim and a pair of very sharp plastic sunglasses, I thought I was Mr Cool. And I was. I remember once at Commiskey Park in Chicago some kids calling to me from behind the first base dug-out, a few yards away. They were big city kids. They looked like they came from the Dead End Gang. I don't know where my brother was this trip, but he wasn't there. The kids said to me, 'Hey, buddy, how come you get to be down there?' and 'Hey, buddy, do me a favour, get me Nellie Fox's autograph, will ya?' But I paid no attention to them because I was . . . Too Cool.

So I was, as I say, desolate to discover that the Twins were a thousand miles away on the east coast and that I couldn't go to a game. My gaze drifted idly over the box scores from the previous day's games and I realised with a kind of dull shock that I didn't recognise a single name. It occurred to me that all these players were in junior high school when I left America. How could I go to a baseball game not knowing any of the players? The essence of baseball is knowing what's going on, knowing who's likely to do what in any given situation. Who did I think I was fooling? I was a foreigner now.

The waitress came over and put a paper mat and cutlery in front of me. 'Hi!' she said in a voice that was more shout than salutation. 'And how are you doin' today?' She sounded as if she really cared. I expect she did. Boy, are Midwestern people wonderful. She wore butterfly glasses and had a beehive hairdo.

'I'm very well, thank you,' I said. 'How are you?'

The waitress gave me a sideways look that was suspicious and yet friendly. 'Say, you don't come from around here, do ya?' she said.

I didn't know how to answer that. 'No, I'm afraid I don't,' I replied, just a trifle wistfully. 'But you know, it's so nice I sometimes kind of wish I did.'

Well, that was my trip, more or less. I visited all but ten of the lower forty-eight states and drove 13,978 miles. I saw pretty much everything I wanted to see and a good deal that I didn't. I had much to be grateful for. I didn't get shot or mugged. The car didn't break down. I wasn't once approached by a Jehovah's Witness. I still had $68 and a clean pair of underpants. Trips don't come much better than that.

I drove on into Des Moines and it looked very large and handsome in the afternoon sunshine. The golden dome of the state capitol building gleamed. Every yard was dark with trees. People were out cutting the grass or riding bikes. I could see why strangers came in off the interstate looking for hamburgers and gasoline and stayed for ever. There was just something about it that looked friendly and decent and nice. I could live here, I thought, and turned the car for home. It was the strangest thing, but for the first time in a long time I almost felt serene.

Neither Here Nor There

To Cynthia

William James describes a man who got the experience
from laughing-gas; whenever he was under its influence,
he knew the secret of the universe, but when he came to,
he had forgotten it. At last, with immense effort,
he wrote down the secret before the vision had faded.
When completely recovered, he rushed to see
what he had written. It was 'A smell of petroleum
prevails throughout'.

Bertrand Russell
A History of Western Philosophy

1. To the North

In winter Hammerfest is a thirty-hour ride by bus from Oslo, though why anyone would want to go there in winter is a question worth considering. It is on the edge of the world, the northernmost town in Europe, as far from London as London is from Tunis, a place of dark and brutal winters, where the sun sinks into the Arctic Ocean in November and does not rise again for ten weeks.

I wanted to see the Northern Lights. Also, I had long harboured a half-formed urge to experience what life was like in such a remote and forbidding place. Sitting at home in England with a glass of whisky and a book of maps, this had seemed a capital idea. But now as I picked my way through the grey, late-December slush of Oslo I was beginning to have my doubts.

Things had not started well. I had overslept at the hotel, missing breakfast, and had to leap into my clothes. I couldn't find a cab and had to drag my ludicrously overweighted bag eight blocks through slush to the central bus station. I had had huge difficulty persuading the staff at the Kreditkassen Bank on Karl Johans Gate to cash sufficient traveller's cheques to pay the extortionate 1,200-kroner bus fare – they simply could not be made to grasp that the William McGuire Bryson on my passport and the Bill Bryson on my traveller's cheques were both me – and now here I was arriving at the station two minutes before departure, breathless and steaming from the endless uphill exertion that is my life, and the girl at the ticket counter was telling me that she had no record of my reservation.

'This isn't happening,' I said. 'I'm still at home in England enjoying Christmas. Pass me a drop more port, will you, darling?' Actually, I said, 'There must be some mistake. Please look again.'

The girl studied the passenger manifest. 'No, Mr Bryson, your name is not here.'

But *I* could see it, even upside-down. 'There it is, second from the bottom.'

'No,' the girl decided, 'that says Bernt Bjornson. That's a Norwegian name.'

'It doesn't say Bernt Bjornson. It says Bill Bryson. Look at the loop of the *y*, the two *l*s. Miss, please.' But she wouldn't have it. 'If I miss this bus when does the next one go?'

'Next week at the same time.'

Oh, splendid.

'Miss, believe me, it says Bill Bryson.'

'No, it doesn't.'

'Miss, look, I've come from England. I'm carrying some medicine that could save a child's life.' She didn't buy this. 'I want to see the manager.'

'He's in Stavanger.'

'Listen, I made a reservation by telephone. If I don't get on this bus I'm going to write a letter to your manager that will cast a shadow over your career prospects for the rest of this century.' This clearly did not alarm her. Then it ocurred to me. 'If this Bernt Bjornson doesn't show up, can I have his seat?'

'Sure.'

Why don't I think of these things in the first place and save myself the anguish? 'Thank you,' I said, and lugged my bag outside.

The bus was a large double-decker, like an American Greyhound, but only the front half of the upstairs had seats and windows. The rest was solid aluminium, covered with a worryingly psychedelic painting of an intergalactic landscape, like the cover of a pulp science-fiction novel, with the words EXPRESS 2000 emblazoned across the tail of a comet. For one giddy moment I thought the windowless back end might contain a kind of dormitory and that at bedtime we would be escorted back there by a stewardess who would invite us to choose a couchette. I was prepared to pay any amount of money for this option. But I was mistaken. The back end, and all the space below us, was for freight. Express 2000 was really just a long-distance lorry with passengers.

We left at exactly noon. I quickly realised that everything about the bus was designed for discomfort. I was sitting beside the heater, so that while chill draughts teased my upper extremities, my left leg grew so hot that I could hear the hairs on it crackle. The seats were designed by a dwarf seeking revenge on full-sized people; there was no other explanation. The young man in front of me put his seat so far back that his head was all but in my lap. He was reading a comic book called *Tommy og Tigern* and he had the sort of face that makes you realise God does have a sense of humour. My own seat was raked at a peculiar angle that induced immediate and lasting neckache. It had a lever on its side, which I supposed might bring it back to a more comfortable position, but I knew from long experience that if I touched it even tentatively the seat would fly back and crush the kneecaps of the sweet little old lady sitting behind me, so I left it alone. The woman beside me, who was obviously a veteran of these polar campaigns, unloaded quantities of magazines, tissues, throat lozenges, ointments, unguents and fruit pastilles into the seat pocket in front of her, then settled beneath a blanket and slept more or less continuously through the whole trip.

We bounced through a snowy half-light, out through the sprawling suburbs of Oslo and into the countryside. The scattered villages and farmhouses looked trim and prosperous in the endless dusk. Every house had Christmas lights burning cheerily in the windows. I quickly settled into that not unpleasant state of mindlessness that tends to overcome me on long journeys, my head lolling loosely on my shoulders in the manner of someone who has lost all control of his neck muscles and doesn't really mind.

My trip had begun. I was about to see Europe again.

The first time I came to Europe was in 1972, skinny, shy, alone. In those days the only cheap flights were from New York to Luxembourg, with a refuelling stop en route at Keflavik Airport at Reykjavik. The aeroplanes were old and engagingly past their prime – oxygen masks would sometimes drop unbidden from their overhead storage compartments and dangle there until a stewardess with a hammer and a mouthful of nails came along to put things right, and the door of the lavatory tended to swing open on you if you didn't hold it shut with a foot, which brought a certain dimension of challenge to anything else you planned to do in there – and they were achingly slow. It took a week and a half to reach Keflavik, a small grey airport in the middle of a flat grey nowhere, and another week and a half to bounce on through the skies to Luxembourg.

Everyone on the plane was a hippie, except the crew and two herring-factory executives in first class. It was rather like being on a Greyhound bus on the way to a folk-singers' convention. People were forever pulling out guitars and mandolins and bottles of Thunderbird wine and forging relationships with their seatmates that were clearly going to lead to lots of energetic sex on a succession of Mediterranean beaches.

In the long, exciting weeks preceding the flight I had sustained myself, I confess, with a series of bedroom-ceiling fantasies that generally involved finding myself seated next to a panting young beauty being sent by her father against her wishes to the Lausanne Institute for Nymphomaniacal Disorders, who would turn to me somewhere over mid-Atlantic and say, 'Forgive me, but would it be all right if I sat on your face for a while?' In the event, my seatmate turned out to be an acned stringbean with Buddy Holly glasses and a line-up of ball-point pens clipped into a protective plastic case in his shirt pocket. The plastic case said GRUBER'S TRU-VALU HARDWARE, FLAGELLATION, OKLAHOMA. IF WE DON'T GOT IT, YOU DON'T NEED IT, or something like that. He had boils on his neck which looked like bullet wounds that had never quite healed and smelled oppressively of Vicks VapoRub.

He spent most of the flight reading holy scripture, moving both sets of fingertips across each line of text as he read and voicing the words just loud enough for me to hear them as a fervid whisper in my right ear. I feared the worst. I don't know why religious zealots have this compulsion to try to convert everyone who passes before them – I don't go around trying to make them into St Louis Cardinals fans, for Christ's sake – and yet they never fail to try.

Nowadays when accosted I explain to them that anyone wearing white socks with Hush Puppies and a badge saying HI! I'M GUS! probably couldn't talk me into getting out of a burning car, much less into making a lifelong commitment to a deity, and ask them to send someone more intelligent and with a better dress sense next time, but back then I was too meek to do anything but listen politely and utter non-committal 'Hmmmm's to their suggestions that Jesus could turn my life around. Somewhere over the Atlantic, as I was sitting taking stock of my 200 cubic centimetres of personal space, as one does on a long plane flight, I spied a coin under the seat in front of me, and with protracted difficulty leaned forward and snagged it. When I sat up, I saw my seatmate was at last looking at me with that ominous glow.

'Have you found Jesus?' he said suddenly.

'Uh, no, it's a quarter,' I answered and quickly settled down and pretended for the next six hours to be asleep, ignoring his whispered entreaties to let Christ build a bunkhouse in my heart.

In fact, I was secretly watching out of the window for Europe. I still remember that first sight. The plane dropped out of the clouds and there below me was this sudden magical tableau of small green fields and steepled villages spread across an undulating landscape, like a shaken-out quilt just settling back onto a bed. I had flown a lot in America and had never seen much of anything from an aeroplane window but endless golden fields on farms the size of Belgium, meandering rivers and pencil lines of black highway as straight as taut wire. It always looked vast and mostly empty. You felt that if you squinted hard enough you could see all the way to Los Angeles, even when you were over Kansas. But here the landscape had the ordered perfection of a model-railway layout. It was all so green and minutely cultivated, so compact, so tidy, so fetching, so . . . European. I was smitten. I still am.

I had brought with me a yellow backpack so enormous that when I went through customs I half expected to be asked, 'Anything to declare? Cigarettes? Alcohol? Dead horse?', and spent the day teetering beneath it through the ancient streets of Luxembourg City in a kind of vivid daze – an unfamiliar mixture of excitement and exhaustion and intense optical stimulation. Everything seemed so vivid and acutely focused and new. I felt like someone stepping out of doors for the first time. It was all so different: the language, the money, the cars, the number plates on the cars, the bread, the food, the newspapers, the parks, the people. I had never seen a zebra-crossing before, never seen a tram, never seen an unsliced loaf of bread (never even considered it an option), never seen anyone wearing a beret who expected to be taken seriously, never seen people go to a different shop for each item of dinner or provide their own shopping bags, never seen feathered pheasants and unskinned rabbits hanging in a butcher's window or a pig's head smiling on a platter, never seen a packet of Gitanes or the Michelin man. And the people – why, they were Luxembourgers. I don't know why this amazed me so, but it did. I kept thinking, That man over there, he's a Luxembourger. And so is that girl. They don't know anything about the New York Yankees, they don't know the theme tune to *The Mickey Mouse Club*, they are from another world. It was just wonderful.

In the afternoon, I bumped into my acned seatmate on the Pont Adolphe, high above the gorge that cuts through the city. He was trudging back towards the centre beneath an outsized backpack of his own. I greeted him as a friend – after all, of the 300 million people in Europe he was the only one I knew – but he had none of my fevered excitement.

'Have you got a room?' he asked gloomily.

'No.'

'Well, I can't find one anywhere. I've been looking all over. Every place is full.'

'Really?' I said, worry stealing over me like a shadow. This was potentially serious. I had never been in a position where I had to arrange for my own bed for the night – I had assumed that I would present myself at a small hotel when it suited me and that everything would be all right after that.

'Fucking city, fucking Luxembourg,' my friend said, with unexpected forthrightness, and trudged off.

I presented myself at a series of semi-squalid hotels around the central station, but they were all full. I wandered further afield, trying other hotels along the way, but without success, and in a not very long time – for Luxembourg City is as compact as it is charming – found myself on a highway out of town. Not sure how to deal with this unfolding crisis, I decided on an impulse to hitch-hike into Belgium. It was a bigger country; things might be better there. I stood for an hour and forty minutes beside the highway with my thumb out, watching with little stabs of despair as cars shot past and the sun tracked its way to the horizon. I was about to abandon this plan as well – and do what? I didn't know – when a battered Citroën 2CV pulled over.

I lugged my rucksack over to find a young couple arguing in the front seat. For a moment I thought they weren't stopping for me at all, that the man was just pulling over to slap the woman around, as I knew Europeans were wont to do from watching Jean-Paul Belmondo movies on public television, but then the woman got out, fixed me with a fiery look and allowed me to clamber into the back, where I sat with my knees around my ears amid stacks of shoeboxes.

The driver was very friendly. He spoke good English and shouted at me over the lawnmower roar of the engine that he worked as a travelling shoe salesman and his wife was a clerk in a Luxembourg bank and that they lived just over the border in Arlon. He kept turning round to rearrange things on the back seat to give me more space, throwing shoeboxes at the back windowsill, which I would have preferred him not to do because more often than not they clonked me on the head, and at the same time he was driving with one hand at seventy miles an hour in heavy traffic.

Every few seconds his wife would shriek as the back of a lorry loomed up and filled the windscreen, and he would attend to the road for perhaps two and a half seconds before returning his attention to my comfort. She constantly berated him for his driving but he acted as if this were some engaging quirk of hers, and kept throwing me mugging, conspiratorial, deeply Gallic looks, as if her squeaky bitching were a private joke between the two of us.

I have seldom been more certain that I was about to die. The man drove as if we were in an arcade game. The highway was a three-lane affair – something else I had never seen before – with one lane going east, one lane going west and a shared middle lane for overtaking from either direction. My new friend did not appear to grasp the system. He would zip into the middle lane and seem genuinely astonished to find a forty-ton truck bearing down on us like something out of a Road Runner cartoon. He would veer out of the way at the last possible instant and then hang out of the window shouting abuse at the passing driver, before being shrieked back to the next crisis by me and his wife. I later learned that Luxembourg has the highest highway fatality rate in Europe, which does not surprise me in the smallest degree.

It took half an hour to reach Arlon, a dreary industrial town. Everything about it looked grey and dusty, even the people. The man insisted that I come to their flat for dinner. Both the wife and I protested – I politely, she with undisguised loathing – but he dismissed our demurrals as yet more engaging quirks of ours and before I knew it I was being bundled up a dark staircase and shown into the tiniest and barest of flats. They had just two rooms – a cupboard-sized kitchen and an everything-else-room containing a table, two chairs, a bed and a portable record player with just two albums, one by Gene Pitney and the other by an English colliery brass band. He asked me which I would like to hear. I told him to choose.

He put on Gene Pitney, vanished into the kitchen, where his wife pelted him with whispers, and reappeared looking sheepish and bearing two tumblers and two large brown bottles of beer. 'Now this will be very nice,' he promised and poured me a glass of what turned out to be very warm lager. 'Oom,' I said, trying to sound appreciative. I wiped some froth from my lip and wondered if I could survive a dive out of an upstairs window. We sat drinking our beer and smiling at each other. I tried to think what the beer put me in mind of and finally decided it was a very large urine sample, possibly from a circus animal. 'Good, yes?' asked the Belgian.

'Oom,' I said again, but didn't lift it to my lips.

I had never been away from home before. I was on a strange continent where they didn't speak my language. I had just travelled 4,000 miles in a chest freezer with wings, I had not slept for thirty hours, or washed for twenty-nine, and here I was in a tiny, spartan apartment in an unknown town in Belgium about to eat dinner with two very strange people.

Madame Strange appeared with three plates, each bearing two fried eggs and nothing else, which she placed in front of us with a certain ringing vehemence. She and I sat at the table. Her husband perched on the edge of the bed. 'Beer and eggs,' I said. 'Interesting combination.'

Dinner lasted four seconds. 'Oom,' I said, wiping the yolk from my mouth and patting my stomach. 'That was really excellent. Thank you very much. Well, I must be going.' Madame Strange fixed me with a look that went well beyond hate, but Monsieur Strange leapt to his feet and held me affectionately by the shoulders. 'No, no, you must listen to the other side of the album and have some more beer.' He adjusted the record and we listened in silence and with small sips of beer. Afterwards he took me in his car to the centre of town, to a small hotel that may once have been grand but was now full of bare light bulbs and run by a man in an undershirt. The man led me on a long trek up flights of stairs and down hallways before abandoning me at a large bare-floored room that contained within its shadowy vastness a chair with a thin towel on its back, a chipped sink, an absurdly grand armoire and an enormous oak bed that had the warp and whiff of 150 years of urgent sex ground into it.

I dropped my pack and tumbled onto the bed, still in my shoes, then realised that the light switch to the twenty-watt bulb hovering somewhere in the murk overhead was on the other side of the room, but I was too weary to get up and turn it off, too weary to do anything but wonder briefly whether my religious-zealot acquaintance was still roomless in Luxembourg and now shivering miserably in a doorway or on a park bench, wearing an extra sweater and stuffing his jeans with pages from the *Luxembourger Zeitung* to keep out the cold.

'Hope so,' I said, and snuggled down for an eleven-hour sleep.

I spent a few days tramping through the wooded hills of the Ardennes. The backpack took some getting used to. Each morning when I donned it I would stagger around for a minute in the manner of someone who has been hit on the head with a mallet, but it made me feel incredibly fit. It was like taking a wardrobe on holiday. I don't know that I have ever felt so content or alive as in those three or four days in the south of Belgium. I was twenty years old and at large in a perfect world. The weather was kind and the countryside green and fetching and dotted with small farms where geese and chickens loitered along roadsides that seldom saw a passing car.

Every hour or two I would wander into some drowsing village where

two old men in berets would be sitting outside a café with glasses of
Bols and would silently watch me approach and pass, responding to
my cheery 'Bonjour!' with the tiniest of nods, and in the evenings
when I had found a room in a small hotel and went to the local
café to read a book and drink beer I would get those same tiny
nods again from a dozen people, which I in my enthusiasm took
as a sign of respect and acceptance. I believe I may even have
failed to notice them edging away when, emboldened by seven or
eight glasses of Jupiler pils or the memorably named Donkle Beer,
I would lean towards one of them and say in a quiet but friendly
voice, 'Je m'appelle Guillaume. J'habite Des Moines.'

And so the summer went. I wandered for four months across the
continent, through Britain and Ireland, through Scandinavia, Germany, Switzerland, Austria and Italy, lost in a private astonishment.
It was as happy a summer as I have ever spent. I enjoyed it so
much that I came home, tipped the contents of my rucksack into
an incinerator, and returned the next summer with a high-school
acquaintance named Stephen Katz, which I quickly realised was a
serious mistake.

Katz was the sort of person who would lie in a darkened hotel
room while you were trying to sleep and talk for hours in graphic,
sometimes luridly perverted, detail about what he would like to do
to various high-school nymphettes, given his druthers and some of
theirs, or announce his farts by saying, 'Here comes a good one. You
ready?' and then grade them for volume, duration and odorosity, as
he called it. The best thing that could be said about travelling abroad
with Katz was that it spared the rest of America from having to spend
the summer with him.

He soon became background noise, a person across the table who
greeted each new plate of food with 'What is *this* shit?', a hyperactive
stranger who talked about boners all the time and unaccountably
accompanied me wherever I went, and after a while I more or less
tuned him out and spent a summer that was almost as enjoyable,
and in a sense as solitary, as the one before.

Since that time, I had spent almost the whole of my adulthood,
fifteen of the last seventeen years, living in England, on the fringe

of this glorious continent, and seen almost none of it. A four-day visit to Copenhagen, three trips to Brussels, a brief swing through the Netherlands – this was all I had to show for my fifteen years as a European. It was time to put things right.

I decided at the outset to start at the North Cape, the northernmost point of the European mainland, and to make my way south to Istanbul, taking in along the way as many of the places Katz and I had visited as I could manage. My intention had been to begin the trip in the spring, but just before Christmas I made a phone call to the University of Tromsø, the northernmost university in the world and hotbed of Northern Lights research, to find out when the best time would be to see this celestial light show. The phone line was so bad that I could barely hear the kindly professor I spoke to – he appeared to be talking to me from the midst of a roaring blizzard; I imagined a door banging open and swirling snow blowing into his frail and lonely hut somewhere out in the wilds – but I did catch enough to gather that the only reliable time to come was now, in the depths of winter, before the sun rose again in late January. This was a very good year for Northern Lights, as it happened – something to do with intense solar activity – but you needed a clear sky to see them, and in northern Norway this could never be guaranteed.

'You should plan to come for at least a month,' he shouted at me.

'A month?' I said with genuine alarm.

'At least.'

A month. A month in the coldest, darkest, bleakest, remotest place in Europe. Everyone I told this to thought it was most amusing. And now here I was heading north on a bouncing bus, inescapably committed.

Not long after leaving Oslo I became aware with a sense of unease that no one on the bus was smoking. I couldn't see any NO SMOKING signs, but I wasn't going to be the first person to light up and then have everyone clucking at me in Norwegian. I was pretty certain that the man in the seat across the aisle was a smoker – he looked suitably out of sorts – and even more sure that the young man ahead of me must be. I have yet to meet a grown-up reader of comic books who does not also have an affection for tobacco and tattoos. I consulted the Express 2000 leaflet that came with each seat and read with horror the words 'tilsammen 2,000 km non-stop i 30 timer'.

Now I don't know Norwegian from alphabet soup, but even I could translate that. Two thousand kilometres! Non-stop! Thirty hours without a cigarette! Suddenly all the discomfort came flooding back. My neck ached, my left leg sizzled like bacon in a skillet, the young man ahead of me had his head closer to my crotch than any man had ever had before, I had less space to call my own than if I had climbed into my suitcase and mailed myself to Hammerfest, and now I was going to go thirty hours without an infusion of nicotine. This was just too much.

Fortunately it wasn't quite as desperate as that. At the Swedish border, some two hours after leaving Oslo, the bus stopped at a customs post in the woods, and while the driver went into the hut to sort out the paperwork most of the passengers, including me and the two I'd forecast, clattered down the steps and stood stamping our feet in the cold snow and smoking cigarettes by the fistful. Who could tell when we would get this chance again? Actually, after I returned to the bus and earned the undying enmity of the lady beside me by stepping on her foot for the second time in five minutes, I discovered from further careful study of the Express 2000 leaflet that three rest stops appeared to be built into the itinerary.

The first of these came in the evening at a roadside cafeteria in Skellefteå, Sweden. It was a strange place. On the wall at the start of the food line was an outsized menu and beside each item was a red button, which when pushed alerted the people in the kitchen to start preparing that dish. Having done this, you slid your empty tray along to the check-out, pausing to select a drink, and then waited with the cashier for twenty minutes until your food was brought out. Rather defeats the purpose of a cafeteria, don't you think? As I was the last in the line and the line was going nowhere, I went outside and smoked many cigarettes in the bitter cold and then returned. The line was only fractionally depleted, but I took a tray and regarded the menu. I had no idea what any of the foods were and as I have a dread of ever inadvertently ordering liver, which I so much detest that I am going to have to leave you here for a minute and go throw up in the wastebasket from just thinking about it, I elected to choose nothing (though I thought hard about pressing *all* the buttons just to see what would happen).

Instead I selected a bottle of Pepsi and some little pastries, but when I arrived at the check-out the cashier told me that my Norwegian money was no good, that I needed Swedish money. This surprised me. I had always thought the Nordic peoples were all pals and freely exchanged their money, as they do between Belgium and Luxembourg. Under the cashier's heartless gaze I replaced the cakes and Pepsi and took instead a free glass of iced water and went to a table. Fumbling in my jacket pocket, I discovered a Dan-Air biscuit left over from the flight from England and dined on that.

When we returned to the bus, sated on our lamb cutlets and vegetables and/or biscuit and iced water, the driver extinguished the interior lights and we had no choice but to try to sleep. It was endlessly uncomfortable. I finally discovered, after trying every possibility, that the best position was to lie down on the seat more or less upside-down with my legs dangling above me. In this manner, I fell into a deep, and surprisingly restful, sleep. Ten minutes later, Norwegian coins began slipping one by one from my pocket and dropping onto the floor behind me, where (one supposes) they were furtively scooped up by the little old lady sitting there.

And so the night passed.

We were woken early for another rest stop, this one in Where The Fuck, Finland. Actually it was called Muonio and it was the most desolate place I had ever seen: a filling station and lean-to café in the middle of a tundra plain. The good news was that the café accepted Norwegian currency; the bad news was that it had nothing that anyone outside a famine zone would want to eat. The driver and his mate were given heaped and steaming platters of eggs, potatoes and ham, but there appeared to be nothing like that on offer for the rest of us. I took a bottle of mineral water and slice of crispbread with a piece of last year's cheese on it, for which I was charged an astonishing twenty-five kroner, and retired to a corner booth. Afterwards, while the driver and his mate lingered over coffees and suppressed contented burps, the other passengers and I milled around in the shop part of the complex, looking at fan belts and snow shovels, and stood in the perishing cold out by the bus and smoked more fistfuls of cigarettes.

We hit the road again at seven-thirty. Only another whole day of this, I thought cheerfully. The landscape was inexpressibly bleak, just mile after tedious mile of snowy waste and scraggly birch forest. Reindeer grazed along the roadside and often on it itself, coming out to lick the salt scattered on the ice. We passed through a couple of Lapp villages, looking frigid and lifeless. There were no Christmas lights in the windows here. In the distance, the sun just peeked over the low hills, lingered uncertainly, and then sank back. It was the last I would see of it for three weeks.

Just after five o'clock we crossed a long, lonely toll bridge on to the island of Kvaløya, home of Hammerfest. We were now as far north as you can get in the world by public transport. Hammerfest is almost unimaginably remote – 1,000 miles north of the Shetlands, 800 miles beyond the Faroes, 150 miles north even of my lonely professor friend at the northernmost university in the world at Tromsø. I was closer now to the North Pole than to London. The thought of it roused me and I pressed my nose to the cold glass.

We approached Hammerfest from above, on a winding coast road, and when at last it pivoted into view it looked simply wonderful – a fairyland of golden lights stretching up into the hills and around an expansive bay. I had pictured it in my mind as a village – a few houses around a small harbour, a church perhaps, a general store, a bar if I was lucky – but this was a little city. A golden little city. Things were looking up.

2. Hammerfest

I took a room in the Håja Hotel near the quay. The room was small but comfortable, with a telephone, a small colour television and its own bathroom. I was highly pleased and full of those little pulses of excitement that come with finding yourself in a new place. I dumped my things, briefly investigated the amenities and went out to look at Hammerfest.

It seemed an agreeable enough town in a thank-you-God-for-not-making-me-live-here sort of way. The hotel was in a dark neighbourhood of shipping offices and warehouses. There were also a couple of banks, a very large police station, and a post office with a row of telephone kiosks in front. In each of these, I noticed as I passed, the telephone books had been set alight by some desperate thrill seeker and now hung charred from their chains.

I walked up to the main street, Strandgatan, which ran for about 300 yards along the harbour, lined on the inland side by an assortment of businesses – a bakery, a bookstore, a cinema (closed), a café called Kokken's – and on the harbour side by the town hall, a few more shops and the dark hulking mass of a Birds Eye–Findus fish-processing plant. Christmas lights were strung at intervals across the street, but all the shops were shut and there wasn't a sign of life anywhere, apart from an occasional cab speeding past as if on an urgent mission.

It was cold out, but nothing like as cold as I had expected. This pleased me because I had very nearly bought a ridiculous Russian-style fur hat – the kind with ear flaps – for 400 kroner in Oslo. Much as I hate to stand out in a crowd, I have this terrible occasional compulsion to make myself an unwitting source of merriment for the world and I had come close to scaling new heights with a Russian hat. Now, clearly, that would be unnecessary.

Beyond the high street, the road curved around the bay, leading out to a narrow headland, and after a half a mile or so it presented a fetching view back to the town, sheltering in a cleft of black mountains, as if in the palm of a giant hand. The bay itself was black and impenetrable; only the whooshing sound of water hinted at what was out there. But the town itself was wonderfully bright and snug-looking, a haven of warmth and light in the endless Arctic night.

Satisfied with this initial reconnaisance, I trudged back to the hotel, where I had a light but astonishingly expensive dinner and climbed gratefully into bed.

In the night I was woken by a storm. I crept to the window and peered out. Snow was blowing wildly, and the wind howled. Lightning lit the sky. I had never seen lightning in a snowstorm. Murmuring, 'Oh, sweet Jesus, where am I?', I climbed back into bed and buried myself deep in the covers. I don't know what time I woke, but I dozed and tossed for perhaps an hour in the dark until it occurred to me that it never was going to get light. I got up and looked out of the window. The storm was still raging. In the police-station car park below, two squad cars marked POLITI were buried in drifts almost to their roofs.

After breakfast, I ventured out into the gale. The streets were still deserted, snow piled in the doorways. The wind was playing havoc with the town. Street lights flickered and swayed, throwing spastic shadows across the snow. The Christmas decorations rattled. A cardboard box sailed across the road ahead of me and was wafted high out over the harbour. It was intensely cold. On the exposed road out to the headland I began to wish again that I had bought the Russian hat. The wind was unrelenting: it drove before it tiny particles of ice that seared my cheeks and made me gasp. I had a scarf with me, which I tied around my face bandit-style and trudged on, leaning heavily into the wind.

Ahead of me out of the swirling snow appeared a figure. He was wearing a Russian hat, I was interested to note. As he drew nearer, I pulled my scarf down to make some cheering greeting – 'Bit fresh out, what?' or something – but he passed by without even looking at me. A hundred yards further on I passed two more people, a man and his wife tramping stolidly into town, and they too passed as if I were invisible. Strange people, I thought.

The headland proved unrewarding, just a jumble of warehouses and small ship-repair yards, loomed over by groaning cranes. I was about to turn back when I noticed a sign pointing the way to something called the Meridianstøtten and decided to investigate. This took me down a lane on the seaward side of the headland. Here, wholly exposed to the pounding sea, the wind was even more ferocious. Twice it all but picked me up and carried me forward several yards. Only the toetips of my boots maintained contact with the ground. I discovered that by holding out my arms I could sail along on the flats of my feet, propelled entirely by the wind. It was the most wonderful fun. Irish windsurfing, I dubbed it. I had a great time until an unexpected burst whipped my feet from under me. I cracked my head on the ice so hard that I suddenly recalled where I put the coal-shed key the summer before. The pain of it, and the thought that another gust might heft me into the sea like the cardboard box I had seen earlier, made me abandon the sport, and I proceeded to the Meridianstøtten with prudence.

The Meridianstøtten was an obelisk on a small elevation in the middle of a graveyard of warehouses. I later learned that it was a memorial erected to celebrate the completion in 1840, on this very spot, of the first scientific measurement of the earth's circumference. (Hammerfest's other historical distinction is that it was the first town in Europe to have electric street lights.) I clambered up to the obelisk with difficulty, but the snow was blowing so thickly that I couldn't read the inscription, and I returned to town thinking I would come back again another day. I never did.

In the evening I dined in the hotel's restaurant and bar, and afterwards sat nursing Mack beers at fifty øre a sip, thinking that surely things would liven up in a minute. It was New Year's Eve, after all. But the bar was like a funeral parlour with a beverage service. A pair of mild-looking men in reindeer sweaters sat with beers, staring silently into space. After a time I realised there was another customer, alone in a dark corner. Only the glow of his cigarette revealed him in the gloom. When the waiter came to take my plate away, I asked him what there was to do for fun in Hammerfest. He thought for a moment and said, 'Have you tried setting fire to the telephone directories by the post office?'

Actually he didn't say that, because just as he was about to speak, the lone figure in the corner addressed some slurred remark to him, which I gathered was something along the lines of 'Hey, you dismal, slope-headed slab of reindeer shit, what does it take to get some service around here?' because the waiter dropped my plate back onto the table with a suddenness that made the silverware jump and went straight to the man and began furiously dragging him by his arm and shoulder from his seat and then pushing him with enormous difficulty to the door, where he finally heaved him out into the snow. When the waiter returned, looking flushed and disconcerted, I said brightly, 'I hope you don't show all your customers out like that!' but he was in no mood for pleasantries and retired sulkily to the bar, so I was unable to determine just what there was to do in Hammerfest to pass the time, other than set telephone books alight, insult the waiter and weep.

At eleven-thirty, with the bar still dead, I went out to see if there was any life anywhere. The wind had died but there was hardly anyone about. Every window in every house blazed with light, but there was no sign of revelry within. Then just before midnight, as I was about to return to the hotel, an odd thing happened. Every person came out of every house and began to set off fireworks – big industrial-sized fireworks that shrieked across the sky and exploded with a sharp bang and filled the night with colour and sparks. For half an hour, from all around the peninsula, fireworks popped and glittered over the harbour and drifted spent into the sea. And then, precisely thirty minutes after it all began, everyone went back inside and Hammerfest slept again.

The days passed. At least three times a day I went for long walks and searched the sky for the Northern Lights, and in the evenings I went out every hour to see if anything was happening yet, but it never was. Sometimes I rose in the night to look out of the window, but I never saw anything. Once or twice a day it would snow – fat, fluffy snowflakes, like the ones you see in a Perry Como Christmas special – but the rest of the time the sky was clear. Everyone told me it was perfect Northern Lights weather. 'You should have been here just before Christmas – ah, fabulous,' they would say and then assure me that tonight would almost certainly be the night. 'About eleven o'clock you go out. Then you'll see.' But it didn't happen.

When I wasn't walking or searching the sky, I sat in the bar of the hotel drinking beer or lay on my bed reading. I tried once or twice to watch television in my room. There is only one network in Norway and it is stupefyingly bad. It's not just that the programmes are dull, though in this respect they could win awards, but that the whole thing is so wondrously unpolished. Films finish and you get thirty seconds of scratchy white circles like you used to get when your home movies ran out and your dad didn't get to the projector fast enough, and then suddenly the lights come up on the day's host, looking faintly startled, as if he had been just about to do something he wouldn't want the nation to see. The host, always a handsome young man or woman with a lively sweater and sculpted hair, fills the long gaps between programmes by showing endless trailers for the rest of the evening's highlights: a documentary on mineral extraction in Narvik, a Napoleonic costume drama in which the main characters wear moustaches that are patently not their own and strut around as if they have had a fence post inserted rectally (but are trying not to let it affect their performance) and a jazz session with the Sigi Wurtmuller Rhythm Cadettes. The best that can be said for Norwegian television is that it gives you the sensation of a coma without the worry and inconvenience.

I began to feel as if a doctor had told me to go away for a complete rest ('someplace really boring, where there's nothing at all to do'). Never had I slept so long and so well. Never had I had this kind of leisure just to potter about. Suddenly I had time to do all kinds of things: unlace my boots and redo them over and over until the laces were *precisely* the same length, rearrange the contents of my wallet, deal with nose hairs, make long lists of all the things I would do if I had anything to do. Sometimes I sat on the edge of the bed with my hands on my knees and just gazed about me. Often I talked to myself. Mostly I went for long, cold walks, bleakly watching the unillumined sky, then stopped for coffee at Kokken's Café, with its steamy windows and luscious warmth.

It occurred to me that this was just like being retired. I even
began taking a small notebook with me on my walks and keeping
a pointless diary of my daily movements, just as my dad had done
when he retired. He used to walk every day to the lunch counter at
our neighbourhood supermarket and if you passed by you would see
him writing in his notebooks. After he died, we found a cupboard
full of these notebooks. Every one of them was filled with entries like
this: 'January 4. Walked to supermarket. Had two cups of decaff.
Weather mild.' Suddenly I understood what he was up to.

Little by little I began to meet people. They began to recognise me
in Kokken's and the post office and the bank and to treat me to
cautious nods of acknowledgement. I became a fixture of the hotel
bar, where I was clearly regarded as a harmless eccentric, the man
from England who came and stayed and stayed.

One day, lacking anything at all to do, I went and saw the Mayor.
I told him I was a journalist, but really I just wanted someone to talk
to. He had an undertaker's face and wore blue jeans and a blue work
shirt, which made him look unsettlingly like a prisoner on day release,
but he was a kind man. He told me at length about the problems of
the local economy and as we parted he said:

'You must come to my house one evening. I have a sixteen-
year-old daughter.' Gosh, that's jolly gracious of you, I thought,
but I'm a happily married man. 'She would like to practise her
English.'

Ah. I'd have gone, but the invitation never came. Afterwards,
I went to Kokken's and wrote in my diary, 'Interviewed Mayor.
Weather cold.'

One Sunday afternoon in the hotel I overheard a man about my
age talking to the proprietor in Norwegian but to his own children
in Home Counties English. His name was Ian Tonkin. He was an
Englishman who had married a Hammerfest girl and now taught
English at the local high school. He and his wife Peggy invited me
to their house for dinner, fed me lavishly on reindeer (delicious) and
cloudberries (mysterious but also delicious) and were kindness itself,
expressing great sympathy for my unluckiness with the Northern

Lights. 'You should have seen it just before Christmas – ah, fabulous,' they said.

Peggy told me a sad story. In 1944 the retreating Germans, in an attempt to deprive the advancing Russian Army of shelter, burned down the town. The residents were evacuated by ship to live out the rest of the war billeted with strangers. As the evacuation flotilla left the harbour, they could see their houses going up in flames. Peggy's father took the house keys from his pocket and dropped them overboard, saying with a sigh, 'Well, we shan't be needing those any more.' After the war the people returned to Hammerfest to find nothing standing but the chapel. With their bare hands and almost nothing else they built their town again, one house at a time. It may not have been much, it may have been on the edge of nowhere, but it was theirs and they loved it and I don't think I have ever admired any group of people quite so much.

From Peggy and Ian and others I met, I learned all about the town – about the parlous state of the fishing industry on which everyone depended in one way or another, about the previous year's exciting murder trial, about accusations of incompetence concerning snow removal. I began to find it engrossing. Hammerfest grew to feel like home. It seemed entirely natural to be there, and my real life in England began to feel oddly distant and dream-like.

On my sixteenth day in Hammerfest, it happened. I was returning from the headland after my morning walk and in an empty piece of sky above the town there appeared a translucent cloud of many colours – pinks and greens and blues and pale purples. It glimmered and seemed to swirl. Slowly it stretched across the sky. It had an oddly oily quality about it, like the rainbows you sometimes see in a pool of petrol. I stood transfixed.

I knew from my reading that the Northern Lights are immensely high up in the atmosphere, something like 200 miles up, but this show seemed to be suspended just above the town. There are two kinds of Northern Light – the curtains of shimmering gossamer that everyone has seen in pictures, and the rather rarer gas clouds that I was gazing at now. They are never the same twice. Sometimes they shoot wraith-like across the sky, like smoke in a wind tunnel, moving at enormous speed, and sometimes they hang like luminous drapes or glittering spears of light, and very occasionally – perhaps once or twice in a lifetime – they creep out from every point on the horizon and flow together overhead in a spectacular, silent explosion of light and colour.

In the depthless blackness of the countryside, where you may be a hundred miles from the nearest artificial light, they are capable of the most weird and unsettling optical illusions. They can seem to come out of the sky and fly at you at enormous speeds, as if trying to kill you. Apparently it's terrifying. To this day, many Lapps earnestly believe that if you show the Lights a white handkerchief or a sheet of white paper they will come and take you away.

This display was relatively small stuff, and it lasted for only a few minutes, but it was the most beautiful thing I had ever seen and it would do me until something better came along.

In the evening, something did – a display of Lights that went on for hours. They were of only one colour, that eerie luminous green you see on radar screens, but the activity was frantic. Narrow swirls of light would sweep across the great dome of sky, then hang there like vapour trails. Sometimes they flashed across the sky like falling stars and sometimes they spun languorously, reminding me of the lazy way smoke used to rise from my father's pipe when he was reading. Sometimes the Lights would flicker brightly in the west, then vanish in an instant and reappear a moment later behind me, as if teasing me. I was constantly turning and twisting to see it. You have no idea how immense the sky is until you try to monitor it all. The eerie thing was how silent it was. Such activity seemed to demand at the very least an occasional low boom or a series of static-like crackles, but there was none. All this immense energy was spent without a sound.

I was very cold – inside my boots I wore three pairs of socks but still my toes were numb and I began to worry about frostbite – but I stayed and watched for perhaps two hours, unable to pull myself away.

The next day I went to the tourist office to report my good news to Hans, the tourism director who had become something of a friend, and to reserve a seat on the following week's bus. There was no longer any need to hang around. Hans looked surprised and said, 'Didn't you know? There's no bus next week. It's going to Alta for its annual maintenance.'

I was crushed. Two more weeks in Hammerfest. What was I going to do with myself for two more weeks?

'But you're in luck,' Hans added. 'You can go today.'

I couldn't take this in. 'What?'

'The bus should have arrived yesterday but it didn't get through because of heavy snows around Kautokeino. It arrived this morning. Didn't you see it out there? They're going back again today.'

'Today? Really? When?'

He looked at his watch with the casualness of someone who has lived for years in the middle of nowhere and will be living there for years more yet. 'Oh, in about ten minutes, I should think.'

Ten minutes! I have seldom moved so quickly. I ran to the bus, begged them not to leave without me, though without any confidence that this plea was understood, ran to the hotel, threw everything into my suitcase, paid the bill, made my thanks and arrived at the bus, trailing oddments of clothes behind me, just as it was about to pull out.

The funny thing is that as we were leaving Hammerfest, just for an instant I had a sudden urge not to go. It was a nice town. I liked the people. They had been kind to me. In other circumstances, I might just have settled down and stayed. But then, I realised, such thinking was crazy. It was time to return to Oslo and the real world. Besides, I had a hat to buy.

3. Oslo

I remember on my first trip to Europe going alone to a movie in Copenhagen. In Denmark you are given a ticket for an assigned seat. I went into the cinema and discovered that my ticket directed me to sit beside the only other people in the place, a young couple locked in the sort of passionate embrace associated with dockside reunions at the end of long wars. I could no more have sat beside them than I could have asked to join in – it would have come to much the same thing – so I took a place a few discreet seats away.

People came into the cinema, consulted their tickets and filled the seats around us. By the time the film started there were about thirty of us sitting together in a tight pack in the middle of a vast and otherwise empty auditorium. Two minutes into the movie, a woman laden with shopping made her way with difficulty down my row, stopped beside my seat and told me in a stern voice, full of glottals and indignation, that I was in her place. This caused much play of flashlights among the usherettes and fretful re-examining of tickets by everyone in the vicinity until word got around that I was an American tourist and therefore unable to follow simple seating instructions and I was escorted in some shame back to my assigned place.

So we sat together and watched the movie, thirty of us crowded together like refugees in an overloaded lifeboat, rubbing shoulders and sharing small noises, and it occurred to me then that there are certain things that some nations do better than everyone else and certain things that they do far worse and I began to wonder why that should be.

Sometimes a nation's little contrivances are so singular and clever that we associate them with that country alone – double-decker buses in Britain, windmills in Holland (what an inspired addition to a flat landscape: think how they would transform Nebraska), sidewalk cafés in Paris. And yet there are some things that most countries do without difficulty that others cannot get a grasp of at all.

The French, for instance, cannot get the hang of queuing. They try and try, but it is beyond them. Wherever you go in Paris, you see orderly lines waiting at bus stops, but as soon as the bus pulls up the line instantly disintegrates into something like a fire drill at a lunatic asylum as everyone scrambles to be the first aboard, quite unaware that this defeats the whole purpose of queuing.

The British, on the other hand, do not understand certain of the fundamentals of eating, as evidenced by their instinct to consume hamburgers with a knife and fork. To my continuing amazement, many of them also turn their fork upside-down and balance the food on the back of it. I've lived in England for a decade and a half and I still have to quell an impulse to go up to strangers in pubs and restaurants and say, 'Excuse me, can I give you a tip that'll help stop those peas bouncing all over the table?'

Germans are flummoxed by humour, the Swiss have no concept of fun, the Spanish think there is nothing at all ridiculous about eating dinner at midnight, and the Italians should never, ever have been let in on the invention of the motor car.

One of the small marvels of my first trip to Europe was the discovery that the world could be so full of variety, that there were so many different ways of doing essentially identical things, like eating and drinking and buying cinema tickets. It fascinated me that Europeans could at once be so alike – that they could be so universally bookish and cerebral, and drive small cars, and live in little houses in ancient towns, and love soccer, and be relatively unmaterialistic and law-abiding, and have chilly hotel rooms and cosy and inviting places to eat and drink – and yet be so endlessly, unpredictably different from each other as well. I loved the idea that you could never be sure of anything in Europe.

I still enjoy that sense of never knowing quite what's going on. In my hotel in Oslo, where I spent four days after returning from Hammerfest, the chambermaid each morning left me a packet of something called Bio Tex Blå, a 'minipakke for ferie, hybel og weekend', according to the instructions. I spent many happy hours sniffing it and experimenting with it, uncertain whether it was for washing out clothes or gargling or cleaning the toilet bowl. In the end I decided it was for washing out clothes – it worked a treat – but for all I know for the rest of the week everywhere I went in Oslo people were saying to each other, 'You know, that man smelled like toilet-bowl cleaner.'

When I told friends in London that I was going to travel around Europe and write a book about it, they said, 'Oh, you must speak a lot of languages.'

'Why, no,' I would reply with a certain pride, 'only English,' and they would look at me as if I were crazy. But that's the glory of foreign travel, as far as I am concerned. I don't *want* to know what people are talking about. I can't think of anything that excites a greater sense of childlike wonder than to be in a country where you are ignorant of almost everything. Suddenly you are five years old again. You can't read anything, you have only the most rudimentary sense of how things work, you can't even reliably cross a street without endangering your life. Your whole existence becomes a series of interesting guesses.

I get great pleasure from watching foreign TV and trying to imagine what on earth is going on. On my first evening in Oslo, I watched a science programme in which two men in a studio stood at a lab table discussing a variety of sleek, rodent-like animals that were crawling over the surface and occasionally up the host's jacket. 'And you have sex with all these creatures, do you?' the host was saying.

'Certainly,' replied the guest. 'You have to be careful with the porcupines, of course, and the lemmings can get very neurotic and hurl themselves off cliffs if they feel you don't love them as you once did, but basically these animals make very affectionate companions, and the sex is simply out of this world.'

'Well, I think that's wonderful. Next week we'll be looking at how you can make hallucinogenic drugs with simple household chemicals from your own medicine cabinet, but now it's time for the screen to go blank for a minute and then for the lights to come up suddenly on the host of the day looking as if he was *just* about to pick his nose. See you next week.'

*

After Hammerfest, Oslo was simply wonderful. It was still cold and dusted with greyish snow, but it seemed positively tropical after Hammerfest, and I abandoned all thought of buying a furry hat. I went to the museums and for a day-long walk out around the Bygdøy peninsula, where the city's finest houses stand on the wooded hillsides, with fetching views across the icy water of the harbour to the downtown. But mostly I hung around the city centre, wandering back and forth between the railway station and the royal palace, peering in the store windows along Karl Johans Gate, the long and handsome main pedestrian street, cheered by the bright lights, mingling with the happy, healthy, relentlessly youthful Norwegians, very pleased to be alive and out of Hammerfest and in a world of daylight. When I grew cold, I sat in cafés and bars and eavesdropped on conversations that I could not understand or brought out my Thomas Cook European Timetable and studied it with a kind of humble reverence, planning the rest of my trip.

The Thomas Cook European Timetable is possibly the finest book ever produced. It is impossible to leaf through its 500 pages of densely printed timetables without wanting to dump a double armload of clothes into an old Gladstone and just take off. Every page whispers romance: 'Montreux – Zweisimmen – Spiez – Interlaken', 'Beograd – Trieste – Venezia – Verona – Milano', 'Göteborg – Laxå – (Hallsberg) – Stockholm', 'Ventimiglia – Marseille – Lyon – Paris'. Who could recite these names without experiencing a tug of excitement, without seeing in his mind's eye a steamy platform full of expectant travellers and piles of luggage standing beside a sleek, quarter-mile-long train with a list of exotic locations slotted into every carriage? Who could read the names 'Moskva – Warszawa – Berlin – Basel – Genève' and not feel a melancholy envy for all those lucky people who get to make a grand journey across a storied continent? Who could glance at such an itinerary and not want to climb aboard? Well, Sunny von Bülow for a start. But as for me, I could spend hours just poring over the tables, each one a magical thicket of times, numbers, distances, mysterious little pictograms showing crossed knives and forks, wine glasses, daggers, miners' pickaxes (whatever could *they* be for?), ferry boats and buses, and bewilderingly abstruse footnotes:

873–4   To/from Storlien – see Table 473.

977   Lapplandspillen – see Table 472. Stops to set down
only. On (7) cars run in train 421.

k   Reservation advisable.

t   Passengers may not join or alight at these stations.

x   Via Västerås on (4), (5), (6), (7).

What does it all mean? I have no idea. You could study the
Thomas Cook book for years and never truly understand its deeper
complexities. And yet these are matters that could affect one's life.
Every year there must be scores of people who end up hundreds
of miles from their destination because they failed to notice the
footnote that said, 'Non-stop to Arctic Circle after Karlskrona –
see Table 721a/b. Hot-water bottle advisable. Hard tack only after
Murmansk. Return journey via Anchorage and Mexicali. Boy oh
boy, have you fucked up this time, pal.'

Hammerfest had been a kind of over-extended limbering-up
exercise, but now I was going to get down to some serious travelling
– and by that I mean the moving-about kind of travelling. I had an
itch to roam. I wanted to wander through Europe, to see movie
posters for films that would never come to Britain, gaze wonderingly
at hoardings and shop notices full of exotic umlauts and cedillas and
No Parking-sign øs, hear pop songs that could not by even the most
charitable stretch of the imagination be a hit in any country but their
own, encounter people whose lives would never again intersect with
mine, be hopelessly unfamiliar with everything, from the workings
of a phone box to the identity of a foodstuff.

I wanted to be puzzled and charmed, to experience the endless,
beguiling variety of a continent where you can board a train and
an hour later be somewhere where the inhabitants speak a different
language, eat different foods, work different hours, live lives that
are at once so different and yet so oddly similar. I wanted to be a
tourist.

But first it was time to go home.

4. Paris

I returned to England and waited for winter to go. I spent an absurd amount of time shopping for things for the trip – a travel clock, a Swiss Army knife, a bright green and yellow rucksack, which my wife assured me would be just the thing if I decided to do any gay camping – and spent a day crawling around the attic searching for my beloved Kümmerly and Frey maps. I bought nearly the whole European set in 1972 and it was one of the few intelligent investments of my younger years. What am I saying? It was *the* intelligent investment of my younger years.

Printed in Switzerland, with all the obsessive precision and expense that that implies, each Kümmerly and Frey map covered one or two countries within its smart blue and yellow folders. Unfolded, they were vast and crisp and beautifully printed on quality paper. Best of all, the explanatory notes were in German and French only, which gave them an exotic ring that appealed to me in 1972 and appeals to me still. There is just something inherently more earnest and worldly about a traveller who carries maps with titles like 'Jugoslawien 1:1 Mio' and 'Schwarzwald 1:250 000'. It tells the world, Don't fuck with me. I'm a guy who knows his maps.

With a stack of K&Fs and the latest Thomas Cook European Timetable, I spent long, absorbed evenings trying to draw up an itinerary that was both comprehensive and achievable, and failed repeatedly on both counts. Europe isn't easy to systematise. You can't go from coast to coast. There are few topographical features that suggest a natural beginning and end, and those that do – the Alps, the Rhine, the Danube – were either physically beyond me or had been done a thousand times. And besides, it's just too big, too packed with things to see. There isn't any place that's not worth going.

In the end, I decided on a fairly random approach. I would return to Oslo to pick up the trail where I had left off and go wherever the fancy took me. Then, a week or so before I was due to fly out, I suddenly had the cold realisation that Oslo was the last place I wanted to be. It was still winter in Oslo. I had been there only two months before. A voice that seemed not to be my own said, 'Hell, Bill, go to Paris.' So I did.

The girl at my travel agency in Yorkshire, whose grasp of the geography of the world south of Leeds is a trifle hazy (I once asked her to book me a plane ticket to Brussels and she phoned back ten minutes later to say, 'Would that be the Brussels in Belgium, Mr Bryson?'), had booked me into a hotel in the 742nd arrondissement, a charmless neighbourhood somewhere on the outskirts of Calais. The hotel was opposite a spanking new sports complex, which had been built to look vaguely like a hill: it had short-cropped grass growing up its sides. Quite what the idea of this was I couldn't say, because the walls sloped so sharply that you couldn't walk on the grass or sit on it, so it had no function. Its only real purpose was to enable the architect to say, 'Look at this, everybody. I've designed a building with grass growing on it. Aren't I something?' This, as we shall see again, is the great failing of Paris architects.

The hotel was one of those sterile, modern places that always put me in mind of a BUPA advertisement, but at least it didn't have those curious timer switches that used to be a feature of hotel hallways in France. These were a revelation to me when I first arrived from America. All the light switches in the hallways were timed to switch off after ten or fifteen seconds, presumably as an economy measure. This wasn't so bad if your room was next to the elevator, but if it was very far down the hall, and hotel hallways in Paris tend to wander around like an old man with Alzheimer's, you would generally proceed the last furlong in total blackness, feeling your way along the walls with flattened palms, and invariably colliding scrotally with the corner of a nineteenth-century oak table put there, evidently, for that purpose. Occasionally your groping fingers would alight on something soft and hairy, which you would recognise after a moment as another person, and if he spoke English you could exchange tips.

You soon learned to have your key out and to sprint like billy-o for your room. But the trouble was that when eventually you re-emerged it was to total blackness once more and to a complete and – mark this – *intentional* absence of light switches, and there was nothing you could do but stumble straight-armed through the darkness, like Boris Karloff in *The Mummy*, and hope that you weren't about to blunder into a stairwell. From this I learned one very important lesson: the French do not like us.

That's OK, because of course nobody likes them much either. It so happens I had just seen a survey in a British paper in which executives had been asked to list their most despised things in the whole universe and the three top ones were, in this order: garden gnomes, fuzzy dice hanging in car windows and the French. I just loved that. Of all the things to despise – pestilence, poverty, tyrannical governments, Michael Fish – they chose garden gnomes, fuzzy dice and the French. I think that's splendid.

On my first trip to Paris I kept wondering, Why does everyone hate me so much? Fresh off the train, I went to the tourist booth at the Gare du Nord, where a severe young woman in a blue uniform looked at me as if I were infectious. 'What do *you* want?' she said, or at least seemed to say.

'I'd like a room, please,' I replied, instantly meek.

'Fill this out.' She pushed a long form at me. 'Not here. Over there.' She indicated with a flick of her head a counter for filling out forms, then turned to the next person in line and said, 'What do *you* want?' I was amazed – I came from a place where *everyone* was friendly, where even funeral directors told you to have a nice day as you left to bury your grandmother – but I soon learned that everyone in Paris was like that. You would go into a bakery and be greeted by some vast slug-like creature with a look that told you you would never be friends. In halting French you would ask for a small loaf of bread. The woman would give you a long, cold stare and then put a dead beaver on the counter.

'No, no,' you would say, hands aflutter, 'not a dead beaver. A loaf of *bread*.'

The slug-like creature would stare at you in patent disbelief, then turn to the other customers and address them in French at much too high a speed for you to follow, but the drift of which clearly was that this person here, this *American tourist*, had come in and asked for a dead beaver and she had given him a dead beaver and now he was saying that he didn't want a dead beaver at all, he wanted a loaf of bread. The other customers would look at you as if you had just tried to fart in their handbags, and you would have no choice but to slink away and console yourself with the thought that in another four days you would be in Brussels and probably able to eat again.

The other thing I have never understood about the French is why they are so ungrateful. I've always felt that, since it was us that liberated them – and let's face it, the French Army couldn't beat a girls' hockey team – they ought to give all Allied visitors to the country a book of coupons good for free drinks in Pigalle and a ride to the top of the Eiffel Tower. But they never thank you. I have had Belgians and Dutch people hug me round the knees and let me drag them down the street in gratitude to me for liberating their country, even after I have pointed out to them that I wasn't even sperm in 1945, but this is not an experience that is ever likely to happen to anyone in France.

In the evening I strolled the eighteen miles to the Île de la Cité and Notre-Dame, through the sort of neighbourhoods where swarthy men in striped Breton shirts lean against lampposts cleaning their teeth with flick knives and spit between your legs as you pass. But it was a lovely March evening, with just the faintest tang of spring in the air, and once I stumbled onto the Seine, at the Pont de Sully, I was met with perfection. There facing me was the Île St-Louis, glowing softly and floating on the river like a vision, a medieval hamlet magically preserved in the midst of a modern city. I crossed the bridge and wandered up and down its shuttered streets, half expecting to find chickens wandering in the road and peasants pushing carts loaded with plague victims, but what I found instead were tiny, swish restaurants and appealing apartments in old buildings.

Hardly anyone was about – a few dawdling customers in the restaurants, a pair of teenage lovers tonguing each other's uvulas in a doorway, a woman in a fur coat encouraging a poodle to leave un doodoo on the pavement. The windows of the upstairs apartments were pools of warm light and from the street gave tantalising glimpses of walls lined with books and sills of sprawling pot plants and decorative antiques. It must be wonderful to live on such streets on such an island and to gaze out on such a river. The very luckiest live at the western end, where the streets are busier but the windows overlook Notre-Dame. I cannot imagine tiring of that view, though I suppose in August when the streets are clogged with tour buses and a million tourists in Bermuda shorts that SHOUT, the sense of favoured ecstasy may flag.

Even now the streets around the cathedral teemed. It was eight o'clock, but the souvenir shops were still open and doing a brisk trade. I made an unhurried circuit of Notre-Dame and draped myself over a railing by the Seine to watch the bateaux-mouches slide by, trimmed with neon like floating jukeboxes. It was hopelessly romantic.

I dined modestly in a half-empty restaurant on a side street and afterwards, accompanied by small burps, wandered across the river to Shakespeare & Co., a wonderfully gloomy English-language bookstore full of cobwebs and musty smells and old forgotten novels by writers like Warwick Deeping. Plump chairs and sagging sofas were scattered about the rooms and on each of them a young person in intellectual-looking glasses was curled up reading one of the proprietor's books, evidently from cover to cover (I saw one owlish young man turn down the corner of a page and replace the book on its shelf before scowling at me and departing into the night). It all had an engagingly clubby atmosphere, but how it stays in business I have no idea. Not only was the guy on the till conspicuously underemployed – only at the most considerable of intervals did he have to stir from his own book to transact a small sale – but its location, on the banks of the Seine in the very shadow of Notre-Dame, surely must push its rent into the stratosphere.

Anywhere else in the world Shakespeare & Co. would be a souvenir emporium, selling die-cast models of the cathedral, Quasimodo ashtrays, slide strips, postcards and OO LA LA T-shirts, or else one of those high-speed cafés where the waiters dash around frantically, leave you waiting forty minutes before taking your order and then make it clear that you have twenty-five seconds to drink your coffee

and eat your rum baba and piss off, and don't even *think* about
asking for a glass of water if you don't want spit in it. How it
has managed to escape this dismal fate is a miracle to me, but it
left me in the right admiring frame of mind, as I wandered back
to my hotel through the dark streets, to think that Paris was a very
fine place indeed.

In the morning I got up early and went for a long walk through the
sleeping streets. I love to watch cities wake up, and Paris wakes up
more abruptly, more startlingly, than any place I know. One minute
you have the city to yourself: it's just you and a guy delivering
crates of bread, and a couple of droning street-cleaning machines.
(It might be worth noting here that Paris spends £58 a year a head on
street-cleaning compared with £17 a head in London, which explains
why Paris gleams and London is a toilet.) Then all at once it's frantic:
cars and buses swishing past in sudden abundance, cafés and kiosks
opening, people flying out of Metro stations like flocks of startled
birds, movement everywhere, thousands and thousands of pairs of
hurrying legs.

By half-past eight Paris is a terrible place for walking. There's
too much traffic. A blue haze of uncombusted diesel hangs over
every boulevard. I know Baron Haussmann made Paris a grand
place to look at, but the man had no concept of traffic flow.
At the Arc de Triomphe alone thirteen roads come together. Can
you imagine that? I mean to say, here you have a city with the
world's most pathologically aggressive drivers – drivers who in other
circumstances would be given injections of thorazine from syringes
the size of bicycle pumps and confined to their beds with leather
straps – and you give them an open space where they can all try to
go in any of thirteen directions at once. Is that asking for trouble
or what?

It's interesting to note that the French have had this reputation
for bad driving since long before the invention of the internal
combustion engine. Even in the eighteenth century British travellers
to Paris were remarking on what lunatic drivers the French were, on
'the astonishing speed with which the carriages and people moved
through the streets . . . It was not an uncommon sight to see a child

run over and probably killed.' I quote from *The Grand Tour* by Christopher Hibbert, a book whose great virtue is in pointing out that the peoples of Europe have for at least 300 years been living up to their stereotypes. As long ago as the sixteenth century, travellers were describing the Italians as voluble, unreliable and hopelessly corrupt, the Germans as gluttonous, the Swiss as irritatingly officious and tidy, the French as, well, insufferably French.

You also constantly keep coming up against these monumental squares and open spaces that are all but impossible to cross on foot. My wife and I went to Paris on our honeymoon and foolishly tried to cross the Place de la Concorde without first leaving our names at the embassy. Somehow she managed to get to the obelisk in the centre, but I was stranded in the midst of a circus maximus of killer automobiles, waving weakly to my dear spouse of two days and whimpering softly while hundreds and hundreds of little buff-coloured Renaults were bearing down on me with their drivers all wearing expressions like Jack Nicholson in *Batman*.

It still happens now. At the Place de la Bastille, a vast open space dominated on its north-eastern side by a glossy new structure that I supposed to be the Paris branch of the Bradford and Bingley Building Society but which proved upon closer inspection to be the new Paris opera house, I spent three-quarters of an hour trying to get from the Rue de Lyon to the Rue de St-Antoine. The problem is that the pedestrian-crossing lights have been designed with the clear purpose of leaving the foreign visitor confused, humiliated and, if all goes to plan, dead.

This is what happens: you arrive at a square to find all the traffic stopped, but the pedestrian light is red and you know that if you venture so much as a foot off the kerb all the cars will surge forward and turn you into a gooey crêpe. So you wait. After a minute, a blind person comes along and crosses the great cobbled plain without hesitating. Then a ninety-year-old lady in a motorised wheelchair trundles past and wobbles across the cobbles to the other side of the square a quarter of a mile away.

You are uncomfortably aware that all the drivers within 150 yards are sitting with moistened lips watching you expectantly, so you pretend that you don't really want to cross the street at all, that actually you've come over here to look at this interesting fin-de-siècle lamppost. After another minute 150 pre-school children are herded across by their teachers, and then the blind man returns from the other direction with two bags of shopping. Finally, the pedestrian light turns green and you step off the kerb and all the cars come charging at you. And I don't care how paranoid and irrational this sounds, but I know for a fact that the people of Paris want me dead.

Eventually I gave up trying to cross streets in any kind of methodical way and instead just followed whatever route looked least threatening. So it was with some difficulty and not a little surprise that I managed to pick my way by early afternoon to the Louvre, where I found a long immobile queue curled around the entrance courtyard like an abandoned garden hose.

I hovered, undecided whether to join the queue, come back later in the faint hope that it would have shrunk, or act like a Frenchman and jump it. The French were remarkably shameless about this. Every few minutes one would approach the front of the queue, affect to look at his wristwatch and then duck under the barrier and disappear through the door with the people at the front. No one protested, which surprised me. In New York, from where many of these people came, judging by their accents and the bullet holes in their trench coats, the queue jumpers would have been seized by the crowd and had their limbs torn from their sockets. I actually saw this happen to a man once at Shea Stadium. It was ugly, but you couldn't help but cheer. Even in London the miscreants would have received a vicious rebuke – 'I say, kindly take your place at the back of the queue, there's a good fellow' – but here there was not a peep of protest.

I couldn't bring myself to jump the queue, but equally I couldn't stand among so much motionless humanity while others were flouting the rule of order and getting away with it. So I passed on, and was rather relieved. The last time I went to the Louvre, in 1973 with Katz, it was swarming with visitors and impossible to see anything. The 'Mona Lisa' was like a postage stamp viewed through a crowd of heads from another building and clearly things had not improved since then.

Besides, there was only one painting I especially wanted to see and that was a remarkable eighteenth-century work, evidently unnoticed by any visitor but me for 200 years among the Louvre's endless corridors. I almost walked past it myself but something about it nicked the edge of my gaze and made me turn. It was a painting of two aristocratic ladies, young and not terribly attractive, standing side by side and wearing nothing at all but their jewels and sly smiles. And here's the thing: one of them had her finger plugged casually – one might almost say absent-mindedly – into the other's fundament. I can say with some certainty that this was an activity quite unknown in Iowa, even among the wealthy and well-travelled, and I went straight off to find Katz, who had cried in dismay fifteen minutes after entering the Louvre, 'There's nothing but pictures and shit in this place,' and departed moodily for the coffee shop, saying he would wait there for me for thirty minutes and no more. I found him sitting with a Coke, complaining bitterly that he had had to pay two francs for it *and* give a handful of centimes to an old crone for the privilege of peeing in the men's room (*'and* she watched me the whole time').

'Never mind about that,' I said. 'You've got to come and see this painting.'

'What for?'

'It's very special.'

'Why?'

'It just is, believe me. You'll be thanking me in a minute.'

'What's so special about it?'

I told him. He refused to believe it. No such picture had ever been painted, and if it had been painted it wouldn't be hanging in a public gallery. But he came. And the thing is, I couldn't for the life of me find it. Katz was convinced it was just a cruel joke, designed to waste his time and deprive him of the last two ounces of his Coke, and he spent the rest of the day in a tetchy frame of mind.

Katz was in a tetchy frame of mind throughout most of our stay in Paris. He was convinced everything was out to get him. On the morning of our second day, we were strolling down the Champs-Elysées when a bird shit on his head. 'Did you know a bird's shit on your head?' I asked a block or two later.

Instinctively Katz put a hand to his head, looked at it in horror –
he was always something of a sissy where excrement was concerned;
I once saw him running through Greenwood Park in Des Moines
like the figure in Edvard Munch's 'The Scream' just because he had
inadvertently probed some dog shit with the tip of his finger – and
with only a mumbled 'Wait here' walked with ramrod stiffness in
the direction of our hotel. When he reappeared twenty minutes
later he smelled overpoweringly of Brut aftershave and his hair was
plastered down like a third-rate Spanish gigolo's, but he appeared to
have regained his composure. 'I'm ready now,' he announced.

Almost immediately another bird shit on his head. Only this time
it *really* shit. I don't want to get too graphic, in case you're snacking
or anything, but if you can imagine a pot of yogurt upended onto
his scalp, I think you'll get the picture. 'Gosh, Steve, that was one
sick bird,' I observed helpfully.

Katz was literally speechless. Without a word he turned and walked
stiffly back to the hotel, ignoring the turning heads of passers-by. He
was gone for nearly an hour. When at last he returned, he was wearing
a windcheater with the hood up. 'Just don't say a word,' he warned
me and strode past. He never really warmed to Paris after that.

With the Louvre packed I went instead to the new – new to me, at
any rate – Musée d'Orsay, on the Left Bank opposite the Tuileries.
When I had last passed it, sixteen years before, it had been a derelict
hulk, the shell of the old Gare d'Orsay, but some person of vision
had decided to restore the old station as a museum and it is simply
wonderful, both as a building and as a collection of pictures. I spent
two happy hours there, and afterwards checked out the situation at
the Louvre – still hopelessly crowded – and instead went to the
Pompidou Centre, which I was determined to try to like, but I
couldn't. Everything about it seemed wrong. For one thing it was
a bit weathered and faded, like a child's toy that has been left out
over winter, which surprised me because it is only a dozen years old
and the government had just spent £40 million refurbishing it, but I
guess that's what you get when you build with plastic. And it seemed
much too overbearing a structure for its cramped neighbourhood. It
would be an altogether different building in a park.

But what I really dislike about buildings like the Pompidou Centre, and Paris is choking on them, is that they are just showing off. Here's Richard Rogers saying to the world, 'Look, I put all the pipes on the *outside*. Am I cute enough to kiss?' I could excuse that if some consideration were given to function. No one seems to have thought what the Pompidou Centre should do — that it should be a gathering place, a haven, because inside it's just crowded and confusing. It has none of the sense of space and light and majestic calm of the Musée d'Orsay. It's like a department store on the first day of a big sale. There's hardly any place to sit and no focal point — no big clock or anything — at which to meet someone. It has no heart.

Outside it's no better. The main plaza on the Rue St-Martin is in the shade during the best part of the day and is built on a slope, so it's dark and the rain never dries and again there's no place to sit. If they had made the slope into a kind of amphitheatre, people could sit on the steps, but now if you sit down you feel as if you are going to slide to the bottom.

I have nothing against novelty in buildings — I am quite taken with the glass pyramid at the Louvre and those buildings at La Défense that have the huge holes in the middle — but I just hate the way architects and city planners and everyone else responsible for urban life seems to have lost sight of what cities are for. They are for people. That seems obvious enough, but for half a century we have been building cities that are for almost anything else: for cars, for businesses, for developers, for people with money and bold visions who refuse to see cities from ground level, as places in which people must live and function and get around. Why should I have to walk through a damp tunnel and negotiate two sets of stairs to get across a busy street? Why should cars be given priority over me? How can we be so rich and so stupid at the same time? It is the curse of our century — too much money, too little sense — and the Pompidou seems to me a kind of celebration of that in plastic.

One evening I walked over to the Place de la République and had a nostalgic dinner at a bistro called Le Thermomètre. My wife and I spent our honeymoon in the Hotel Moderne across the way (now a Holiday Inn, alas, alas) and dined nightly at the Thermomètre because it was cheap and we had next to no money. I had spent the whole of my savings, some £18, on a suit for the wedding – a remarkable piece of apparel with lapels that had been modelled on the tail fins of a 1957 Coupe de Ville and trousers so copiously flared that when I walked you didn't see my legs move – and had to borrow £12 spending money from my father-in-law in order, as I pointed out, to keep his daughter from starving during her first week of married life.

I expected the Thermomètre to be full of happy memories, but I couldn't remember anything about it at all, except that it had the fiercest toilet attendant in Paris, a woman who looked like a Russian wrestler – a male Russian wrestler – and who sat at a table in the basement with a pink dish full of small coins and craned her head to watch you while you had a pee to make sure you didn't dribble on the tiles or pocket any of the urinal cakes. It is hard enough to pee when you are aware that someone's eyes are on you, but when you fear that at any moment you will be felled by a rabbit chop to the kidneys for taking too much time, you seize up altogether. My urine turned solid. You couldn't have cleared my system with Draino. So eventually I would hoist up my zip and return unrelieved to the table, and spend the night doing a series of Niagara Falls impressions back at the hotel. The toilet attendant, I'm pleased to say, was no longer there. There was no toilet attendant at all these days. No urinal cakes either, come to that.

It took me two or three days to notice it, but the people of Paris have become polite over the last twenty years. They don't exactly rush up and embrace you and thank you for winning the war for them, but they have certainly become more patient and accommodating. The cab drivers are still complete jerks, but everyone else – shopkeepers, waiters, the police – seemed almost friendly. I even saw a waiter smile once. And somebody held open a door for me instead of letting it bang in my face.

It began to unsettle me. Then on my last night, as I was strolling near the Seine, a well-dressed family of two adults and two teenage children swept past me on the narrow pavement and without breaking stride or interrupting their animated conversation flicked me into the gutter. I could have hugged them.

On the morning of my departure I trudged through a grey rain to the Gare de Lyon to get a cab to the Gare du Nord and a train to Brussels. Because of the rain, there were no cabs so I stood and waited. For five minutes I was the only person there, but gradually other people came along and took places behind me.

When at last a cab arrived and pulled up directly in front of me, I was astonished to discover that seventeen grown men and women believed they had a perfect right to try to get in ahead of me. A middle-aged man in a cashmere coat who was obviously wealthy and well-educated actually laid hands on me. I maintained possession by making a series of aggrieved Gallic honking noises – 'Mais non! Mais non!' – and using my bulk to block the door. I leaped in, resisting the chance to catch the pushy man's tie in the door and let him trot along with us to the Gare du Nord, and just told the driver to get me the hell out of there. He looked at me as if I were a large, imperfectly formed piece of shit, and with a disgusted sigh engaged first gear. I was glad to see some things never change.

5. Brussels

I got off at the wrong station in Brussels, which is easy to do if you are a little bit stupid and you have been dozing and you awake with a start to see a platform sign outside the window that says BRUXELLES. I leaped up in a mild panic and hastened to the exit, knocking passengers on the head with my rucksack as I passed, and sprang Peter Pan-like onto the platform just as the train threw a steamy *whoosh!* at my legs and pulled out.

It didn't strike me as odd that I was the only passenger to alight at the station, or that the station itself was eerily deserted, until I stepped outside, into that gritty drizzle that hangs perpetually over Brussels, and realised I was in a part of the city I had never seen before: one of those anonymous neighbourhoods where the buildings are grey and every end wall has a three-storey advertisement painted on it and the shops sell things like swimming-pool pumps and signs that say NO PARKING − GARAGE IN CONSTANT USE. I had wanted Bruxelles Centrale and would have settled for the Gare du Nord or the Gare du Midi or even the obscure Gare Josaphat, but this was none of these, and I had no idea where I was. I set my face in a dogged expression and trudged towards what I thought might be the downtown − a hint of tall buildings on a distant, drizzly horizon.

I had been to Brussels a couple of times before and thought I knew the city reasonably well, so I kept telling myself that any minute I would start to recognise things, and sometimes I even said, 'Say, that looks kind of familiar,' and would trudge a quarter of a mile to what I thought might be the back of the Palais de Justice but which proved in the event to be a dog-food factory. I walked and walked down long streets that never changed character or even acquired any, just endless blocks of grey sameness, which Brussels seems to possess in greater abundance than almost anywhere else in Europe.

I hate asking directions. I am always afraid that the person I approach will step back and say, 'You want to go *where*? The centre of Brussels? Boy, are you lost. This is *Lille*, you dumb shit,' then stop other passers-by and say, 'You wanna hear something classic? Buddy, tell these people where you think you are,' and that I'll have to push my way through a crowd of people who are falling about and wiping tears of mirth from their eyes. So I trudged on. Just when I reached the point where I was beginning to think seriously about phoning my wife and asking her to come and find me ('And listen, honey, bring some Yorkies and the Sunday papers'), I turned a corner and there to my considerable surprise was the Manneken-Pis, the chubby little statue of a naked boy having a pee, the inexpressibly naff symbol of the city, and suddenly I knew where I was and all my little problems melted. I celebrated by buying a Manneken-Pis cake plate and a family-sized Toblerone at one of the 350 souvenir shops that line the street, and felt better still.

Fifteen minutes later, I was in a room at the Hotel Adolphe Sax, lying on the bed with my shoes on (disintegrating into a hermitic slobbiness is one of the incidental pleasures of solitary travel), breaking my teeth on the Toblerone (who invented those things?) and watching some daytime offering on BBC 1 – a panel discussion involving people who were impotent or from Wolverhampton or suffering some other personal catastrophe, the precise nature of which eludes me now – and in half an hour was feeling sufficiently refreshed to venture out into Brussels.

I always stay in the Sax because it gets BBC 1 on the TV and because the lifts are so interesting, a consideration that I was reminded of now as I stood in the corridor beside an illuminated Down button, passing the time, as one does, by humming the Waiting for the Elevator Song ('Doo dee doo dee doo dee doo doo') and wondering idly why hotel hallway carpet is always *so* ugly.

Generally speaking, they don't understand elevators in Europe. Even in the newer buildings the elevators are almost always painfully slow and often lack certain features that are elsewhere considered essential, like an inside door, so that if you absent-mindedly lean forward you are likely to end up with one arm twenty-seven feet longer than the other. But even by these standards the lifts at the Sax are exceptional.

You get in intending to go downstairs for breakfast, but find that the lift descends without instructions past the lobby, past the underground garage and basement and down to an unmarked sub-basement where the doors open briefly to reveal a hall full of steam and toiling coolies. As you fiddle uselessly with the buttons (which are obviously not connected to anything), the doors clang shut and, with a sudden burst of vigour, the elevator shoots upwards to the eleventh floor at a speed that makes your face feel as if it is melting, pauses for a tantalising half-second, drops ten feet, pauses again and then freefalls to the lobby. You emerge, blood trickling from your ears, and walk with as much dignity as you can muster into the dining-room.

So you can perhaps conceive my relief at finding now that the lift conveyed me to my destination without incident apart from an unscheduled stop at the second floor and a brief, but not unpleasant, return trip to the fourth.

Brussels, it must be said, is not the greatest of cities for venturing. After Paris, it was a relief just to cross a street without feeling as if I had a bull's-eye painted on my butt, but once you've done a couple of circuits of the Grand-Place and looked politely in the windows of one or two of the many thousands of shops selling chocolates or lace (and they appear to sell nothing else in Brussels), you begin to find yourself glancing at your watch and wondering if nine-forty-seven in the morning is too early to start drinking.

I settled instead for another circuit of the Grand-Place. It is fetching, no doubt about it. It is the centrepiece of the city, a nicely proportioned cobbled square surrounded by grand and ornate buildings: the truly monumental Hôtel de Ville and opposite it the only slightly less grand Maison du Roi (which despite its name has never been a royal palace – don't say you never learned anything from me), all of them linked by narrow, ornately decorated guild houses. The ground floors of these guild houses almost all contain dark, cosy cafés, full of wooden furniture and crackling fires, where you can sit over a coffee or beer and gaze out on this most beguiling of backdrops. Many people seem to spend whole days doing little else.

I opted for De Gulden Boot, even though on a previous visit I had been shamelessly short-changed there by a waiter who mistook me for a common tourist just because I was wearing a Manneken-Pis tracksuit, and I had to put on my severest Don't-fuck-with-me-Gaston look in order to get my full complement of change. But I don't bear grudges, except against Richard Nixon, and didn't hesitate to go in there now. Besides, it's the nicest café on the square and I believe that a little elegance with a cup of coffee is worth paying for. But watch your change, ladies.

I spent two and a half days seeing the sights – the grand and splendid Musée d'Art Ancien, the Musée d'Art Moderne, the two historical museums in the ponderously named Parc du Cinquantenaire (the museums were a bit ponderous, too), the Musée Horta, and even the gloomy and wholly forgotten Institut des Sciences Naturelles – and in between times just shuffled around among the endless office complexes in a pleasantly vacant state of mind.

Brussels is a seriously ugly place, full of wet litter, boulevards like freeways and muddy building sites. It is a city of grey offices and faceless office workers, the briefcase capital of Europe. It has fewer parks than any city I can think of, and almost no other features to commend it – no castle on a hill, no mountainous cathedral, no street of singularly elegant shops, no backdrop of snowy peaks, no fairy-lighted seafront. It doesn't even have a river. How can a city not at least have a river? They did once have some city walls, but all that remains is a crumbly fragment stuck next door to a bowling alley on the Rue des Alexiens. The best thing that can be said for Brussels is that it is only three hours from Paris. If I were in charge of the EEC, and frankly you could do worse, my first move would be to transfer the capital to Dublin or Glasgow or possibly Naples, where the jobs would be appreciated and where the people still have some pride in their city, because in Brussels, alas, they simply haven't.

It would be hard to think of a place that has shown less regard for its heritage. Example: Brussels was home for thirty-five years to the father of art nouveau architecture, Victor Horta, who was so celebrated in his lifetime that they made him a baron – he was to Brussels what Mackintosh was to Glasgow and Gaudi to Barcelona – but even so the sluggardly city authorities over the years allowed developers to demolish almost all his finest buildings: the Anspach

Department Store, the Maison du Peuple, the Brugmann Hospital, the Roger house. Now there is remarkably little in Brussels worth looking at. You can walk for hours and not see a single sight to lift the heart.

I am assured that things are getting better. It used to be that when you emerged from the central station your first view was looking downhill across the roofs of the old town, and in the very centre of this potentially arresting setting, in the sort of open space into which other cities would have inserted a golden cathedral or baroque town hall, sat a parking lot and gas station. Now both of those have been torn down and some new brick buildings – not brilliant architecturally, but certainly an improvement on the gas station – have been erected in their place, and I was assured again and again by locals that the city government has at last recognised its slack attitude towards development and begun to insist on buildings of some architectural distinction, but the evidence of this so far is rather less than overwhelming.

The one corner of charm in the city is a warren of narrow, pedestrian-only streets behind the Grand-Place called, with a mildly pathetic dash of hyperbole, the Sacred Isle. Here the little lanes and passageways are packed with restaurants and crowds of people wandering around in the happy state of deciding where to eat, nosing around the iced barrows of lobsters, mussels and crayfish that stand outside each establishment. Every doorway issues a warm draught of grilled aromas and every window reveals crowds of people enjoying themselves at almost any hour of the day or night. It is remorselessly picturesque and appealing, and it has been like this since the Middle Ages, and yet even this lovable, clubby little neighbourhood came within an ace of being bulldozed in the 1960s. Wherever you go in Europe, you find yourself wondering what sort of brain-wasting disease it was that affected developers and architects in the 1960s and 70s, but nowhere is this sensation stronger than in Brussels.

Yet Brussels has its virtues. It's the friendliest big city in Europe (which may or may not have something to do with the fact that a quarter of its residents come from abroad), it has a couple of good museums, the oldest shopping arcade in Europe, the small but pleasurable Galeries St-Hubert, lots of terrific bars and the most wonderful restaurants. Eating out is the national sport in Belgium, and Brussels alone has 1,500 restaurants, twenty-three of them carrying Michelin rosettes. You can eat incredibly well there for less than almost anywhere else on the continent. I dined in the Sacred Isle every night, always trying a new restaurant and always achieving the gustatory equivalent of a multiple orgasm. The restaurants are almost always tiny – to reach a table at the back you have to all but climb over half a dozen diners – and the tables are squeezed so tightly together that you cannot cut your steak without poking your neighbour in the cheek with an elbow or dragging your sleeve through his sauce Béarnaise, but in an odd way that's part of the enjoyment. You find that you are effectively dining with the people next to you, sharing bread rolls and little pleasantries. This is a novel pleasure for the lone traveller, who usually gets put at the darkest table, next to the gents, and spends his meal watching a procession of strangers pulling up their flies and giving their hands a shake as they pass.

After dinner each night I would go for a necessarily aimless stroll – there is nothing much to aim for – but, like most cities, Brussels is always better at night. I walked one evening up to the massive Palais de Justice, which broods on a small eminence overlooking the old town and looks like an American state capitol building that has been taking steroids. It is absolutely enormous – it covers 280,000 square feet and was the largest building constructed anywhere in the world in the nineteenth century – but the only truly memorable thing about it is its bulk. Another evening, I walked out to the headquarters of the EEC. In a city of buildings so ugly they take your breath away, the headquarters of the EEC at Rond Point Schuman manages to stand out. It was only six o'clock, but there wasn't a soul about, not a single person working late, which made me think of the old joke: Question: How many people work in the European Commission? Answer: About a third of them. You cannot look at all those long rows of windows without wondering what on earth goes on in there. I suppose there are whole wings devoted to making sure that post-office queues are of a uniform length throughout the community and that a soft-drinks machine in France dispenses the same proportion of upside-down cups as one in Italy.

As an American, it's interesting to watch the richest countries in Europe enthusiastically ceding their sovereignty to a body that appears to be out of control and answerable to no one. Did you know that because of its Byzantine structure, the European Commission does not even know 'how many staff members it has or what they all do'? (I quote from *The Economist*.) I find this worrying. For my part I decided to dislike the EEC when I discovered that they were taking away those smart hardback navy blue British passports and replacing them with flimsy red books that look like the identity papers of a Polish seaman. This is always the problem with large institutions. They have no style.

I don't know much about how the EEC works, but I do know one interesting fact that I think gives some perspective to its achievements: in 1972 the European Conference on Post and Telecommunications called for a common international telephone code for Common Market nations, namely oo. Since then the various member states have been trying to reach agreement. So far not one of them has adopted the code, but give them another eighteen years and things may start to happen.

6. Belgium

I spent a couple of pleasantly pointless days wandering around Belgium by train. As countries go, Belgium is a curiosity. It's not one nation at all, but two, northern Dutch-speaking Flanders and southern French-speaking Wallonia. The southern half possesses the most outstanding scenery, the prettiest villages, the best gastronomy and, withal, a Gallic knack for living well, while the north has the finest cities, the most outstanding museums and churches, the ports, the coastal resorts, the bulk of the population and most of the money.

The Flemings can't stand the Walloons and the Walloons can't stand the Flemings, but when you talk to them a little you realise that what holds them together is an even deeper disdain for the French and the Dutch. I once walked around Antwerp for a day with a Dutch-speaking local and on every corner he would indicate to me with sliding eyes some innocent-looking couple and mutter disgustedly under his breath, 'Dutch.' He was astonished that I couldn't tell the difference between a Dutch person and a Fleming.

When pressed on their objections, the Flemings become a trifle vague. The most common complaint I heard was that the Dutch drop in unannounced at mealtimes and never bring gifts. 'Ah, like our own dear Scots,' I would say.

I learned much of this in Antwerp, where I stopped for an afternoon to see the cathedral and stayed on into the evening wandering among the many bars, which must be about the finest and most numerous in Europe: small, smoky places, as snug as Nigel Lawson's waistcoat, full of dark panelling and dim yellowy light and always crowded with bright, happy-looking people having a good time. It is an easy city in which to strike up conversations because the people are so open and their English is nearly always perfect. I talked for an hour to two young street sweepers who had stopped for a drink on their

way home. Where else but northern Europe could an outsider talk
to street sweepers in his own tongue?

It struck me again and again how much they know about us and how
little we know about them. You could read the English newspapers
for months, and the American newspapers for ever, and never see a
single article about Belgium, and yet interesting things happen there.

Consider the Gang of Nijvel. This was a terrorist group which for
a short period in the mid-1980s roamed the country (to the extent
that it is possible to roam in Belgium) and from time to time would
burst into supermarkets or crowded restaurants and spray the room
with gunfire, killing at random – women, children, anyone who
happened to be in the way. Having left bodies everywhere, the
gang would take a relatively small sum of money from the tills and
disappear into the night. The strange thing is this: the gang never
revealed its motives, never took hostages, never stole more than a
few hundred pounds. It didn't even have a name that anyone knew.
The Gang of Nijvel label was pinned on it by the press because its
getaway cars were always Volkswagen GTi's stolen from somewhere
in the Brussels suburb of Nijvel. After about six months the attacks
abruptly stopped and have never been resumed. The gunmen were
not caught, their weapons were never found, the police haven't the
faintest idea who they were or what they wanted. Now is that strange
or what? And yet you probably never read about it in your paper. I
think that's pretty strange or what, too.

I went to Bruges for a day. It's only thirty miles from Brussels and
so beautiful, so deeply, endlessly gorgeous, that it's hard to believe
it could be in the same country. Everything about it is perfect –
its cobbled streets, its placid bottle-green canals, its steep-roofed
medieval houses, its market squares, its slumbering parks, everything.
No city has been better favoured by decline. For 200 years Bruges – I
don't know why we persist in calling it this because to the locals it's
spelled Brugge and pronounced 'Brooguh' – was the most prosperous
city in Europe, but the silting-up of the River Zwyn and changing
political circumstances made it literally a backwater, and for 500
years, while other cities grew and were endlessly transformed, Bruges
remained forgotten and untouched. When Wordsworth visited in the

nineteenth century he found grass growing in the streets. Antwerp, I've been told, was more beautiful still, even as late as the turn of this century, but developers moved in and pulled down everything they could get their hands on, which was pretty much everything. Bruges was saved by its obscurity.

It is a rare place. I walked for a day with my mouth open. I looked in at the Groeninge Museum and visited the beguinage, its courtyard lawns swimming in daffodils, but mostly I just walked the streets, agog at such a concentration of perfection. Even the size of the place was perfect – big enough to be a city, to have bookstores and interesting restaurants, but compact enough to feel contained and friendly. You could walk every street within its encircling canal in a day or so. I did just that and never once saw a street I wouldn't want to live on, a pub I wouldn't like to get to know, a view I wouldn't wish to call my own. It was hard to accept that it was real – that people came home to these houses every night and shopped in these shops and walked their dogs on these streets and went through life thinking that this is the way of the world. They must go into a deep reverberating shock when they first see Brussels.

An insurance claims adjuster I got talking to in a bar on St Jacobstraat told me sadly that Bruges had become insufferable for eight months of the year because of the tourists, and related to me what he clearly thought were disturbing anecdotes about visitors peeking through his letterbox and crushing his geraniums in the pursuit of snapshots. But I didn't listen to him, partly because he was the most boring fart in the bar – possibly in Flanders – and partly because I just didn't care to hear it. I wanted my illusions intact.

For that reason I left early in the morning, before any tour buses could arrive. I went to Dinant, a riverside town on the banks of the stately Meuse, crouched on this day beneath a steady rain. It was an attractive place and I would doubtless have been highly pleased with it if I hadn't just come from Bruges and if the weather hadn't been so dreadful. I stood on the bridge across the river and watched raindrops the size of bullets beat circles in the water. My intention had been to hike through the southern Ardennes for a couple of days to see if I could recognise any of the little villages and roads I had walked around on my first trip, but I hadn't packed for this kind of weather – I was already soaked through and shivering as if I had forgotten to take my malaria tablets – and instead, after only an hour in Dinant, I walked back to the station, caught the first train to Namur and travelled on to Spa. One of the virtues of Belgium is that its tininess allows you to be anywhere else within an hour or two. It takes a while to get used to the idea that the whole country is effectively a suburb of Brussels.

I had no particular reason to go to Spa, except that it always sounded to me like a nice place, and indeed it proved to be, set in a bowl of green hills, with a wooded park, the Parc de Sept Heures, a grand casino out of all proportion to the modest town and a pair of big white hotels standing around a little island of green called the Place Verte. I liked it immediately. The rain had stopped and left the town with a clean, fresh feel, vaguely reminiscent of sheets lifted warm from a tumble dryer, and it had an eerily timeless air of convalescence about it. I half expected to see limbless soldiers in brown uniforms being pushed through the park in wheelchairs.

Spa is the original spa town, the one from which all the others take their name, and for 200 years it was the haunt of Europe's royalty. Even up to the First World War it catered to aristocrats and grandees. It was from Spa that Kaiser Wilhelm abdicated, a milestone that marked its decline as much as his own. Today it didn't seem to cater to anyone much, at least not at this time of year. I went to the tourist information centre in the park and, after browsing politely at the displays, asked the man behind the counter where all the kings and queens were.

'Ah, they do not come any more,' he said with a sad smile. 'Not so much since Peter the Great.'

'Why not?'

He shrugged. 'Fashions change. Now they want the sunshine, the sea. We still get the odd baron, but mostly it is wealthy Germans. There are many treatments available if you are interested.' He waved a hand over a selection of brochures and went off to help a new caller.

The brochures were all for places with no-nonsense names like The Professor Henrijean Hydrology Institute and The Spa Therm Institution's Department of Radiology and Gastro-Enterology. Between them they offered an array of treatments that ran from immersion in 'natural carbogazeous baths' and slathering in hot and gooey mudpacks, to being connected to a free-standing electrical sub-station and briskly electrocuted, or so it looked from the photograph. These treatments were guaranteed to do a number of things I didn't realise it was desirable to do – 'dilate the dermal vessels', 'further the repose of the thermoregulatory centres' and 'ease periarticular contractures', to name but three.

I decided without hesitation that my thermoregulatory centres were reposed enough, if not actually deceased, and although I do have the occasional periarticular contracture and pitch forward into my spaghetti, I decided I could live with this after seeing what the muscular, white-coated ladies of the Spa institutes do to you if they detect so much as a twinge in your periarticulars or suspect any backsliding among the dermals. The photographs showed a frankly worried-looking female patient being variously covered in tar, blown around a shower stall with a high-pressure hose, forced to recline in bubbling copper vats and otherwise subjected to a regimen that in other circumstances would bring ineluctably to mind the expression 'war crimes'. I looked at the list of the town's approved doctors to see if Josef Mengele appeared anywhere, but the only memorable name was a Dr Pitz. Resisting the impulse to ring him up and say, 'Well, are you?', I went instead to a small hotel recommended to me by the man in the tourist office.

I showered, dined, had a diverting stroll through the town and repaired to a convivial little bar on the Rue Royale for an evening with Martin Gilbert's grave and monumental *Second World War*. It is not a pub book, I can tell you now. You read a bit and before long you find yourself staring vacantly around you and longing for a conversation.

But hardly anyone in Wallonia speaks English. I began to regret that I didn't understand French well enough to eavesdrop. I took three years of French in school, but learned next to nothing. The trouble was that the textbooks were so amazingly useless. They were always written by somebody clearly out of touch with the Francophile world – Prof. Marvis Frisbee of the Highway 68 State Teachers College at Windsock, North Dakota, or something – and at no point did they intersect with the real world. They never told you any of the things you would need to know in France – how to engage a bidet, deal with a toilet matron or kneecap a queue jumper. They were always tediously preoccupied with classroom activities: hanging up coats in the cloakroom, cleaning the blackboard for the teacher, opening the window, shutting the window, setting out the day's lessons. Even in the seventh grade I could see that this sort of thing would be of limited utility in the years ahead. How often on a visit to France do you need to tell someone you want to clean a blackboard? How frequently do you wish to say, 'It is winter. Soon it will be spring'? In my experience, people know this already.

I could never understand why they couldn't make the textbooks more relevant to the adolescent mind and give us chapters with topics like 'Gerard et Isabelle Engage dans some Heavy Petting' or 'Claude a son Premier Wet Dream. C'est Magnifique!'. At the very least they could have used comic books.

I woke to find rain streaming down the windows. The streets were half flooded and the cars below whooshed as they passed. I went out to cash a traveller's cheque and window shopped along the Place Verte, sheltering beneath awnings on which the rain drummed steadily and rather soothingly. Every shop was filled with the most tempting foodstuffs – La Raclette Fromagerie, with cheeses the size of automobile tyres; the Boucherie Wagener, where strings of sausages hung in the window and slices of smoked Ardennes ham lay stacked in pink piles; La Gâterie, where the window was a delirium of marzipan fruits, hyperventilating cream cakes and other frothy delights. How clever these continentals are with their shop windows. Even the windows of chemists are so tidy and clean and scrupulously arranged that you find yourself gazing longingly at corn plasters and incontinence pads.

When I reached the last shop, I stared emptily at the Place Verte, not certain what to do with myself, and decided impulsively to push on to Durbuy in the hope that the weather would be better there. This was unlikely, considering that Durbuy was only fifteen miles away. None the less, thanks to the bewildering peculiarities of the Belgian railway system, to get to Durbuy took most of the morning and required three separate (albeit short) journeys and even then I couldn't quite get there, as Durbuy has no station. The closest I could get was Barvaux, which on the map is about half a millimetre to the left of Durbuy, but which in reality is four kilometres away, with a momumentally steep hill in between. Even from the station I could hear trucks straining to climb it. But at least the rain had stopped.

I thought I'd take a cab, but there was none at the station, so I walked into the town – a large village really – looking for a bus stop or a cab office, and went into a hotel on the main street and discovered from the dour patroness that Barvaux had neither cabs nor buses. In my best schoolboy French I asked how one then gets to Barvaux when one is sans l'auto. I braced for the lady to put a dead beaver on the counter, but instead she just said, 'À pied, monsieur,' and gave me one of those impassive Gallic shrugs – the one where they drop their chin to belt level and try to push their ears to the top of their head with their shoulders. You have to be Gallic to do it. It translates roughly as 'Life is a bucket of shit, monsieur, I quite agree, and while I am prepared to acknowledge this fact, I shall offer you no sympathy because, monsieur, this is your bucket of shit.'

Thanking her for playing such a small and passing role in my life, I walked to the edge of town and was confronted by a feature of landscape that was more wall than hill. The road was lined by the sort of unappealing houses that get built along any busy road and always look as if they are being slowly shaken to pieces by heavy lorries. Each yard was enclosed with a chain-link fence, behind each of which dozed a dog named Spike, who would leap to life and come flying down the front path as I approached and fling himself repeatedly at the gate, barking and baring his teeth and wanting to strip the flesh from my flanks in the worst way.

I don't know why it is but something about me incites dogs to a frenzy. I would be a rich man if I had a nickel for every time a dog tried to get at the marrow in my ankle bone while the owner just stood there and said, 'Well, I don't understand it, he's never done anything like this before. You must have said something to him.' That always knocks me out. What would I say to the dog? 'Hello, boy, like to open a vein in my leg?'

The only time a dog will not attack me with a view to putting me in a wheelchair is when I'm a guest at someone's house sitting on a deep sofa with a glass filled to the brim. In this case the dog – it's always a large dog with a saliva problem – will decide he doesn't want to kill me but to have sex with me. 'Come on, Bill, get your pants off. I'm *hot*,' he seems to be saying. The owner always says, 'Is he bothering you?' I love that, too. 'No, Jim, I adore it when a dog gets his teeth around my balls and frantically rubs the side of my head with his rear leg.'

'I can put him out if he's bothering you,' the owner always adds. 'Hey,' I want to reply, 'don't put him out, put him *down*.'

It wouldn't bother me in the least (and I realise I am sounding dangerously like Bernard Levin here, which God forbid) if all the dogs in the world were placed in a sack and taken to some distant island – Greenland springs attractively to mind – where they could romp around and sniff each other's anuses to their hearts' content and never bother or terrorise me again. The only kind of dog I would excuse from this round-up is poodles. Poodles I would shoot.

I don't like most animals, to tell you the truth. Even goldfish daunt me. Their whole existence seems a kind of reproach. 'What's it all about?' they seem to be saying. 'I swim here, I swim there. What for?' I can't look at a goldfish for more than ten seconds without feeling like killing myself, or at least reading a French novel.

To my mind, the only possible pet is a cow. Cows love you. They are harmless, they look nice, they don't need a box to crap in, they keep the grass down and they are so trusting and stupid that you cannot help but lose your heart to them. Where I live there's a herd of cows down the lane. You can stand by the wall at any hour of the day or night and after a minute the cows will all waddle over and stand with you, much too stupid to know what to do next, but happy just to be with you. They will stand there all day, as far as I can tell, possibly till the end of time. They will listen to your problems and never ask a thing in return. They will be your friends for ever. And when you get tired of them, you can kill them and eat them. Perfect.

Durbuy lay, at the foot of a startlingly steep road, on the other side of the hill. It looked to be about a half a mile below me. It was the kind of hill that, once you started down it, you couldn't guarantee to stop. I walked with an increasing loss of control, my legs moving beneath me as if on stilts. By the last bend I was really just a passenger on a pair of alien stumps which were frantically scissoring me towards a stone barn at the foot of the road. I could see myself going through it like a character in a cartoon, leaving a body-shaped hole, but instead I did a more interesting thing. I stepped heavily into a wobbly drain, spectacularly spraining my ankle – I'm sure I heard a crack as of splintering wood – did a series of graceless pirouettes which even as they were occurring put me in mind of the Frankenstein monster on roller skates, spun across the road, smacked face-first into the barn wall and, after teetering theatrically for a moment, fell backwards.

I lay still in the tall grass, taking a minute to accommodate the idea that down at the bottom of my right leg there was an unusual measure of agony going on. At intervals I raised my chin to my chest and gazed down the length of my body to see if my right foot was facing backwards or otherwise composed in a way that would account for the vividness of the pain, but it looked normal enough. From where I lay I could also see back up the hill and I spent some time wondering, in a curiously abstract way, how I was going to get back up there with no buses or cabs to call on.

Eventually, I hauled myself upright, using the barn as support, and hobbled erratically to a café, where I fell into a chair near the door and ordered a Coca-Cola. I took off my boot and sock and examined my ankle, expecting – and indeed, in that perverse manner of the injured male, rather hoping – to find some splintered bone straining at the skin like a tent pole, making everyone who saw it queasy. But it was just faintly bluish and tender and very slightly swollen, and I realised that once more in my life I had merely achieved acute pain and not the sort of grotesque injury that would lead to a mercy flight by helicopter and a fussing-over by young nurses in erotically starched uniforms. I sat glumly sipping my Coke for half an hour and discovered upon rising that the worst of the pain had subsided and I was able to walk after a fashion.

So I had a limping look round Durbuy. It was exceptionally pretty, with narrow back streets and houses built of stone beneath slate roofs. At one end stood a château lifted wholesale from a fairy tale and beneath it was a shallow, racing river, the Ourthe. All around were the strangely overbearing green hills that had for centuries kept the outside world out. I gathered from the size of the car parks that this was a popular spot with trippers, but there was hardly anyone about now and most of the shops were shut. I spent a couple of hours in the town, mostly sitting on a bench by the river, absorbed by scenery and birdsong. It was impossible to imagine in any sensible way that this perpetually tranquil place had, almost within my lifetime, been the epicentre, more or less, of the Battle of the Bulge. I lugged out Gilbert's magisterial history of the Second World War and skimmed through the index. Durbuy and Barvaux didn't get a mention, but many of the other neighbouring towns and villages did – Malmédy, where seventy-two captured American soldiers were taken into a field by an SS unit and machine-gunned rather than be kept as prisoners; Stavelot, where two days later the ever-busy subhumans of the SS killed 130 Belgian civilians, including twenty-three children; Bastogne, where American forces were besieged for a month and hundreds lost their lives; and many others. I simply couldn't take it in – that these terrible, savage things had happened here, in these hills and woods, to people as close to me in time as my father. And yet now it was as if it had never happened. Germans who had once slaughtered women and children in these villages could now return as tourists, with cameras around their necks and wives on their arms, as if it had all just been a Hollywood movie. I have been told more than once in fact that one of the more trying things about learning to live with the Germans after the war was having to watch them return with their wives and girlfriends to show off the places they had helped to ruin.

At about three o'clock it occurred to me that I had better head back to Barvaux. It took me until just after six to reach the station because of the pained slowness of my walking and the frequent rests I took along the way. The station was dark and untended when I arrived. No other passengers were about and the walls were without timetables.

I sat on the platform on the opposite side from which I had arrived, not knowing when the next train might come along, not knowing indeed if there might be a next train. It was as lonely a station as you could imagine in such a small and crowded country as Belgium. The tracks stretched in a straight line for two or three miles in either direction. I was cold and tired and my ankle throbbed. Even more than this, I was hungry. I hadn't eaten all day.

In my lonely, enfeebled state I began to think longingly about my old home-town diner. It was called the Y Not Grill, which everyone assumed was short for Y Not Come In and Get Food Poisoning. It was a strange place. I was about to say it was an awful place, but in fact, like most things connected with one's adolescence, it was wonderful and awful at the same time. The food was terrible, the waitresses notoriously testy and stupid, and the cooks were always escaped convicts of doubtful hygiene. They always had one of those permanent, snuffly colds that mark a dissolute lifestyle, and there was invariably a droplet of moisture suspended from the tip of their nose. You always knew, with a sense of stoic doom, that when the chef turned around and put your food before you, the drip would be gone from his nose and glistening on the top of your hamburger bun, like a bead of morning dew.

The Y Not had a waitress named Shirley who was the most disagreeable person I have ever met. Whatever you ordered, she would look at you as if you had asked to borrow her car to take her daughter to Tijuana for a filthy weekend.

'You want *what?*' she would say.

'A pork tenderloin and onion rings,' you would repeat apologetically. 'Please, Shirley. If it's not too much trouble. When you get a minute.'

Shirley would stare at you for up to five minutes, as if memorising your features for the police report, then scrawl your order on a pad and shout out to the cook in that curious dopey lingo they always used in diners, 'Two loose stools and a dead dog's schlong,' or whatever.

In a Hollywood movie Shirley would have been played by Marjorie Main. She would have been gruff and bossy, but you would have seen in an instant that inside her ample bosom there beat a heart of pure gold. If you unexpectedly gave her a birthday present she would blush and say, 'Aw, ya shouldana oughtana done it, ya big palooka.' If you gave Shirley a birthday present she would just say, 'What the fuck's this?' Shirley, alas, didn't have a heart of gold. I don't think she had a heart at all, or indeed any redeeming features. She couldn't even put her lipstick on straight.

Yet the Y Not had its virtues. For one thing, it was open all night, which meant that it was always there if you found yourself having a grease crisis or just wanted to be among other people in the small hours. It was a haven, a little island of light in the darkness of the downtown, very like the diner in Edward Hopper's painting 'The Nighthawks'.

The Y Not is long gone, alas. The owner, it was said, ate some of his own food and died. But even now I can see it: the steam on the windows, the huddled clusters of night workers, Shirley lifting a passed-out customer's head up by his hair to give the counter a wipe with a damp cloth, a lone man in a cowboy hat lost in daydreams with a cup of coffee and an untipped Camel. And I still think of it from time to time, especially in places like southern Belgium, when it's dark and chilly and an empty railway line stretches out to the horizon in two directions.

7. Aachen and Cologne

I took a train to Aachen. I hadn't been there before, but it was only a short journey from Liège, where I had spent the night, and I had always wanted to see Aachen Cathedral. This is an odd and pleasantly neglected corner of Europe. Aachen, Maastricht and Liège are practically neighbours – only about twenty miles separate them – but they are in three countries, speaking three distinct languages (namely Dutch, French and German), yet the people of the region employ a private dialect that means they can understand each other better than they can understand their fellow countrymen.

I got a room in a small hotel across from the station, dumped my rucksack and went straight out. I had a lunch of burger and fries in a hamburger chain called Quick (short for 'Quick – a bucket'), then set off to see the town.

My eagerness surprised me a little, but I hadn't been to Germany in seventeen years and I wanted to see if it had changed. It had. It had grown even richer. It was rich enough in 1973, but now – golly. Even prosperous Flanders paled beside this. Here, almost every store looked rich and busy and was full of stylish and expensive goods like Mont Blanc pens and Audemars Piguet watches. Even the stores selling mundane items were riveting – J. von der Driesel, for instance, a stockist of kitchenware and other household goods at the top of a hill near the old market square. Its large windows displayed nothing more exciting than ironing boards, laundry baskets and pots and pans, but every pan gleamed, every piece of plastic shone. A little further on I passed not one but two shops selling coffins, which seemed a bit chillingly Germanic to me, but even they looked sleek and inviting and I found myself staring in admiration at the quality of the linings and the shine on the handles.

I couldn't get used to it. I still had the American habit of thinking of Europe as one place and Europeans as essentially one people. For all that you read that Denmark's per capita gross domestic product is forty per cent higher than Britain's, the Danes don't look forty per cent richer than the British, they don't wear forty per cent shinier shoes or drive forty per cent bigger cars. But here people *did* look rich and different, and by a factor of much more than forty per cent. Everyone was dressed in clothes that looked as if they had been purchased that morning. Even the children's trainers weren't scuffed. Every car had a showroom shine on it. Even the taxis were all Mercedes. It was like Beverly Hills. And this was just an obscure little city on the edge of the country. The Germans were leaving the rest of us standing.

Not everything was perfect. Much of the architecture in the city centre was blatantly undistinguished, especially the modern shopping precinct, and the bars and restaurants didn't have the snug and convivial air of those in Holland and Belgium. But then I found my way to the calm of the cathedral close and warmed to Aachen anew. I went first to the Schatzkammer, the treasury, which contained the finest assortment of reliquaries I ever expect to see, including the famous life-size golden bust of Charlemagne, looking like a god; a carved sixteenth-century triptych depicting Pope Gregory's mass, which I think I could look at almost for ever; and assorted other baubles of extraordinary beauty and craftsmanship.

The whole collection is displayed in three small, plain, feebly lit rooms, but what a collection. Next door was the octagonal cathedral, modelled on the church of San Vitale at Ravenna, and all that remains of a palace complex mostly destroyed during the Second World War. The cathedral was small and dark but exquisite, with its domed roof, its striped bands of contrasting marble and its stained glass, so rich that it seemed almost liquid. It must have been cramped even in Charlemagne's day – it couldn't seat more than a hundred or so – but every inch of it was superb. It was one of those buildings that you don't so much look at as bathe in. I would go to Aachen tomorrow to see it again.

Afterwards I passed the closing hours of the afternoon with a gentle stroll around the town, still favouring my sore ankle. I looked at the large cobbled Marktplatz and tottered out to the preternaturally quiet residential streets around the Lousberg park. It was curious to think that this pleasant backwater was once one of the great cities of

Europe, the seat of the Holy Roman Empire, Charlemagne's capital. I didn't realise until I turned again to Gilbert's history of the Second World War a day or so later that Aachen was the first German city to fall to the Allies, after a seven-day street battle in 1944 that left almost the whole of it in ruins. You would never guess it now.

In the evening I went looking for a restaurant. This is often a problem in Germany. For one thing, there's a good chance that there will be three guys in lederhosen playing polka music, so you have to look carefully through the windows and question the proprietor closely to make sure that Willi and the Bavarian Boys won't suddenly bound onto a little stage at half-past eight, because there is nothing worse than being just about to tuck into your dinner, a good book propped in front of you, and finding yourself surrounded by ruddy-faced Germans waving beer steins and singing the 'Horst Wessel Lied' for all they're worth. It should have been written into the armistice treaty at the end of the war that the Germans would be required to lay down their accordions along with their arms.

I went up to six or eight places and studied the menus by the door but they were all full of foods with ominous Germanic names – Schweinensnout mit Spittle und Grit, Ramsintestines und Oder Grosser Stuff, that sort of thing. I expect that if ordered they would turn out to be reasonably digestible, and possibly even delicious, but I can never get over this nagging fear that I will order at random and the waiter will turn up with a steaming plate of tripe and eyeballs. Once in Bavaria Katz and I recklessly ordered Kalbsbrann from an indecipherable menu and a minute later the proprietor appeared at our table, looking hesitant and embarrassed, wringing his hands on a slaughterhouse apron.

'Excuse me so much, gentlemens,' he said, 'but are you knowing what Kalbsbrann *is*?'

We looked at each other and allowed that we did not.

'It is, how you say, what ze little cow thinks wiz,' he said.

Katz swooned. I thanked the man profusely for his thoughtfulness in drawing this to our attention, though I dare say it was a self-interested desire not to have two young Americans projectile-vomiting across his dining-room that brought him to our table, and asked him to provide us something that would pass for food in middle America. We then spent the intervening period remarking on what a close shave that had been, shaking our heads in wonder like two people who have stepped unscathed from a car wreck, and discussing what curious people the Europeans are. It takes a special kind of vigilance to make your way across a continent on which people voluntarily ingest tongues, kidneys, horsemeat, frogs' legs, intestines, sausages made of congealed blood, and the brains of little cows.

Eventually, after walking some distance, I found an Italian restaurant called Capriccio just around the corner from my hotel on Theaterstrasse. The food was Italian, but the staff were all German. (I could tell from the jackboots – only joking!) My waitress spoke no English at all and I had the most extraordinary difficulty getting myself understood. I asked for a beer and she looked at me askance.

'Wass? Tier?'

'Nein, beer,' I said, and her puzzlement grew.

'Fear? Steer? Queer? King Leer?'

'Nein, nein, *beer*.' I pointed at the menu.

'Ah, *beer*,' she said, with a private tut, as if I had been intentionally misleading her. I felt abashed for not speaking German, but comforted myself with the thought that if I did understand the language I would know what the pompous man at the next table was boasting about to his wife (or possibly mistress) and then I would be as bored as she clearly was. She was smoking heavily from a packet of Lord's and looking with undisguised interest at all the men in the room, except of course me. (I am invisible to everyone but dogs and Jehovah's Witnesses.) Her companion didn't notice this. He was too busy telling her how he had just sold a truckload of hula hoops and Leo Sayer albums to the East Germans, and basking in his cunning.

When he laughed, he looked uncannily like Arvis Dreck, my junior high school woodwork teacher, which was an unsettling coincidence since Mr Dreck was the very man who had taught me what little German I knew.

I had only signed up for German because it was taught by a walking wet dream named Miss Webster, who had the most magnificent breasts ever and buttocks that adhered to her skirt like melons in shrink wrap. Whenever Miss Webster stretched to write on the blackboard, eighteen adolescent boys would breathe hard and let their hands slip below the table. But two weeks after the school year started Miss Webster departed in mysterious circumstances – mysterious to us anyway – and Mr Dreck was drafted in to take over until a replacement could be appointed.

This was a catastrophe. Mr Dreck knew slightly less than bugger-all about German. The closest he had come to Germany was a beerfest in Milwaukee. I'm sure he wasn't even remotely qualified to teach the language. He taught it to us from an open book, running a stubby finger over the lines and skipping anything that got too tricky. I don't suppose he needed a lot in the way of advanced degrees to teach junior high school woodwork, but it was clear that even there he was operating on the outer limits of his mental capabilities. I learned more German from watching *Hogan's Heroes.*

I hated Mr Dreck as much as I have ever hated anyone. For two long years he made my life hell. I used to sit during his endless monotone lectures on hand tools, their use and care, genuinely trying to pay attention, but after a few minutes I would find my gaze drifting helplessly out the window to where a girls' gym class was romping around – thirty-six adolescent girls, all wearing little blue pleated skirts that didn't *quite* cover their pert little asses – and my imagination would break free, like a dog off its lead, and scamper playfully among them, sniffing and panting around all those long, tanned legs. After a minute or two I would turn back to the class with a dreamy leer tugging at my lips to find that everyone was watching me. Mr Dreck had evidently just launched a question in my direction.

'Pardon, Mr Dreck?'

'I said what kind of blade is this, Mr Bryson?'

'That's a sharp blade, Mr Dreck.'

Mr Dreck would emit one of those exasperated sighs that stupid people reserve for those happy occasions when they chance upon someone even more stupid than they, and say in a wearied voice, 'It's a fourteen-inch Hungarian dual nasal borer, Mr Bryson.' Then he would make me stand for the rest of the hour at the back of the room holding a piece of coarse sandpaper to the wall with my nose.

I had no gift for woodwork. Everyone else in the class was building things like cedar chests and ocean-going boats and getting to play with dangerous and noisy power tools, but I had to sit at the Basics Table with Tubby Tucker and a kid who was so stupid that I don't think we ever learned his name. We just called him Drooler. The three of us weren't allowed anything more dangerous than sandpaper and Elmer's Glue, so we would sit week after week making little nothings out of offcuts, except for Drooler who would just eat the glue. Mr Dreck never missed a chance to humiliate me. 'And what is *this*?' he would say, seizing some mangled block of wood on which I had been labouring for the last twenty-seven weeks and holding it aloft for the class to titter at. 'I've been teaching shop for sixteen years, Mr Bryson, and I have to say that this is the worst bevelled edge I've ever seen.' He held up a birdhouse of mine once and it just collapsed in his hands. The class roared. Tubby Tucker laughed so hard that he almost choked. He laughed for twenty minutes, even when I whispered to him across the table that if he didn't stop it I would bevel his testicles.

The waitress brought my beer and I became uncomfortably aware that I had spent the last ten minutes adrift in a little universe of my own, very possibly chuckling quietly and murmuring to myself in the manner of people who live in bus stations. I looked around and was relieved to see that no one appeared to have noticed. The man at the next table was too busy boasting to his wife/mistress how he had sold 2,000 Jason King video tapes, 170 Sinclair electric cars and the last 68,000 copies of the American edition of *The Lost Continent* to the Romanians for loft insulation. His companion meanwhile was making love with her eyes to a man dining alone across the room — or rather masturbating with her eyes, since the man was too busy struggling with three-foot-long strands of tangled spaghetti to notice that he was being used as a sex aid.

I took a big draught of my beer, warmed by my reminiscences, and quietly jubilant at the thought that my schooldays were for ever behind me, that never again for as long as I lived would I have to bevel an edge or elucidate the principles of the Volstead Act in not less than 250 words or give even a mouse-sized shit about which far-flung countries produce jute and what they do with it. It is a thought that never fails to cheer me.

On the other hand, never again would I experience the uniquely satisfying sensation of driving a fist into the pillow-like softness of Tubby Tucker's abdomen. I don't wish to suggest that I was a bully, but Tubby was different. God put Tubby on earth for no other reason than to give other kids someone to beat up. Girls beat him up. Kids four years younger than him beat him up. It sounds cruel – it was cruel – but the thing is he *deserved* it. He never learned to keep his mouth shut. He would say to the toughest kid in the school, 'God, Buckley, where'd you get that hair-cut? I didn't know the Salvation Army offered a hair-styling service,' or 'Hey, Simpson, was that your mom I saw cleaning the toilets at the bus station? You ought to tell her those cigarette butts would smoke better if she dried them out first.'

So every time you saw him he was being given a Chinese burn or having his wobbly pink butt mercilessly zinged with damp towels in the locker-room or standing in his underpants beneath a school-yard oak endeavouring with a long stick to get his trousers down from one of the branches, where they had recently been deposited by a crowd of up to four hundred people, which sometimes included passing motorists and the residents of nearby houses. There was just something about him that brought out the worst in everyone. You used to see pre-school kids chasing him down the street. I bet even now strangers come up to him on the street and for no reason smash his hot dog in his face. I would.

In the morning I went to the station to catch a train to Cologne. I had half an hour to kill, so I wandered into the station café. It was a little one-woman operation. The woman running it saw me take a seat, but ignored me and instead busied herself tidying the shelves behind the counter. She was only a foot or so from me. I could have leaned over and used her buttocks as bongos, but it gradually dawned on me that if I wanted service I would have to present myself at the counter and make a formal request. It would never occur to her to conclude that I was a foreign visitor who didn't know the drill and say to me in a pleasant voice, 'Coffee, mein Liebschen?' or even just signal to me that I should step to the counter. No, I was breaking a rule and for this I had to be ignored. This is the worst characteristic of the Germans. Well, actually a predilection for starting land wars in Europe is their worst characteristic, but this is up there with it.

I know an English journalist living in Bonn who was phoned at work by his landlady and instructed to come home and take his washing down from the line and rehang it in a more systematic manner. He told her, in so many words, to go fuck herself, but every time he put washing out after that he would return home to find it had all been taken down and rehung. The same man came in one weekend from cutting the grass to find an anonymous note on the doormat informing him that it was illegal to mow one's lawn in North Rhine-Westphalia between noon on Saturday and 9 a.m. on Monday, and that any further infractions would be reported to the lawnmower police or whatever. Eventually he was transferred to Bogotá and he said it was the happiest day of his life.

Cologne is a dismal place, which rather pleased me. It was comforting to see that the Germans could make a hash of a city as well as anyone else, and they certainly have done so with Cologne. You come out of the station and there, at the top of an outdoor escalator, is the cathedral, the largest Gothic structure in the world. It is awesome and imposing, no question, but it stands in the midst of a vast, windswept, elevated concrete plaza that is just heart-numbingly barren and forlorn. If you can imagine Salisbury Cathedral dropped into the car park of the Metro Centre you may get the picture. I don't know what they were thinking of when they built it. Certainly it wasn't people.

I had been to Cologne briefly once before, the summer I travelled alone, but I could remember little of it, except for the massive presence of the cathedral, and staying in a guesthouse somewhere on a back street in the permanent shadow of an iron bridge across the Rhine. I remembered the guesthouse much better than the city. In the hallway outside my room stood a table stacked high with German weekly magazines, all of which seemed to be concerned exclusively with sex and television, and since television in Germany seemed also to be concerned almost exclusively with sex, sex was something of a feature in these publications. There was nothing pornographic about them, you understand. They just covered sex the way British magazines cover gardening. I spent much of an afternoon and a whole evening travelling between my room and the table with armloads of these diverting periodicals for purposes of cultural study.

I was particularly fascinated by a regular feature in, I think, *Neue Review*, which focused on a young couple each week – a truck mechanic from Duisburg named Rudi and his dishy librarian wife Greta, that sort of thing. Each week it was a different couple, but they all looked as if they had been squeezed from the same tube of toothpaste. They were all young and good-looking and had superb bodies and dazzling smiles. Two or three of the photographs would show the couple going about their daily business – Rudi lying under a DAF truck with a spanner and a big smile, Greta at the local supermarket beaming at the frozen chickens. But the rest of the pictures treated us to the sight of Rudi and Greta without any clothes on doing things around the house: standing together at the sink washing the dishes, sharing a spoonful of soup from the stove, playing Scrabble buttocks-up on a furry rug.

There was never anything overtly sexual about the pictures. Rudi never got a hard on – he was having much too good a time drying those dishes and tasting that soup! He and Greta looked as if every moment of their existence was bliss. They smiled straight at the camera, as happy as anything to have their neighbours and workmates and everyone else in the Federal Republic of Germany see them chopping vegetables and loading the washing machine in their birthday suits. And I thought then what curious people the Germans are.

That was about all I could remember of Cologne, and I began to fear, as I lingered on the precipice of the cathedral plaza looking down on the grim shopping streets below, that that was about all that was worth remembering. I went and stood at the base of the cathedral and gazed up at it for a long time, impressed by its sheer mass. It is absolutely immense, over 500 feet long and more than 200

feet wide, with towers that soar almost as high as the Washington
Monument. It can hold 40,000 people. You can understand why it
took 700 years to build – and that was with German workers. In
Britain they would still be digging the foundations.

I went inside and spent a half-hour looking dutifully at the contents,
but without feeling any of that sense of exhilaration that the vastly
smaller cathedral at Aachen had stirred in me the day before,
then wandered back outside and went to the edge of the terrace
overlooking the Rhine, broad and brown and full of long fleets of
barges. This done, I wandered over to the main shopping street,
Hohe Strasse, a long, straight pedestrian artery which is one of the
two most expensive streets in Europe on which to rent retail space
(the other is Kaufingerstrasse in Munich). It's more expensive even
than Bond Street in London or the Rue du Faubourg-St-Honoré in
Paris. Bernard Levin wrote glowingly of Hohe Strasse in *To the End of
the Rhine*, but to me it just looked like any shopping street anywhere
– a succession of C&A-type department stores, shoe stores, record
stores, places selling cameras and video recorders. It was aswarm
with Saturday shoppers, but they didn't look particularly discerning
and nothing like as well-dressed as the citizens of Aachen. I could
have been in Milton Keynes or Doncaster.

I stopped outside one of the many electronics shops and looked
over the crowded window, idly wondering if the goods on offer
would be German-made, but no, they were the same Japanese videos
and cameras you see everywhere else, apart from the odd Grundig
slide projector or some other relic of a simpler age. Having grown up
in a world dominated by American goods I used to get patriotically
chagrined seeing Japanese products appearing everywhere and I
would read with sympathy articles in magazines about how these
wily little orientals were taking over the world.

Then one time, while I was flying on a Boeing 747, I plugged in
a pair of earphones that offered the audio quality of a paper cup at
the end of a length of string and watched a film that looked as if it
were being projected onto a bath mat, and I had a shocking thought –
namely, that this was as far as American consumer electronics ever
got. We got up to about 1972 and then just stopped. If we had
left the field to RCA and Westinghouse and the other American

companies we would now all be wheeling around personal stereos the size of suitcases and using video recorders that you would have to thread yourself. And since that moment I have been grateful to the Japanese for filling my life with convenient items like a wristwatch that can store telephone numbers, calculate my overdraft and time my morning egg.

Now my only complaint is that we have to live with all the embarrassing product names the Japanese give us. No one ever seems to remark on this – on what a dumb and misguided name Walkman is, for instance. I've never understood it. It doesn't walk, it's not a man. It sounds like something you'd give a blind person to keep him from bumping into walls ('You want to turn up the bleeper on your Walkman, Harry'). If it had been developed in America it would have been given a name like the SoundBlaster or MuzixMaster or Dynam-O-Box or something with a little zip to it. But these things aren't developed in America any longer, so we have to accept the sort of names that appeal to Japanese engineers – the Sony Handy-Cam, the Panasonic Explorer, the Toyota Tercel. Personally, I would be embarrassed to buy a car that sounds like a new kind of polyester, but I imagine that to the Japanese these names are as exciting and stellar as all-get-out. I suppose that's what you have to expect from people who wear white shirts every day of their lives.

I returned to the station, where I had left my bag in a locker, and couldn't decide what to do with myself. My intention had been to spend a couple of days in Cologne going to the museums – it has some excellent ones – but now I couldn't muster much enthusiasm for the idea. And then I saw something that gave me an instant urge to get out of there. It was a non-stop porno cinema, and quite a gross one at that to judge by the candid glossy pictures on display by the ticket booth. The cinema was in the station, one of the services permitted to travellers by the thoughtful management of Deutsche Bundesbahn. I don't know precisely why, but I found this hugely repellent. I have no especial objection to pornography, but in a station? There was just something so seedy about the idea of a businessman stopping off at the end of the day to watch twenty minutes of heaving bonking before catching the 17.40 to his home

and family in Bensberg, and there was something seedier still in the
thought of a national railway endorsing it.

Just then the huge timetable board high above me went *chickata
chickata* in that appealing way of theirs, announcing an express train
to Amsterdam. 'Hold that train!' I muttered, and scurried off to the
ticket window.

8. Amsterdam

Arriving at Amsterdam's Centraal Station is a strange experience. It's in the middle of town on a sunny plaza at the foot of the main street, the Damrak. You step out of the front door and there in front of you is – gosh! – every hippie that's left. I had no idea there were still so many of them, but there were scores, if not hundreds, lounging around in groups of six or eight, playing guitars, passing reefers, sunning themselves. They look much as you would expect someone to look who has devoted a quarter of a century to lounging around in public places and smoking dope. A lot of them seemed to be missing teeth and hair, but they had compensated somewhat by acquiring large numbers of children and dogs. The children amused themselves by frolicking barefoot in the sun and the dogs by nipping at me as I passed.

I walked up the Damrak in a state of high anticipation. Amsterdam had been Katz's and my favourite European city by a factor too high to compute. It was beautiful, it was friendly, it had excellent bars and legal dope. If we had lingered another week I could well be there yet, sitting on the station plaza with an acoustic guitar and some children named Sunbeam and Zippity Doo-Dah. It was that close.

The Damrak was heaving with tourists, hippies and Saturday shoppers, all moving at different speeds: the tourists shuffling as if their shoelaces were tied together, looking everywhere but where they were going, the hippies hunched and hurried, and the shoppers scurrying around among them like wind-up toys. It was impossible to walk with any kind of rhythm. I tried several of the hotels along the street, but they were all full, so I dodged behind the prison-like royal palace at Dam Square and branched off into some side streets, where I had vague recollections of there being a number of small hotels. There were, but these too were full. At most of them it wasn't even necessary to enquire because a sign in the window announced NO VACANCY in half a dozen languages.

Things had clearly changed since my day. Katz and I had stepped off the train at the height of summer, asked our way to the Sailors' Quarter and got a room in the first hotel we came to. It was a wonderful little place called the Anco, in a traditional Amsterdam house: narrow and gabled, with steep, dark staircases and a restful view of the O.Z. Voorburgwal canal four floors below. It cost $5 a night, with an omelette for breakfast thrown in (almost literally), though we did have to share a room with two slightly older guys.

Our first meeting was inauspicious. We opened the door to find them engaged in a session of naked bed-top wrestling – an occurrence that surprised the four of us equally.

'Pardon us, ladies!' Katz and I blurted and scuffled backwards into the hallway, closing the door behind us and looking confounded. Nothing in twenty years of life in Iowa had quite prepared us for this. We gave them a minute to disengage and don bathrobes before we barged back in, but it was clear that they considered us boorish intruders, an opinion reinforced by our knack, developed over the next two days, of always returning to the room in the middle of one of their work-outs. Either these guys never stopped or our timing was impeccable.

They spoke to us as little as was humanly possible. We couldn't place their accents but we thought the smaller one might be Australian since he seemed so at home down under. Their contempt for us became irredeemable in the middle of the second night, when Katz stumbled heavily from his bed after a gala evening at the Club Paradiso and, with an enormous sigh of relief, urinated in the wastebasket.

'I thought it was the sink,' he explained, a trifle lamely, the next morning. Our room-mates moved out after breakfast and for the rest of the week we had the room to ourselves.

We quickly fell into a happy routine. We would rise each morning for breakfast, then return to the room, shut out every trace of daylight and go back to bed for the day. At about four o'clock we would stir again, have a steaming shower in a cubicle down the hall, change into fresh clothes, press our hair flat against our heads and descend to the bar of the Anco, where we would sit with Oranjebooms in the window seat, watching the passing scene and remarking on what fine people the Dutch were to fill their largest city with pleasant canals, winsome whores and plentiful intoxicants.

The Anco had a young barman with a Brillo-pad beard and a red jacket three sizes too snug for him who had clearly taken one toke too many some years earlier and now looked as if he should carry a card with his name on it in case he needed to remember it in a hurry. He sold us small quantities of hash and at six o'clock we would have a reefer, as a sort of appetiser, and then repair to an Indonesian restaurant next door. Then, as darkness fell over the city and the whores took up their positions on the street corners, and the evening air filled with the heady smells of cannabis and frites, we would wander out into the streets and find ourselves being led gently into mayhem.

We went frequently to the Paradiso, a nightclub converted from an old church, where we tried without success to pick up girls. Katz had the world's worst opening line. Wearing an earnest, almost worried look, he would go up to a girl and say, 'Excuse me, I know you don't know me, but could you help me move something six inches?'

'What?' the girl would reply.

'One and a half fluid ounces of sperm,' Katz would say with a sudden beam. It never worked, but then it was no less successful than my own approach, which involved asking the least attractive girl in the room if I could buy her a drink and being told to fuck off. So instead we spent the nights getting ourselves into a state of what we called ACD – advanced cognitive dysfunction. One night we fell in with some puzzled-looking Africans whom Katz encouraged to foment rebellion in their homeland. He got so drunk that he gave them his watch (he semed to think that punctual timekeeping would make all the difference in the revolution), a Bulova that had belonged to his grandfather and was worth a fortune, and for the rest of the summer whenever I forgot and asked him the time he would reply sourly, 'I don't know. I have a man in Zululand who looks after these things for me.' At the end of the week we discovered we had spent exactly half our funds of $700 each and concluded that it was time to move on.

The Dutch are very like the English. Both are kind of slobby (and I mean that in the nicest possible way): in the way they park their cars, in the way they set out their litter bins, in the way they dump their bikes against the nearest tree or wall or railing. There is none of that obsessive fastidiousness you find in Germany or Switzerland, where the cars on some residential streets look as if they were lined up by somebody with a yardstick and a spirit level. In Amsterdam they just sort of abandon their cars at the canalside, often on the brink of plunging in.

They even talk much the same as the English. This has always puzzled me. I used to work with a Dutch fellow on *The Times*, and I once asked him whether the correct pronunciation of the artist's name was Van Go or Van Gok. And he said, a little sharply, 'No, no, it's Vincent Van –' and he made a sudden series of desperate hacking noises, as if a moth had lodged in his throat. After that, when things were slow around the desk, I would ask him how various random expressions were said in Dutch – International Monetary Fund, poached eggs, cunnilingus – and he would always respond with these same abrupt hacking noises. Passing people would sometimes slap him on the back or offer to get him a glass of water.

I've tried it with other Dutch people – it's a good trick if you've got a Dutch person at a party and can't think what to do with him – always with the same result. Yet the odd thing is that when you hear Dutch people speaking to each other they hardly hack at all. In fact, the language sounds like nothing so much as a peculiar version of English.

Katz and I often noticed this. We would be walking down the street when a stranger would step from the shadows and say, 'Hello, sailors, care to grease my flanks?' or something, and all he would want was a light for his cigarette. It was disconcerting. I found this again now when I presented myself at a small hotel on the Prinsengracht and asked the kind-faced proprietor if he had a single room. 'Oh, I don't believe so,' he said, 'but let me check with my wife.' He thrust his head through a doorway of beaded curtains and called, 'Marta, what stirs in your leggings? Are you most moist?'

From the back a voice bellowed, 'No, but I tingle when I squirt.'

'Are you of assorted odours?'

'Yes, of beans and sputum.'

'And what of your pits – do they exude sweetness?'

'Truly.'

'Shall I suckle them at eventide?'

'Most heartily!'

He returned to me wearing a sad look. 'I'm sorry, I thought there might have been a cancellation, but unfortunately not.'

'A smell of petroleum prevails throughout,' I said by way of thanks and departed.

There were no rooms to be had anywhere. In the end, despondent, I trudged back to the station plaza, to the office of the VVV, the state tourist bureau, where I assumed there would be a room-finding service. I went inside and up some stairs and found myself in a hall that brought to mind Ellis Island. There were eight straggly lines of weary tourists, with at least thirty people in each queue. The VVV staff were sending people all over – to Haarlem, to Delft, to Rotterdam, to The Hague – because there was not a single hotel room left in Amsterdam at any price. This was only April. What on earth can it be like in July? They must send people to Iceland. A big sign on the wall said NO TICKETS FOR THE VAN GOGH EXHIBITION. SOLD OUT. That was great, too. One of the reasons I had come when I did was to see the exhibition.

I took a place in one of the lines. Progress was glacial. I was hot, I was sweaty, I was tired, I was hungry. My feet hurt. I wanted a bath. I wanted a large dinner and several beers. There wasn't a single part of me that was happy.

Almost every one of us in the room was an American. Upon reaching the front of the line, each new customer had to be interviewed regarding his or her requirements in terms of toilet facilities, breakfast arrangements, room amenities, accessibility by public transport and price. This took ages because of all the permutations involved. Then almost invariably the customer had to turn to his or her mate – who had been standing there all along *seeming* to take it in but evidently not – and explain all the possibilities all over again. This would prompt a lengthy discussion and a series of supplementary questions – Can we get there by bus instead of by train? Are there any vegetarian restaurants near the hotel? Does the hotel have no-smoking rooms? Will there be a cab at the station when we get there or do we have

to call one, and if we have to call one can you give us the number?
Is there a laundromat in Delft? What time does the last train run?
Do you think I should be taken outside and shot for having such
an enormous butt and asking so many stupid questions? It just went
on and on.

Once they had arrived at a kind of agreement in principle, the VVV
person would make anything up to twenty phone calls to outlying
hotels, with a look of infinite patience and low expectations – most
hotels weren't even bothering to answer their phones by now – before
announcing that nothing was available in that price range. So then
they would have to discuss another more expensive or more distant
set of options. It all took so long that you felt like applauding
whenever anyone left the window and the queue pushed forward
six inches.

The one lucky thing was that the VVV girl at the head of my
queue was beautiful – not just extraordinarily good-looking, with
the sort of bottom that made your palms sweat when she went to
the filing cabinet, but intelligent, sweet-natured, patient, sympathetic,
and with that exquisite, dusky Dutch accent that simply melts your
heart. She dealt with every customer gracefully and expertly, and
switched effortlessly between French, German, English and Dutch
– all with that delectable accent. I was infatuated. I freely admit it.
Stuck in a line that was going nowhere, there was nothing I could
do but just stare dumbly at her and admire everything about her –
the way she hooked her hair behind her ear, the way she wrinkled
her nose when she looked in the phone book, the way she dialled
the phone with the eraser end of her pencil. By the time I reached
her window it was all I could do to keep from blurting, 'Can we have
sex a few times and then talk marriage?' But all I did was shyly ask
for a hotel room somewhere in the northern hemisphere. She found
me one in Haarlem.

Haarlem was very pleasant. People ahead of me in the line had been
falling into swoons when told they would have to leave Amsterdam
to get a room, but I was rather pleased. Haarlem was only twenty
minutes away by train and it was a handsome little city with a
splendid cathedral and cosy cathedral square, and lots of good

restaurants that were cheaper and emptier than those in Amsterdam. I had a steak the size of a hot-water bottle, went for a long walk around the town, stood impressed in the shadow of the cathedral, returned to the hotel, showered steamily and went to bed a happy man.

In the morning I returned to Amsterdam. I used to love walking in cities on Sunday mornings, but it gets more and more dispiriting. All the things left over from Saturday night – vomit slicks, litter, twisted beer cans – are still lying around, and everywhere now there are these depressing grilles and iron shutters on all the shop fronts. They make every street look dangerous and forbidding, which is just absurd in Europe. On an innocuous pedestrian street called Heiligeweg almost every store front was completely hidden behind a set of iron blinds – even the Aer Lingus office. What on earth is anyone going to steal from an Aer Lingus office – the little model aeroplane in the window?

I found my way to the canals – the Singel, Herengracht, Keizersgracht and Prinsengracht – and things were immediately better. I roamed along them in a happily random way, shuffling through leaves and litter, cocooned by the tall narrow houses and old trees. Along its canals Amsterdam is an immensely beautiful city, especially on a Sunday morning when there is almost no one about. A man sat in a patch of sun on his stoop with a cup of coffee and a newspaper, another was returning from somewhere with a bottle of wine, a young couple passed entwined in a post-coital glow, and the occasional unhurried cyclist crossed from one side street to another somewhere up ahead, like extras employed to lend colour to the scene, but in two hours of wandering around I saw not another soul but them.

Again and again, I found myself leaning on a railing on a small humpbacked bridge just gazing into the shimmering green water, lost in a simple-minded reverie until a tour boat would chunter by, full of tourists with cameras, slicing through the mirrored street scene below me to break the spell. In its wake there would always be a little festival of bestirred litter – a Fairy Liquid bottle, some cigarette packets, assorted cartons from McDonald's and Burger King – and I would be reminded that Amsterdam is also a dirty city. It's full of dog shit and litter and graffiti. The graffiti is everywhere – on phone boxes, on park benches, on the walls of almost every building, even on the marbled vaults of the passageway that runs like a tunnel beneath the Rijksmuseum. I have never seen so much graffiti. And it's not even good graffiti. It's just random squiggles, sprayed by people with brains the size of a Cheerio. The Dutch seem to have a problem with mindless crime. You may never get mugged in Amsterdam, but I'm told you can't park a car on the streets anywhere in the centre of the city in the evening without a strong probability of someone scoring the paintwork from end to end with a screwdriver.

When I was twenty I liked Amsterdam – indeed admired it passionately – for its openness, its tolerance, its relaxed attitude to dope and sex and all the other sins that one can't get enough of at twenty. But I found it oddly wearisome now. The people of Amsterdam were rather stuck with their tradition of tolerance, like people who take up a political stance and then have to defend it no matter how untenable it gets. Because they have been congratulating themselves on their intelligent tolerance for all these centuries, it is now impossible for them not to be nobly accommodating to graffiti and burned-out hippies and dog shit and litter. Of course, I may be completely misreading the situation. They may like dog shit and litter. I sure hope so, because they've certainly got a lot of it.

Here and there I would pass a house braced with timbers, awaiting urgent repairs. Amsterdam was built on a swamp, and just keeping the canalside houses from sinking into it is an unending task. My *Times* colleague's brother bought a house on one of the lesser canals and discovered after moving in that the pilings on which it had been built three hundred years before were rotting away and the house was sinking into the underlying ooze at a rate that would make most of it basement within a short while. Putting new pilings under several tons of existing structure is not the easiest job in the world and it cost him almost twice as much to have the house shored up as it did to buy it in the first place. This was almost twenty years ago, and he still wears socks with holes in them because of the debt.

I suppose the same experience has been repeated in countless buildings all over the city, so you have to admire the good people of Amsterdam for keeping the houses standing, and even more for having the sense to keep the canal streets residential. In Britain the ground floors would long ago have been filled with kebab houses and building-society offices and Sketchley dry cleaners, all with big picture windows, as if anybody in the world cares to see what's going on inside a dry cleaner's or a building society.

I've never understood this. The first thing a building society does when it acquires a Victorian building in Britain is gut the ground floor and put in a lot of plate glass. Why? As you may have noticed, building societies have *nothing* to put in their windows. So they make a fan-shaped arrangement of brochures informing you that you can borrow money there 'Christ, thanks, I thought you sold sausages' – and insert some dreadful watercolours by the manager's wife. So I am full of admiration for the Dutch for preserving their finest streets and insisting that people live on them.

The one problem is that it makes the occasional catastrophe all the more unbearable, as I discovered with a cry of pain as I reached the far end of Nieuwezijds Voorburgwal. There, where once a fine gabled house must have stood, squatted a new Holiday Inn, a building so ugly, so characterless, so *squat*, that it stopped me in my tracks, left me standing agog. Everything about it was cheap and unimaginative – the cardboard-box shape, the shit-brown bricks, the empty, staring windows, the acrylic canopy over the entrance, the green plastic signs, the wall-mounted video cameras peering at every passer-by. It looked like a parking ramp. Not the tiniest effort had been made to give it any distinction.

It would have been painful enough out by an airport, but this was in the heart of one of the great cities of Europe on a street otherwise lined with handsome, patrician houses. How could an architect walk through such a city and allow himself to design a building of such utter indistinction? How could the city authorities let him? How could anyone sleep in it? I found myself turning dumbstruck to people passing on the sidewalk as if to say 'Do you see this building here?', but they all just hunched past, quite unmoved by its existence. I just don't understand the world.

Evening came. A light rain began to fall. Pulling my collar round my ears, I walked to the dark streets of the red-light district and squinted through rain-spattered glasses at the goods on offer. The red-light district had changed since my day. In 1973, the most outspoken thing was a club with a sign that said, LIVE ON STAGE – REAL FOCKY-FOCKY SHOW. Now everything was much more explicit. The shop windows were filled with a boggling array of plastic phalluses, vibrators, whips, video tapes, unguents, magazines, leatherwear and other exotica not to be found in your average Woolworth's. One window contained a plastic, life-size, astonishingly realistic woman's reproductive region, complete with dilated labia. It was *awful*. It looked like something that would be used in an anatomy lesson, and even then you could imagine students fainting.

The magazines were even grosser. They showed every conceivable variety of couple doing messy and urgent things to each other – heterosexuals, gays, sado-masochists, grotesquely fat people (a little comic relief, I guess) and even animals. The cover of one showed a woman providing – how shall I put this? – a certain oral service to a horse that a horse wouldn't normally expect to get, even from another horse. I was astounded. And this was just the stuff in the windows. God knows what they keep under the counters.

The whores were still there. They sat in luminous body stockings in windows lit with a pinkish glow, and winked at me as I passed. ('Hey, they like me!' I thought, until I realised that they do this for everybody.) Behind them, I could sometimes glimpse the little cells where they conduct their business, looking white and clinical, like someplace you would go to have your haemorrhoids seen to. Twenty years ago the prostitutes were all Dutch. They were friendly and sweet-natured and often heart-breakingly attractive. But now all the prostitutes were Asian or African, and they looked mean and weathered, even when they were pouting and blowing kisses in their most coquettish come-hither manner.

There was a whole street of this stuff, several blocks long, with a spill-over into neighbouring side streets. I couldn't believe that there could be that many people in Amsterdam – that many people in the *world* – requiring this sort of assistance just to ejaculate. Whatever happened to personal initiative?

I spent the morning of my last day in the Rijksmuseum. 'The Night Watch' wasn't on view because a few days earlier some crazy person had attacked it with a knife, and both he and it had been taken away for rehabilitation, but the museum is so massive – 250 rooms – and so filled with wonderful pictures that there was plenty else to look at.

Afterwards I strolled on to the Anne Frank House on Prinsengracht. It was packed, but moving none the less. Eight people spent three years hiding in a secret flat above Otto Frank's spice business, and now an endless line of visitors shuffles through it every day, to see the famous bookcase that hid the secret entrance and the five rooms in which they lived. The tragic part is that when the Franks and their companions were anonymously betrayed and finally captured in August 1944, the Allies were on the brink of liberating Holland. A few more weeks and they would have been saved. As it was, seven of the eight died in concentration camps. Only Anne's father survived.

The Anne Frank museum is excellent at conveying the horror of what happened to the Jews, but it is a shame that it appears not to give even a passing mention to the Dutch people who risked their own lives in helping the Franks and others like them. Miep Gies, Otto Frank's secretary, had to find food each day for eight people, as well as herself and her husband, for three years at a time of the strictest rationing. It must have been extremely trying, not to mention risky. Yet this was hardly a rare act: twenty thousand people in Holland sheltered Jews during the war at considerable peril to themselves. They deserve to be remembered too.

What must it have been to be a Jew in Europe in the 1930s? From the beginning they were subjected to the grossest indignities: forbidden to sit in parks or cafés or to ride on trams, required to give up their cars and bicycles, even their children's bicycles. If it had ended there, it would have redounded to Germany's shame for ever, but of course it grew unspeakably worse, as the photographs and documents in the museum's other rooms gruesomely testify – people being herded onto cattle trains, piles of stick-like corpses, the gaunt faces of the living dead, all the pictures you have seen a thousand times.

One picture I hadn't seen transfixed me. It was a blurry photo of a German soldier taking aim with a rifle at a woman and the baby she was clutching as she cowered beside a trench of bodies. I couldn't stop staring at it, trying to imagine what sort of person could do such a thing.

It probably wasn't the best picture to look at just before heading to the station and catching a train to Germany.

9. Hamburg

I travelled to Hamburg, by way of Osnabrück and Bremen, and arrived in the early evening. I hadn't been to Hamburg before. Katz and I passed through it by train on our way to Scandinavia, but it was late at night and all I recalled was a dark city and a dark station where we stopped for half an hour while more carriages were hooked on. The station was much as I remembered it, vaulted and echoing, but brighter and busier at six in the evening. People were everywhere, hurrying to catch trains.

I threaded my way through the crowds to the tourist information desk and, having had so much trouble finding a room in Amsterdam, gladly paid a handsome fee to have accommodation found for me, and then was chagrined to discover that the Hotel Popp, the establishment to which the pleasant and well-spoken young man directed me after relieving me of a handful of notes and a selection of coins, was directly opposite the station. I could have found it on my own in thirty seconds and applied the money to a night of abandon in the Reeperbahn. Still, it was convenient and had a bar and restaurant, so I couldn't complain. Actually I could. The room was tiny and depressingly basic, with a twenty-watt bulb in the reading light, no carpet, no television and a bed that could have passed for an ironing board. But at least with a place called the Hotel Popp I wouldn't forget the name and end up, as I often do in strange cities, asking a cabbie to just drive around until I spotted it.

I went out for a stroll before dinner. Lounging at intervals along the side streets around the station were some of the most astonishingly unattractive prostitutes I had ever seen — fifty-year-old women in mini-skirts and black fishnet stockings, with crooked lipstick and tits that grazed their kneecaps. Where on earth they get their trade from I couldn't begin to guess. One of them gave me a 'Hello, dearie' look and I was nearly crushed by a bus as I faltered backwards into the street. But within a block or two things improved considerably.

I had left my city map behind in the hotel so I had no idea where I was going, but it all looked inviting in every direction. It was a warm spring evening, with dusk settling cosily over the city, like a blanket around one's shoulders, and people were out walking aimlessly and browsing in shop windows. I was pleased to find myself among them.

I had expected Hamburg to be grimmer, a sort of German Liverpool, full of crumbling flyovers and vacant lots – I already knew that it had the highest unemployment rate in Germany, over twelve per cent, half as high again as the national average, so I expected the worst – but Hamburg proved to be anything but struggling, at least on the surface. The department stores along the Mönckebergstrasse, the main shopping street, were bright and spotless and full of fancy goods – much finer than anything on Oxford Street – and the side streets glowed with restaurants and bistros through whose yellowy windows I could see people dining elegantly and well.

I walked through the big town hall square and around the darkened streets of the warehouse district, handsome and silent, then rounded a corner to find one of the more arresting city sights I have ever seen – the Inner Alster, the smaller of the two lakes around which Hamburg is built. I knew from maps that Hamburg had these lakes, but nothing I had read or seen in pictures had prepared me for just how beautiful they were. The Inner Alster is much the smaller of the two, but it is still large enough to present a great rectangular pool of silence and darkness in the midst of the city. The lakeside is agreeably lined with trees and benches, overlooked by office buildings and a couple of hotels of the old school, the sort of places where the doormen are dressed like Albanian admirals and rich old ladies in furs constantly go in and out with little dogs under their arms.

I sat on a bench in the darkness for perhaps half an hour just watching the lights shimmering on the surface and listening to the lapping of water, then stirred myself enough to walk over to the Kennedybrücke, a bridge across the channel where the two lakes meet. The Outer Alster, seen from here, was more massive and irregular and even more fetching, but I would leave that for tomorrow.

Instead, famished, I strolled back to the welcoming glow of the Popp, where I dined amply and surprisingly well for what was after all just a small station hotel, bloating my cheeks with bread rolls and salad and meat and potatoes till I could eat no more, and then filled all the remaining space inside me with good German beer and read half a book, until at last, at about half-past midnight, I arose from my table, nodded genteelly to the six Turkish waiters who had been waiting hours for me to go and ascended in a tiny slow-motion lift to the fourth floor, where I spent no more than half an hour stabbing at the keyhole with my key before bursting unexpectedly into the room, pushing the door shut with the back of my foot, shedding some clothes (one sock, half a shirt) and falling onto the bed, where I dropped more or less immediately into a deep, contented and, I dare say, grotesquely blubbery sleep.

I woke in a square of sunshine, too hot and bright to sleep through, and stumbled to the window to find a gorgeous morning blazing away outside, much too gorgeous to waste. The Hauptbahnhoff concourse and the street below, the Kirchenallee, were so brightly bathed in sunlight that I had to shield my eyes. I had a hangover you could sell to science, but after two cups of strong coffee at a sunny table outside the Popp, a handful of aspirins, two cigarettes and a cough so robust that I tapped into two new seams of phlegm, I felt tolerably human and was able to undertake a gentle stroll to the waterfront through the dappled sunshine of St Pauli Park. There wasn't much to see upon arrival, just cranes and dockyards and the broad, sluggish estuary of the Elbe. I thought of what Konrad Adenauer used to say: 'You can smell Prussia when you get to the Elbe.' I could only smell dead fish, or at least I assumed it was dead fish. Maybe it was Prussians.

In the 1930s, the docks at Hamburg employed 100,000 people. Now the number is barely 1,200, though it is still the second busiest port in Europe (after Rotterdam), with a volume of trade equal to the whole of Austria's. Until just a couple of weeks before, I could have witnessed the interesting sight of freighters unloading grain from their aft holds and redepositing it in their forward holds as a way of extracting additional funds from the ever-beneficent EEC. With its flair for grandiose fuck-ups, the EEC for years paid special subsidies to shippers for grain that was produced in one part of the Common Market and re-exported from another, so shippers taking a consignment from, say, France to Russia discovered that they could make a fortune by stopping off at Hamburg en route and pointlessly unloading the cargo and then reloading it. This little ruse enriched the shippers by a mere £42 million before the bureaucrats of the EEC realised that the money could be much better spent on something else – themselves, say – and put a stop to the practice.

I walked a few hundred yards inland and uphill to the Reeperbahn, that famed mile-long avenue of sin. It looked disappointingly unlusty. Of course, sinful places never look their best in daylight. I remember thinking even in Las Vegas that it all looked rather endearingly pathetic when viewed over a cup of coffee and a doughnut. All that noise and electric energy that is loosed at dusk vanishes with the desert sun and it all suddenly seems as thin and one-dimensional as a film set. But even allowing for this, the Reeperbahn looked tame stuff, especially after Amsterdam. I had envisioned it as a narrow, pedestrianised street packed on both sides with bars, sex shops, peep shows, strip clubs and all the other things a sailor needs to revive a salty dick, but this was almost a normal city street, busy with traffic flowing between the western suburbs and the downtown. There was a fair sprinkling of seamy joints, but also a lot of more or less normal establishments – restaurants, coffee shops, souvenir stores, jeans shops, even a furniture store and a theatre showing the inescapable *Cats*. Almost the only thing that told you this was a neighbourhood of dim repute was the hard look on the people's faces. They all had that gaunt, washed-out look of people who run funfair stalls.

The really seedy attractions were on the side streets, like Grosse Freiheit, which I turned up now. I walked as far as the Kaiserkeller at No. 36, where the Beatles used to play. Most of the other businesses along the street were given over to live sex shows, and I was interested to note that the photos of the artistes on display outside were unusually – I am tempted to say unwisely – candid. In my experience, places such as these always show pictures of famously beautiful women like Christie Brinkley and Raquel Welch, which I dare say even the most inexperienced sailor from Tristan da Cunha must realise is not what he's likely to encounter inside, but at least they leave you wondering what you *are* going to find. These pictures, however, showed gyrating women of frightfully advanced years – women with maroon hair and thighs that put me in mind of flowing lava. These ladies must have been past their best when the Beatles were playing. They weren't just over the hill; they were pinpricks on the horizon.

The sex shops, too, were as nothing compared to those of Amsterdam, though they did do a nice line in inflatable dolls, which I studied closely, never having seen one outside a Benny Hill sketch. I was particularly taken with an inflatable companion called the Aphrodite, which sold for 129 marks. The photograph on the front was of a delectably attractive brunette in a transparent négligé. Either this was cruelly misleading or they have made more progress with vinyl in recent years than I had realised.

In large, lurid letters the box listed Aphrodite's many features: LIFE SIZED!, SOFT FLESH-LIKE SKIN!, INVITING ANUS! (Beg pardon?), MOVEABLE EYES! (Ugh) and LUSCIOUS VAGINA THAT VIBRATES AT YOUR COMMAND!

Yeah, but can she cook? I thought.

There was another one called a Chinese Love Doll 980. 'For a Long-Lasting Relationship,' it promised sincerely, and then in bolder letters added: EXTRA THICK VINYL RUBBER. Kind of takes the romance out of it, don't you think? This was clearly a model for the more practical types. On the other hand it also had a VIBRATING VAGINA AND ANUS and TITS THAT GET HOT!! Below this it promised: SMELL LIKE A REAL WOMAN.

All these claims were given in a variety of languages. It was interesting to see that the German versions all sounded coarse and bestial: LEBENGROSSE, VOLLE JUNGE BRUSTE, LIEBENDER MUND. The same words in Spanish sounded delicate and romantic: ANO TENTADOR, DELICIOSA VAGINA QUE VIBRA A TU ORDEN, LABIOS AMOROSOS. You could almost imagine ordering these in a restaurant ('I'll have the Ano Tentador lightly grilled and a bottle of Labios Amorosos '88'). The same things in German sounded like a wake-up call at a prison camp.

I was fascinated. Who buys these things? Presumably the manufacturers wouldn't include a vibrating anus or tits that get hot if the demand wasn't there. So who's clamouring for them? And how does anyone bring himself to make the purchase? Do you tell the person behind the counter it's for a friend? Can you imagine taking it home on the tram and worrying all the time that the bag will split and it will flop out or self-inflate or, worse still, that you'll be killed in a crash and all the next week the papers will be full of headlines like 'POLICE IDENTIFY RUBBER-DOLL MAN' above a smiling picture of you from your high-school year book? I couldn't handle the tension. Imagine having friends drop in unexpectedly when you were just about to pop the champagne cork and settle down for a romantic evening with your vinyl companion and having to shove her up the chimney and then worry for the rest of the evening that you've left the box on the bed or some other give-away lying around. ('By the way, who's the other place setting for, Bill?')

Perhaps it's just me. Perhaps these people aren't the least embarrassed about their abnormal infatuations. Perhaps they talk about it freely with their friends, sit around bars saying, 'Did I tell you I just traded up to an Arabian Nights Model 280? The eyes don't move, but the anus gives good action.' Maybe they even bring them along. 'Helmut, I'd like you to meet my new 440. Mind her tits. They get hot.'

With this intriguing thought to chew on, I strolled back to the city centre past the massive law courts and concert hall and along an avenue interestingly named Gorch-Fock-Wall, which sounded to me like the answer to a riddle ('What does Gorch do when he can't find his inflatable doll?'), and had a look around the shopping streets and classy arcades packed into the area between the huge town hall and Inner Alster.

It was getting on for midday and people were sitting out in the sunny plazas having lunch or eating ice-creams. Almost without exception they looked healthy and prosperous and often were strikingly good-looking. I remembered German cities from twenty years before being full of businessmen who looked just as Germans were supposed to look — fat and arrogant. You would see them gorging themselves on piles of sausages and potatoes and gulping with full mouths from litre tankards of golden beer at all hours of the day, but now they seemed to be picking delicately at salads and fish, and looking fit and tanned — and, more than that, friendly and happy. Maybe this was just a Hamburg trait. Hamburg is after all closer to Denmark and Sweden and even England than it is to Munich, so perhaps it is atypical of Germany.

At all events, this relaxed and genial air was something that I hadn't associated with Germans before, at least not those aged over twenty-five. There was no whiff of arrogance here, just a quiet confidence, which was clearly justified by the material wealth around them. All those little doubts we've all had about the wisdom of letting the Germans become the masters of Europe evaporated in the Hamburg sunshine. Forty-five years ago Hamburg was rubble. Virtually everything around me was new, even when it didn't look it. The people had made their city, and even themselves, rich and elegant and handsome through their cleverness and hard work, and they had every right to be arrogant about it, but they were not, and I admired them for that.

I don't think I can ever altogether forgive the Germans their past, not as long as I can wonder if that friendly old waiter who brings me my coffee might have spent his youth bayonetting babies or herding Jews into gas ovens. Some things are so monstrous as to be unpardonable. But I don't see how anyone could go to Germany now and believe for a moment that that could ever happen again. Germans, it struck me, are becoming the new Americans – rich, ambitious, hard-working, health-conscious, sure of their place in the world. Seeing Hamburg now, I was happy to hand them my destiny – happier, at any rate, than leaving it to those who have spent the last forty years turning Britain into a kind of nation-state equivalent of Woolworth's.

One thing hadn't changed: the women still don't shave their armpits. This has always puzzled me in a vague sort of way. They all look so beautiful and stylish, and then they lift up their arms and there's a Brillo pad hanging there. I know some people think it's earthy, but so are turnips and I don't see anyone hanging those in their armpits. Still, if failure to deal with secondary pubic hairs is the worst trait the Germans take with them into the closing years of the century, then I for my part shall be content to let them lead us into the new millennium. Not that we will have the slightest fucking choice, mind you.

All these lithe and attractive bodies began to depress me, especially after I caught sight of myself reflected in a store window and realised that I was the fat one now. After spending the first twenty-five years of my life looking as if my mother had mated with a stick insect, these sudden reflected glimpses of rolling blubber still come as a shock. Even now I have to stop myself from giving a good-morning smile to the fat guy every time I get into a mirrored lift. I tried a diet once, but the trouble is they so easily get out of control. I lost four pounds in the first week and was delighted until it occurred to me that at this rate in only a little over a year I would vanish altogether. So it came as something of a relief to discover that in the second week I put all the weight back on (I was on a special diet of my own devising called the Pizza and Ice-Cream Diet) and I still draw comfort from the thought that if there is ever a global famine I will still be bounding around, possibly even playing a little tennis, while the rest of you are lying there twitching your last.

I devoted the afternoon to a walk around the immense Outer Alster. I hadn't intended to spend the whole afternoon there, but it was so beautiful that I couldn't pull myself away. Sailing boats dotted the water, and little red and white ferries plied endlessly beneath a sky of benign clouds, taking passengers between the rich northern quarters of the city and the distant downtown. A narrow park, full of joggers and lovers and occasional benchloads of winos (who looked remarkably fit and prosperous considering their vocation), encircled the lake and offered one enchantment after another. Every view across the water was framed by sturdy oaks and trembling willows, and offered distant prospects of the city: the space-needle eminence of a TV tower, a few scattered skyscrapers, and for the rest copper roofs and church spires that looked as if they had been there for ever.

On the streets around the perimeter of the lake, and as far back into the surrounding streets as you cared to wander, stood huge houses of every architectural style, with nothing in common but their grandness. Where the lake occasionally wandered off into placid backwaters, the houses had immense shady lawns running down to the water's edge, with gazebos and summer houses and their own jetties. It must be very agreeable to live on a lake in a grand house and go to work by foot or bike around the lake or by ferry across it or even aboard your own boat and to emerge at the other end at such a rich and handsome city centre. What a perfect life you could lead in Hamburg.

10. Copenhagen

I took a train to Copenhagen. I like travelling by train in Denmark because you are forever getting on and off ferries. It takes longer, but it's more fun. I don't know how anyone could fail to experience that frisson of excitement that comes with pulling up alongside a vast white ship that is about to sail away with you aboard it. I grew up a thousand miles from the nearest ocean, so for me any sea voyage, however brief, remains a novelty. But I noticed that even the Danes and Germans, for whom this must be routine, were peering out of the windows with an air of expectancy as we reached the docks at Puttgarden and our train was shunted onto the ferry, the *Karl Carstens*.

Here's a tip for you if you ever travel on a Scandinavian ferry. Don't be the first off the train, because everyone will follow you, trusting you to find the way into the main part of the ship. I was in a group of about 300 people following a flustered man in a grey trilby who led us on a two-mile hike around the cargo deck, taking us up and down long avenues of railway carriages and huge canvas-sided trucks, casting irritated glances back at us as if he wished we would just go away, but we knew that our only hope was to stick to him like glue and, sure enough, he eventually found a red button on the wall, which when pressed opened a secret hatch to the stairwell.

Overcome with new frissons of excitement, everyone clambered hurriedly up the metal stairs and made straight for the buffet. You could tell the nationality of the people by what they went for. The Germans all had plates piled high with meat and potatoes, the Danes had Carlsbergs and cream cakes, the Swedes one piece of Ryvita with a little dead fish on it. The queues were too much for me, so I went up on the top deck and stood out in the sunshine and gusty breeze as the boat cast off and, with a sound oddly like a washing machine on its first cycle, headed across the twelve miles of white-capped water between northern Germany and the Danish island of Lolland. There

were about eight of us, all men, standing in the stiff breeze, pretending
we weren't perishing. Slowly Puttgarden receded behind us in a wake
of foam and before long Lolland appeared over the horizon and began
to glide towards us, like a huge low-lying sea monster.

You cannot beat sea travel, if you ask me, but there's not much
of it left these days. Even now grand plans are under way to run
bridges or tunnels between all the main islands of Denmark and
between Copenhagen and Sweden, and even across this stretch of
water between Puttgarden and Rödbyhavn, so that people will be
able to zip across it in ten minutes and scarcely notice that they have
moved from one country to another. This new European impulse to
blur the boundaries between countries seems a mite misguided to me.

At Rödbyhavn, our frissons spent, we all reboarded the train and
rode listlessly through the rest of the afternoon to Copenhagen. Denmark was much neater and emptier than northern Germany had been.
There were no factories as there had been in Germany and none of
that farmyard clutter of abandoned tractors and rusting implements
that you see in Belgium and Holland. Big electricity-generating wind
turbines, their three-bladed fans spinning sluggishly, were dotted
around the low hillsides and stood in ranks in the shallow coastal
bays. It was a pity, I thought with that kind of distant casualness
that comes with looking at things that are already sliding from view,
that they hadn't made them more attractive – like scaled-up Dutch
windmills perhaps.

It seemed odd and sad that mankind could for centuries have so
effortlessly graced the landscape with structures that seemed made for
it – little arched bridges and stone farmhouses, churches, windmills,
winding roads, hedgerows – and now appeared quite unable to do
anything to the countryside that wasn't like a slap across the face.
These days everything has at best a sleek utility, like the dully practical
windmills slipping past with the scenery outside my train window,
or else it looks cheap and temporary, like the tin sheds and concrete
hangars that pass for superstores on the edge of every medium-sized
town. We used to build civilisations. Now we build shopping malls.

We reached Copenhagen's central station at a little after five, but the
station tourist office was already closed. Beside it stood a board with

the names of thirty or so hotels and alongside each hotel was a small red light to indicate whether it was full or not. About two-thirds of the lights were lit, but there was no map to show where the hotels stood in relation to the station. I considered for a moment jotting down some of the names and addresses, but I didn't altogether trust the board and in any case the addresses were meaningless unless I could find a map of the city.

Perplexed, I turned to find a Danish bag lady clasping my forearm and addressing me in a cheerful babble. These people have an uncanny way of knowing when I hit town. They must have a newsletter or something. We wandered together through the station, I looking distractedly for a map of the city on a wall, she holding onto my arm and sharing demented confidences with me. I suppose we must have looked an odd sight. A businessman stared at us over the top of a newspaper as we wandered past. 'Blind date,' I explained confidentially, but he just kept staring.

I could find no map of the city, so I allowed the lady to accompany me to the front entrance, where I disengaged her grip and gave her some small coins of various nations. She took them and wandered off without a backward glance. I watched her go and wondered why crazy people like train and bus stations so much. It is as if it's their office ('Honey, I'm off to the station to pick through the litter bins and mumble at strangers. See you at five!'). I can never understand why they don't go to the beach or the Alps or someplace more agreeable.

I went to half a dozen hotels in the immediate neighbourhood of the station and they were all full. 'Is there some reason for this?' I asked at one. 'Some convention or national holiday or something?'

'No it's always like this,' I was assured.

Am I wrong to find this exasperating? Surely it shouldn't be too much, on a continent that thrives on trade and tourism, to arrange things so that a traveller can arrive in a city in late afternoon and find a room without having to traipse around for hours like a boat person. I mean here I was, ready to spend freely in their hotels and restaurants, subsidise their museums and trams, shower them with foreign exchange and pay their extortionate VAT of twenty-two per cent, all without a quibble, and all I asked in return was a place to lay my head.

Like most things when you are looking for them, hotels were suddenly thin on the ground in Copenhagen. I walked the length of the old part of the city without luck and was about to trudge back to the station to begin again when I came across a hotel by the waterfront called the Sophie Amalienborg. It was large, clean, modern and frightfully expensive, but they could give me a single room for two nights and I took it without hesitation. I had a steamy shower and a change of clothes and hit the streets a new man.

Is there anything, apart from a really good chocolate cream pie and receiving a large, unexpected cheque in the post, to beat finding yourself at large in a foreign city on a fair spring evening, loafing along unfamiliar streets in the long shadows of a lazy sunset, pausing to gaze in shop windows or at some church or lovely square or tranquil stretch of quayside, hesitating at street corners to decide whether that cheerful and homy restaurant you will remember fondly for years is likely to lie down this street or that one? I just love it. I could spend my life arriving each evening in a new city.

You could certainly do worse than Copenhagen. It is not an especially beautiful city, but it's an endlessly appealing one. It is home to one and a half million people – a quarter of the Danish population – but it has the pace and ambience of a university town. Unlike most great cities, it is refreshingly free of any delusions of self-importance. It has no monuments to an imperial past and little to suggest that it is the capital of a country that once ruled Scandinavia. Other cities put up statues of generals and potentates. In Copenhagen they give you a little mermaid. I think that's swell.

I walked along Nyhavn, a three-block-long street with a canal in the middle filled with tall-masted ships and lined with narrow, step-gabled seventeenth- and eighteenth-century houses, looking for all the world like a piece of Amsterdam gone astray. The neighbourhood was in fact originally settled by Dutch sailors and remained the haunt of jolly tars until recent times. Even now it has a vaguely raffish air in parts – a tattoo parlour and one or two of the sort of dive bars through whose windows you expect to see Popeye and Bluto trading blows – but these are fading relics. For years, restaurateurs have been dragging Nyhavn almost forcibly upmarket and most of the places now are yuppie bars and designer restaurants, but very agreeable places for all that, since the Danes don't seem to be the least bit embarrassed about living well, which is after all how it should be.

The whole length of Nyhavn was lined with outdoor tables, with young, blond, gorgeous people drinking, eating and enjoying the unseasonably warm weather. I always wonder in Copenhagen what they do with their old people – they must put them in cellars or send them to Arizona – because everyone, without exception, is youthful, fresh-scrubbed, healthy, blond and immensely good-looking. You could cast a Pepsi commercial in Copenhagen in fifteen seconds. And they all look so happy.

The Danes are so full of joie de vivre that they practically sweat it. In a corner of Europe where the inhabitants have the most blunted concept of pleasure (in Norway, three people and a bottle of beer is a party; in Sweden the national sport is suicide), the Danes' relaxed attitude to life is not so much refreshing as astonishing. Do you know how long World War II lasted for Denmark? It was over in a day – actually less than a day. Hitler's tanks crossed the border under cover of darkness and had taken control of the country by dawn. As a politician of the time remarked, 'We were captured by telegram.' By evening they were all back in the bars and restaurants.

Copenhagen is also the only city I've ever been in where office girls come out at lunchtime to sunbathe topless in the city parks. This alone earns it my vote for European City of Culture for any year you care to mention.

I dined in a crowded, stylish basement restaurant half-way along Nyhavn. I was the only person who didn't look as if he had just come from the set of *Miami Vice*. All the men wore shirts buttoned to the throat and the women had big earrings and intentionally distressed hair, which they had to shove out of the way each time they went to their plate. Every one of them was beautiful. I felt like Barney Rubble. I kept expecting the manger to come to the table and say, 'Excuse me, sir, but would you mind putting some of this mousse on your hair?' In the event, the staff treated me like an old friend and the food was so superb that I didn't mind parting with the six-inch wad of banknotes that any meal in Copenhagen occasions.

When I climbed the steps to the street, darkness had fallen and the air had chilled, but people still sat outside at tables, drinking and talking enthusiastically, jackets draped over their shoulders. I crossed Kongens Nytorv, one of the city's principal squares, sleepy and green, passed beneath the soft lights of the Hotel D'Angleterre, full of yet more happy diners, and headed up Strøget, Copenhagen's main shopping street. Strøget is the world's longest pedestrian street. Actually it's five streets that run together for a little over a mile between Kongens Nytorv and the city's other main square, Raadhuspladsen, at the Tivoli end. Every travel article you read about Copenhagen talks rapturously about Strøget, but I always feel vaguely disappointed by it. Every time I see it, it seems to have grown a tiny bit seedier. There are still many swish and diverting stores down at the Kongens Nytorv end – Georg Jensen for silver, Brødrene Andersen for clothes, Holmegaard for china and glass – but as you pass the half-way point Strøget swiftly deteriorates into tatty gift shops and McDonald's, Burger Kings and other brightly lit temples of grease. The whole thing could do with a lot more in the way of benches and flagstones (it's all patched asphalt now) and even – dare I say it? – the odd tub of geraniums. It's a shame that in a country as wealthy and design-conscious as Denmark they can't make the whole street – the words tumble involuntarily from my lips – more picturesque.

Still, it is pleasant to walk from one end of the downtown to the other without encountering cars, and just as you reach the western end, when you think that this is too, too dreary and you really should turn back, you step into the large and colourful Raadhuspladsen, or town hall square. One of the things they do in Europe that has always impressed me is let advertisers put colourful neon signs all over the roofs and top floors of the buildings around their main squares. You don't notice the signs in the daytime because they are so high up, so the buildings preserve that air of stern magnificence appropriate to their function, but when darkness falls and you could do with a little gaiety, the same buildings suddenly light up with bright advertisements that illuminate the square and colour the faces of the people below.

I walked across to Tivoli, even though I could see from a distance that it was shut and darkened, as if under dust sheets. A sign on the gate said it wouldn't open for a couple of weeks. As I walked back across the square towards Strøget I encountered a small crowd by the town hall and stopped to have a look.

Two police officers, a man and a woman, both young and blond and as gorgeous as everyone else in the city, were talking softly and with sympathy to a boy of about seventeen who had clearly ingested the sort of drugs that turn one's brain into an express elevator to Pluto. Disorientated by this sudden zip through the cosmos, he had apparently stumbled and cracked his head; a trickle of blood ran from above his hairline to his downy cheek. The police officers were wearing the smartest commando-style uniforms I have ever seen – navy blue jump suits with lots of zips and velcro pockets and loops holding torches and notebooks and portable telephones and, for all I know, grappling hooks and rocket launchers. They looked as if between them they could handle any contingency, from outbreaks of Lassa fever to disarming a nuclear submarine.

And the thing is, this was probably the biggest thing they would have to deal with all evening. The Danes are almost absurdly law-abiding. The most virulent crime in the country is bike theft. In 1982, a year for which I just happen to have the facts at my fingertips, there were six murders in Copenhagen, compared with 205 in Amsterdam, a city of similar size, and 1,688 in New York. The city is so safe that Queen Margarethe used to walk from Amalienborg Palace to the shops every morning to buy flowers and vegetables just like a normal citizen. I once asked a Dane who guarded her in such circumstances, and he looked at me with surprise and replied, 'Why, we all do,' which I thought was rather sweet.

The police officers helped the boy to his feet and led him to the patrol car. The small crowd dispersed, but I found myself following them, almost involuntarily. I don't know why I was so fascinated, except that I had never seen such gentle police. At the patrol car, I said in English to the female officer, 'Excuse me, what will you do with the boy?'

'We'll take him home,' she said simply, then raised her eyebrows a fraction and added: 'I think he needs his bed.'

I was impressed. I couldn't help thinking of the time I was stopped by police in America, made to stand with my arms and legs spread against a wall and frisked, then taken to a police station and booked because of an unpaid parking ticket. I was about seventeen myself at the time. God knows what they would have done to me if they had found me in a drugged stupor on a city bench. I suppose I'd be getting out of jail about now. 'Will he be in trouble for this?' I asked.

'With his father, I think so, yes. But not with us. We are all young and crazy sometimes, you know? Good-night. Enjoy your stay in Copenhagen.'

'Good-night,' I said, and with the deepest admiration watched them go.

In the morning I felt like going to some museums. Copenhagen has splendid museums, which are strangely neglected, even by the Danes. I went first to the immense National Museum, opposite Christiansborg Palace, and had it more or less to myself. National museums, especially in small countries, are often feeble affairs – department-store mannequins dressed in sixteenth-century peasant costumes and a display case containing six Roman coins found in somebody's back garden. But the Danish National Musuem is both vast and richly endowed, and I spent a morning happily wandering through its miles of echoing rooms.

Afterwards I went to the Ny Carlsberg Glyptotek. Some museums have great treasures but are dull buildings and some have dull treasures but are great buildings, but the Glyptotek succeeds on both counts. It has an outstanding collection of Roman statuary and some of the finest Impressionist paintings to be seen anywhere, but the building itself is a joy – light, airy, impeccably decorated, with a warm and tranquil palm court full of gently dozing old people. (So that's where they put them!)

But the best museum of all I saved for last – the Hirschsprung Collection in Østre Anlaeg Park. Everything about it is wonderful. It's a pleasant and gentle stroll from the city centre and Østre Anlaeg is the best park in the city, in my experience (which is short but in this case attentive), for seeing secretaries sunning their breasts, but even without these huge and novel inducements it is worth seeking out because it is such a terrific and little-visited museum. It contains 884 paintings, assembled over forty years by one man, almost all of them from the nineteenth-century Skagen school of Danish painting, and all packed densely into twenty or so mostly small rooms. The paintings are all concerned with simple themes – summer landscapes, friends enjoying a casual dinner, a view of the sea from an open window, a woman at a sink – but the effect is simply enchanting, and you come away feeling as if you have spent the afternoon in some kind of marvellous and refreshing ioniser.

Afterwards, my spirits lifted, I had a long, happy walk through the surrounding park, moving methodically from one sunbathing blonde to another, enquiring if they needed any assistance with their suntan lotion. Actually, that's not true. It wasn't warm enough for sunbathing and in any case it was four in the afternoon and all the secretaries in Copenhagen were tucked away in their dark offices, their lovely breasts bagged away for at least another day, so I just walked around the park and imagined.

Early in the evening I went for a stroll along the city's curiously uninspiring waterfront: a dull vista of fish-processing factories and industrial cranes. Far away across the still water a ship-repair yard was working late doing something shrill and drastic to a rusted freighter, which defended itself with hideous shrieks and a shower of sparks. I walked as far as the statue of the Little Mermaid perched forlornly but rather prettily on her rock at the harbour's edge, and then strolled around a neighbouring park called Castellet, named for its star-shaped fortress guarding the harbour mouth, before finally stopping for a light and cheapish dinner at a café/bistro on Stockholmsgade.

The food was not remarkable, but the beer was good and the service was excellent since I was the only customer in the place. I had only to look up and smile hopefully and a fresh beer would be hustled to me. After a bit I didn't even have to look up. A new bottle would magically appear as the last drop fell from the old one. This was my kind of bistro.

So I sat contentedly for two hours looking at some Danish newspapers that had been left on the table, trying to discern from the mass of unfamiliar words whether Margaret Thatcher had perchance fallen

out of a moving car or World War III had started yet. But planet Earth
seemed to be much as I had left it three weeks before, so instead I
gazed out of the window at the passing traffic and lost myself in
those aimless reveries that are the lone traveller's equivalent of a
night on the town.

Eventually I rose, paid the enormous bill and tottered a trifle
wobbily out into the night. It was a fair hike back to my hotel, but I
sustained myself en route by stopping at any place that looked bright
and friendly and dispensed beer, of which Copenhagen possesses a
gratifying plenitude, and thus passed the evening sitting alone in a
series of corners, drinking far too many beers, smiling inanely at
strangers and dribbling ash down my shirt. Sometime around one
in the morning, as I was weaving down Strøget, suppressing the
urge to break into song, I encountered an Irishman reeling down
the street towards me, swearing crazily at anyone who passed.

'You fucking cunts!' he screamed at a genteel-looking couple whose
pace immediately quickened. 'You shit-head! You great Danish turd!'
he shouted at a young man who lowered his head and hurried on.

The odd thing was that the Irishman was dressed in a dapper grey
suit. He looked like a successful businessman. God knows what was
going on inside his addled head. He caught sight of me, but seemed to
recognise me as a fellow drunk and let me pass with a listless wave of
the hand, but immediately perked up to rain abuse on a middle-aged
man. 'You're a piece of crap for sure, you stupid old twat!' he said,
to the man's considerable surprise, then added mysteriously: 'And I
bet you're staying in a fucking posh hotel!' I stood with my arms
crossed and watched as the Irishman reeled off down the street,
shouting abuse at the buildings now, before he lurched abruptly
to the left, as if yanked on a long rope, and disappeared down a
side street, taking his expletives into the night.

I awoke in the morning feeling as if I had spent the night with my head
attached to one of those machines they use to test shock absorbers. I
looked at my watch. It was a quarter to ten. I had intended to catch
a train to Sweden at half-past, and I had yet to pack and check out.
I went to the bathroom to struggle through the morning hygiene and
make low death noises, then wandered around the room dealing with

personal effects as I chanced upon them – a sock went onto my foot, a map was forced into the rucksack, a Big Mac box that I had no recollection of acquiring went into the wastebasket – until at last I had assembled my possessions. I needed coffee the way Dan Quayle needs help with an IQ test.

I arrived at the front desk just in time to take up a position behind twenty-seven Italian visitors who, in that interesting way of the Italians, were all trying to check out at once. This didn't help my fragile mood any. At last the Italians departed, moving across the lobby as if surgically linked, and the last I saw of them they were all trying to go out of the revolving door together. I gave my key to the young woman and waited as the computer hummed for a minute, as if getting up steam, and then abruptly spewed out several feet of paper, which was shorn of its sprocket holes and separated into sixteen sheets, the faintest of which was presented to me for inspection.

I was surprised to see that the bill contained a charge for phone calls. The night before – it all seemed so long ago now – I had tried to phone home, but all I got was a recording in Danish which I presumed was telling me that the international lines were engaged or that I was dialling wrongly or possibly that I should just go and fuck myself. In any case, I couldn't get anywhere with it, and after three tries gave up. So I was taken aback to see myself billed for three phone calls. I explained this to the girl.

'Yes,' she said. 'You must pay for any phone calls you try to make, whether or not you are connected.'

'But that's insane.'

She shrugged, as if to say, Maybe it is, maybe it isn't.

'You're telling me,' I said slowly, my head feeling like the gong in a Rank movie, 'that I have to pay for phone calls I didn't make?'

'Yes, that is correct.'

'I didn't use the spare blanket in the cupboard. Do I have to pay you for that, too?' She looked steadily at me, clearly unaware that she was dealing with a person who could tip over the edge into violent insanity at any moment. 'I didn't use the shower cap,' I went on. 'Shall I give you a little something for that? I didn't use one of the bars of soap or the trouser press. This is going to cost me a fortune, isn't it?'

The girl continued to gaze levelly at me, though with a certain noticeable diminishment of goodwill. She had obviously weathered these storms before. 'I am sorry you find these small charges inconvenient, but it is the normal practice in Copenhagen.'

'Well, I think it stinks!' I barked, then caught a glimpse of a seriously demented person in the mirror – wild hair, red face, Parkinson-like shakiness – and recognised myself. I gave her my credit card, scratched a wild signature on the bill, and with a haughty turn exited, regretting only that I didn't have a cape to sling over my shoulder and an ebony stick with which to scatter the doormen.

I should have gone immediately to a café and had two cups of coffee and caught a later train. That would have been the sensible thing to do. Instead, still steaming, I proceeded towards the station at a pace that did my body no good at all, stopping en route at a bank on Strøget to cash a traveller's cheque. It was for only $50 – a snippet in Scandinavia, mere pocket money until I reached Sweden in the evening and would require some serious cash – but for this I was charged the whopping sum of thirty-five kroner, well over ten per cent of the total. I suddenly realised why the Irishman from the night before was swearing at everyone. He had paid one Danish bill too many. 'That's an outrage,' I said, clutching the bank receipt like bad news from a doctor. 'I don't know why I don't just pin money to my jacket and let you people pick it off me!' I shrilled, leaving a row of clerks and customers looking at each other as if to say, What's his problem? Not enough coffee?

And it was in this dim and unfortunate frame of mind that I boarded the morning express to Gothenburg, abused a hapless young conductor for giving me the unwelcome news that it had no buffet car, and sat morosely in a corner, watching the garden-like suburbs of Copenhagen slip past, every nerve ending in my body tingling for caffeine.

11. Gothenburg

On the ferry across the Öresund between Denmark and Sweden, I drank a cup of coffee and began to feel human again. I passed the time staring out at the slate-grey sea and studying my Kümmerly and Frey 'Sudskandinavien' map. Denmark looks like a plate that has been dropped onto a hard floor: it is fractured into a thousand pieces, forming deep bays and scorpion-tail peninsulas and seas within seas. The villages and towns sounded inviting – Aerösköbing, Skaerbaek, Holstenbro, the intriguingly specific Middelfart – and from dozens of them dotted red lines led out to cosily forlorn islands like Anholt and Endelave and above all Bornholm, adrift in the Baltic, closer to Poland than to Denmark. It was my sudden earnest wish to visit them all. There would never be enough time. There never is in life. There wasn't even time for another cup of coffee.

A reddish-brown train was waiting at Helsingborg to take us on to Gothenburg, 152 miles to the north along the west coast. We travelled through a landscape of low hills, red barns, small towns with mustard-coloured town halls, impenetrable pine forests, scattered lakes dotted with clapboard holiday cottages, jetties, upturned rowing boats. Occasionally the train would swing near the coast and give a glimpse through the trees of a cold sea. After a while rain began to streak the window.

I shared a compartment with a tanned young man, blond as only a Swede can be, in wire-rimmed glasses and a pony tail, who was returning to Gothenburg from Marrakech, where he had been wisiting a girlfriend, as he put it. Actually she was a former girlfriend and he hadn't exactly wisited her because upon arriving he discovered she was living with a Moroccan rug merchant – she had somehow neglected to mention this in her postcards – who had pulled out a scimitar and threatened to send the Swede home with his goolies in a sandwich bag if he didn't clear off instantly.

Considering that he had just made a pointless journey of a couple of thousand miles, the young man seemed remarkably equable and spent almost the entire journey sitting cross-legged spooning purple yoghurt into his mouth from an enormous jar and reading a novel by Thomas Mann.

At Ängelholm we were joined by two more people, a grim-looking older woman all in black who looked as if she hadn't smiled since 1937 and who spent the entire journey watching me as if she had seen my face on a wanted poster, and by a fastidious older man who I guessed to be a recently retired schoolmaster and to whom I took an instant dislike.

The young Swede was sitting in the schoolmaster's reserved seat. Not only did the schoolmaster make him move, but instructed him to transfer all his personal effects from the luggage rack above the seat to the rack on the other side, which takes a particular kind of pettiness, don't you think? The schoolmaster then spent an endless period fussily sorting out his things – extracting a folded newspaper and a small bag of plums from his case, arranging the case on the rack, examining the seat minutely for anything unpleasant and giving it a brush with the back of his hand, folding his jacket and his jumper with ritualistic care, adjusting the window in consultation with the lady but without reference to me or the young Swede, getting his case down again for some forgotten item, checking his hankie, readjusting the window. Every time he bent over, his ass bobbed in my face. How I longed for a Smith & Wesson. And every time I looked round there would be that old crone watching me like the Daughter of Death.

And so the morning passed.

I fell into one of those drooly, head-lolling dozes that seem to be more and more a feature of my advancing years. When I woke, I discovered that my companions were also snoozing. The schoolmaster was snoring raspingly, his mouth hugely agape. I noticed that my swaying foot had rubbed against him, leaving a dusty mark on his navy trousers. I further discovered, with cautious movements of my foot, that it was possible to extend the mark from just above his knee almost to his ankle, leaving an interesting streak on the trouser leg. In this means I amused myself for some minutes until I turned my head a fraction and discovered that the old lady was watching me. Immediately, I pretended to be asleep, knowing that if she uttered a sound I would have to smother her with my jacket. But she said nothing.

And so the afternoon passed.

I hadn't eaten since my snackette supper of the night before and I was so hungry that I would have eaten almost anything, even a plate of my grandmother's famous creamed ham and diced carrots, the only dish in history to have been inspired by vomit. Late in the afternoon, a porter came along with a creaking trolley carrying a coffee urn and snackstuffs, and everyone stirred to a kind of frisky wakefulness and examined the fare keenly. I had twenty-four kronor of Swedish money, which I thought a handsome sum, but it proved sufficient to buy just one hopelessly modest open-faced sandwich, like the bottom half of a hamburger bun with a menopausal piece of lettuce and eight marble-sized meatballs on top of it. Eating in Sweden is really just a series of heart-breaks.

I bought the sandwich and carefully peeled away the cellophane, but just as I lifted it to my mouth the train lurched violently over some points, making the bottles clatter in the drinks trolley and causing all the meatballs to jump off the bun, like sailors abandoning a burning ship. I watched with dismay as they hit the floor and bounced to eight dusty oblivions.

I'd have scarcely thought it possible, but the lady in black found a look of even deeper contempt for me. The schoolmaster skittishly slid his feet out of the way, lest a meatball come to rest against his glossy brogues. Only the young Swede and the trolley attendant took a sympathetic interest and pointed helpfully as I gathered up the meatballs and deposited them in the ashtray. This done, I nibbled bleakly on my piece of lettuce and dry bun and dreamed of being almost anywhere else in the universe. Only another two and a half hours to go, I told myself, and fixed the old lady with a hard stare that I hoped somehow conveyed to her what pleasure, what deep and lasting pleasure, it would give me to haul her off her seat and push her out of the window.

*

We reached Gothenburg just after six. Rain was belting down, drumming on the pavements and coursing in torrents through the gutters. I sprinted across the open square outside the station, jacket over head, dodging tramcars with split-second if largely inadvertent precision, skirted a large puddle, feinted between two parked cars, head-faked a lamppost and two startled elderly shoppers (once I start running, I can't stop myself from pretending I'm returning a kick-off for the Chicago Bears. It's a compulsion – a sort of Tourette's syndrome of the feet), and darted breathless and sodden into the first hotel I came to.

I stood in the lobby, a vertical puddle, wiped the steam from my glasses with a corner of shirt tail and realised with a touch of horror, as I hooked my glasses back around my ears, that this was much too grand a place for me. It had potted palms and everything. For a moment I considered bolting, but I noticed that a reptilian young reception clerk was watching me narrowly, as if he thought I might roll up a carpet and try to carry it out under my arm, and I became instantly obstreperous. I was damned if some nineteen-year-old pipsqueak with zits and a clip-on tie was going to make me feel loathsome. I marched to the front desk and enquired the price of a single room for one night. He quoted me the sort of sum that would necessitate a trip to the bank with a wheelbarrow if paid in cash.

'I see,' I said, trying to sound casual. 'I assume it has a private bath and colour TV?'

'Of course.'

'Free shower cap?'

'Yes, sir.'

'Assortment of complimentary bath gels and unguents in a little wicker basket by the sink?'

'Certainly, sir.'

'Sewing kit? Trouser press?'

'Yes, sir.'

'Hair dryer?'

'Yes, sir.'

I played my trump card. 'Magic-wipe disposable shoe sponge?'

'Yes, sir.'

Shit. I had been counting on his saying no to at least one of these so that I could issue a hollow guffaw and depart shaking my head, but he did not and I had no choice but to slink away or sign in. I signed in.

The room was pleasant and business-like, but small, with a twenty-watt reading light – when will Europeans learn that this is just not good enough? – a small TV, a clock radio, a good bath with a shower. I tipped all the lotions from the bathroom into my rucksack, then tossed in the little wicker basket, too – well, why not? – and went through the room harvesting matchbooks, stationery and all the other items that were either complimentary or portable. This done, I ventured out into Gothenburg, still famished.

The rain was falling in sheets. I had thought I might stroll out towards the famous Liseberg Gardens, but I got no more than a couple of hundred yards before I was turned back by the pitiless downpour. I trudged back to the city centre and tried to have a look around the main shopping district, sprinting squelchily from doorway to doorway and from one dripping awning to another, but it was hopeless. I wanted a restaurant, one simple, wholesome restaurant, but there seemed to be none. I was soaked and shivering, and was about to return in a desultory spirit to my hotel to take whatever food was offered there at whatever price, when I noticed an indoor shopping centre and darted in, shaking myself out like a dog. The shops were mostly dreary Woolworth's-type places and they were all shut, but there was a surprising number of people wandering around, as if this were some kind of marvellous place to take an evening stroll. There were a lot of young drunks staggering about too, most of them at that noisy and unattractive stage where they might want to be your pal or pick a fight or just throw up on you, so I gave them a wide berth.

One of the more striking features of Sweden and Norway is how much public drunkenness there is. I mean here you have two countries where you cannot buy a beer without taking out a bank loan, where successive governments have done everything in their power to make drinking not worth the cost and effort, and yet everywhere you go you see grossly intoxicated people –

in stations, on park benches, in shopping centres. I don't begin to understand it.

But then I don't begin to understand a lot of things about Sweden and Norway. It's as if they are determined to squeeze all the pleasure out of life. They have the highest income-tax rates, the higest VAT rates, the harshest drinking laws, the dreariest bars, the dullest restaurants, and television that's like two weeks in Nebraska. Everything costs a fortune. Even the purchase of a bar of chocolate leaves you staring in dismay at your change, and anything larger than that brings tears of pain to your eyes. It's bone-crackingly cold in the winter and it does nothing but rain the rest of the year. The most fun thing to do in these countries is walk around semi-darkened shopping centres after they have closed, looking in the windows of stores selling wheelbarrows and plastic garden furniture at prices no one can afford.

On top of that, they have shackled themselves with some of the most inane and restrictive laws imaginable, laws that leave you wondering what on earth they were thinking about. In Norway, for instance, it is illegal for a barman to serve you a fresh drink until you have finished the previous one. Does that sound to you like a matter that needs to be covered by legislation? It is also illegal in Norway for a bakery to bake bread on a Saturday or Sunday. Well, thank God for that, say I. Think of the consequences if some ruthless Norwegian baker tried to foist fresh bread on people at the weekend. But the most preposterous law of all, a law so pointless as to scamper along the outer margins of the surreal, is the Swedish one that requires motorists to drive with their headlights on during the daytime, even on the sunniest summer afternoon. I would love to meet the guy who thought up that one. He must be head of the Department of Dreariness. It wouldn't surprise me at all if on my next visit to Sweden all the pedestrians are wearing miner's lamps.

I ended up dining in a Pizza Hut in the basement of the shopping centre, the only customer in the place. I had forgotten to bring anything to read with me, so I passed the time waiting for my pizza by staring thoughtfully at the emptiness around me, sipping a glass of water and making up Scandinavian riddles –

Q. How many Swedes does it take to paint a wall?
A. Twenty-seven. One to do the painting and twenty-six to organise the spectators.

Q. What does a Norwegian do when he wants to get high?
A. He takes the filter off his cigarette.

Q. What is the quickest way in Sweden of getting the riot police to your house?
A. Don't take your library book back on time.

Q. There are two staples in the Swedish diet. One is the herring. What is the other?
A. The herring.

Q. How do you recognise a Norwegian on a Mediterranean beach?
A. He's the one in the snowshoes.

– and chuckling quietly in the semi-demented manner of someone who finds himself sitting alone in damp clothes in an empty restaurant in a strange country waiting for a $25 pizza.

Afterwards, just to make an evening of it, I went to the station to purchase a ticket on the next morning's express to Stockholm. You cannot just hop onto a train in Sweden, but must think about it carefully and purchase a ticket in advance. The ticket hall had one of those systems where you take a number from a machine by the door and wait for it to appear above one of the ticket windows. My number was 415, and the highest number seeing action was 391. I waited for twenty minutes and the numbers advanced only to 393, so I wandered off to the station newsagent to look at girlie magazines. The newsagent, alas, was closed, so I looked at a couple of travel posters, and then wandered back. Not entirely to my surprise, I discovered that there had been a frenzy of activity in my absence, and number 415 had come and gone. So I took another number – 432 this time – and a seat and waited for half an hour. When at last my number came I presented myself at the window and asked the man for a ticket on the 10.05 to Stockholm the next morning.

He regarded me sadly. 'I'm sorry, I do not speak English,' he said.

I was taken aback. 'Everybody in Sweden speaks English,' I protested feebly.

His sadness grew. 'I don't. Please you must to go to window sree.' He indicated a window further down the line. 'She speaks vair good English.'

I went to window three and asked for a ticket to Stockholm the next morning. The woman, seeing the number 432 crumpled in my fist, pointed to the number above her window. 'You have the wrong number. This window is for number 436.' Even as she spoke a ferocious-looking lady with grey hair and a dicky hip was hoisting herself out of her chair and charging towards me. I tried to explain my problem with the monoglot at window five, but the ticket lady just shook her head and said, 'You must take another ticket. Then maybe I will call you. Now I must deal with this lady.'

'You are at zer wrong window!' the old lady announced in the bellow of someone whose hearing is going. 'This is *my* window,' she added, and tossed a haughty look to the rest of the room as if to say, Are foreigners stupid as shit, or what?

Forlornly I shuffled over to the machine and took another number. In fact, I took three – I figured this would give me some insurance – then retired to a new seat to watch the board. What a lot of fun I was having! Eventually my number came around again. It directed me to return to window number five – home of the only man in Sweden who speaks no English. I crumpled this ticket and waited for the next to be called. But he called the next one, too. I scampered to his window and begged him not to call my remaining number, but he did.

I couldn't bear to start the whole thing all over again. 'Please,' I said, speaking carefully, 'I just want a one-way ticket to Stockholm for tomorrow morning at 10.05.'

'Certainly,' he said, as if he had never seen me before, took my money and gave me a ticket. It's no wonder so many Swedes kill themselves.

12. Stockholm

In the morning it was still raining, and I gave up hope of exploring Gothenburg before catching my train. Instead I went to the station and spent my children's inheritance on two cups of coffee and a leaden iced bun. The train left promptly at 10.05 and after four hours and twenty minutes of riding through the endless pine forest that is Sweden, I was making my way through the throngs at Stockholm's pleasantly gloomy central station.

I went to the station tourist office to have a room found for me. I had to fill out a form with about 700 questions on it, but it was worth it because the hotel, the Castle on Riddargatan, about a mile from the station, was a charming little find, friendly, clean, and reasonably priced – in so far as that statement can be made about anything in Sweden.

I headed first for Gamla Stan, the old town, on the far side of the Strömbron bridge. It had an oddly Central European feel to it: narrow, hilly streets lined by severe, heavy buildings the colour of faded terracotta, sometimes with chunks of plaster missing, as if they had been struck a glancing blow by tank fire, and often with pieces knocked off the corners where trucks had carelessly backed into them. It had a kind of knocked-about charm, but was surprisingly lacking in any air of prosperity. Most of the windows were dirty, the brass name plates and door knockers were generally unpolished, and almost every building was in serious need of a good coat of paint. It looked much as I would expect Cracow or Bratislava to look. Maybe it was just the rain, which was falling steadily again, bringing its inevitable grey gloom to the city. Did it never stop raining in Sweden?

I walked with shoulders hunched and eyes cast down, avoiding the water that rushed down the steep, slickly cobbled lanes, glancing in the windows of antique shops, wishing I had a hat or an umbrella or a ticket to Bermuda. I retreated into a dark coffee shop, where I sat

shivering, drinking a $3 cup of coffee with both hands, watching the
rain through the window, and realised I had a cold coming on.

I returned to the hotel, had a lavishly steamy bath and a change
of clothes and felt marginally better. I spent the closing hours of
the afternoon studying a map of Stockholm and waiting for the
weather to clear. At about five the sky brightened. I immediately
pulled on my damp sneakers and went out to explore the streets
between Norrmalmstorg, a nearby square, and Kungsträdgården, a
small rectangular park that ran down to the waterfront. Everything
was much better now. It was a Saturday evening and the streets
were full of people meeting friends or partners and repairing in
high spirits to the little restaurants and bistros scattered around the
neighbourhood.

Starving as ever, I looked carefully at several and finally selected
what looked to be the cheeriest and most popular of all, a cavernous
bistro overlooking Norrmalmstorg called Matpalatset. It was friendly
and crowded and wonderfully warm and snug, but the food was
possibly the worst I have ever had outside a hospital cafeteria – a
grey salad with watery cucumber and mushrooms that tasted of old
newspaper, and a lasagne that was not so much cooked as scorched.
Each time I poked it with my knife and fork, the lasagne recoiled
as if I were tormenting it. I was quietly agog. Nowhere else in
Europe could a place serve food this bad and stay in business,
and yet people were queuing at the door. I ate it all because I
was hungry and because it was costing me as much as a weekend
in Brighton, but seldom have I felt more as if I were engaged in a
simple refuelling exercise.

Afterwards I went for a long walk and felt more charitably
disposed to Stockholm now that the rain had stopped. It really is
an exceptionally beautiful city, more watery even than Venice, and
with more parkland per person than any other city in Europe. It is
built on fourteen islands and within a few miles of the city there are
25,000 more, almost all of them dotted with cottages into which the
city drains its population every weekend. I walked far out onto the
broad and leafy avenues and narrower side streets to the north of
the downtown, all of them lined with six-storey apartment buildings,
stern and stolid and yet oddly homy, and at least three-quarters of

the windows were darkened. It must be a burglar's paradise between Friday evening and Sunday afternoon.

I grew up wanting to live in buildings like these. It needn't necessarily have been in Europe – it could have been in Buenos Aires or Dar es Salaam, say – but it had to be in the midst of a big foreign city, full of noises and smells and sights unknown in Iowa. Even now I find myself drawn to these neighbourhoods and able to walk for hours through their anonymous streets, which is what I did now, and I returned to the city centre feeling pleased with Stockholm and content everywhere but in my stomach.

I passed the cinema on Sveavägen where Olof Palme, the Prime Minister, was gunned down in March 1986. He had walked with his wife from their flat nearby to see a movie about Mozart and they had just emerged from the cinema to stroll home when some madman stepped from the shadows and shot him. It seemed to me one of the tragedies of our age because this must have been almost the last important place in the world where a prime minister could be found walking the streets unguarded and standing in movie lines just like a normal person.

The Swedish police did not exactly distinguish themselves. Palme was killed at 11.21 p.m., but the order to watch the roads didn't go out until 12.50 and even then the police in patrol cars weren't told what they were looking for, and the airports were not closed until 1.05 a.m. The police cordoned off a large area outside the cinema and brought in forensic experts to make a minute search of the scene, but both of the assassin's bullets were picked up and handed in by passers-by. A 300-member police unit spent eleven months and $6 million investigating the murder before finally arresting an innocent man. They still don't know who did it.

I strolled aimlessly along Kungsgatan, one of the main shopping streets, past the PUB department store where Greta Garbo used to work in the millinery department, and along the long pedestrian shopping street called Drottninggatan, and felt as if I were entering a different city. Drottninggatan is a mile and a half of concrete charmlessness, and it was awash with rain-sodden litter. There were drunks everywhere, too, stumbling about. I paused to look in some shop window and realised after a moment that a middle-aged man a few yards to my right was peeing down the front of it, as discreetly as he could on a lighted street, which wasn't very discreetly at all. He was seriously intoxicated, but he had a suit on and looked prosperous and educated, and I felt immensely disappointed in him, and in all the hundreds of people who had dropped hamburger boxes and crisp packets all over the streets. This was unworthy of the Swedes. I expected better than that.

I grew up admiring Sweden because it managed to be rich and socialist at the same time, two things I believe everyone ought to be. Coming from a country where no one seemed to think it particularly disgraceful that a child with a brain tumour could be sent home to die because his father didn't have the wherewithal to pay a surgeon, or where an insurance company could be permitted by a state insurance commissioner to cancel the policies of its 14,000 sickest patients because it wasn't having a very good year (as happened in California in 1989), it seemed to me admirable beyond words that a nation could dedicate itself to providing equally and fairly for everyone, whatever the cost.

Not only that, but the Swedes managed to be rich and successful as well, unlike Britain, say, where the primary goal of socialists always seemed to be to make everyone as poor and backward as a shop steward in a British Leyland factory. For years, Sweden was to me the perfect society. It was hard enough to come to terms with the fact that the price to be paid for this was a scandalously high cost of living and an approach to life that had all the gusto of an undertakers' convention, but to find now that there was litter everywhere and educated people peeing on shop fronts was almost too much.

Still starving, I stopped at a mobile fast-food stand near the waterfront and paid a small fortune for the sort of hamburger that leaves you wondering if this could mark the start of a long period on a life-support machine. To say that it was crappy would be to malign faeces. I ate a third of it and dropped the rest in a bin. The rain began to fall again. On top of that my cold was growing worse. I returned to my room in grim spirits.

I woke with my head full of snot and my sneakers full of water, but Stockholm looked better than ever. The sun was out, the air was clean and crisp, more like late October than early April, and the water of the harbour sparkled, as blue as a swimming pool. I walked along Strandvägen, a grand residential boulevard with the boat-lined harbour on one side and imposing apartment houses on the other, out towards Djurgården, an island given over entirely to parkland in the midst of the city. It is the most wonderful place.

Essentially it is just a city park full of grassy knolls and woodland, but scattered through it are all kinds of diversions – a museum of Nordic life, a funfair, a permanent circus, a 'Komedie Teatern', a biological museum, a vast open air museum called Skansen, a technological museum, and much else. Everything was just stirring to life when I arrived. Kiosk awnings outside Skansen were being cranked into place, chairs were being set out at little open-air cafés, ticket booths readied for the happy crowds that would soon be arriving.

I pushed on into the depths of the island, warmed by the morning sunshine. Every couple of hundred yards the road would branch into three or four side roads and whichever one I took would lead through some new and captivating landscape – a view across the water to the green copper roofs of the downtown, a statue of some hero named Gustavus or Adolphus or both astride a prancing horse, a wooded dell full of infant leaves and shafts of golden sunshine. Occasionally I would pass things I wouldn't expect to find in a public park – a boarding school, the Italian embassy, even some grand and very beautiful wooden houses on a hill above the harbour.

One of the many wonderful things about European cities is how often they have parks – like Tivoli, the Bois de Boulogne, the Prater in Vienna – that are more than just parks, that are places where you can not only go for fresh air and a stroll, but also go for a decent meal or visit an amusement park or explore some interesting observatory or zoo or museum. Djurgården is possibly the finest of them all. I spent half a day there, making a lazy circuit of the island, constantly pausing, knuckles on hips, to survey the views, having a coffee outside Skansen, watching the families arriving, and came away admiring Stockholm all over again.

I walked back into the city to Drottninggatan, and it didn't look half so bad in the spring sunshine. Two street-sweeping machines were collecting up the Saturday-night litter, which I was heartened to see, though in fact they were only playing at it because anything that was in a doorway or under a bench or trapped against a wall or in any of the hundreds of other places where most litter ends up was beyond the reach of the machines' brushes, so they left behind as much as they gathered up. And people passing by were already depositing fresh litter in their wake.

I thought I would treat myself to an English newspaper and I needed some tissues for my leaking nose, but there were no shops open anywhere that I could see. Stockholm must be the deadest city in Europe on a Sunday. I stopped for coffee at a McDonald's and helped myself to about seventy-five napkins, then strolled over a low bridge to Skeppsholmen and Kastellholmen, two lovely, sleeping islands in the harbour, and thence back to Gamla Stan, now magically transformed by the sunshine. The mustard- and ochre-coloured buildings seemed positively to glow and the deep shadows in the doorways and windows gave everything a texture and richness it had entirely lacked the day before.

I made a circuit of the colossal royal palace (and I mean colossal – it has 600 rooms), which may be one of the most boring buildings ever constructed. I don't mean that it is ugly or unpleasant. It is just boring, featureless, like the buildings children make by cutting window-holes in cardboard boxes. Still, I enjoyed the sentries, who must be the most engagingly wimpish-looking in the world. Sweden has been at peace for 150 years and remains determinedly unmilitaristic, so I suppose they don't want their soldiers to look too macho and ferocious; as a result they make them wear a white helmet that looks disarmingly like a bathing cap, and white spats straight out of Donald Duck. It's very hard not to go up to one of them and say, sotto voce out of the side of the mouth, 'You know, Lars, you look *quite* ridiculous.'

I walked back down the hill to the waterfront and crossed the Strömbron bridge, stopping midway to lean on the railing and be hypnotised once again by the view of bridges, islands and water. As I stood there a raindrop from out of nowhere struck me on the head, and then another and another.

I looked up to see a turmoil of grey clouds rolling in from the west. Within seconds the sky was black and the rain was in a sudden freefall. People who a moment before had been walking lazily hand in hand in the mild sunshine were now dashing for cover with newspapers over their heads. I stayed where I was, too dumbfounded by the fickleness of the Swedish weather to move, staring out over the now grey, rain-studded water, blowing my nose expansively on McDonald's napkins and thinking in passing that if there were a market for snot I could be a very wealthy man. At length I gazed up at the unkind sky and took an important decision.

I was going to Rome.

13. Rome

Well, I'm sorry. I had intended to reach Rome as you would expect me to, in a logical, systematic way, progressing diligently down the length of Germany, through Austria and Switzerland, across a corner of France and finally arriving, dusty and weary and in desperate need of a launderette, by way of Lombardy and Tuscany. But after nearly a month beneath the endlessly damp skies of northern Europe, I longed for sunshine. It was as simple as that. I wanted to walk down a street in shirtsleeves, to sit out of doors with a cappuccino, to feel the sun on my face. So it was with only the odd wrenching spasm of guilt that I abandoned my planned itinerary and bounded with a single leap across 1,500 miles of Europe. Travelling is more fun – shit, life is more fun – if you can treat it as a series of impulses.

I hadn't been to Rome before, but I had been wanting to go there for about as long as I could remember, certainly since I first saw *La Dolce Vita* as a teenager. I love Italian movies, especially the truly crummy ones – the ones that are dubbed by people who bravely refuse to let a total absence of acting skills stand in the way of a good career. They always star Giancarlo Giannini and the delectable Ornella Muti and have titles that tell you just how bad they are going to be – *A Night Full of Rain, That Summer in Naples, When Spring Comes* – so you have no anxieties that you will be distracted by plots and can concentrate instead on the two important things, namely waiting for Ornella Muti to shed her clothes and looking at the scenery. Italian films are always full of good background shots – usually of Ornella and Giancarlo riding a buzzing Vespa past the Colosseum and the Piazza Navona and the other tourist sights of Rome on the way to having either a brisk bonk or a soulful discussion about how they can't go on like this, usually because one of them is living with Marcello Mastroianni.

Movies everywhere used to be full of this kind of local colour – every film shot in Britain in the 1960s was required by law, if I am not mistaken, to show four laughing swingers in an open-topped Morgan roadster crossing Tower Bridge, filmed from a helicopter at a dizzy angle – but now everyone but the Italians seems to have abandoned the practice, which I think is a huge pity because my whole notion of the world was shaped by the background scenes in films like *To Catch a Thief* and *Breathless* and *Three Coins in a Fountain* and even the Inspector Clouseau movies. If I hadn't seen these pictures, I would be living in Peoria now and thinking that that was about as rich as life gets.

Rome was as wonderful as I had hoped it would be, certainly a step up from Peoria. It was everything Stockholm was not – warm, sunny, relaxed, lively, full of good food and cheap drink. I went to dinner on the first night with an American expatriate friend who had lived there for twenty years and he complained the whole time about how expensive and impossible it had become, but it seemed wonderfully cheap after Stockholm and in any case, as I asked him, how could you sit in the open air on a warm evening eating a splendid meal and bitch about anything at all?

'Sure, sure, but you should try to get your plumbing fixed,' he said, as if that settled everything. After dinner he took me on a brisk walk around the city and showed me how everything had deteriorated – how the bars of the Via Veneto had no class any longer and were full of German and American tourists too stupid and sluggish to know that they were being mercilessly ripped off, how Rugantino's, the nightclub near the Spanish Steps made famous by *La Dolce Vita*, is now a McDonald's, how some once-charming restaurant or hotel had been vandalised by tasteless proprietors whose only motivation was greed.

I listened, but I didn't hear. Everything seemed wonderful to me, even the monumentally impassive waiters, even the cab drivers, even the particular cab driver who bilked me out of the better part of 30,000 lire – the price he quoted to take me from Roma-Termini to my hotel, without bothering to inform me that it was two and a half blocks away and could be walked in thirty seconds – because he did it with such simplicity and charm, forgiving me my stupidity for letting him do this to me. I was so touched that I tipped him.

My hotel was in a battered, out-at-the-elbow district just off the

Via Cavour – it was the sort of neighbourhood where you could pee on the buildings and it would be all right – but it had the compensating virtue of being central. You could walk anywhere in the city from there, and that's what I did, day after day, just walked and walked. I rose daily just after dawn, during that perfect hour when the air still has a fresh, unused feel to it, and watched the city come awake – whistling shopkeepers slopping out, sweeping up, pulling down awnings, pushing up shutters.

I walked through the gardens of the Villa Borghese, up and down the Spanish Steps, window-shopped along the Via dei Condotti, admired the Colosseum and Forum, crossed the river by the Isola Tiberina to tramp the hilly streets of Trastevere, and wandered up to the lofty heights of the Gianicolo, where the views across the city were sensational and where young couples entwined themselves in steamy embraces on the narrow ledges. The Italians appear to have devised a way of having sex without taking their clothes off and they were going at it hammer and tongs up here. I had an ice-cream and watched to see how many of them tumbled over the edge to dash themselves on the rocks below, but none did, thank goodness. They must wear suction cups on their backs.

For a week, I just walked and walked. I walked till my feet steamed. And when I tired I sat with a coffee or sunned myself on a bench, until I was ready to walk again.

Having said this, Rome is not an especially good city for walking. For one thing, there is the constant danger that you will be run over. Zebra crossings count for nothing in Rome, which is not unexpected but takes some getting used to. It is a shock to be strolling across some expansive boulevard, lost in an idle fantasy involving Ornella Muti and a vat of Jell-O, when suddenly it dawns on you that the six lanes of cars bearing down upon you at speed have no intention of stopping.

It isn't that they want to hit you, as they do in Paris, but they just will hit you. This is partly because Italian drivers pay no attention to anything happening on the road ahead of them. They are too busy tooting their horns, gesturing wildly, preventing other vehicles from cutting into their lane, making love, smacking the children in the back seat and eating a sandwich the size of a baseball bat, often all at once. So the first time they are likely to notice you is in the rear-view mirror as something lying in the road behind them.

Even if they do see you, they won't stop. There is nothing personal in this. It's just that they believe that if something is in the way they must move it, whether it is a telephone pole or a visitor from the Middle West. The only exception to this is nuns. Even Roman drivers won't hit a nun – you see groups of them breezing across eight-lane arteries with the most amazing impunity, like scraps of black and white paper borne along by the wind – so if you wish to cross some busy place like the Piazza Venezia your only hope is to wait for some nuns to come along and stick to them like a sweaty T-shirt.

I love the way the Italians park. You turn any street corner in Rome and it looks as if you've just missed a parking competition for blind people. Cars are pointed in every direction, half on the pavements and half off, facing in, facing sideways, blocking garages and side streets and phone boxes, fitted into spaces so tight that the only possible way out would be through the sun roof. Romans park their cars the way I would park if I had just spilled a beaker of hydrochloric acid on my lap.

I was strolling along the Via Sistina one morning when a Fiat Croma shot past and screeched to a smoky halt a hundred feet up the road. Without pause the driver lurched into reverse and came barrelling backwards down the street in the direction of a parking space that was precisely the length of his Fiat, less two and a half feet. Without slowing even fractionally, he veered the car into the space and crashed resoundingly into a parked Renault.

Nothing happened for a minute. There was just the hiss of escaping steam. Then the driver leaped from his car, gazed in profound disbelief at the devastation before him – crumpled metal, splintered tail lights, the exhaust pipe of his own car limply grazing the pavement – and regarded it with as much mystification as if it had dropped on him from the sky. Then he did what I suppose almost any Italian would do. He kicked the Renault in the side as hard as he could, denting the door, punishing its absent owner for having the gall to park it there, then leaped back in his Fiat and drove off as madly as he had arrived, and peace returned once again to the Via Sistina, apart from the occasional clank of a piece of metal dropping off the stricken Renault. No one but me batted an eye.

Italians will park anywhere. All over the city you see them bullying their cars into spaces about the size of a sofa cushion, holding up traffic and prompting every driver within three miles to lean on his horn and give a passable imitation of a man in an electric chair. If the opening is too small for a car, the Romans will decorate it with litter – an empty cigarette packet, a wedge of half-eaten pizza, twenty-seven cigarette butts, half an ice-cream cone with an ooze of old ice-cream emerging from the bottom, danced on by a delirium of flies, an oily tin of sardines, a tattered newspaper and something truly unexpected, like a tailor's dummy or a dead goat.

Even the litter didn't especially disturb me. I know Rome is dirty and crowded and the traffic is impossible, but in a strange way that's part of the excitement. Rome is the only city I know, apart from New York, that you can say that about. In fact, New York is just what Rome reminded me of – it had the same noise, dirt, volubility, honking, the same indolent cops standing around with nothing to do, the same way of talking with one's hands, the same unfocused electric buzz of energy. The only difference is that Rome is so wondrously chaotic. New York is actually pretty well ordered. People stand patiently in queues and for the most part obey traffic signals and observe the conventions of life that keep things running smoothly.

Italians are entirely without any commitment to order. They live their lives in a kind of pandemonium, which I find very attractive. They don't queue, they don't pay their taxes, they don't turn up for appointments on time, they don't undertake any sort of labour without a small bribe, they don't believe in rules at all. On Italian trains every window bears a label telling you in three languages not to lean out of the window. The labels in French and German instruct you not to lean out, but in Italian they merely suggest that it might not be a good idea. It could hardly be otherwise.

Even kidnappers in Italy can be amazingly casual. In January 1988, a gang of them kidnapped an eighteen-year-old named Carlo Celadon. They put him in a six-foot-deep pit in the earth and fed him, but they didn't bother sending a ransom demand until – listen to this – the following October, nine months after they took him. Can you believe that? The kidnappers demanded five billion lire (£2.5 million) and the desperate parents immediately paid up, but the kidnappers then asked for more money. This time the parents balked. Eventually, two years and 100 days after they took him, the kidnappers released him.

At the time of my visit, the Italians were working their way through their forty-eighth government in forty-five years. The country has the social structure of a banana republic, yet the amazing thing is that it thrives. It is now the fifth biggest economy in the *world*, which is a simply staggering achievement in the face of such chronic disorder. If they had the work ethic of the Japanese they could be masters of the planet. Thank goodness they haven't. They are too busy expending their considerable energies on the pleasurable minutiae of daily life – children, good food, arguing in cafés – which is just how it should be.

I was in a neighbourhood bar on the Via Marsala one morning when three workmen in blue boiler suits came in and stopped for coffees at the counter. After a minute one of them started thumping another emphatically on the chest, haranguing him about something, while the third flailed his arms, made mournful noises and staggered about as if his airway were obstructed, and I thought that at any moment knives would come out and there would be blood everywhere, until it dawned on me that all they were talking about was the quality of Schillaci's goal against Belgium the night before or the mileage on a Fiat Tipo or something equally innocuous, and after a minute they drained their coffees and went off together as happy as anything.

What a wonderful country.

I went one morning to the Museo Borghese. I knew from a newspaper clipping that it had been shut in 1985 for two years of repairs – the villa was built on catacombs and for years has been slowly collapsing in on itself – but when I got there it was still covered in scaffolding and fenced off with warped and flimsy sheets of corrugated iron and looked to be nowhere near ready for the public – this a mere five years after it was shut and three years after its forecast reopening.

This is the sort of constant unreliability that must be exasperating to live with (especially if you left your umbrella in the cloak-room the day before it shut), but you quickly take it as an inevitable part of life, like the weather in England.

The care of the nation's cultural heritage is not, it must be said, Italy's strong suit. The country spends $200 million a year on maintenance and restoration, which seems a reasonable sum until it is brought to your attention that that is less than the cost of a dozen new miles of highway, and a fraction of what was spent on stadiums for the 1990 World Cup. Altogether it is less than 0.2 per cent of the national budget. As a result, two-thirds of the nation's treasures are locked away in warehouses or otherwise denied to the public, and many others are crumbling away for want of attention – in March 1989, for instance, the 900-year-old civic tower of Pavia collapsed, just keeled over, killing four people – and there are so many treasures lying around that thieves can just walk off with them. In 1989 alone almost 13,000 works of art were taken from the country's museums and churches, and as I write some 90,000 works of art are missing. Eighty per cent of all the art thefts in Europe take place in Italy.

This casual attitude to the national heritage is something of a tradition in Rome. For a thousand years, usually with the blessings of the Roman Catholic Church (which had a share in the profits and a lot to answer for generally, if you ask me), builders and architects looked upon the city's ancient baths, temples and other timeless monuments as quarries. The Colosseum isn't the hulking ruin it is today because of the ravages of time, but because for hundreds of years people knocked chunks from it with sledgehammers and carted them off to nearby lime kilns to turn into cement. When Bernini needed a load of bronze to build his sumptuous baldacchino in St Peter's, it was stripped from the roof of the Pantheon. It is a wonder that any of ancient Rome survives at all.

Deprived of the opportunity to explore the interior of the Borghese, I wandered instead through the surrounding gardens, now the city's largest and handsomest public park, full of still glades and piercing shafts of sunlight, and enjoyed myself immensely, except for one startled moment when I cut through a wooded corner and encountered a rough-looking man squatted down crapping against a tree, regarding me dolefully. I hadn't thought about this much before, but Europeans do seem to have a peculiar fondness for alfresco excretion. Along any highway in France or Belgium you can see somebody standing beside a parked car having a whizz in the bushes only a foot from the road. In America these people would be taken away and beaten. And in Paris you can still find those extraordinary pissoirs, gun-metal-grey barriers which are designed to let the whole word see who's in there and what he's doing. I could never understand why we passers-by had to be treated to the sight of the occupant's lower legs and upper body. Why couldn't they build the sides six feet high? If a guy went in there we knew what he was doing; we didn't have to keep an eye on him, did we?

I remember once watching a man and two women – office colleagues on their way to lunch, I guessed – carrying on an animated three-way conversation while the man was standing in one of these contraptions. It seemed very odd to me that they were talking as if nothing extraordinary was going on. In England, if such a thing as a pissoir existed, the women would have turned away and talked between themselves, affecting not to be aware of what their colleague was up to in there. But then, according to Reay Tannahill's *Sex in History*, in eighteenth-century France aristocratic men and women thought nothing of going to the toilet together, and sometimes would repair en masse to the privy after dinner in order not to interrupt their lively discussions. I think this explains a lot about the French. As for the Italians, in the working-class argot of Rome if you see an acqaintance on the street, you do not say 'How are you?' or 'How's it going?' but 'Had a good crap today?' Honestly.

And at the end of that enlightening digression, let us make our way to the Vatican City and St Peter's – the world's largest church in its smallest country, as many a guidebook has observed. I had always thought of the Vatican City as being ancient, but in fact as an institution it dates only from 1929, when Mussolini and the Pope signed the Lateran Treaty. I arrived wondering vaguely if I would have to pass through some sort of border control and pay a steep fee, but in fact the only obstacle I encountered were two dozen jabbering men all trying to sell me slide strips or take my photograph with a Polaroid. I directed them to a lady in a Denver Broncos warm-up jacket fifteen feet away saying that she was my wife and had all my money, and they all rushed off to her and I was thus able to cross the great piazza unmolested, pausing only to attach myself briefly to an American tour group, where I learned the aforementioned fact about Mussolini and the Lateran Treaty and was informed which balcony the Pope would come out on if he were going to come out, which he wasn't. This was interesting stuff and I would have stayed with them longer, but the guide quickly spotted me because I wasn't wearing a baseball cap, a warm-up jacket and trousers in one of the livelier primary colours. She informed me that this was a private party, and clearly wasn't going to continue until I had slunk off.

St Peter's doesn't look all that fabulous from the outside, not at least from the piazza at its foot, but step inside and it's so senational that your mouth falls open whether you want it to or not. It is a marvel, so vast and beautiful and cool and filled with treasures and airy heights and pale beams of heavenly light that you don't know where to place your gaze. It is the only building I have ever been in where I have felt like sinking to my knees, clasping my hands heavenward and crying, 'Take me home, Lord.' No structure on earth would ever look the same to me again.

I wandered down the wide central aisle, agog at the scale of the place. It is 730 feet long, 364 feet wide and 438 feet from the floor to the top of the dome. But as Mark Twain noted in *The Innocents Abroad*, the trouble is that because every bit of it is built to such a scale you have to remind yourself continually of its immensity. The four grand pillars that support the dome don't look that mighty in such a setting until you find yourself backing up to one and suddenly realise that it is fifty feet wide, and the baldacchino does indeed look, as Twain said, like nothing more than a magnified bedstead, but it is more than half as high as Niagara Falls. It was only when I looked back down the length of the church to where more visitors were coming in, and I saw that they were like insects, that I had a sudden, crushing sense of just how big this place was. It occurred to me, too, that although the building was nearly silent and seemed almost empty – every clutch of visitors had an area of floor space about the size of a football field – there were none the less hundreds and hundreds of us in there.

I had a look at the 'Pietà' – in a side vault behind a glass screen and a barrier that keeps you so far back you can barely see it, which seemed a bit harsh just because some madman attacked it once years ago – then went to the Sistine Chapel and the museums, and they were naturally impressive, but I confess that all visual experiences were largely wasted on me after the spacious grandeur of St Peter's.

I walked back towards the neighbourhood of my hotel along the Via della Conciliazione and was pleased to find the street crowded with souvenir shops. I have a certain weakness for tacky memorabilia, and in my experience no place is more reliable in this regard than shops specialising in religious curios. Once in Council Bluffs, Iowa, I agonised for an hour over whether to pay $49.95 for a back-lit electric portrait of Christ which when switched on gave the appearance of blood flowing perpetually from his wounds, before finally concluding that it was too tasteless even for me and at any rate I couldn't afford it. So I thought I might find some suitably tasteless compensation here – crucifix corn-on-the-cob holders or a Nativity pen and pencil set or a musical 'Last Supper' toilet-roll holder or at the very least a crucifix paperweight that said MY DAD WENT TO THE VATICAN CITY AND ALL HE BROUGHT ME WAS THIS LOUSY CRUCIFIX. But all the shops sold a more or less identical assortment of rosary beads, crucifixes in 120 sizes, plaster models of the basilica and Pope John Paul dinner plates, none of them in remotely bad taste (unless you really went to town and bought a dozen papal plates for use at dinner parties, but that would cost a fortune), and so I trudged on. One of the worst parts about living in the 1990s is that crappy souvenirs are *so* hard to find these days.

On my final morning I called at the Capuchin monks' mausoleum in the church of Santa Maria della Concezione on the busy Piazza Barberini. This I cannot recommend highly enough. In the sixteenth century some monk had the inspired idea of taking the bones of his fellow monks when they died and using them to decorate the place. Is that rich enough for you? Half a dozen gloomy chambers along one side of the church were filled with such attractions as an altar made of rib cages, shrines meticulously concocted from skulls and leg bones, ceilings trimmed with forearms, wall rosettes fashioned from vertebrae, chandeliers made from the bones of hands and feet. In the odd corner there stood a complete skeleton of a Capuchin monk dressed like the Grim Reaper in his hooded robe, and ranged along the other wall were signs in six languages with such cheery sentiments as WE WERE LIKE YOU. YOU WILL BE LIKE US, and a long poem engagingly called 'My Mother Killed Me!!'. These guys must have been a barrel of laughs to be around. You can imagine every time you got the flu some guy coming along with a tape measure and a thoughtful expression.

Four thousand monks contributed to the display between 1528 and 1870 when the practice was stopped for being just too tacky for words. No one knows quite why or by whom the designs were made, but the inescapable impression you are left with is that the Capuchins once harboured in their midst a half-mad monk with time on his hands and a certain passion for tidiness. It is certainly a nice little money spinner for the church. A constant stream of tourists came in, happy to pay over a stack of lire for the morbid thrill of it all. My only regret, predictably, was that they didn't have a gift shop where you could purchase a boxed set of vertebrae napkin rings, say, or back scratchers made from real arms and hands, but it was becoming obvious that in this respect I was to be thwarted at every turn in Rome.

14. Naples, Sorrento and Capri

I checked out of my hotel and walked to Roma-Termini. It was, in the way of most public places in Italy, a madhouse. At every ticket window customers were gesturing wildly. They didn't seem so much to be buying tickets as pouring out their troubles to the monumentally indifferent and weary-looking men seated behind each window. It is amazing how much emotion the Italians invest in even the simplest transactions.

I had to wait in line for forty minutes while a series of people ahead of me tore their hair and bellowed and eventually were issued with a ticket and came away looking suddenly happy. I couldn't guess what their problems were, and in any case I was too busy fending off the many people who tried to cut in front of me, as if I were holding a door open for them. One of them tried twice. You need a pickaxe to keep your place in a Roman queue.

Finally, with only a minute to spare before my train left, my turn came. I bought a second-class single to Naples – it was easy; I don't know what all the fuss was about – then raced around the corner to the platform and did something I've always longed to do: I jumped onto a moving train – or, to be slightly more precise, fell into it, like a mailbag tossed from the platform.

The train was crowded, but I found a seat by a window and caught my breath and mopped up the blood trickling down my shins as we lumbered slowly out through the endless tower-block suburbs of Rome, picked up speed and moved on to a dusty, hazy countryside full of half-finished houses and small apartment buildings with no sign of work in progress. It was a two-and-a-half-hour journey to Naples and everyone on the train, without apparent exception, passed the time by sleeping, stirring to wakefulness only to note the location when we stopped at some drowsing station or to show a ticket to the conductor when he passed through. Most of the passengers looked poor and unshaven (even several of the women), which was a notable contrast after the worldly elegance of Rome. These, I supposed, were mostly Neopolitan labourers who had come to Rome for the work and were now heading home to see their families.

I watched the scenery – a low plain leading to mountains of the palest green and dotted with occasional lifeless villages, all bearing yet more unfinished houses – and passed the time dreamily embroidering my Ornella Muti fantasy, which had now grown to include a large transparent beach ball, two unicycles, a trampoline and the massed voices of the Mormon Tabernacle Choir. The air in the carriage was warm and still and before long I fell into a doze myself, but was startled awake after a few minutes by a baleful wailing. A gypsy woman, overweight and in a headscarf, was passing along the carriage with a filthy baby, loudly orating the tale of her troubled life and asking for money, but no one gave her any. She pushed the baby in my face – he was covered in chocolaty drool and so startlingly ugly that it was all I could do to keep from going 'Aiieee!' and throwing my hands in front of my face – and I gave her a thousand lire as fast as I could drag it out of my pocket before Junior loosed a string of gooey brown dribble onto me. She took the money with the indifference of a conductor checking a ticket and without thanks proceeded on through the train shouting her troubles anew. The rest of the journey passed without incident.

At Naples, I emerged from the train and was greeted by twenty-seven taxi-drivers, all wanting to take me someplace nice and probably distant, but I waved them away and transferred myself by foot from the squalor of the central station to the squalor of the nearby Circumvesuviana station, passing through an uninterrupted stretch of squalor en route. All along the sidewalks people sat at wobbly tables selling packets of cigarettes and cheap novelties. All the cars parked along the street were dirty and battered. All the stores looked gloomy and dusty and their windows were full of items whose packaging had faded, sometimes almost to invisibility, in the brilliant sunshine. My plan had been to stop in Naples for a day or two before going on to Sorrento and Capri, but this was so awful that I decided to press on at once and come back to Naples when I thought I might be able to face it better.

It was getting on for rush hour by the time I got to Circumvesuviana and bought a ticket. The train was packed with sweating people and very slow. I sat between two fat women, all wobbling flesh, who talked across me the whole time, making it all but impossible for me to follow my book or do any useful work on my Ornella Muti fantasy, but I considered myself lucky to have a place to sit, even if it was only six inches wide, and the women were marvellously soft, it must be said. I spent most of the journey with my head on one or the other of their shoulders, gazing adoringly up at their faces. They didn't seem to mind at all.

We travelled out of the slums of Naples and through the slums of the suburbs and onwards into a slummy strip of countryside between Vesuvius and the sea, stopping every few hundred feet at some suburban station where 100 people would get off and 120 would get on. Even Pompeii and Herculaneum, or Ercolano as they call it nowadays, looked shabby, all washing lines and piles of crumbled concrete, and I could see no sign of the ruins from the train. But a few miles further on we climbed higher up a mountainside and into a succession of tunnels. The air was suddenly cool and the villages – sometimes no more than a few houses and a church in a gap between tunnels – were stunningly pretty with long views down to the blue sea.

I fell in love with Sorrento in an instant. Perhaps it was the time of day, the weather, the sense of relief at being out of Naples, but it seemed perfect: a compact town tumbling down from the station to the Bay of Naples. At its heart was a small, busy square called the Piazza Tasso, lined with outdoor cafés. Leading off the square at one end was a network of echoing alleyways, cool and shadowy and richly aromatic, full of shopkeepers gossiping in doorways and children playing and the general tumult of Italian life. For the rest, the town appeared to consist of a dozen or so wandering streets lined with agreeable shops and restaurants and small, pleasant, old-fashioned hotels hidden away behind heavy foliage. It was lovely, perfect. I wanted to live here, starting now.

I got a room in the Hotel Eden, a medium-sized 1950s establishment on a side street, expensive but spotless, with a glimpse of sea above the rooftops and through the trees, and paced the room manically for five minutes, congratulating myself on my good fortune, before abruptly switching off the lights and returning to the streets. I had a look around, explored the maze of alleyways off the Piazza Tasso and gazed admiringly in the neat and well-stocked shop windows along the Corso Italia, then repaired to an outdoor seat at Tonino's Snack Bar on the square, where I ordered a Coke and watched the passing scene, radiating contentment.

The town was full of middle-aged English tourists having an off-season holiday (i.e. one they could afford). Wisps of conversation floated to me across the tables and from couples passing on the sidewalk. It was always the same. The wife would be in noise-making mode, that incessant, pointless, mildly fretful chatter that overtakes Englishwomen in mid-life. 'I was going to get tights today and I forgot. I asked you to remind me, Gerald. These ones have a ladder in them from here to Amalfi. I suppose I *can* get tights here. I haven't a clue what size to ask for. I knew I should have packed an extra pair . . .' Gerald was never listening to any of this, of course, because he was secretly ogling a braless beauty leaning languorously against a lamppost and trading quips with some local yobbos on Vespas, and appeared to be aware of his wife only as a mild, chronic irritant on the fringe of his existence. Everywhere I went in Sorrento I kept seeing these English couples, the wife looking critically at everything, as if she was working undercover for the Ministry of Sanitation, the husband dragging along behind her, worn and defeated.

I had dinner at a restaurant just off the square. It was packed, but super-friendly and efficient and the food was generous and superb – ravioli in cream, a heap of scallopine alla Sorrentino, a large but simple salad and an over-ample bowl of home-made ice-cream that had tears of pleasure welling in my eye sockets.

Afterwards, as I sat bloated with a coffee and a cigarette, resting my stomach on the tabletop, an interesting thing happened. A party of eight people came in, looking rich and self-important and distinctly shady, the women in furs, the men in cashmere coats and sunglasses, and within a minute a brouhaha had erupted, sufficiently noisy to make the restaurant fall silent as everyone, customers and waiters alike, looked over.

Apparently the new arrivals had a reservation, but their table wasn't ready – there wasn't an empty table in the place – and they were engaged in various degrees in making a stink about it. The manager, wringing his hands, soaked up the abuse and had all his waiters dashing around like scene shifters, with chairs and tablecloths and vases of flowers, trying to assemble a makeshift table for eight in an already crowded room. The only person not actively involved in this was the head of the party, a man who looked uncannily like Adolfo Celli and stood aloof, a £500 coat draped over his shoulders. He said nothing except to make a couple of whispered observations into the ear of a pock-faced henchman, which I assumed involved concrete boots and the insertion of a dead fish in someone's mouth.

The head waiter dashed over and bowingly reported that they had so far assembled a table for six, and hoped to have the other places shortly, but if in the mean time the ladies would care to be seated . . . He touched the floor with his forehead. But this was received as a further insult. Adolfo whispered again to his henchman, who departed, presumably to get a machine gun or to drive a bulldozer through the front wall.

Just then I said, 'Scusi' (for my Italian was coming on a treat), 'you can have my table. I'm just going.' I drained my coffee, gathered my change and stood up. The manager looked as if I had saved his life, which I would like to think I may have, and the head waiter clearly thought about kissing me full on the lips but instead covered me with obsequious 'Grazie's. I've never felt so popular. The waiters beamed and many of the other diners regarded me with, if I say it myself, a certain lasting admiration. Even Adolfo inclined his head in a tiny display of gratitude and respect. As my table was whipped away, I was escorted to the door by the manager and head waiter who bowed and thanked me and brushed my shoulders with a whisk broom and offered me their daughters' hands in marriage or just for some hot sex. I turned at the door, hesitated for a moment, suddenly boyish and good-looking, a Hollywood smile on my face, tossed a casual wave to the room and disappeared into the evening.

Weighted down with good pasta and a sense of having brought peace to a troubled corner of Sorrento, I strolled through the warm twilight along the Corso Italia and up to the coast road to Positano, the high and twisting Via del Capo, where hotels had been hacked into the rock-face to take advantage of the commanding view across the Bay of Naples. All the hotels had names that were redolent of another age – the Bel Air, the Bellevue Syrene, the Admiral, the Caravel – and looked as if they hadn't changed a whit in forty years. I spent an hour draped over the railings at the roadside, staring transfixed across the magical sweep of bay to Vesuvius and distant Naples and, a little to the left, floating in the still sea, the islands of Procida and Ischia. Lights began to twinkle on around the bay and were matched by early-evening stars in the grainy blue sky. The air was warm and kind and had a smell of fresh-baked bread. This was as close to perfection as anything I had ever encountered.

On the distant headland overlooking the bay was the small city of Pozzuoli, a suburb of Naples and home town of Sophia Loren. The citizens of Pozzuoli enjoy the dubious distinction of living on the most geologically unstable piece of land on the planet, the terrestrial equivalent of a Vibro-Bed. They experience up to 4,000 earth tremors a year, sometimes as many as a hundred in a day. People in Pozzuoli are so used to having pieces of plaster fall into their ragù and tumbling chimney stacks knock off their grannies that they hardly notice it any more.

This whole area is like an insurance man's worst nightmare. Earthquakes are a way of life in Calabria – Naples had one in 1980 that left 120,000 people homeless, and another even fiercer one could come at any time. It's no wonder they worry about earthquakes. The towns are built on hills so steep that they look as if the tiniest rumble would send them sliding into the sea. And on top of that, quite literally, there's always Vesuvius grumbling away in the background, still dangerously alive. It last erupted in 1944, which makes this its longest period of quiescence since the Middle Ages. Doesn't sound too promising, does it?

I stared for a long time out across the water at Pozzuoli's lights and listened intently for a low boom, like scaffolding collapsing, or the sound of the earth tearing itself apart, but there was nothing, only the mosquito buzz of an aeroplane high above, a blinking red dot moving steadily across the sky, and the soothing background hum of traffic.

In the morning I walked through bright sunshine down to the Sorrento marina along a perilously steep and gorgeous road called the Via da Maio, in the shadow of the grand Excelsior Vittoria Hotel, and took a nearly empty hover-ferry to Capri, a mountainous outcrop of green ten miles away off the western tip of the Sorrentine peninsula.

Up close, Capri didn't look much. Around the harbour stood a dozing, unsightly collection of shops, cafés and ferry booking offices. All of them appeared to be shut, and there was not a soul about, except for a sailor with Popeye arms lazily coiling rope at the quayside. A road led steeply off up the mountain. Beside it stood a sign saying CAPRI 6 KM.

'Six kilometres!' I squeaked.

I had with me two incredibly useless guidebooks to Italy, so useless in fact that I'm not even going to dignify them by revealing their titles here, except to say that one of them should have been called *Let's Go Get Another Guidebook* and the other was Fodor's (I was lying a moment ago) and neither of them so much as hinted that Capri town was miles away up a vertical mountainside. They both made it sound as if all you had to do was spring off the ferry and there you were. But from the quayside Capri town looked to be somewhere up in the clouds.

The funicolare up the mountainside wasn't running. (Natch.) I looked around for a bus or a taxi or even a donkey, but there was nothing, so I turned with a practised sigh and began the long trek up. It was a taxing climb, mollified by some attractive villas and sea views. The road snaked up the mountain in a series of long, lazy S-bends, but a mile or so along some steep and twisting steps had been hewn out of the undergrowth and they appeared to offer a more direct, if rather more precipitate, route to Capri town. I ventured up them. I have never seen such endless steps. They just went on and on. They were closed in by the whitewashed walls of villas on both sides and overhung by tumbling fragrant shrubs – highly fetching, but after about the three-hundredth step I was gasping and sweating so much that the beauty was entirely lost on me.

Because of the irregular geography of the hillside, it always looked as if the summit might be just ahead, but then I would round a turning to be confronted by another expanse of steps and yet another receding view of the town. I stumbled on, reeling from wall to wall, gasping and wheezing, shedding saliva, watched with solemn interest by three women in black coming down the steps with the day's shopping. The only thing sustaining me was the thought that clearly I was going to be the only person tenacious enough to make the climb to Capri. Whatever lay up there was going to be mine, all mine. Eventually the houses grew closer together until they were interconnected, like blocks of Lego, and the steps became a series of steep cobbled alleyways. I passed beneath an arch and stepped out into one of the loveliest squares I have ever seen. It was packed with German and Japanese tourists. The tears streamed down my cheeks.

I got a room in the Hotel Capri. 'Great name! How long did it take you to come up with it?' I asked the manager, but he just gave me that look of studied disdain that European hotel managers reserve for American tourists and other insects. I don't know why he was so snooty because it wasn't a great hotel. It didn't even have a bell-boy, so the manager had to show me to my room himself, though he left me to deal with my baggage. We went up a grand staircase, where two workmen were busy dribbling a nice shade of ochre on the marble steps and occasionally putting some of it on the wall, to a tiny room on the third floor. As he was the manager, I wasn't sure whether to give him a tip, as I would a bellboy, or whether this would be an insult to his lofty position. In the event, I settled on what I thought was an intelligent compromise. I tipped him, but I made it a very small tip. He looked at it as if I had dropped a ball of lint into his palm, leading me to conclude that perhaps I had misjudged the situation. 'Maybe you'll laugh at my jokes next time,' I remarked cheerfully, under my breath, as I shut the door on him.

Capri town was gorgeous, an infinitely charming little place of villas and tiny lemon groves and long views across the bay to Naples and Vesuvius. The heart of the town was a small square, the Piazza Umberto I, lined with cream-coloured buildings and filled with tables and wicker chairs from the cafés ranged around it. At one end, up some wide steps, stood an old church, dignified and white, and at the other was a railinged terrace with an open view to the sea far below.

I cannot recall a more beguiling place for walking. The town consisted almost entirely of a complex network of white-walled lanes and passageways, many of them barely wider than your shoulders, and all of them interconnected in a wonderfully bewildering fashion, so that I would constantly find myself returning unexpectedly to a spot I had departed from in an opposing direction ten minutes before. Every few yards an iron gate would be set in the wall and through it I could glimpse a white cottage in a jungle of flowery shrubs and, usually, a quarry-tiled terrace overlooking the sea. Every few yards a cross-passageway would plunge off down the hillside or a set of steps would climb half-way to the clouds to a scattering of villas high above. I wanted every house I saw.

There were no roads at all, apart from the one leading from the harbour to the town and onward to Anacapri, on the far side of the island. Everywhere else had to be got to on foot, often after an arduous trek. Capri must be the worst place in the world to be a washing-machine delivery man.

Most of the shops lay beyond the church, up the steps from the central piazza, in yet another series of lanes and little squares of unutterable charm. They all had names like Gucci and Yves St Laurent, which suggested that the summertime habitués must be rich and insufferable, but mercifully most of the shops were still not open for the season, and there was no sign of the yachting-capped assholes and bejewelled crinkly women who must make them prosper in the summer.

A few of the lanes were enclosed, like catacombs, with the upper

storeys of the houses completely covering the passageways. I followed
one of these lanes now as it wandered upward through the town and
finally opened again to the sky in a neighbourhood where the villas
began to grow larger and enjoy more spacious grounds. The path
meandered and climbed, so much so that I grew breathless again
and propelled myself onwards by pushing my hands against my
knees, but the scenery and setting were so fabulous that I was
dragged on, as if by magnets. Near the top of the hillside the
path levelled out and ran through a grove of pine trees, heavy with
the smell of rising sap. On one side of the path were grand villas
– I couldn't imagine by what method they got the furniture there
when people moved in or out – and on the other was a giddying
view of the island: white villas strewn across the hillsides, half
buried in hibiscus and bougainvillaea and a hundred other types
of shrub.

It was nearly dusk. A couple of hundred yards further on the
path rounded a bend through the trees and ended suddenly, breathtakingly, in a viewing platform hanging out over a precipice of rock –
a little patio in the sky. It was a look-out built for the public, but
I had the feeling that no one had been there for years, certainly no
tourist. It was the sheerest stroke of luck that I had stumbled on it.
I have never seen anything half as beautiful: on one side the town
of Capri spilling down the hillside, on the other the twinkling lights
of the cove at Anacapri and the houses gathered around it, and in
front of me a sheer drop of – what? – 200 feet, 300 feet, to a sea
of the lushest aquamarine washing against outcrops of jagged rock.
The sea was so far below that the sound of breaking waves reached
me as the faintest of whispers. A sliver of moon, brilliantly white,
hung in a pale blue evening sky, a warm breeze teased my hair and
everywhere there was the scent of lemon, honeysuckle and pine.
It was like being in the household-products section of Sainsbury's.
Ahead of me there was nothing but open sea, calm and seductive, for
150 miles to Sicily. I would do anything to own that view, anything.
I would sell my mother to Robert Maxwell for it. I would renounce
my citizenship and walk across fire. I would swap hair – yes! – with
Andrew Neil.

Just above me, I realised after a moment, overlooking this secret place was the patio of a villa set back just out of sight. Somebody *did* own that view, could sit there every morning with his muesli and orange juice, in his Yves St Laurent bathrobe and Gucci slippers, and look out on this sweep of Mediterranean heaven. It occurred to me that it probably was owned by Donald Trump, or the Italian equivalent, some guy who only uses it for about two minutes a decade and then is too busy making deals and screwing people by telephone to notice the view. Isn't it strange how wealth is always wasted on the rich? And with this discouraging thought I returned to the town.

I had dinner in a splendid, friendly, almost empty restaurant on a back street, sitting in a window seat with a view over the sea, and had the chilling thought that I was becoming stupefied with all this ease and perfection. I began to feel that sort of queasy guilt that you can only know if you have lived among the English – a terrible sense that any pleasure involving anything more than a cup of milky tea and a chocolate digestive biscuit is somehow irreligiously excessive. I knew with a profound sense of doom that I would pay for this when I got home – I would have to sit for whole evenings in an icy draught and go for long tramps over wild, spongy moors and eat at a Wimpy at least twice before I began to feel even the tiniest sense of expiation. Still, at least I was feeling guilty for enjoying myself so much, and that made me feel slightly better.

It was after eight when I emerged from the restaurant, but the neighbouring businesses were still open – people were buying wine and cheese, picking up a loaf of bread, even having their hair cut. The Italians sure know how to arrange things. I had a couple of beers in the Caffè Funicolare, then wandered idly into the main square. The German and Japanese tourists were nowhere to be seen, presumably tucked up in bed or more probably hustled back to the mainland on the last afternoon ferry. Now it was just locals, standing around in groups of five or six, chatting in the warm evening air, beneath the stars, with the black sea and far-off lights of Naples as a backdrop. It seemed to be the practice of the townspeople to congregate here after supper for a half-hour's conversation. The teenagers all lounged on the church steps, while the smaller children raced among the grown-ups' legs. Everyone seemed incredibly happy. I longed to be part of it, to live on this green island with its wonderful views and friendly people and excellent food and to stroll nightly here to this handsome square with its incomparable terrace and chat to my neighbours.

I stood off to one side and studied the dynamics of it. People drifted about from cluster to cluster, as they would at a cocktail party. Eventually they would gather up their children and wander off home, but then others would come along. No one seemed to stay for more than half an hour, but the gathering itself went on all evening. A young man, who was obviously a newcomer to Capri, stood shyly on the fringe of a group of men, smiling at their jokes. But after a few moments he was brought into the conversation, literally pulled in with an arm, and soon he was talking away with the rest of them.

I stood there for ages, perhaps for an hour and a half, then turned and walked back towards my hotel and realised that I had fallen spectacularly, hopelessly and permanently in love with Italy.

I awoke to a gloomy day. The hillsides behind the town were obscured by a wispy haze and Naples across the bay appeared to have been taken away in the night. There was nothing but a plane of dead sea and beyond it the sort of tumbling fog that creatures from beyond the grave stumble out of in B-movies. I had intended to walk to the hilltop ruins of Tiberius's villa, where the old rascal used to have guests who displeased him hurled over the ramparts onto the rocks hundreds of feet below, but when I emerged from the hotel a cold, slicing rain was falling, and I spent the morning wandering from café to café, drinking cappuccinos and scanning the sky. Late in the morning, out of time to see the villa unless I stayed another day, which I could scarce afford to do, I checked reluctantly out of the Hotel Capri and walked down the steep and slippery steps to the quay where I purchased a ticket on a slow ferry to Naples.

Naples looked even worse after Sorrento and Capri than it had before. I walked for half a mile along the waterfront, but there was no sign of happy fishermen mending their nets and singing 'Santa Lucia', as I had fervently hoped there might be. Instead there were just menacing-looking derelicts and mountains – and I mean mountains – of rubbish on every corner and yet more people selling lottery tickets and trinkets from cardboard boxes.

I had no map and only the vaguest sense of the geography of the city, but I turned inland hoping that I would blunder onto some shady square lined with small but decent hotels. Surely even Naples must have its finer corners. Instead I found precisely the sort of streets that you automatically associate with Naples – mean, cavernous, semi-paved alleyways, with plaster peeling off walls and washing hung like banners between balconies that never saw sunlight. The streets were full of overplump women and unattended children, often naked from the waist down, in filthy T-shirts.

I felt as if I had wandered onto another continent. In the centre of Naples some 70,000 families live even now in cramped bassi – tenements without baths or running water, sometimes without even a window, with up to fifteen members of an extended family living together in a single room. The worst of these districts, the Vicaria, where I was now, is said to have the highest population density in Europe, possibly in the world now that the Forbidden City in Hong Kong is being demolished. And it has crime to match – especially the pettier crimes like car theft (29,000 in one year) and muggings. Yet I felt safe enough. No one paid any attention to me, except occasionally to give me a stray smile or, among the younger people, to shout some smart-ass but not especially hostile wisecrack. I was clearly a tourist with my rucksack, and I confess I clutched the straps tightly, but there was no sign of the scippatori, the famous bag snatchers on Vespas, who doubtless sensed that all they would get was some dirty underpants, half a bar of chocolate and a tattered copy of H. V. Morton's *A Traveller in Southern Italy*.

They are used to having a hard time of it in Naples. After the war, people were so hungry that they ate everything alive in the city, including all the fish in the aquarium, and an estimated third of the women took up prostitution, at least part-time, just to survive. Even now the average worker in Naples earns less than half of what he would receive in Milan. But it has also brought a lot of problems on itself, largely through corruption and incompetence.

As of 1986, according to *The Economist*, the city had not paid

its own street-lighting bill for three years and had run up a debt of
$1.1 billion. Every service in the city is constantly on the brink of
collapse. It has twice as many dustmen as Milan, a bigger city, but
the streets are filthy and the service is appalling. The city has become
effectively ungovernable.

I passed the Istituto Tecnico Commerciale, where a riot seemed to
be in progress both inside and outside the building. Students inside
were hanging out of the upstairs windows, tossing down books and
papers, and holding shouted exchanges with their colleagues on the
ground. Whether this was some sort of protest or merely part of the
daily routine I couldn't tell. All I know is that everywhere I went there
was rubbish and pandemonium – people shouting, horns honking,
ambulances bleating.

After Capri the din and filth were hard to take. I walked and
walked and it never got any better. I found the main shopping
street, the Via Roma, and though the shops were generally smart,
it was thronged with people and litter and all but impossible to
walk along without stepping down off the pavement and into the
edge of the lunatic traffic. Not once did I see a hotel that looked as
if its beds were occupied for more than twenty minutes at a time.

Eventually, to my considerable surprise, I found myself in the
Piazza Garibaldi, in front of the central railway station. I had
walked right the way across Naples. Sweat-streaked and footsore, I
looked back at the city I had just walked through and thought about
giving it one more try. But I couldn't face it. Instead I went into the
station, waving off the twenty-seven taxi drivers, and bought a ticket
to Florence. Things would have to be better there.

15. Florence

I went on the world's slowest train to Florence. It limped across the landscape like a runner with a pulled muscle, and it had no buffet. At first it was crowded, but as afternoon gave way to evening and evening merged into the inkiness of night, there were fewer and fewer of us left, until eventually it was just a businessman buried in paperwork and a guy who looked as if he was on his way to an Igor look-alike competition and me. Every two or three miles the train stopped at some darkened station where no train had stopped for weeks, where grass grew on the platforms and where no one got on and no one got off.

Sometimes the train would come to a halt in the middle of nowhere, in the black countryside, and just sit. It would sit for so long that you began to wonder if the driver had gone off into the surrounding fields for a pee and fallen down a well. After a time the train would roll backwards for perhaps thirty yards, then stop and sit again. Then suddenly, with a mighty *whoomp* that made the carriage rock and the windows sound as if they were about to implode, a train on the parallel line would fly past. Bright lights would flash by – you could see people in there dining and playing cards, having a wonderful time, moving across Europe at the speed of a laser – and then all would be silence again and we would sit for another eternity before our train gathered the energy to creep onwards to the next desolate station.

It was well after eleven when we reached Florence. I was starving and weary and felt that I deserved any luxury that came my way. I saw with alarm, but not exactly surprise, that the restaurants around the station were all closed. One snack bar was still lighted and I hastened to it, dreaming of a pizza the size of a dustbin lid, drowning in mushrooms and salami and olive oil, but the proprietor was just locking up as I reached the door.

Dejected, I went to the first hotel I came to, a modern concrete box half a block away. I could tell from the outside that it was going to be expensive, and it contravened all my principles to patronise a hotel of such exquisite ugliness, especially in a city as historic as Florence, but I was tired and hungry and in serious need of a pee and a face-wash and my principles were just tapped out.

The receptionist quoted me some ludicrous figure for a single room, but I accepted with a surrendering wave and was shown to my room by a 112-year-old porter who escorted me into the world's slowest lift and from whom I learned, during the course of our two-day ascent to the fifth floor, that the dining-room was closed and there was no room service – he said this with a certain smack of pride – but that the bar would be open for another thirty-five minutes and I might be able to get some small snackstuff there. He waggled his fingers cheerfully to indicate that this was by no means a certainty.

I was desperate for a pee and to get to the bar before it shut, but the porter was one of those who feel they have to show you everything in the room and required me to follow him around while he demonstrated the shower and television and showed me where the cupboard was. 'Thank you, I would never have found that cupboard without you,' I said, pressing thousand-lire notes into his pocket and more or less bundling him out the door. I don't like to be rude, but I felt as if I were holding back the Hoover Dam. Five more seconds and it would have been like trying to deal with a dropped fire hose. As it was I only barely made it, but oh my, the relief. I washed my face, grabbed a book and hastened to the lift. I could hear it still descending. I pushed the Down button and looked at my watch. Things weren't too bad. I still had twenty-five minutes till the bar closed, time enough for a beer and whatever snacks they could offer. I pushed the button again and passed the time by humming the Waiting for an Elevator Song, puffing my cheeks for the heck of it and looking speculatively at my neck in the hallway mirror.

Still the elevator didn't come. I decided to take the fire stairs. I bounded down them two at a time, the whole of my existence dedicated to the idea of a beer and a sandwich, and at the bottom found a padlocked door and a sign in Italian that said IF THERE IS EVER A FIRE HERE, THIS IS WHERE THE BODIES WILL PILE UP. Without pause, I bounded back up to the first floor. The door there was locked, too. Through a tiny window I could see the bar, dark and cosy and still full of people. Somebody was playing a piano. What's more, there were little bowls of peanuts and pistachios on each table. I'd settle for that! I tapped on the door and scraped it with my fingernails, but nobody could hear me, so I bounded up to the second floor and the door there was unlocked, thank goodness. I went straight to the lift and jabbed the Down button. An instant later the Up light dinged on and the doors slid open to reveal three Japanese men in identical blue suits. I indicated to them, as best I could in my breathless state, that they were going the wrong direction for me and that my reluctance to join them had nothing to do with Pearl Harbor or anything like that. We exchanged little bows and the door closed.

I pushed the Down button again and immediately the doors popped open to reveal the Japanese men. This was repeated four times until it dawned on me that I was somehow cancelling out their instructions to ascend, so I stood back and let them go away. I waited a full two minutes; caught my breath, counted my remaining traveller's cheques, hummed the Elevator Song, glanced at my watch – ten minutes till closing! – and pushed the Down button.

Immediately the doors opened to reveal the Japense men still standing there. Impulsively I jumped in with them. I don't know if it was the extra weight that kick-started it or what but we began to rise, at the usual speed of about one foot every thirty seconds. The lift was tiny. We were close enough together to be arrested in some countries and as I was facing them, all but rubbing noses, I felt compelled to utter some pleasantry.

'Businessmen?' I asked.

One of them gave a small, meaningless bow from the shoulders.

'In Italy on business?' I elaborated. It was a stupid question. How many people go on holiday in blue suits?

The Japanese man bowed again and I realised he had no idea what I was saying.

'Do you speak English?'

'Ahhhr . . . no,' said the second man, as if not certain, swaying just a tiny bit, and it dawned on me that they were all extremely drunk. I looked at the third man and he bowed before I could say anything.

'You guys been to the bar?' A small uncomprehending bow. I was rather beginning to enjoy this one-way conversation. 'You look like you've had a few, if you don't mind me saying so. Hope nobody's going to be sick!' I added jauntily.

The elevator crept on and eventually thudded to a halt. 'Well, here we are, gentlemen, eighth floor. Alight here for all stations to Iwo Jima.'

They turned to me in the hallway and said simultaneously, 'Buon giorno.'

'And a very buon giorno to you,' I riposted, jabbing button number one anxiously.

I got to the bar two minutes before it shut, though in fact it was effectively shut already. An over-zealous waiter had gathered up all the little dishes of nuts and the pianist was nowhere to be seen. It didn't really matter because they didn't serve snacks there anyway. I returned to my room, rummaged in the mini-bar and found two tiny foil bags containing about fourteen peanuts each. I searched again, but this was the only food among the many bottles of soft drinks and intoxicants. As I stood eating the peanuts one at a time, to make the pleasure last, I idly looked at the mini-bar tariff card and discovered that this pathetic little snack was costing me $4.80. Or at least it would have if I'd been foolish enough to tell anyone about it.

In the morning I transferred to the Hotel Corallo on the Via Nazionale. The room had no TV, but there was a free showercap and it was 50,000 lire a day cheaper. I have never seen a smaller bathroom. It was so small that there was no stall for the shower. You just shut the door to the bedroom and let the shower spray all over everything – over the toilet, over the sink, over yesterday's copy of the *Guardian*, over your fresh change of underwear.

I went first to the cathedral, the centrepiece of the town. I defy anyone to turn the corner into the Piazza del Duomo and not have his little heart leap. It is one of Europe's great sights.

But it was packed with tourists and with people trying to sell them things. When I was there in 1972, Florence was crowded, but it was August and you expected it. But this was a weekday in April, in the middle of the working year, and it was far worse. I walked down to the Uffizi Palace and around the Piazza della Signoria and the other

fixtures of the old part of town and it was the same everywhere –
throngs of people, almost all of them from abroad, shuffling about in
that aimless, exasperating way of visitors, in groups of five and six,
always looking at something about twenty feet above ground level.
What is it they see up there?

In my adolescent years whenever I was in crowded places I often
pretended I had a ray gun with me, which I could use to vaporise
anyone I didn't like the look of – dawdlers, couples in matching
outfits, children called Junior and Chip. I always imagined myself
striding through the crowd, firing the gun at selected targets and
shouting, 'Make way, please! Culling!' I felt a little like that now.

There were hundreds of Japanese – not just the traditional busloads
of middle-aged camera-toters but also students and young couples
and backpackers. They were at least as numerous as the Americans,
and the Americans were everywhere, plus hordes of Germans and
Australians and Scandinavians and Dutch and British and on and
on. You wonder how many people one city can absorb.

Here's an interesting statistic for you: in 1951, the year I was
born, there were seven million international airline passengers in
the world. Nowadays that many people fly to Hawaii every year.
The more popular tourist places of Europe routinely receive numbers
of visitors that dwarf their own populations. In Florence, the annual
ratio of tourists to locals is 14:1. How can any place preserve any
kind of independent life when it is so manifestly overwhelmed? It
can't. It's as simple as that.

It is of course hypocritical to rail against tourists when you are
one yourself, but none the less you can't escape the fact that mass
tourism is ruining the very things it wants to celebrate. And it can
only get worse as the Japanese and other rich Asians become bolder
travellers. When you add in the tens of millions of eastern Europeans
who are free at last to go where they want, we could be looking back
on the last thirty years as a golden age of travel, God help us all.

Nowhere is the decline in quality in Florence more vivid than on
the Ponte Vecchio, the shop-lined bridge across the Arno. Twenty
years ago the Ponte Vecchio was home to silversmiths and artisan
jewellers and it was quiet enough, even in August, to take a picture
of a friend (or in my case a picture of Stephen Katz) sitting on the

bridge rail. Now it's like the stowage deck of the *Lusitania* just after somebody's said, 'Say, is that a torpedo?' It was covered with Senegalese immigrants selling semi-crappy items of jewellery and replica Louis Vuitton luggage spread out on blankets or pieces of black velvet. And the crowds of tourists pushing among them were unbelievable. It took me half an hour to bull my way through, and I didn't try again for the rest of the week. Far easier, I concluded, to make a quarter-mile detour to the Ponte di Santa Trinita, the next bridge downriver, and cross from there.

The city fathers of Florence could do a great deal more to ease the pressures – like allow museums to be open for more than a couple of hours a day, so that everybody doesn't have to go at once. I went to the Uffizi now and had to stand in line for forty minutes and then had to shuffle around amid crowds of people straining to see the paintings. Several rooms were roped off and darkened. Again, surely, they could spread the crowds around by opening more rooms and showing more paintings. In 1900 the Uffizi had 2,395 paintings on display. Today it shows just 500. The others are locked away, almost never seen.

Still, few galleries are more worth the frustration. The Uffizi must have more perfect paintings than any other gallery on the planet – not just Tintorettos and Botticellis, but the most sumptuous and arresting works by people quite unknown to me, like Gentile da Fabriano and Simone Martini. It struck me as odd that the former pair could be so much more famous than the latter. Then again, a hundred years from now it could easily be the other way around. Old masters come and go. Did you know, for instance, that Piero della Francesca was all but unknown a century ago? It seems to me impossible to look at his portraits of the Duke of Urbino and not see them instantly as masterpieces, but Ruskin in all his writings mentioned him only once in passing, and Walter Pater mentioned him not at all, and the bible of the nineteenth-century art world, Heinrich Wolfflin's *Classic Art*, appears to be unaware of his existence. It wasn't until 1951, with a study by Kenneth Clark, that people really began to appreciate him again. The same was true of Caravaggio and Botticelli, whose works spent much of two centuries tucked away in attics, quite unloved. Caravaggio's 'Bacchus' was found in an Uffizi store-room in 1916.

*

I spent four days wandering around Florence, trying to love it, but mostly failing. The famous view of the rooftops from the Boboli Gardens – the one that graces a thousand postcards – was splendid and entrancing, and I liked the long walks along the Arno, but mostly it was disappointing. Even when I made allowance for the hordes of tourists, I couldn't help feeling that much of it was tawdrier than any city this beautiful and historic and lavishly subsidised by visitors like me had any right to be. There was litter everywhere and gypsy beggars constantly importuning and Senegalese street vendors cluttering every sidewalk with their sunglasses and Louis Vuitton luggage, and cars parked half on the narrow pavements so that you constantly had to step in the road to get past them. You don't so much walk around Florence as pick your way among the obstacles. Everything seemed dusty and in need of a wash. The trattorias were crowded and dear and often unfriendly, especially in the city centre. Nobody seemed to love the city. Even rich people dropped litter without qualm. The buildings around the Duomo seemed to grow progressively dustier and shabbier each time I walked past them.

Why is it that the cities people most want to see are the ones that so often do the least to make it agreeable to do so? Why can't the Florentines see that it would be in their own interest to sweep up the litter and put out some benches and force the gypsies to stop being so persistent in their panhandling and spend more on brightening the place up? Florence has more treasures than any city in the world – twenty-one palaces, fifty-five historic churches, eight galleries, twenty museums – more than the whole of Spain, according to a UNESCO report, and yet the annual restoration budget for the entire city is less than £5 million. (The Archaeological Museum alone has 10,000 pieces still awaiting cleaning from the great flood of 1966.) It's no wonder so much of it looks unloved.

Where neglect doesn't come into play, incompetence and corruption often do. In 1986, the long-overdue decision was taken to restore the cobbles of the Piazza della Signoria. The ancient stones were dug up and taken away for cleaning. When they were returned they looked brand new. They were brand new. The originals, or so it was alleged, had been taken away and sold for a fortune and could now be found as driveways to rich people's houses.

It was the gypsies who got to me the most. They sit along almost every street calling out to passers-by, with heart-breakingly filthy children of three and four stuck on their laps, made to sit there for hour after hour just to heighten the pathos. It's inhuman, as scandalous as forcing the children to work in a sweatshop, and yet the carabinieri, who strut through the streets in groups of three and four looking smart and lethal in their uniforms, pay them not the slightest notice.

The only gypsy I didn't mind, curiously enough, was the little girl who picked my pocket as I was leaving the city. The kid was magic. It was a Sunday morning, brilliantly sunny. I had just checked out of the hotel and was heading for the station to catch a train to Milan. As I reached the street opposite, three children carrying wrinkled day-old newspapers approached trying to sell them to me. I waved them away. One of them, a jabbering and unwashed girl of about eight, was unusually persistent and pressed the paper on me to such an extent that I stopped and warned her off with a firm voice and a finger in her face and she slunk off abashed. I walked on, with the cocksure strut of a guy who knows how to handle himself on the street, and ten feet later knew without even feeling my pockets that something was missing. I looked down and the inside breast pocket of my jacket was unzipped and gaping emptily. The kid had managed in the time it had taken me to give her a five-second lecture on street etiquette to reach into my jacket, unzip the pocket, dip a hand inside, withdraw two folders of traveller's cheques and pocket them. I wasn't angry. I was impressed. I couldn't have been more impressed if I'd found myself standing in my underwear. I took inventory of my rucksack and other pockets, but nothing else had been disturbed. It hardly needed to be. The girl, who of course was now nowhere to be seen – she was probably at that moment sitting down to a feast of truffles and Armagnac with her seventy-four nearest relatives at a campground somewhere in the hills – had got $1,500 worth of traveller's cheques, not bad for five seconds' work.

I went to the police office at the railway station, but the policeman there, sitting with his feet evidently nailed to the desk, did not want his Sunday morning disturbed and indicated that I should go to the Questura, the central police office. It never entered his mind to go out and try to find the little culprits. Only with reluctance did he write down the address on a scrap of paper I provided for him.

Outside I climbed into a cab and told the driver where to take me. 'Peekpockets?' he said, looking at me in the rear-view mirror as we whizzed through the streets. This Questura run was obviously part of his Sunday-morning routine.

'Yes,' I said, a bit sheepishly.

'Geepsies,' he added with disgust and made a spitting sound, and that was the end of our conversation.

I presented myself at the guard-room of the Questura and was directed upstairs to a waiting-room, a bare cell with grey, flaking walls and a high ceiling. There were three others ahead of me. Occasionally, a policeman or policewoman would come and summon one of them. I waited an hour. Others came and were seen ahead of me. Eventually I presented myself at one of the cubicles around the corner and was told curtly to return to the waiting-room.

I had with me *Fodor's Guide to Italy* which contained an appendix of Italian—English phrases and I looked through it now to see if it offered anything applicable to encounters with sticky-fingered gypsy children. But it was just full of the usual guidebook type of sentences, like 'Where can I buy silk stockings, a map of the city, films?' (my shopping list exactly!) and 'I want: razor blades, a hair-cut, a shave, a shampoo, to send a telegram to England (America)'. The utter uselessness of the language appendices in guidebooks never fails to fascinate me. Take this sentence from Fodor's, which I quote here verbatim: 'Will you prepare a bath for seven o'clock, ten o'clock, half-past ten, midday, midnight, today, tomorrow, the day after tomorrow?' Think about it. Why would anyone want to order a bath for midnight the day after tomorrow? The book doesn't tell you how to say 'Good-night' or 'Good-afternoon', but it does tell you how to ask for silk stockings and get baths drawn around the clock. What sort of world do they think we're living in?

Not only are you unlikely ever to need the things described, but they overlook the somewhat elementary consideration that even if you do by some wild chance require tincture of paregoric, three opera tickets and water for your radiator, and even if you sit up all night committing to memory the Italian for these expressions, you are not going to have the faintest idea what the person says to you in reply.

Yet I find myself studying them with an endless sense of wonder. Consider this instruction: 'We would like a bathing cabin for two, a beach umbrella, three deck chairs'. Why three deck chairs, but a bathing cabin for two? Who is being made to change outside? It must be the old roué in the party who used the book for private purposes and shamed the family by going into a pharmacy and saying leeringly to the lady behind the counter, 'I'd like these two enlarged,' then adding with a suggestive whisper: 'Will you put some air in my tyres?'

I always end up trying to imagine the person who compiled the list. In this case it was obviously a pair of those imperious, middle-aged, lesbian Englishwomen with stout shoes and Buster Brown hair-cuts you often see at foreign hotels, banging the desk bell and demanding immediate attention. They despise all foreigners, assume that they are being cheated at every step and are forever barking out orders: 'Take this to the cloak-room', 'Come in!', 'I want this dress washed (ironed)', 'Bring me soap, towels, iced water', 'How much, including all taxes?' The evidence also clearly pointed to a secret drinking problem: 'Is there a bar in the station?', 'Bring a bottle of good local wine', 'A glass (a bottle) of beer to take away', 'Twenty litres'.

The only phrase book I've ever come across that was of even the remotest use was a nineteenth-century volume for doctors, which I found years ago in the library of the county hospital in Des Moines. (I worked there part-time while I was in college and used to go into the library on my dinner break to see if I could find a medical condition that would get me excused from Phys. Ed.) In five languages the book offered such thoughtful expressions as 'Your boils are septic. You should go to a hospital without delay' and 'How long has your penis been distended in this way?' Knowing that I was about to summer in Europe, I committed several of them to memory, thinking they might come in handy with truculent waiters. At the very least I thought it might be useful, upon finding oneself on a crowded train or in a long queue, to be able to say in a variety of languages, 'Can you kindly direct me to a leprosy clinic? My skin is beginning to slough.' But

I never found a use for any of them and sadly they are forgotten to me now.

Eventually, with the waiting-room empty and nothing happening, I presented myself at the nearest interrogation cubicle. The young policeman who was taking down details from a woman with a bruised face looked at me irritably for disturbing him twice in two hours. 'Do you speak Italian?' he said.

'No.'

'Then come back tomorrow. There will be an English-speaking policeman here then.' This rather overlooked the fact that his own English was accomplished.

'Why didn't you tell me this two hours ago?' I enquired in the semi-shrill voice of someone challenging an armed person.

'Come back tomorrow.'

I checked back into the Hotel Corallo and spent a festive afternoon dealing with the Italian telephone system and trying to get through to the claims office in London. I had two types of traveller's cheques, Visa and American Express, which meant that I got to do everything twice. I spent the afternoon on telephone lines that sounded as if they were full of water reading out lists of serial numbers:

'RH259 –'

I would be interrupted by a tiny voice shouting at me from a foot locker at the bottom of a very deep lake, 'Is that R A 2 9 9 . . . ?'

'No, it's R H 2 five nine –'

'Can you speak up, please?'

'IT'S R H TWO FIVE NINE!!'

'Hello? Are you still there, Mr Byerson? Hello? Hello?'

And so the afternoon went. American Express told me I could get my refund at their Florence office in the morning. Visa wanted to sleep on it.

'Look, I'm destitute,' I lied. They told me they would have to wire the details to an associate bank in Florence, or elsewhere in Europe, and I could have the money once the paperwork was sorted out at my end. I already knew from experience how byzantine Italian banks were – you could have a heart attack in an Italian bank and they wouldn't call an ambulance until you had filled out a Customer Heart Attack Form and had it stamped at at least three windows –

so I unhesitatingly told her to give me the name of a bank in Geneva.
She did.

In the morning I returned to the Questura and after waiting an
hour and a half was taken into a room called the Ufficio Denuncie.
I just loved that. The Office of Denunciations! It made me feel like
making sweeping charges: 'I denounce Michael Heseltine's barber!
I denounce the guy who thought Hereford & Worcester would make
a nifty name for a county! I denounce every sales assistant at every
Dixons I've ever been in!'

I was introduced to a young lady in jeans who sat at a desk
behind a massive and ancient manual typewriter. She had a kind,
searching face and asked me lots and lots of questions – my name
and address, where I came from, my passport number, what I did for
a living, my ten favourite movies of all time, that sort of thing – and
then typed each response with one finger and inordinate slowness,
searching the half-acre keyboard for long minutes before tentatively
striking a key, as if fearful of receiving an electric shock. After each
question she had to loosen the typewriter platen and move the sheet
of paper around to get the next answer in the vicinity of the blank
space for it. (This was not her strongest skill.) The whole thing
took ages. Finally, I was given a carbon copy of the report to use
in securing a refund. The top copy, I have no doubt, went straight
into a wastebasket.

I walked the couple of miles to the American Express office – I
was now out of money – wondering if I would be lectured like a
schoolboy who has lost his lunch money. There were seven or eight
people, all Americans, in the single queue and it became evident
as we chatted together that we had all had our pockets picked
by children of roughly the same description, though at different
places in the city. And this of course was just the American Express
cheques. If you added in all the Visa and other kinds of traveller's
cheques that were taken, and all the cash, then it was obvious
that the gypsies must clear at a minimum $25,000–$30,000
every Sunday afternoon. Presumably the cheques are then laundered
through friendly exchange bureaux around the country. Why do
the police care so little about this racket (unless of course they
get a cut)? At all events, American Express replaced my cheques

with commendable dispatch, and I was back on the street fifteen minutes later.

Outside a gypsy woman with a three-year-old on her lap asked me for money. 'I gave already,' I said, and walked on to the station.

16. Milan and Como

I arrived in Milan in mid-afternoon, expecting great things. It is after all the richest city in Italy, the headquarters of many of the most famous names of Italian commerce: Campari, Benetton, Armani, Alfa-Romeo, the Memphis design group, and the disparate empires of Silvio Berlusconi and Franco Maria Ricci. But this, as I should have realised beforehand, is its problem. Cities that are dedicated to making money, and in Milan they appear to think about little else, seldom have much energy left for charm.

I got a room in an expensive but nondescript hotel across from the monumental white marble central railway station – like something built for Mussolini to give a strutting address to massed crowds – and embarked on a long, hot walk into town along the Via Pisani. This was a broad, modern boulevard, more American than European. It was lined with sleek glass and chrome office buildings, but the central grass strip was scrubby and uncared-for and the few benches where you could rest had syringes scattered beneath them. As I moved further into the city the buildings became older and rather more pleasing, but there was still something lacking. I paused to consult my map in a tiny park on a pleasant residential street near the cathedral square and it was depressingly squalid – grassless and muddy, with broken benches, and pigeons picking among hundreds of cigarette butts and disused tram tickets. I find that hard to excuse in a rich city.

Two blocks on and Milan blossomed. Clustered together were the city's three glories: La Scala, the Duomo and the Galleria Vittorio Emanuele. I went first to the cathedral – cavernous and Gothic, the third-largest church in the world – begrimed on the outside and covered in scaffolding, and so gloomy within that it took me whole minutes to find the ceiling. It was quite splendid in a murky sort of way and entirely free of tourists, which was a happy novelty after Florence. Here it was just a constant stream of locals popping in to add a candle to the hundreds already burning and say a quick

'Ave Maria' before heading home for supper. I liked that. It is such an unusual sight to find a grand church being used for its intended purpose.

Afterwards I crossed the cathedral square to the Galleria Vittorio Emanuele and spent a happy hour wandering through it, hands behind my back, browsing in the windows and noting with unease the occasional splats from the pigeons that had managed to sneak in and were now leading a rewarding life gliding among the rafters and shitting on the people below. It is an imposing shopping arcade, four storeys high, built in the grandiose style of the 1860s and still probably the most handsome shopping mall in the world, with floors of neatly patterned tiles, a vaulted latticework roof of glass and steel, and a cupola rising 160 feet above a rotunda where the two interior avenues intersect. It has the loftiness and echoing hush, and even the shape, of a cathedral, but with something of the commercial grandness of a nineteenth-century railway station thrown in. Every shopping centre should be like this.

Needing my afternoon infusion of caffeine, I took a table outside one of the three or four rather elegant cafés scattered among the shops. It was one of those typically European places where they have seventy tables and one hopelessly overworked waiter, who dashes around trying to deliver orders, clear tables and take money all at the same time, and who has the cheerful, nothing's-too-much-trouble attitude that you would expect of someone in such an interesting and remunerative line of work. You don't get a second chance in these places. I was staring at nothing in particular, chin in hand, idly wondering if Ornella Muti had ever done any mud wrestling, when it filtered through to my consciousness that the waiter was making one of his rare visits to my vicinity and had actually said to me, 'Prego?'

I looked up. 'Oh, an espres –' I said, but he was gone already and I realised that I was never going to get this close to him again unless I married his sister. So with a sigh of resignation I pulled myself up, moved sideways through the tiny gaps between the tables, grimacing apologetically as I caused a succession of unforgiving people to slop their coffee or plunge their noses into their gateaux, and returned unrefreshed to the streets.

I strolled along the Corso Vittorio Emanuele II, a wide pedestrian shopping street, looking for an alternative café and finding none. For a moment I thought I had died and been sent by mistake to yuppie heaven. Unlike the Galleria Vittorio Emanuele, where at least there were a couple of bookshops and an art gallery or two, here and on the neighbouring streets there was nothing to sustain the mind or soul, just boutiques selling expensive adornments for the body: shoes, handbags, leather goods, jewellery, designer clothing that hung on the body like sacking and cost a fortune. Things reached a kind of understated intensity on the Via Montenapoleone, an anonymous-looking side street but none the less the most exclusive shopping artery in the country, and lined with ritzy stores where the password was clearly 'Money's no object'. Apart from the old shopping arcade, Milan appeared to have no café life at all. There were a few establishments, but they were all hole-in-the-wall stand-up places, where people would order a small coffee, toss it back and return to the street all in five seconds. That wasn't what I was looking for.

After southern Italy, Milan seemed hardly Italian at all. People walked quickly and purposefully, swinging shopping bags with names like Gucci and Ferragamo on them. They didn't dawdle over espressos and tuck into mountainous plates of pasta, napkins bibbed into their collars. They didn't engage in passionate arguments about trivialities. They took meetings. They made deals. They talked into car phones. They drove with restraint, mostly in BMWs and Porsches, and parked neatly. They all looked as if they had just stepped off the covers of *Vogue* or *GQ*. It was like an outpost of southern California in Italy. I don't know about you, but I find southern California hard enough to take in southern California. This was Italy – I wanted pandemonium and street life, people in sleeveless vests on front stoops, washing hanging across the streets, guys selling things from pushcarts, Ornella Muti and Giancarlo Giannini zipping past on a Vespa. Most of all, I wanted a cup of coffee.

In the morning I went to the Brera Gallery, hidden away on a back street and reached through a courtyard in a scaffolding-covered palazzo. Big things were going on here: plaster dust hung in the air and there was a commotion of hammering and drilling. The gallery seemed to be only half open. Several of the rooms were closed off and even in the open rooms there were lots of rectangles of unfaded wallpaper where pictures had been lent out or sent away for restoration. But what remained was not only sensational but familiar – Mantegna's foreshortened body of Christ, a Bellini madonna, two Canalettos recently and glowingly restored, and Piero della Francesca's gorgeously rich but decidedly bizarre 'Madonna with Christ Child, Angels, Saints and Federico da Montefeltro' – our old friend the Duke of Urbino again.

I didn't understand this picture at all. If it was painted after the Duke died and here he was now in heaven, why was Christ a baby again? On the other hand, were we to take it that the Duke had somehow managed to fly through the centuries in order to be present at Christ's birth? Whatever the meaning, it was a nifty piece of work. One man liked it so much that he had brought his own folding chair and was just sitting there with arms crossed looking at it. The best thing about the Brera was that there was hardly anyone there, just a few locals and no foreign tourists but me. After Florence, it was bliss to be able to see the paintings without having to ask somebody to lift me up.

Afterwards I walked a long way across the city to see Leonardo's 'Last Supper' in the refectory beside the church of Santa Maria delle Grazie. You pay a load of money at a ticket window and step into a bare, dim hall and there it is, this most famous of frescoes, covering the whole of the far wall. A railing keeps you from approaching any closer than about twenty-five feet, which seems unfair since it is so faint that you could barely see it from five feet and must strain to the utmost to see anything at all from twenty-five feet. It's like a ghost image. If you hadn't seen it reproduced a thousand times before, you probably wouldn't be able to recognise it at all. One end was covered with scaffolding and a great deal of gleaming Dr Who-like restoration equipment. A lone technician was on a platform scratching away. They have been working on the 'Last Supper' for years, but I couldn't see any sign that the thing was actually coming to life.

Poor old Leonardo hasn't been too well served by history. The wall began to crumble almost immediately (some of it had been built with loose dirt) after he finished painting it, and some early friars cut a door into it, knocking off Christ's feet. Then over time the chamber stopped being a refectory and became in turn a stable (can you imagine that – a roomful of donkeys with the greatest painting in history on the wall?), a storage-room, a prison and a barracks. Much of the earlier restoration work was not, to put it charitably, terribly accomplished. One artist gave Saint James six fingers. It is a wonder that it survived at all. In point of fact, it hasn't really. I don't know what it will be like after another ten or fifteen years of restoration work, but for now it would be more accurate to say that this is where the 'Last Supper' used to be.

I slotted 1,000 lire into a machine on the wall, knowing that it would be a mistake, and was treated to a brief and ponderous commentary about the history of the fresco related by a woman on Mogadon whose command of English pronunciation was not altogether up to the task ('Da fresk you see in fronna you iss juan of da grettest works of art in da whole worl . . .'), then looked around for any other ways to waste my money and, finding none, stepped blinking out into the strong sunshine.

I strolled over to the nearby Museo Tecnica, where I paid another small fortune to walk through its empty halls. I was curious to see it because I had read that it had working models of all Leonardo's inventions. It did – small wooden ones – but they were surprisingly dull and, well, wooden, and for the rest the museum was just full of old typewriters and oddments of machinery that meant nothing to me because the labels were in Italian. And anyway, let's be frank, the Italians' technological contribution to humankind stopped with the pizza oven.

I took a late-afternoon train to Como for no other reason than that it was nearby and on a lake and I didn't wish to spend another night in a city. I remembered reading that Lake Como was where Mussolini was found hiding out after Italy fell, and I figured it must have something going for it if it was the last refuge of a desperate man.

It did. It was a lovely little city, clean and perfect, in a cupped hand of Alpine mountains at the southern end of the narrow, thirty-mile-long lake of the same name. It is only a small place, but it boasts two cathedrals, two railway stations (each with its own line to Milan), two grand villas, a fetching park, a lakeside promenade overhung with poplars and generously adorned with green wooden benches, and a maze of ancient pedestrian-only streets filled with little shops and secret squares. It was perfect, perfect.

I found a room in the Hotel Plinius in the heart of town, had two coffees at a café on the Piazza Roma overlooking the lake, ate a splendid meal in a friendly restaurant on a back street and fell in love with Italy all over again. Afterwards I spent a long, contented evening just walking, shuffling with hands in pockets along the apparently endless lakeside promenade and lolling for long periods watching evening sneak in. I walked as far as the Villa Geno, on a promontory at a bend in the lake, and strolled back round to the opposite bank to the small lakeside park with its museum, built in the likeness of a temple, in commemoration of Allesandro Volta, who lived in Como from 1745 to 1827, and there I lolled some more. I walked back to the hotel through empty streets, browsing in shop windows, and thinking how very lucky the Italians are not to have Boots and Dixons and Rumbelows filling their shopping streets with tat and glare, and retired to bed a happy man.

In the morning, I visited the two main churches. The Basilica of San Fidele, begun in 914, was much the more ancient, but the domed cathedral, 500 years younger, was larger and more splendid – indeed, more splendid than any provincial church I had seen since Aachen. It was dark and I had to stand for a minute to adjust to the dimness for fear of walking into a pillar. Morning sunlight flowed through a lofty stained-glass window, but was swallowed almost immediately by the gloom among the high arches. The church was not only surprisingly large for its community, but richly endowed – it was full of subtle tapestries and ancient paintings and some striking statuary, including a Christ figure that is said to weep. (They must show it a Jimmy Tarbuck video beforehand.) I spent an hour sitting out of the way, gazing at the interior and watching people lighting candles. Very restful. This done, I felt content to return to the station and climb aboard the first train to Switzerland.

The train went north, through steep and agreeable countryside, but without the lake views I had been hoping for. We left the country at Chiasso, at the southernmost tip of a pointed length of Switzerland that plunges into Italy like a diver into water. Chiasso looked an unassuming border town, but it was the setting of one of Europe's greatest bank frauds, when in 1979 five men at the small local branch of Credit Suisse managed to syphon off the better part of a $1 billion before anyone back at head office in Zurich noticed this slight drain on the bank's liquidity.

Switzerland and Italy are threaded together like the fingers of clasped hands all along the southern Alps and I spent much of the day passing from one to the other, as I headed for Brig. The train climbed sluggishly through ever-higher altitudes to Lugano and thence Locarno.

At Locarno I had to change trains and had an hour to kill, so I went for a look around the town and a sandwich. It was an immaculate, sunny place, with a lakeside walk even finer than Como's. They still spoke Italian here, but you could tell you were in Switzerland just from the zebra crossings and the glossy red benches, which all looked as if they had been painted that morning, and the absence of even a leaf on the paths of the little lakeside park. Street sweepers were at work everywhere, sweeping up leaves with old-fashioned brooms, and I had the distinct feeling that if I dropped a chewing-gum wrapper someone in uniform would immediately step out from behind a tree and sweep it up or shoot me, or possibly both.

They don't seem to eat sandwiches in Locarno. I walked all around the business district and had trouble finding even a bakery. When at last I did find one it seemed to sell nothing but gooey pastries, though they did have a pile of what I took to be sausage rolls. Starving, I ordered three, at considerable expense, and went outside with them. But they turned out to contain mashed figs – a foodstuff that only your grandmother would eat, and only then because she couldn't find her dentures – and tasted like tea leaves soaked in cough syrup. I gamely nibbled away at one of them, but it was too awful and I put them in my rucksack with the idea that I might try them again later. In the event I forgot all about them and didn't rediscover them until two days later when I pulled my last clean shirt from the rucksack and found the rolls clinging to it.

I went into the station buffet for a glass of mineral water to wash away the stickiness. It was possibly the unfriendliest place in Switzerland. It had eight customers but was so quiet you could hear the clock ticking. The waiter stood at the counter lazily reaming beer glasses with a cloth. He made no move to serve me until I held up a finger and called for a mineral water. He brought a bottle and a glass, wordlessly placed them on the table and returned to his cloth and wet glasses. He looked as if he had just learned that his wife had run off with the milkman and taken all his Waylon Jennings albums, but then I noticed that the other customers were wearing the same sour expression. It seemed chilling after the boundless good humour of Italy. Across from me sat an old lady with a metal crutch, which clattered to the floor as she tried to get up. The waiter just stood there watching, clearly thinking, Now what are you going to do, you old cripple? I sprang to her aid and for my pains was given a withering look and the teensiest of 'Grazie's, then she got up and hobbled out.

Locarno, I decided, was a strange place. I bought a ticket on the two o'clock train to Domodossala, a name that can be pronounced in any of thirty-seven ways. The man in the ticket window made me try out all of them, furrowing his brow gravely as if he couldn't for the life of him think what nearby community had a name that might cause an American difficulty, until finally I stumbled on the approximate pronunciation. 'Ah, Domodossala!' he said, pronouncing it a thirty-eighth way. As a final act of kindness he neglected to tell me that because of work on the railway lines the service was by bus for the first ten kilometres.

I waited and waited on the platform, but the train never came and it seemed odd that no one else was waiting with me. There were only a couple of trains a day to Domodossala. Surely there would be at least one or two other passengers? Finally, I went and asked a porter and he indicated to me, in that friendly why-don't-you-go-fuck-yourself way of railway porters the world over, that I had to take a bus and, when pressed as to where I might find this bus, motioned vaguely with the back of his hand in the direction of the rest of the world. I went outside just in time to see the bus to Domodossala pulling out. Fortunately, I was able to persuade the driver to stop by clinging to the windscreen for two hundred yards. I was desperate to get out of there.

A few miles outside Locarno we joined a waiting train at a little country station. It climbed high into the jagged mountains and took us on a spectacular ride along the lips of deep gorges and forbidding passes, where farmhouses and hamlets were tucked away in the most inaccessible places, on the edge of giddy eminences. It would be hard to imagine a more difficult place to be a farmer. One misstep and you would be falling for a day and a half. Even from the train it was unnerving, an experience more akin to wing-walking than rail travel.

It struck me as inconceivable that anyone could be confronted by such grandeur and not be overwhelmed by the beauty of it and yet, according to Kenneth Clark, almost no visitor to the Alps before the eighteenth century remarked on the scenery. They seemed not to see it. Now, of course, the problem is the reverse. Fifty million tourists a year trample through the Alps, delighting in and despoiling its beauty all at the same time. All the encroachments associated with tourism – resorts, hotels, shops, restaurants, holiday homes, ski runs, ski lifts and new highways – are not only altering the face of the Alps irreparably but undermining their very foundations. In 1987, just a few miles east of where I was now, sixty people died when a flash flood raced through the Valtellina valley, sweeping houses and hotels away like matchboxes before a broom. In the same summer, thirty people died in a landslide at Annecy in France. Without the mountainsides being denuded of trees for new housing and resorts, neither would have happened.

I was sitting on the wrong side of the train to see the scenery – outside my window there was nothing but a wall of rock – but a kindly bespectacled lady sitting across the aisle saw me straining to see and invited me to take the empty seat opposite her. She was Swiss and spoke excellent English. We chatted brightly about the scenery and our modest lives. She was a bank clerk in Zurich but was visiting her mother in a village near Domodossola and had just had a day shopping in Locarno. She showed me some flowers she had bought there. It was wonderful. It seemed like weeks – it *was* weeks – since I had held a normal conversation with anyone, and I was so taken with the novel experience of issuing sounds through a hole in my head that I talked and talked, and before long she was fast asleep and I was back once again in my own quiet little world.

17. Switzerland

I reached Brig, by way of Domodossala and the Simplon Pass, at about five in the evening. It was darker and cooler here than it had been in Italy, and the streets were shiny with rain. I got a room in the Hotel Victoria overlooking the station and went straight out to look for food, having had nothing to eat since my two bites of Mashed Fig Delight in Locarno at lunchtime.

All the restaurants in Brig were German. You never know where you are in Switzerland. One minute everything's Italian, then you travel a mile or two and everyone is talking German or French or some variety of Romansch. All along an irregular line running the length of east-central Switzerland you can find pairs of villages that are neighbours and yet clearly from different linguistic groups – St Blaise and Erlach, Les Diablerets and Gsteig, Delémont and Laufen – and as you head south towards Italy the same thing happens again with Italian. Brig was a nipple of German speakers, so to speak, between the two.

I examined six or seven restaurants, mystified by the menus, wishing I knew the German for liver, pig's trotters and boiled eyeball, before chancing upon an establishment called the Restaurant de la Place at the top of the town. Now this is a nice surprise, I thought, and went straight in, figuring that at least I'd have some idea what I was ordering, but the name Restaurant de la Place was just a heartless joke. The menu here was in German, too.

It really is the most unattractive language for foodstuffs. If you want whipped cream on your coffee in much of the German-speaking world, you order it 'mit Schlag'. Now does that sound to you like a frothy and delicious pick-me-up, or does that sound like the sort of thing smokers bring up first thing in the morning? Here the menu was full of items that brought to mind the noises of a rutting pig: Knoblauchbrot, Schweinskotelett ihrer Wahl, Portion Schlagobers (and that was a dessert).

I ordered Entrecôte and Frites, which sounded a trifle dull after Italy (and indeed so it proved to be), but at least I wouldn't have to hide most of it in my napkin rather than face that awful, embarrassing cry of disappointment that waiters always give when they find you haven't touched your Goat's Scrotum En Croûte. At all events, it was an agreeable enough place, as much bar as restaurant: dark and plain, with a tobacco-stained ceiling, but the waitress was friendly and the beer was large and cold.

In the middle of the table sat a large cast-iron platter, which I assumed was an ashtray, and then I had the awful thought that perhaps it was some kind of food receptacle and that the waitress would come along in a minute and put some bread in it or something. I looked around the room to see if any of the other few customers were using theirs as an ashtray and no one seemed to be, so I snatched out my cigarette butt and dead match and secreted them in a pot plant beside the table, and then tried to disperse the ash with a blow, but it went all over the tablecloth. As I tried to brush it away I knocked my glass with the side of my hand and slopped beer all across the table.

By the time I had finished, much of the tablecloth was a series of grey smudges outlined in a large, irregular patch of yellow that looked distressingly like a urine stain. I casually tried to hide this with my elbow and upper body when the waitress brought my dinner, but she saw instantly what a mess I had made of things and gave me a look not of contempt, as I had dreaded, but – worse – of sympathy. It was the look you might give a stroke victim who has lost control of the muscles in his mouth but is still gamely trying to feed himself. It was a look that said, 'Bless him, poor soul.'

For one horrible moment I thought she might tie a napkin around my neck and cut my food up for me. Instead, she retreated to her station behind the bar, but she kept a compassionate eye on me throughout the meal, ready to spring forward if any pieces of cutlery should clatter from my grasp or if a sudden spasm should cause me to tip over backwards. I was very pleased to get out of there. The cast-iron pot was an ashtray, by the way.

Brig was a bit of a strange place. Historically it was a staging post on the road between Zurich and Milan, and now it looked as if it didn't quite know what to do with itself. It was a reasonably sized town but it appeared to offer little in the way of diversions. It was the kind of place where the red-light district would be in a phone box. All the shops sold unarresting products like refrigerators, vacuum cleaners and televisions from behind shiny plate-glass windows. Then it occurred to me that the shops in most countries sell unarresting items from behind plate-glass windows. It was simply that I was no longer in Italy, which caused me a passing pang of grief. This is the problem with travelling: one day you are sitting with a cappuccino on a terrace by the sea and the next you are standing in the rain in the dullest town in Switzerland looking at Zanussis.

It dawned on me that I hadn't seen a refrigerator, vacuum cleaner or other truly functional thing on sale anywhere in Italy. I presume they don't all drive to Brig to buy them, that they must be able to purchase them somewhere in their own country, but I couldn't recall seeing any. In Brig, however, there was nothing else. I walked the empty streets trying to work up an interest in white goods, but the mood wouldn't take me, and I retired instead to the bar of my hotel, where I drank some beer and read Philip Ziegler's classic account of the black death, imaginatively entitled *The Black Death* – just the thing for those lonely, rainy nights in a foreign country.

Actually, it was fascinating, not least because it dealt with places I had just passed through – Florence, for instance, where 100,000 people, half the populace, lost their lives in just four months, and Milan, where the news from Florence so terrified the locals that families suspected of harbouring a victim were walled up inside their houses.

There's nothing like reading about people being entombed alive to put your own problems in perspective. I tend to think of life as bleak when I can't find a parking space at Sainsbury's, but imagine what it must have been to be an Italian in the fourteenth century. For a start, in 1345 it rained non-stop for six months, turning much of the country into a stagnant lake and making planting impossible. The economy collapsed, banks went bust and thousands died in the ensuing famines. Two years later the country was rocked with terrible earthquakes – in Rome, Naples, Pisa, Padua, Venice – which brought further death and chaos. And then, just when people were surely thinking that things *had* to get better now, some anonymous sailor stepped ashore at Genoa and said, 'You know, I don't feel so hot,' and within days the great plague was beginning its long sweep across Europe.

And it didn't stop there. The plague returned for a mop-up operation in 1360–61, and yet again in 1368–69, 1371, 1375, 1390 and 1405. The odd thing to me is that this coincided with one of the great periods of church-building in Europe. I don't know about you, but if I lived in an age when God was zinging every third person in my town with suppurating bubos, I don't think I'd look on Him as being on my side.

In the morning I took a fast train to Geneva. We rattled through a succession of charmless industrial towns – Sierra, Sion, Martigny – places that seemed to consist almost entirely of small factories and industrial workshops fringed with oildrums, stacks of wooden pallets and other semi-abandoned clutter. I had forgotten that quite a lot of Switzerland is really rather ugly. And everywhere there were pylons. I had forgotten about those, too. The Swiss are great ones for stringing wires. They thread them across the mountainsides for electricity and suspend them from endless rows of gibbets along every railway track and hang them like washing lines on all their city streets for the benefit of trams. It seems not to have occurred to them that there might be a more attractive way of arranging things.

We found the shore of Lake Geneva at Villeneuve and spent the next hour racing along its northern banks at a speed that convinced me the driver was slumped dead on the throttle. We shot past the castle of Chillon – *shoomp*: a picturesque blur – flew through the stations at Montreux and Vevey, scattering people on the platforms, and finally screeched to a long, slow stop at Lausanne, where the body of the driver was presumably taken away for recycling (I assume the fanatically industrious Swiss don't bury their dead but use them for making heating oil) and his place taken by someone in better health. At all events, the final leg into Geneva was made at a more stately pace.

Just outside my carriage were two young Australians who spent the passage from Lausanne to Geneva discussing great brawls they had taken part in over the years. I couldn't quite see them, but I could hear every breathless word. They would say things like, 'D'ya remember the time Muscles Malloy beat the crap out of the Savage triplets with a claw hammer? There was blood and guts all over the place, man.'

'I was picking pieces of brain out of my beer!'

'Yeah, it was fan-tas-tic! D'ya remember that time Muscles rammed that snooker cue up Jason Brewster's nose and it came out the top of his head?'

'That Muscles was an animal, wasn't he?'

'Not half!'

'Did you ever see him eat a live cat?'

'No, but I saw him pull the tongue out of a horse once.'

It went on like this all the way to Geneva. These guys were serious psychopaths, in urgent need of a clinic. I kept expecting one of them to look in at me and say, 'I'm bored. Let's hang this asshole upside-down out the window and see how many times we can hit his head on the sleepers.' Eventually, I peeked out. They were both about four feet two inches tall and couldn't have beaten up a midget in a blindfold. I followed them off the train at Geneva and out of the station, chattering excitedly as they went about people having their heads stuck in a waffle iron or their tongues nailed to the carpet.

I watched them go, then turned and, with an instinct that seldom fails to let me down, checked into the dreariest and unfriendliest hotel in its class in Geneva, the aptly named Terminus.

Finding nothing to detain me there, I went straight to the Union Bank of Switzerland offices on the Rue du Rhône to claim my refund on my Visa traveller's cheques. I was directed to a small room in the basement, where international transactions were dealt with. I had assumed that things would be painlessly efficient here, but I hadn't allowed for the fact that the Swiss national motto is 'Trust No One'. It took most of the afternoon.

First, I had to stand in a long queue, full of veiled women and men in nightshirts, all involved in complicated transfers of funds from one Arab sandpit to another, requiring the production of parchment documents, the careful counting of huge stacks of brightly coloured money and occasional breaks to pray to Allah and slaughter a goat. All of this was presided over by a blonde woman who clearly hated her job and every living thing on the planet. It took an hour for me just to reach the window, where I was required to do no more than establish my identity and reveal, in a low voice and with significant sidelong glances, the secret reclaim number I had been given over the phone in Florence. This done, the woman told me to take a seat.

'Oh, thanks, but I'd never get it in my suitcase,' I said with my best Iowa smile. 'Can't I just have my cheques?'

'You must take a seat and wait. Next.'

I sat for three-quarters of an hour before I was summoned to the window and handed a claim form packed with questions and sent back to my seat to fill them in. It was an irritating document. It required me not only to explain in detail how I had been so reckless as to have lost the traveller's cheques with which Visa had trustingly endowed me, and to give all manner of trifling detail including the number on the police report and the address of the police station at which the report was made, but also contained long sections of irrelevant questions concerning things like my height, weight and complexion. 'What the fuck does my complexion have to do with traveller's cheques?' I said, a trifle wildly, causing a pleasant-looking matron sitting next to me to put some space between us. Finally it instructed me to give two financial references and one personal reference.

I couldn't believe it. By what mad logic should I have to give references to reclaim something that was mine? 'American Express doesn't ask for anything like this,' I said to the matronly lady, who looked at me and shifted her butt another two inches towards safety. I lied on all the answers. I said I was four feet two inches tall, weighed 400 pounds, was born in Abyssinia and busted broncos for a living. I put 'amber' for complexion and Michael Milken and Ivan Boesky for my financial references. For a personal reference, I gave myself, of course. Who better? I was spluttering with indignation when I rejoined the queue, which had now grown to include a delegation of Rwandan diamond merchants and two guys with camels.

'Why do I have to answer all these stupid questions?' I demanded as I turned in my claim form. 'This is the most stupid thing I've ever seen. It's really . . . *stupid*.' I get eloquent like that when I'm angry. The woman pointed out that it was nothing to do with her, that she was just following instructions. 'That's what Himmler said!' I cried, both feet leaving the ground at once. Then I realised it was pointless, that she would only make me take a seat again and wait there until Michaelmas if I didn't act calm and Swiss about it all, so I accepted my replacement traveller's cheques with nothing stronger than sulky indignation.

But from now on it's American Express traveller's cheques for me, boy, and if the company wishes to acknowledge this endorsement with a set of luggage or a skiing holiday in the Rockies, then let the record show that I am ready to accept it.

I spent two days in Geneva, wandering around with an odd, empty longing to be somewhere else. I don't know why exactly, because Geneva is an agreeable enough place – compact, spotless, eminently walkable, with a steep and venerable old town, some pleasant parks and its vast blue lake, glittering by day and even more fetching at night with the multi-coloured lights of the city stretched across it. But it is also a dull community: expensive, business-like, buttoned up, impossible to warm to. Everyone walked with a brisk, hunched, out-of-my-way posture. It was spring on the streets, but February on people's faces. It seemed to have no young people enlivening the bars and bistros, as they do in Amsterdam and Copenhagen. It had no exuberance, no sparkle, no soul. The best thing that could be said for it was that the streets were clean.

I suppose you have to admire the Swiss for their industriousness. Here, after all, is a country that is small, mountainous, has virtually no natural resources and yet has managed to become the richest nation on earth. (Its per capita GDP is almost twenty-five per cent higher than even Japan's and more than double Britain's.) Money is everything in Switzerland – the country has more banks than dentists – and their quiet passion for it makes them cunning opportunists. The country is land-locked, 300 miles from the nearest sniff of sea, and yet it is home to the largest manufacturer of marine engines in the world. The virtues of the Swiss are legion: they are clean, orderly, law-abiding and diligent – so diligent that in a national referendum in the 1970s they actually voted against giving themselves a shorter working week.

And this of course is the whole problem. They are so desperately dull, and wretchedly conservative. A friend of mine who was living in Geneva in 1968, when students all over Europe were tearing the continent apart, once told me that the students of Geneva decided to hold a riot of their own, but called it off when the police wouldn't give them permission. My friend swears it's a true story. It is certainly true that women didn't get the vote in Switzerland until 1971, a mere half-century after they got it everywhere else, and in one of the cantons, Appenzell Innherhoden, women were excluded from cantonal votes until 1990. They have a terrible tendency to be smug and ruthlessly self-interested. They happily bring in hundreds of thousands of foreign workers – one person in every five in Switzerland is a foreigner – but refuse to offer the security of citizenship. When times get tough they send the workers home – 300,000 of them during the oil shocks of 1973, for instance – making them leave their homes, pull their children from schools, abandon their comforts, until times get better. Thus the Swiss are able to take advantage of cheap labour during boom times without the inconvenient social responsibilities of providing unemployment benefit and health care during bad times. And by this means they keep inflation low and preserve their own plump, complacent standard of living. I can understand it, but I don't have to admire it.

On the second day, I went for a long stroll along the lakeside – leafy, spacious, empty – past the old and largely derelict League of Nations building, where young boys with stones were trying without much success to break the windows, through the tranquil Jardin Botanique, and to the gates of the vast Palais des Nations (larger than Versailles, according to the tourist brochures), now home to the United Nations Organisation. I hesitated by the gate, thinking about paying the multi-franc entrance fee to go in for a guided tour, and aren't you glad I didn't? I am.

Instead I noticed on my city map that just up the road was the Musée International de la Croix-Rouge et du Croissant-Rouge (International Museum of the Red Cross and Red Breakfast Roll), which sounded much more promising to me. And so it proved to be. It really was a surprisingly nice place, if that isn't too inappropriate a term to apply to a museum dedicated to human suffering in all its amazing and manifold variety. I mean that it was thoughtfully laid out, with a confident and accomplished use of multi-media resources, as I believe they would call it in the trade. It was virtually empty, too, and generally effective at putting its story across, considering that everything had to be explained in four languages and that they couldn't be too graphic in their depictions of disasters and human cruelty lest it unsettle young visitors.

Clearly too the organisation's hands were tied by certain political considerations. One of the displays was a replica of a cell no bigger than a cupboard in which Red Cross workers had discovered seventeen prisoners being held in conditions of unspeakable discomfort, unable even to lie down, for no reason other than that their political views did not accord with those of the rulers. But nowhere did it hint in what country this cell had been found. At first I thought this constant discretion craven, but on reflection I supposed that it was necessary and prudent. To name the country would have jeopardised the Red Cross's operations there, wherever it was. The scary thing was to realise just how many countries it might have been.

I spent the rest of the day shuffling around the city, wandering through department stores, fingering the merchandise (this drives Swiss sales clerks crazy), dining on the only affordable food in town (at McDonald's), visiting the cathedral, exploring the old town and gazing in the windows of antique shops that sold the sort of over-ornate objects you would expect to see in, say, a *House Beautiful* article on Barry Manilow's Malibu hacienda – life-sized porcelain tigers, oriental vases you could put a large child in, oversized Louis-Quatorze bureaux and sideboards with gilt gleaming from every curl and crevice.

In the evening, having scrubbed the mashed figs of Locarno out of my last clean shirt, I went for a beer in a dive bar around the corner, where I waited weeks for service and then spent the next hour gaping alternately at the largeness of the bill and the smallness of the beer, holding the two side by side for purposes of comparison. Declining the advance of Geneva's only prostitute ('Thanks, but I've just been fucked by the management'), I moved to another semi-seamy bar down the street, but found precisely the same experience, and so returned with heavy feet to my hotel room.

I went into the bathroom to see how my shirt was drying. The purply mashed-fig stains, I noted with the steady gaze of someone who knows his way around disappointment, were coming back, like disappearing ink. I dropped the shirt in the wastebin then went back to the bedroom, switched on the TV and fell onto the bed all in one movement and watched a 1954 film called *The Sands of Iwo Jima*, featuring John Wayne killing Japanese people while talking in French using someone else's voice – an acting skill I never knew he possessed.

It occurred to me, as I lay there watching this movie of which I could understand nary a word other than 'Bonjour', 'Merci bien' and 'Aaaargh!' (what the Japanese said when John stuck them in the belly with his bayonet), that this was almost boring enough to cause brain damage, and yet at the same time – and here's the interesting thing – I was probably having as much fun as anyone in Switzerland.

I took a morning train to Bern, two hours away to the east. Bern was a huge relief. It was dignified and handsome, and full of lively cafés and young people. I picked up a city map at the station's tourist office and with its aid found a room in the Hotel Kreuz in the centre of town. I dumped my bag and went straight back out, not only eager to see the town but delighted at my eagerness. I had begun to fear in Geneva that my enthusiasm for travel might be seeping away and that I would spend the rest of the trip shuffling through museums and along cobbled streets in my Willy Loman posture. But, no, I was perky again, as if I'd just been given a booster shot of vitamins.

Bern is built on a bluff above a broad loop of the River Aare, and the views from the bridges and vantage points are quite splendid, especially back towards the old town – a jumble of orangcish tiled roofs broken up with church spires and towers that look like mutant cuckoo clocks. Most of the streets are arcaded in a way I've never seen before: the ground floors are set back and the upper floors jut out over them, their heavy weight supported by thick arched buttresses,

creating a covered walkway over the pavements. The shops along
them were infinitely more varied and interesting – even more classy
– than those in Geneva. There were antiquarian bookstores and art
galleries and antique shops specialising in everything from wind-up
toys to clocks and binoculars to Etruscan pottery.

Culturally, Bern is on the dividing line between French-speaking
Switzerland and German-speaking Switzerland, and there is a mildly
exotic blending of the two. Waiters greeet you with 'Bitte', for
instance, but thank you with 'Merci'. Architecturally, it is stolidly Swiss-German, with severe (though not disagreeable) sandstone
buildings that look as if they were built to withstand a thousand
earthquakes. Bern has the air of a busy provincial market town. You
would never guess that it is a national capital. This is partly because
of the peculiar nature of Swiss politics. So many powers are devolved
to the cantons and to national referenda that Switzerland doesn't even
feel the need to have a prime minister, and the presidency is such a
nominal and ceremonial position that it changes hands every year.
They wouldn't have a president at all except that they need somebody
to greet visiting heads of state at the airport. The Bundeshaus, the
national parliament, looks like a provincial town hall, and nowhere
in the city – even in the bars on the nearby streets – do you have a
sense of being among bureaucrats and politicians.

I spent a day and a half wandering through the streets of the
old town and across the high bridges to the more modern, but still
handsome, residential streets on the far side of the Aare. It was a
wonderful city for random walking. There were no freeways, no
industry, no sterile office parks, just endless avenues of fine homes
and small parks.

I attempted just two touristy diversions and failed at both. I crossed
the high, arched Nydegg Bridge to see the famous bear pits – the city
name derives from the German word for bear, so they like to keep
several bears as mascots – but the pits were empty. There was no
sign to explain why and locals who arrived with their children were
clearly as surprised and perplexed as I was.

I tried also to go to the Albert Einstein museum, housed in his old
flat on Kramgasse, one of the main arcaded streets. I walked up and
down the street half a dozen times before I found the modest entrance

to the building, tucked away between a restaurant and a boutique. The door was locked – it was dusty and looked as if it hadn't been opened for weeks, perhaps years – and no one answered the bell, though according to the tourist brochure it should have been open. It struck me as odd that nowhere in the town had I encountered any indication that Einstein had ever lived there: no statue in a park or square, no street named in his honour, not even his kindly face on postcards. There wasn't so much as a plaque on the wall to tell the world that in one year, 1905, while working as an obscure clerk in the Swiss patent office and living above this door, Einstein produced four papers that changed for ever the face of physics – on the theory of Brownian motion, on the theory of relativity, on the photon theory of light and on the establishment of the mass-energy equivalence. I have no idea what any of that means, of course – my grasp of science is such that I don't actually understand why electricity doesn't leak out of sockets – but I would have liked to see where he lived.

In the evening I had a hearty meal, which is about as much as the visitor can aspire to in Switzerland, and went for another long walk down darkened streets and through empty squares. As I returned to the city centre along Marktgasse, one of the main pedestrian venues, I discovered that all the bars were shutting. Waiters were taking chairs and tables inside and lights were going out. It was nine-twenty in the evening. This gives you some idea of what a heady night-life Bern offers.

Quietly distraught, I wandered around and with relief found another bar still open a couple of blocks away on Kochegasse. It was crowded, but had an aimable, smoky air, and I was just settling in with a tall glass of golden Edelweiss and the closing chapters of The Black Death, when I heard a familiar voice behind me saying, 'D'ya remember that time Blane Brockhouse got the shits and went crazy with the Uzi in the West Gollagong Working Men's Club?'

I turned around to find my two friends from the Geneva train sitting on booster seats behind frothy beers. 'Hey, how you guys doing?' I said before I could stop myself.

They looked at me as if I were potentially insane. 'Do we know you, mate?' said one of them.

I didn't know what to say. These guys had never seen me before in their lives. 'You're Australian, huh?' I burbled stupidly.

'Yeah. So?'

'I'm an American.' I was quiet for a bit. 'But I live in England.'

There was a long pause. 'Well, that's great,' said one of the Australians with a measured hint of sarcasm, then turned to his friend and said, 'D'ya remember the time Dung-Breath O'Leary hacked that waitress's forearms off with a machete because there was a fly in his beer?'

I felt like an asshole, which of course is a pretty fair description of my condition. Something about their diminutive size and warped little minds heightened the sense of quiet humiliation. I turned back to my beer and my book, the tips of my ears warm to the touch, and took succour in the plight of the poor people of Bristol, where in 1349 the plague so raged through the city that 'the living were scarce able to bury the dead' and the grass grew calf-high in the city streets.

Before long, with the aid of two more beers and 120,000 agonised deaths in the west country of England, my embarrassment was past and I was feeling much better. As they say, time heals all wounds. Still, if you wake up with a bubo on your groin, better see a doctor all the same.

18. Liechtenstein

You know when you are entering the German-speaking part of Switzerland because all the towns have names that sound like someone talking with his mouth full of bread: Thun, Leuk, Bülach, Plaffeien, Flims, Gstaad, Pfäffikon, Linthal, Thusis, Fluelen, Thalwil.

According to my rail ticket I was headed for the last of these, which puzzled me a little, since Thalwil didn't appear on my much-trusted Kümmerly and Frey 'Alpenländer Strassenkarte'. Where Thalwil should have been was given instead as Horgen. I couldn't conceive that the conscientious draughtspeople at Kümmerly and Frey could have made an error of this magnitude in their own country, but equally it was unthinkable that the conservative burghers of this corner of Switzerland would have elected at some time during the last eighteen years to change the name of one of their towns, so I put it down to an act of God and turned my attention instead to spreading out the map on my knees in its full crinkly glory, to the undisguised irritation of the old lady next to me, who hoomphed her bosom and made exasperated noises every time a corner of the paper waggled in her direction.

What is it about maps? I could look at them all day, earnestly studying the names of towns and villages I have never heard of and will never visit, tracing the course of obscure rivers, checking elevations, consulting the marginal notes to see what a little circle with a flag on its signifies (a Burg or Schloss) and what's the difference between a pictogram of an airplane with a circle around it and one without (one is a Flughafen, the other a Flugplatz), issuing small profound 'Hmmmm's and nodding my head gravely without having the faintest idea why.

I noticed now that I might alternatively have gone from Brig to Geneva on a more southerly route, by way of Aosta, Mont Blanc and Chamonix. It would almost certainly have been much more scenically exciting. What a fool I was to miss the chance to see

Aosta and Mont Blanc. How could I have come this far and failed to travel through the heart of the Alps? What a mighty dick-head I am. 'Hmmmm,' I said, nodding gravely and folding up the map.

We chuntered pleasantly through a landscape of small farms and steep wooded hills, beside a shallow river, stopping frequently at isolated villages where half a dozen people would climb aboard with empty shopping baskets. When the train was full, we would call at a busy little market town like Langnau or Zug and all the passengers would pour off, leaving me all alone, and then the slow, steady refilling process would begin again. It was not a bad way to spend a day.

I left the train at Sargans, just short of Liechtenstein. The railway runs through Liechtenstein, but, in line with the national policy of being ridiculous in every possible way, it doesn't stop there. You must instead get off at Sargans or Buchs and transfer to Vaduz, the diminutive Liechtenstein capital, on a yellow post bus.

One was conveniently waiting at the station. I purchased a ticket and took a seat midway along, the only passenger not clutching bagloads of shopping, and sat high on the seat, eager to see the little country. It is only about seven miles from Sargans to Vaduz, but the journey takes an hour or so because the bus goes all over the place, darting down every side road and making cautious, circuitous detours around back lanes, as if trying to sneak into Vaduz. I watched carefully out of the window, but never did know at what point we entered Liechtenstein — indeed wasn't certain that we were there at all until I saw the city-limit sign for Vaduz.

Everything about Liechtenstein is ridiculous. For a start it is ridiculously small: it is barely 1/250th the size of Switzerland, which of course is itself ridiculously small. It is the last remaining fragment of the Holy Roman Empire, and so obscure that its ruling family didn't even bother to come and see it for 150 years. It has two political parties, popularly known as the Reds and the Blacks, which have so few ideological differences that they share a motto: 'Faith in God, Prince and Fatherland'. Liechtenstein's last military engagement was in 1866, when it sent eighty men to fight against the Italians. Nobody was killed. In fact — you're going to like this — they came back with eighty-one men, because they made a friend on the way.

Two years later, realising that the Liechtensteiners could beat no one, the Crown Prince disbanded the army.

More ridiculousness: it is the world's largest producer of sausage skins and false teeth. It is a notorious tax haven, the only country in the world with more registered companies than people (though most of these companies exist only as pieces of paper in someone's desk). It was the last country in Europe to give women suffrage (in 1984). Its single prison is so small that prisoners' meals are sent over from a nearby restaurant. To acquire citizenship, a referendum must be held in the applicant's village and, if that passes, the Prime Minister and his cabinet must then vote on it. But this never happens, and hundreds of families who have lived in Liechtenstein for generations are still treated as foreigners.

Vaduz is not terribly picturesque, but the setting is arresting. The town nestles at the very foot of Mount Alpspitz, 6,700 feet high. On an outcrop directly above the town is the gloomy and fortress-like royal Schloss, looking uncannily like the Wicked Witch's castle in *The Wizard of Oz*. Every time I looked up at it I expected to see those winged monkeys flying in and out. Curiously, despite centuries as a backwater, Vaduz retains almost no sense of antiquity. The whole town looks as if it were built twenty years ago in a hurry – not exactly ugly, but certainly undistinguished.

It was a Saturday and the main road through the town was backed up with big Mercedes from Switzerland and Germany. The rich must come at the weekends to visit their money. There were only four hotels in the central area. Two were full and one was closed, but I managed to get a room at the fourth, the Engel. It was friendly but outrageously expensive for what it offered, which wasn't much – a lumpy bed, a reading light with a twenty-watt bulb, no TV, and a radio so old that I half expected to hear Edward R. Murrow broadcasting details of the Battle of Monte Cassino. Instead, all I could get was polka music, mercifully interrupted at frequent intervals by a German-speaking disc jockey who had evidently overdosed on sleeping pills (or possibly on polka music), judging by the snappiness of his delivery. He . . . talked . . . like . . . this, like someone trapped in a terrible dream, which I suppose in a sense he was.

The sole virtue of the room was that it had a balcony with a view

over the main church and town square (really just a strip of lawn
with a car park) and beyond that a handsome prospect of mountains.
By leaning perilously out over the street and craning my neck at a
peculiar angle, I could just see the Schloss high above me. It is still
the home of the Crown Prince, one of the richest men in Europe
and possessor of the second-finest private collection of paintings in
the world, outdone only by the Queen of England. He has the only
Leonardo in private hands and the largest collection of Rubenses,
but a fat lot of good that does the eager visitor, because the castle is
completely off limits, and plans to build a modest national gallery to
house a few of the paintings have yet to get off the ground. Parliament
has been debating the matter for almost twenty years, but the thought
of parting with the necessary funds has proved too painful so far
and evidently no one would dare to ask the royal family (worth an
estimated $1.3 billion) to dip into their treasure chest and pass down
some bauble to get the ball rolling.

I went out for a walk and to check out the possibilities for dinner,
which were not abundant. The business district was only a couple
of blocks square and the shops were so pedestrian and small-town
– a newsagent's, a chemist's, a gift shop selling the sort of gifts that
you dread receiving at Christmas from your in-laws – that it was
impossible to linger. Restaurants were thin on the ground and either
very expensive or discouragingly empty. Vaduz is so small that if you
walk for fifteen minutes in any direction you are deep in the country.
It occurred to me that there is no reason to go to Liechtenstein except
to say that you have been there. If it were simply part of Switzerland
(which in fact it is in all but name and postage stamps – and even
then it uses the Swiss postal service) nobody would ever dream of
visiting it.

I wandered down a pleasant but anonymous residential street
where the picture windows of every living-room offered a ghostly
glow of television, and then found myself on a straight, unpaved and
unlit road through flat, still-fallow fields. The view back to Vaduz
was unexpectedly lovely. Darkness had fallen with that suddenness
you find in the mountains and a pale moon with a chunk bitten out
of it hung in the sky. The Schloss, bathed in yellow floodlights, stood
commandingly above the town looking impregnable and draughty.

The road ended in a T-junction to nowhere and I turned back for another look around the town. I settled for dinner in the dining-room of the Vaduzerhof Hotel. Two hours earlier I had been solemnly assured that the hotel was closed, but the dining-room was certainly open, if not exactly overwhelmed with customers, and people also seemed to be coming in through the front door, taking keys off hooks in the hallway and going upstairs to bedrooms. Perhaps the people at the hotel just didn't like the look of me, or maybe they correctly suspected that I was a travel writer and would reveal to the world the secret that the food at the Vaduzerhof Hotel at No. 3 Städtlestrasse in Vaduz is Not Very Good. Who can say?

In the morning I presented myself in the dining-room of the Engel for breakfast. It was the usual continental breakfast of bread and butter and cold cuts and cheese, which I didn't really want, but it was included in the room charge and with what they were charging me I felt bound to empty a couple of little tubs of butter and waste some cheese, if nothing else. The waiter brought me coffee and asked if I wanted orange juice.

'Yes, please,' I said.

It was the strangest orange juice I've ever seen. It was a peachy colour and had red stringy bits suspended in it like ganglia. They looked unnervingly like those deeply off-putting red squiggles you sometimes find in the yolks of eggs. It didn't even taste like orange juice and after two polite sips I pushed it to one side and concentrated on my coffee and cutting slices of ham into small, unreusable pieces.

Twenty minutes later I presented myself at the check-out desk and the pleasant lady there handed me my bill to review while she did brusque things with my credit card in a flattening machine. I was surprised to see that there was a charge of four francs for orange juice. Four francs is a lot of money.

'Excuse me, but I've been charged four francs for orange juice.'

'Did you not have orange juice?'

'Yes, but the waiter never said I'd be charged for it. I thought it was part of the breakfast.'

'Oh no, our orange juice is very special. Fresh-squeezed. It is –'

she said some German word which I assume translates as 'full of stringy red bits' then added – 'and as it is *razzer* special we charge four francs for it.'

'Fine, splendid, but I really feel you should have told me.'

'But, sir, you ordered it and you drank it.'

'I didn't drink it – it tasted like duck's urine – and besides I thought it was free.'

We were at an impasse. I don't usually make a scene in these circumstances – I just come back at night and throw a brick through the window – but this time I was determined to take a stand and refused to sign the bill until the four-franc charge was removed. I was even prepared to be arrested over it, though for one unsettling moment I confess I had a picture of me being brought my dinner in jail and taking a linen cloth off the tray to find a glass of peach-coloured orange juice and a single slice of ham cut into tiny pieces.

Eventually she relented, with more grace than I probably deserved, but it was clear from the rigid all-is-forgiven smile she gave me as she handed me back my card that there will never be a room for me at the Hotel Engel in Vaduz, and with the Vaduzerhof also evidently barred to me for life, it was obvious that I had spent my last night in Liechtenstein.

As it was a Sunday, there was no sign of any buses running, so I had no choice but to walk to Buchs, half a dozen miles to the north, but I didn't mind. It was a flawless spring morning. Church bells rang out all over the valley, as if a war had just ended. I followed the road to the nearby village of Schaan, successfully gambled that a side lane would lead me to the Rhine, and there found a gravel footpath waiting to conduct me the last half-mile to the bridge to Switzerland. I had never crossed a border by foot before and felt rather pleased with myself. There was no border post of any kind, just a plaque in the centre of the bridge showing the formal dividing line between Liechtenstein and Switzerland. No one was around, so I stepped back and forth over the line three or four times just for the novelty of it.

Buchs, on the opposite bank of the river, wasn't so much sleepy as comatose. I had two hours to kill before my train, so I had a good look around the town. This took four minutes, including rest stops. Everything was geschlossen.

I went to the station and bought a ticket to Innsbruck, then went and looked for the station buffet. It was shut, but a news-stand was open and I had a look at it. I was ready for some-thing to read – Ziegler's relentless body-count of fourteenth-century European peasants was beginning to lose its sparkle – but the only thing they had in English was the weekend edition of *USA Today*, a publication that always puts me in mind of a news-paper we used to get in primary school called *My Weekly Reader*. I am amazed enough that they can find buyers for *USA Today* in the USA, but the possibility that anyone would ever present himself at the station kiosk in Buchs, Switzerland, and ask for it seemed to me to set a serious challenge to the laws of probability. I thought about stealing a look at the paper, just to check the Major League baseball standings, but the kiosk lady was watching me with a look that suggested this could be a punishable offence in Switzerland.

Instead I found the way to my platform, unburdened myself of my rucksack and took a seat on a bench. I allowed my eyelids to droop and passed the time by composing Swiss riddles.

Q. What is the best way to make a Swiss roll?
A. Take him to a mountaintop and give him a push.

Q. How do you make a Swiss person laugh?
A. Hold a gun to his head and say, 'Laugh.'

Q. What do you call a great lover in Switzerland?
A. An immigrant.

Q. How can you spot a Swiss anarchist?
A. He doesn't use the post code.

Q. What do you call a gathering of boring people in Switzerland?
A. Zurich.

Tiring of this, I switched, for no explainable reason, to multiple-choice Adolf Hitler–Eva Braun jokes, but I had only completed one –

Q. What were Adolf Hitler's last words to Eva Braun?
a. Did you remember to cancel the milk?
b. Bang! OK, it's your turn.
c. All right, all right, I'll see to it that they name a range of
   small electrical appliances after you.

– when the train pulled in. With more than a little relief, I boarded
it, pleased to be heading for yet another new country.

19. Austria

I walked through the station at Innsbruck with an almost eerie sense of familiarity, a sensation half-way between déjà vu and actual memory. I hadn't been to Innsbruck for eighteen years and hadn't thought about it more than once or twice in that time, but finding myself there now it was as if it had been no more than a day or two and the years in between had never happened. The station appeared not to have changed at all. The buffet was where I remembered it and still serving goulash with dumplings, a meal that I ate four times in three days because it was the cheapest and most substantial food in town. The dumplings were the size of cannonballs and just as filling. About as tasty as well.

I took a room in a small hotel in the centre, the Goldene Krone, and spent the dying hours of the afternoon walking through slanting sunshine that bathed the town in golden light. Innsbruck really is an ideal little city, with solid baroque buildings and a roofscape of bulbous towers. It is carefully preserved without having the managed feel of an open-air museum, and its setting is as near to perfection as could be imagined. At the end of every street you are confronted by a towering backdrop of mountains, muscular and snow-peaked beneath intensely clear skies.

I walked the paved footpath along the River Inn, swift and shallow and clear as polished glass, passed through a small park called the Hofgarten and drifted out into the residential avenues beyond: long, straight, shaded streets lined with stolid three-storey houses that disappeared in the treetops. Many of them – too many surely for such a small city – contained doctors' surgeries and had shiny brass plates on the walls or gates announcing DR G. MUNSTER/ZAHNARZT or DR ROBERT SCHLUGEL/PLASTISCHE CHIRURGIE – the sort of offices where you know that you would be ordered, whatever the complaint, to undress, climb onto the table and put your feet in the stirrups. Bright trams, empty but for the driver, trundled heavily past from time to time, but all the rest was silence.

It occurred to me that one of my first vivid impressions of Europe was a Walt Disney movie I saw as a boy. I believe it was called *The Trouble With Angels*. It was a hopelessly sentimental and naff fictionalised account of how a group of cherry-cheeked boys with impish instincts and voices like angels made their way into the Vienna Boys' Choir. I enjoyed the film hugely, being hopelessly sentimental and naff myself, but what made a lasting indent on me was the Europeanness of the background – the cobbled streets, the toytown cars, the corner shops with a tinkling bell above the door, the modest, lived-in homyness of each boy's familial flat. It all seemed so engaging and agreeably old-fashioned compared with the sleek and modern world I knew, and it left me with the unshakeable impression that Austria was somehow more European than the rest of Europe. And so again it seemed to me here in Innsbruck. For the first time in a long while, certainly for the first time on this trip, I felt a palpable sense of wonder to find myself here, on these streets, in this body, at this time. I was in Europe now. It seemed an oddly profound notion.

I found my way back to my hotel along the city's main street, Maria-Theresien-Strasse. It is a handsome thoroughfare and well worth an amble, so long as you don't let your gaze pause for one second on any of the scores of shop windows displaying dirndls and lederhosen, beer mugs with pewter lids, peaked caps with a feather in the brim, long-stemmed pipes and hand-carved religious curios. I don't suppose any small area of the world has as much to answer for in the way of crappy keepsakes as the Tyrol, and the sight of so much of it brings a depressing reminder that you are among a nation of people who like this sort of thing.

This is the down-side of Austria. The same impulse that leads people to preserve the past in their cities leads them also to preserve it in their hearts. No one clings to former glories as the Austrians do, and since these former glories include one of the most distasteful interludes in history, this is not their most attractive feature.

They are notoriously red-necked. I remember that Katz and I, while hitch-hiking through Austria, made friends with two Germans of a similar age, Thomas and Gerhard, who were making their way by thumb from Berlin to India with a view to finding spiritual enlightenment and good drugs. We camped together in a high Alpine pass, somewhere along the road between Salzburg and Klagenfurt, and in the evening walked into the nearest village, where we found awaiting us a perfect inn, full of black panelled wood and a log fire with a sleeping dog before it and ruddy-faced yeoman customers swinging steins of beer. We ate sausages with dabs of mustard and drank many beers. It was all most convivial.

I remember sitting there late in the evening, glowing with drink and thinking what a fine place this was and what good, welcoming people the Austrians were – they were smiling warmly at us and occasionally raising glasses to us in a toast – when the Germans leaned forward and told us in low voices that we were in danger. The Austrians, it seemed, were mocking us. Unaware that two of our party could understand every word they said, they were talking freely – every one of them: the men, the women, the landlord, the landlord's wife, the whole fucking village – about taking us out back and, as Gerhard translated, 'of giving us a hair-cut and running us through with zer pitchforks'.

A roar of laughter passed across the room. Gerhard showed a flicker of smile. 'Zey say zat perhaps zey should also make us to eat of zer horse dung.'

'Oh, swell,' said Katz. 'As if I haven't eaten enough shit on this trip already.'

My head swivelled like a periscope. Those cheery smiles had become demonic leers. A man opposite toasted me again and gave me a wink that said, Hope you like horse shit, kid.

I turned to Gerhard. 'Should we call the police?'

'I sink zat man over zere *is* zer police.'

'Oh, swell,' said Katz again.

'I sink maybe we should just go to zer door as *quietly* as we can and zen run like, how you say, zer clappers.'

We rose, leaving behind unfinished beers, strolled casually to the door, nodding to our would-be assailants as we passed, and ran like hell. We could hear a fresh roar of laughter lift the inn roof off its moorings, but no one followed us and the soft squish of horse shit between the teeth remains for me – thank you, God, thank you, thank you, thank you – for ever in the realms of the imagined.

As we lay in our sleeping bags in a dewy meadow beneath a thousand stars, with the jagged mountains outlined against a fractionally less black sky and the smell of mown hay hanging on the still night air, I remarked to no one in particular that I had never seen such a beautiful place as this.

'Zat's zer whole trouble wiz Austria,' said Thomas with sudden passion, in one of the few times I actually heard him speak. 'It's such a lovely country, but it's full of fucking Austrians.'

I travelled the next day to Salzburg. I found it hard to warm to, which surprised me because I had fond, if somewhat hazy, memories of the place. It was full of tourists and, worse still, full of shops selling things that only a tourist could want: Tyrolean crap and Alpine crap and crap crap and, above all, Mozart crap – Mozart chocolates, Mozart marzipan, Mozart busts, Mozart playing-cards, Mozart ashtrays, Mozart liqueurs. Building and roadworks seemed to be in progress everywhere, filling the town with dust and noise. I seemed to be forever walking on planks over temporary ditches.

The streets of the old town, crammed into a compact space between the River Salzach and the perpendicular walls of the Mönchsberg mountain, are undeniably quaint and attractive, but so overbearingly twee as to bring on frequent bouts of dry heaving. Along Getreidegasse, the site of Mozart's birthplace, every shop had one of those hanging pretzel signs above the door, including, God help us, the local McDonald's (the sign had a golden-arches M worked into its filigree), as if we were supposed to think that they have been dispensing hamburgers there since the Middle Ages. I sank to my knees and beat my poor head on the cobbled pavement.

I'm all for McDonald's in European cities, I truly am, but we should never forget that any company that chooses a half-witted clown named Ronald McDonald as its official public face cannot be relied on to exercise the best judgement in matters of corporate presentation.

The people of McDonald's need guidance. They need to be told that Europe is not Disneyland. They need to be instructed to take suitable premises on a side street and given, without option, a shop design that is recognisable, appropriate to its function and yet reasonably subdued. It should look like a normal European bistro, with perhaps little red curtains and a decorative aquarium and nothing to tell you from the outside that this is a McDonald's except for a discreet golden-arches transfer on each window and a steady stream of people with enormous asses going in and out of the door. While we're at it, they should be told that they will no longer be allowed to provide each customer with his own weight in styrofoam boxes and waste paper. And finally they have to promise to shoot Ronald. When these conditions are met, McDonald's should be allowed to operate in Europe, but not until.

The main square in Salzburg, the Mozartplatz, was quite astonishingly ugly for a city that prides itself on its beauty – a big expanse of asphalt, as charming as a Tesco car park, one extraordinarily begrimed statue of the great man, and a few half-broken benches, around every one of which was crowded a noisy cluster of thirteen-year-old Italians in whom the hormonal imbalances of adolescence were clearly having a deleterious effect. It was awful.

What surprised me was that I remembered Salzburg as being a beautiful place. It was in Salzburg that Katz and I met Gerhard and Thomas, in a bar around the corner from the Mozartplatz, and it was such a thrill to have someone to dilute Katz's company that I think my enthusiasm may have coloured my memory of the city. In any case, I could find nothing now in the old town but these wretched souvenir shops and restaurants and bars whose trade was overwhelmingly non-local and thus offered about as much charm and local colour as a Pizza Hut on Carnaby Street.

When I crossed the river to the more modern right bank, I found I liked Salzburg much better. A long, quiet street of big houses stood overlooking the Salzach and the views across to the old town were splendid: the ancient roofs, the three domed spires of the cathedral and the vast, immensely heavy-looking Hohensalzburg fortress sinking into the low mountain-top at its back. The shopping streets of the modern town were to my mind much more interesting and appealing and certainly more real than their historic counterparts across the river. I had a coffee in a Konditorei on Linzer Gasse, where every entering customer got a hearty 'Grüss Gott!' from every member of the staff. It was like on *Cheers* when Norm comes in, only they did it for everybody, including me, which I thought was wonderful. Afterwards I had a good dinner, a couple of beers and a long evening walk along the river and felt that Salzburg wasn't such a bad place at all. But it wasn't the Salzburg that most people come to see.

Vienna is a little under 200 miles east of Salzburg and it took all morning and half the afternoon to get there. There is this curiously durable myth that European trains are wonderfully swift and smooth and a dream to travel on. The trains in Europe are in fact often tediously slow and for the most part the railways persist in the antiquated system of dividing the carriages into compartments. I used to think this was rather jolly and friendly, but you soon discover that it is like spending seven hours in a waiting-room waiting for a doctor who never arrives. You are forced into an awkward intimacy with strangers, which I always find unsettling. If you do anything at all – take something from your pocket, stifle a yawn, rummage in your rucksack – everyone looks over to see what you're up to. There is no scope for privacy and of course there is nothing like being trapped in a train compartment on a long journey to bring all those unassuageable little frailties of the human body crowding to the front of your mind – the withheld fart, the three and a half square yards of boxer short that have somehow become concertinaed between your buttocks, the Kellogg's cornflake that is teasingly and unaccountably lodged deep in your left nostril. It was the cornflake that I ached to get at. The itch was all-consuming. I longed to thrust a finger so far up my nose that it would look as if I were scratching the top of my head from the inside, but of course I was as powerless to deal with it as a man with no arms.

You even have to watch your thoughts. For no reason I can explain, except perhaps that I was inordinately preoccupied with bodily matters, I began to think of a sub-editor I used to work with on the business section of *The Times*. I shall call him Edward, since that was his name. Edward was crazy as fuck, which in those palmy pre-Murdoch days was no impediment to employment, or even promotion to high office, on the paper, and he had a number of striking peculiarities, but the one I particularly remember was that late at night, after the New York markets had shut and there was nothing much to do, he would straighten out half a dozen paper clips and probe his ears with them. And I don't mean delicate little scratchings. He would really jam those paper clips home and then twirl them between two fingers, as if tuning in a radio station. It looked excruciating, but Edward seemed to derive immense satisfaction from it. Sometimes his eyes would roll up into his head and he would make ecstatic little gurgling noises. I suppose he thought no one was watching, but we all sat there fascinated. Once, during a particularly intensive session, when the paper clip went deeper and deeper and looked as if it might be stuck, John Price, the chief sub-editor, called out, 'Would it help, Edward, if one of us pulled from the other side?'

I thought of this as we went *tracketa-tracketa* across the endless Austrian countryside and I laughed out loud – a sudden lunatic guffaw that startled me as much as my three companions. I covered my mouth with my hand, but more laughter – embarrassed, helpless – came leaking out. The other passengers looked at me as if I had just been sick down my shirt. It was only by staring out of the window and concentrating very hard for twenty minutes that I was able to compose myself and return once again to the more serious torments of the cornflake in my nostril.

At Vienna's huge Westbahnhof I paid to have a room found for me, then walked to the city centre along the long and ugly Mariahilfer Strasse, wondering if I had been misled about the glories of Vienna. For a mile and a half, from the station to the Ringstrasse, the street was lined with seedy-looking discount stores – the sort of places that sell goods straight out of their cardboard boxes – and customers to match. It was awful, but then near the Hofburg palace I passed into the charmed circle of the Ringstrasse and it was like the sun breaking out from behind clouds. Everything was lovely and golden.

My hotel, the Wandl, was not particularly charming or friendly, but it was reasonably cheap and quiet and it had the estimable bonus of being in almost the precise geographical centre of the city, just behind the baroque Schottenkirche and only half a block from Graben, one of the two spacious pedestrian shopping streets that dominate the heart of Vienna. The other is Kärntnerstrasse, which joins Graben at a right angle by the cathedral square. Between them, they provide Vienna with the finest pedestrian thoroughfare in Europe. Strøget may be a hair longer, others may have slightly more interesting buildings, and a few may be fractionally more elegant, but none is all of these things. I knew within minutes that I was going to like Vienna.

I went first to the cathedral. It is very grand and Gothic outside, but inside I found it oddly lifeless – the sort of place that gives you a cold shiver – and rather neglected as well. The brass was dull and unpolished, the pews were worn, the marble seemed heavy and dead, as if all the natural luminescence had been drained from it. It was a relief to step back outside.

I went to a nearby Konditorei for coffee and a 15,000-calorie slice of cake and planned my assault on the city. I had with me the *Observer Guide to Vienna*, which included this piece of advice: 'In Vienna, it is best to tackle the museums one at a time.' Well, *thank* you, I thought. All these years I've been going to museums two at a time and I couldn't figure out why I kept getting depressed.

I decided to start at the top with the Kunsthistorisches Museum. It was fabulous – vast, grand, full of great paintings. They employ a commendable system there. In every room is a rack of cards giving histories of the paintings in that room in a choice of four languages. You wander around with a card looking at the paintings and reading the notes and then replace it in the rack before passing on to the next room where you collect another. I thought it was a great idea.

The only problem with the Kunstmuseum is that it is so enormous. Its lofty halls just run on and on, and before I was a third of the way through it I was suffering museum fatigue. In these circumstances, especially when I have paid a fortune to get in and feel that there are still a couple of hours standing between me and my money's worth, I find myself involuntarily supplying captions to the pictures: Salome, on being presented the head of John the Baptist on a salver, saying, 'No, I ordered a double cheeseburger,' and an exasperated St Sebastian whining, 'I'm warning you guys, the next person who shoots an arrow is going to get reported.' But this time I did something that astonished even me. I left, deciding that I would come back for a second sweep later in the week, in spite of the cost.

Instead, for a change of pace, I went to the Tobacco Museum, not far away behind the Messepalast. This was expensive, too. Most things in Vienna are. The entrance charge was twenty schillings, two-thirds as much as the Kunstmuseum, but it was hardly two-thirds as good. In two not-very-large rooms I was treated to a couple of dozen display cases packed with old pipes (including a few grotesquely anti-Semitic ones), cigars, matches, cigarettes and cigarette boxes. Around the larger of the two rooms was an elevated gallery of paintings with little artistic merit and nothing in common except that one or more of the people portrayed was smoking. Not recommended.

Nor, I have to say, is the Albertina. This was even more expensive – forty-five schillings. For that kind of money, I would expect to be allowed to take one of the drawings away with me. But I paid without a whimper because I had read that the Albertina has one of the world's great collections of graphic art, which I just happen to like a lot, but in fact there was hardly anything on show. It was a huge building, but the public gallery was confined to eight small rooms at the back, all with creaking floors and sketching students and unmemorable drawings by mostly obscure artists.

The postcard-stand outside was full of drawings 'from the Albertina collection' by artists like Rubens and Dürer, but I had seen none of these. The woman running the stall didn't speak English and when I held up a Dürer postcard and asked her where the original was, she just kept saying, with that irritableness for which the Viennese are noted, 'Ja, ja, das ist ein *postcard*,' as if I had said, 'Pardon me, is this a postcard or is it a snack food?' and refused to try to grasp my question until finally I had no choice but to slap her to the ground and leave.

Apart from her, however, I didn't find the Viennese especially rude and pushy, which rather disappointed me, because I had heard many times that they are the most disagreeable people in Europe. In *The Double Eagle*, Stephen Brook's excellent account of Vienna, Budapest and Prague, he notes that he met many foreign residents of the city who reported being stopped on the streets by strangers and rebuked for crossing against the lights or letting their children walk with their coats unbuttoned.

Brook also promised that at the famous Café Landtmann, on the Ringstrasse next to the Burgtheater, 'the waiters and cloak-room attendants treat you like shit' and in this he was certainly closer to my experience. I didn't feel *precisely* like excrement, but the waiters certainly did have that studied air of superiority that you find among a certain class of European waiter. When I was younger this always cowed me, but now I just think, Well, if you're so hot how come I'm sitting down and you're doing the fetching? Let's be honest, if your career consists of nothing more demanding than conveying trays of food back and forth between a kitchen and a dining-room all day, there's not really much of anyone you are superior to, is there? Except perhaps estate agents.

On the whole, the cafés were the biggest disappointment of Vienna to me. I've reached the time of life where my idea of a fabulous time is to sit around for half a day with a cup of coffee and a newspaper, so a city teeming with coffee houses seemed made for me. I had expected them to be more special, full of smoky charm and eccentric characters, but they were just restaurants really. The coffee was OK, but not sensational, and the service was generally slow and always unfriendly. They provide you with newspapers, but so what? I can provide newspapers.

Even the Café Central, where Trotsky used to hang out, sitting for long hours every day doing bugger-all, was a disappointment. It had some atmosphere – vaulted ceilings, marble tables, a pianist – but coffee was thirty-four schillings a throw and the service was indifferent. Still, I do like the story about the two Viennese who were sitting in the Central with coffees, discussing politics. One of them, just back from Moscow, predicted a revolution in Russia before long. 'Oh, yeah?' said the other doubtfully, and flicked his head in the direction of the ever-idle Trotsky. 'And who's going to lead it – him?'

The one friendly café I found was the Hawalka, around the corner from my hotel. It was an extraordinary place, musty, dishevelled and so dark that I had to feel my way to a table. Lying everywhere were newspapers on racks like carpet beaters. An old boy who was dressed more like a house painter than a waiter brought me a cup of coffee without asking if I wanted one and, upon realising that I was an American, began gathering up copies of *USA Today*.

'Oh no, please,' I said as he presented me with half a dozen, 'put these on the fire and bring me some newspapers.' But I don't think his hearing was good, and he scuttled around the room collecting even more and piling them on the table. 'No, no,' I protested, 'these are for lining drawers.' But he kept bringing them until I had a stack two feet high. He even opened one up and fixed it in front of me, so I drank my coffee and spent half an hour reading features about Vanna White, Sylvester Stallone and other great thinkers of our age.

Vienna is certainly the grandest city I have ever seen. All along the Ringstrasse colossal buildings proclaim an imperial past – the parliament, the Palace of Justice, the Natural History Museum, the Kunsthistorisches Museum, the opera house, the Burgtheater and above all the Hofburg, with its 2,600 rooms. They all look much the same – mighty piles of granite and sandstone with warlike statuary crowded along the roofs and pediments. A Martian coming to earth would unhesitatingly land at Vienna, thinking it the capital of the planet.

The one thing you soon learn to adjust to in Vienna is that the Danube is entirely incidental to the city. It is so far from the centre that it doesn't even appear on most tourist maps. I tried walking to it one afternoon and never made it. I got as far as the Prater, the vast and famous park, which is bordered by the Danube on its far side, but the Prater is so immense that after a half-hour it seemed pointless to continue walking on aching feet just to confirm with my own eyes what I have read a hundred times: that the Danube isn't blue at all. Instead, I plodded lengthwise through the park along the long straight avenue called Hauptallee, passing busy playing-fields, swings, a sports stadium, cafés and restaurants and eventually the amusement park with its ferris wheel – the one made famous by Orson Welles and Joseph Cotton in *The Third Man*.

A sign by the ferris wheel, the famous Riesenrad, gave a history of it in German. It was built in 1896–97 by an Englishman named Walter Basset, I noted with a touch of pride on behalf of my friends and neighbours. I assume old Walter had some help because it's a pretty good size. It cost twenty-five schillings to go up, but it wasn't operating. The rest of the park, however, was doing brisk business, though I am hard pressed to explain why, since it seemed to be rather a dump.

Late one afternoon I went to the Sigmund Freud museum, in his old apartment on Berggasse, a mile or so to the north of the city centre. Berggasse is now a plain and rather dreary street, though the Freuds lived in some style. Their apartment had sixteen rooms, but of these only four are open to the public and they contain almost no furniture, original or otherwise, and only a few trifling personal effects of Freud's: a hat and walking stick, his medical bag and a steamer trunk. Still, this doesn't stop the trust that runs the museum from charging you thirty schillings to come in and look around.

The four rooms are almost entirely bare but for the walls, which are lined with 400 photographs and photocopies of letters and other documents relating to Freud's life – though some of these, it must be said, are almost ludicrously peripheral: a picture of Michelangelo's Moses, which Freud had admired on a trip to Italy, and a photograph of Sarah Bernhardt, included not because Freud treated her or slept with her or even met her, but because he once saw her perform. Almost all of the personal effects Freud collected during half a century of living in this apartment – his library, his 2,500 pieces of classical statuary, his furniture, his famous consulting couch – are now in a far superior museum in Hampstead because, of course, Freud was driven from Vienna by the Nazis two years before he died.

The wonder to me is that it took him so long to go. By well before the turn of the century Freud was one of the most celebrated figures in world medicine, and yet he wasn't made a professor at the University of Vienna until 1902, when he was nearly fifty, simply because he was a Jew.

Before the war there were 200,000 Jews in Vienna. Now there are hardly any. As Jane Kramer notes in her book *Europeans*, most Austrians now have never met an Austrian Jew and yet Austria remains the most ferociously anti-Semitic country in Europe. According to Kramer, polls repeatedly show that about seventy per cent of

Austrians do not like Jews, a little over twenty per cent actively loathe them and not quite a tenth find Jews so repulsive that they are 'physically revolted in a Jew's presence'. I'd have thought this scarcely credible except that I saw another poll in the *Observer* revealing that almost forty per cent of Austrians thought the Jews were at least partly responsible for what happened to them during the war and forty-eight per cent believed that the country's 8,000 remaining Jews who, I should point out, account for just a little over 0.001 per cent of the Austrian population – still enjoy too much economic power and political influence.

The Germans, however unseemly their past, have made some moving attempts at atonement – viz., Willy Brandt weeping on his knees in the Warsaw ghetto and Richard von Weizsäcker apologising to the world for the sins of his country on the fiftieth anniversary of the start of the war. What do the Austrians do? They elect a former Wehrmacht officer as President.

I thought about this as I was walking from the Freud museum to my hotel along the Karl-Lueger-Strasse. At a set of traffic lights, a black limousine led by a single motor-cycle policeman pulled up. In the back seat, reading some papers, was – I swear to God – the famous Dr Kurt Waldheim, the aforementioned Wehrmacht officer and now President of Austria.

A lot of people aren't sure of the difference between the Chancellor and the President in Austria, but it's quite simple. The Chancellor decides national policy and runs the country, while the President rounds up the Jews. I'm only joking, of course! I wouldn't suggest for a moment that President Waldheim would have anything to do with the brutal treatment of innocent people – not these days, certainly. Moreover, I fully accept Dr Waldheim's explanation that when he saw 40,000 Jews being loaded onto cattle trucks at Salonica, he genuinely believed they were being sent to the seaside for a holiday.

For the sake of fairness, I should point out that Waldheim insists he never even knew that the Jews of Salonica were being shipped off to Auschwitz. And let's be fair – they accounted for no more than *one-third of the city's entire population* (italics theirs), and it is of course entirely plausible that a high-ranking Nazi officer in the district could have been quite unaware of what was happening within his area of command.

Let's give the man a break. I mean to say, when the Storm Troopers burned down forty-two of Vienna's forty-three synagogues during Kristallnacht, Waldheim did wait a whole week before joining the unit. And after the Anschluss, he waited *two whole weeks* before joining the Nazi Student Union. Christ, the man was practically a resistance hero. I don't know what all the fuss is about.

Austria should be proud of him and proud of itself for having the courage to stand up to world opinion and elect a man of his calibre, pugnaciously overlooking the fact that he is a pathological liar, that he has been officially accused of war crimes, that he has a past so murky and mired in mistruths that no one but he knows what he has done. It takes a special kind of people to stand behind a man like that.

What a wonderful country.

20. Yugoslavia

I flew to Split, half-way down the Adriatic coast in Yugoslavia. Katz and I had hitch-hiked there from Austria. It took four days of standing on baking roadsides on the edge of a series of nowheres watching carloads of German tourists sweep past, so there was a certain pleasure even now in covering the same ground in hours. I had no choice: I was running out of time. I had to be in Bulgaria in six days or my visa would lapse.

I caught a bus into town from the airport and was standing at the harbourside in that state of mild indecisiveness that comes with the sudden arrival in a strange country, when a woman of late middle years approached and said quietly, as if offering something illicit, 'Zimmer? Room? You want?'

'Yes, please,' I said, suddenly remembering that this was how Katz and I had found a room in Split. 'How much?'

'Ten t'ousan' dinar,' she said.

Five dollars. This sounded like my kind of a deal. I considered the possibility that she might have four grown sons at home waiting to throttle me and take my money – I have long assumed that this is how I will die: trussed up and dumped into the sea after following a stranger offering an unbeatable bargain – but she looked honest enough. Besides, she had to trust that I wasn't an axe murderer. 'Sure,' I said. 'Let's go.'

We took a bus to her neighbourhood, twenty minutes away up a long hill, and stepped off on a nondescript residential street somewhere at the back of the town. The lady led me down a complicated series of steps and sunny alleyways full of scrawny cats. It was the sort of route you would follow if you were trying to give someone the slip. It wouldn't have altogether surprised me if she had asked me to put on a blindfold. Eventually we crossed a plank over a narrow ditch, made our way across a grassless yard and entered a four-storey building that looked only half-finished. A cement mixer was standing by the stairwell. I was beginning to have my doubts. This was just the place for an ambush.

'Come,' she said, and I followed her up the stairs to the top floor and into her apartment. It was small and plainly furnished, but spotless and airy. Two men in their twenties, both vaguely thuggish-looking, were sitting in T-shirts at the table in the kitchen/living-room. Uh-oh, I thought, casually sliding my hand into my pocket and fingering my Swiss Army knife, but knowing that even in ideal circumstances it takes me twenty minutes to identify a blade and prise it out. If these guys came at me I would end up defending myself with a toothpick and tweezers.

In fact, they turned out to be nice fellows. Isn't the world a terrific place? They were her sons and knew a little English because they worked as waiters in town. One of them, in fact, was just off for work and would give me a lift if I wanted. I gratefully accepted on account of the distance and my considerable uncertainty as to where I was. He donned a red waiter's jacket and walked me to a dusty blue Skoda parked on a nearby street, where he fired up the engine and took off at a speed that had the back of the car fish-tailing and me holding the armrest with both hands. It was like being in one of those movie chase scenes where the cars scatter dustbins and demolish vegetable carts. 'I'm a little bit late,' he explained as he chased a flock of elderly pedestrians off a zebra crossing and turned on two wheels into a busy avenue without pausing to see if any cars were coming. There were, but they generously made way for him by veering sideways into buildings. He dropped me by the marketplace and was gone before I could barely get out a 'Thank you'.

Split is a wonderful place, with a pretty harbour overlooking the Adriatic and a cluster of green islands lurking attractively a mile or two offshore. Somewhere out there was Vis, where Katz and I had spent an almost wonderful week. We were sitting at an outdoor café one morning, trying to anaesthetise hangovers with coffee, when two Swedish girls came up to us and said brightly, 'Good-morning! How are you today? Come with us. We're going on the bus to a beach on the other side of the island.'

Unquestioningly we got up and followed. If you had seen these girls, you would have, too. They were gorgeous: healthy, tanned, deliciously fresh-smelling, soft all over, with good teeth and bodies shaped by a loving god. I whispered to Katz as we walked along behind, massaging our eyeballs on the perfect hemispheres of their backsides, 'Do we know them?'

'I dunno. I think maybe we talked to them last night at that bar by the casino.'

'We didn't go to the bar by the casino.'

'Yes we did.'

'We *did*?'

'Yeah.'

'*Really?*' I could remember nothing of the night before other than a series of Bip Pivo beers passing before me, as if on a bottling line. I shrugged it off, youthfully unaware that I was in a single summer disabling clusters of brain cells at a pace that would leave me seventeen years later routinely standing in places like a pantry or toolshed, gazing at the contents and trying to remember what the hell it was that had brought me there.

We went on a bouncing bus to the far side of the island, to a fishing village called Komiža, had a long swim in a warm sea, a couple of beers at a beachside taverna, caught a bouncing bus back to Vis town, had some more beers, ordered dinner, had some more beers, told stories, compared lives, fell in love.

Well, I did anyway. Her name was Marta. She was eighteen, dark and from Uppsala and she seemed to me the fairest creature I had ever run eyes over – though it must be said that by this stage of the trip even Katz, in certain lights, was beginning to look not half bad. In any case, I thought she was lovely and the miracle was that she appeared to find a certain charm in me. She and the other girl, Trudi, grew swiftly drunk and loquacious and spent half the time talking in Swedish, but it didn't matter. I sat with my chin in my hands, just gazing at this Swedish fantasy, hopelessly besotted, stirring to my senses from time to time just long enough to suck back drool and take a sip of beer. Occasionally she would lay a hand on my bare forearm, sending my hormones into delirious turmoil, and once she glanced over and absently stroked my cheek with the back of her hand. I would have sold my mother as a galley slave and plunged a dagger into my thigh for her.

Late in the evening, when Katz and Trudi had gone off for pees, Marta turned to me, abruptly pulled my head to hers and swabbed my throat with her tongue. It felt as if a fish were flopping around in my mouth. She released me, wearing a strange, dreamy expression and breathed, 'I'm fool of lust.'

I couldn't find words to communicate my appreciation. Then the most awful thing happened. An abrupt startled look seized her, as if she had been struck by a sniper's bullet. Her eyes snapped shut and she slid bonelessly from her chair.

I gaped for a long moment and cried, 'Don't do this to me, God, you prick!' But she was gone, as dead to the world as if she had been hit broadside by a Mack truck. I looked at the sky. 'How could you do this to me? I'm a *Catholic*.'

Trudi reappeared, tutting in a sudden maternal fashion and saying, 'Well, well, well, we'd better get this one to bed.' I offered to carry Marta to their hotel for her, thinking that at the very least I might manage to lay my tingling mitts on her splendid buttocks – only for a moment, you understand, just a little something to sustain me till the end of the century – but Trudi, doubtless sensing my intent, wouldn't hear of it. She was as strong as a steam train and before I could blink she had hoisted Marta over her shoulder and was disappearing down the street, leaving behind a fading 'Good-night'.

I watched them go, then stared moodily into my beer. Katz arrived and saw from my face that there would be no naked twining in the moonlit surf this night. 'What am I supposed to do now?' he said, sinking into his chair. 'She was coming on to me outside the men's room. I've got a boner like Babe Ruth's bat. What am I supposed to do?'

'You'll just have to take matters into your own hands,' I said, but he failed to see any humour in the situation, as indeed, on reflection, did I, and we spent the rest of the evening drinking in silence.

We never saw the Swedish girls again. We had no idea which was their hotel, but Vis town was not a big place and we were certain that we would run into them. For three days we went everywhere, peered in restaurant windows, walked up and down the beaches, but we never saw them. After a time I half began to wonder if it wasn't all a product of an overheated imagination. Maybe Marta had never even said, 'I'm fool of lust.' Maybe she had said, 'I'm fit to bust.' I didn't know. And as it became clearer and clearer that she was gone for ever, it didn't really seem to matter.

I wandered along the quayside looking at the sailing boats, then ventured into the sun-warmed lanes and courtyards that form the heart of Split. Once this area, roughly a quarter of a mile square, was the Palace of Diocletian. But after the fall of the Roman Empire, squatters moved in and started building houses inside the crumbling palace walls. Over the centuries a little community grew up. What were once corridors became streets. Courtyards and atriums evolved into public squares. Now the lanes – some so narrow you have to turn sideways to pass through them – are mostly lined with houses and shops, and yet there is this constant, disarming sense of being *inside* a palace. Incorporated into many of the façades are parts of the original structure – stairways that go nowhere, columns supporting nothing, niches that once clearly held Roman busts. The effect is that the houses look as if they grew magically out of the ruins. It is entrancing and there is no other place in Europe like it.

I walked around for a couple of hours, then had an early dinner on a square bounded on three sides by old buildings with outdoor restaurants and on the fourth by the quay. It was a fine summery evening, with the kind of still air on which aromas hang – in this case a curious but not displeasing mixture of vanilla, grilled meat and fish. Swifts circled and darted overhead and the masts of yachts rocked lazily on the water. It was such a pleasant spot and dusk was settling in so nicely that I sat for some time drinking Bips and watching the nightly promenade, the korzo.

Every person in town dresses up in his best clothes and goes for an evening stroll along the main street – families, hunched groups of furtive-looking teenage boys, giggling clumps of dolled-up, over-fragranced teenage girls, young couples with heavy-footed toddlers, old men and their wives. It had the same chatty, congenial air of the gatherings around the square in Capri, except that here they kept moving, marching up and down the long quayside in their hundreds. It seemed to go on for much of the night.

As I drank my fourth or possibly fifth beer, I suddenly felt drowsy

– drowsy enough to lay my head on my arms and just sleep. I looked at the label on my beer bottle and discovered with alarm that the alcohol content was twelve per cent. It was as strong as wine and I had drunk a bucket of it. No wonder I felt tired. I called the waiter and paid the bill.

Solitary drinking is a strange and dangerous thing. You can drink all night and not feel the remotest sense of intoxication, but when you rise you discover that while your head feels clear enough, your legs have suddenly decided to go in for a little moonwalking or some other involuntary embarrassment. I moved across the square, dragging one reluctant leg behind me, as if under the strain of a gunshot wound, and realised I was too far gone to walk anywhere.

I found a cab at the quayside, climbed in the front passenger seat, waking the driver, and realised I had no idea where I was going. I didn't know the name of the street, the name of the woman to whom I had entrusted my personal effects, the part of town in which she lived. I just knew it was up a hill. Suddenly Split seemed to be full of hills.

'Do you speak English?' I asked the driver.

'Nay,' he said.

'Okay, let's not panic. I want to go sort of that direction. Do you follow me?'

'Nay.'

'Over there – just drive that way.' We went all over the place. His meter spun like the altimeter on a crashing plane. Occasionally I would spot a corner that looked familiar, grab his arm and cry, 'Left here! Left here!' A minute later we would find ourselves coming up against the gates of a prison or something. 'No, I think we may have gone wrong here,' I would say, not wanting to let his spirits down. 'It was a good try though.' Eventually, when it became apparent that he was convinced I was insane as well as drunk and was considering pushing me out, we blundered onto the correct street. At least I thought it was correct. I gave him a pile of dinars and stumbled out. It was correct – I recognised a corner shop – but I still had to find my way along the steps and alleys. Everything looked different at night and I was drunk and weary. I wandered blindly, occasionally frightening the crap out of myself by stepping on a cat, and peered through the darkness for a four-storey building with a plank of wood outside.

Finally I found it. The plank was thinner and wobblier than I remembered. I shuffled along it and was about half-way across when it turned sideways and my footing went. I fell through black space for an instant – it seemed longer and was really rather pleasant – unaware that my feet were either side of the plank and that I was about to break my fall with my reproductive organs.

Well, it was a surprise, let me say that much. I teetered for a moment, gasping, then fell heavily sidelong into the ditch. I lay on my back for a long minute waiting for my lungs to reflate, wondering in an oddly detached way if the dull, unspeakable ache in my midsection indicated permanent damage and the embarrassing burden of a catheter bag, until it occurred to me that there might be rats in the ditch and that they might find me of interest. Abruptly I rose, scrabbled my way to the top against the loose dirt, slipped back, scrabbled again and tumbled out. I hobbled into the building and up to the fourth floor, where I tapped on the door to the lady's flat. A minute later a woman in hair curlers opened the door to find an American man, dishevelled, covered in dirt, swaying slightly and clutching his scrotum with both hands, standing on her threshold. We had never seen each other before. It was the wrong flat.

I tried to think of words to explain the situation, but could not, and wandered wordlessly off down the hall, with an ambiguous wave as I went. I found the right flat and knocked, and after a minute knocked again. Eventually I heard shuffling inside and the door was opened by my lady acquaintance. She was wearing a nightdress and a frightening array of hair curlers, and she said something cross to me about, I guess, the lateness of the hour. I tried to explain things but she was looking at me as if I had brought shame into her home, and I gave up. She showed me to my room, her slippers flopping ahead of me down the hall. Her sons were also in there, fast asleep. My bed was an upper bunk. Suddenly $5 seemed like a lot of money. She shut the door and plodded off.

Still dressed, I crossed the room in the dark, and hoisted myself onto the upper bunk, stepping inadvertently on the stomach of one of the sleeping brothers. 'Oomph,' he went, like a deflated punchbag, but he seemed not to wake. I lay on the bed and took ten minutes to push my nuts back into place, locating them somewhere up around my shoulders and cautiously working them back down my body, as with a coin trapped in the lining of a jacket. That done, I tried to sleep, but without much success.

In the morning I sat up to find the brothers gone. I went into the kitchen with my rucksack. The flat was silent but for an insistently ticking clock and a periodic *bloop bloop* of a dripping tap, which somehow made the silence more intense. I didn't know if the patroness was out or still in bed. I brushed my teeth quietly in the sink and made myself fractionally more presentable with the application of a little cold water and a tea towel. Then I took out a five-dollar bill and put it on the table, then took out another and put it on the table, too. And then I left.

I walked into the city centre and went to the bus station. I had intended taking the bus to Belgrade, as Katz and I had done, but discovered that there was no longer a direct daytime bus. I would have to travel to Sarajevo, half-way along, and hope that I could make a connection there. I bought a ticket for the ten o'clock bus and, with two hours to kill, went off to find some coffee. Midway along the quay, directly across the street from two of the city's grandest hotels, I noticed a gloopy sound and a smell as of a slurry wagon. I peered over the quay edge. A small outfall pipe was disgorging raw sewage straight into the harbour. You could see everything – turds, wriggling condoms, pieces of toilet paper. It was awful, and it was only feet from the main street, mere yards from the cafés and hotels. I decided not to have coffee at my usual spot, and instead found a café well inside the old town where the view wasn't so good but the chances of cholera were presumably slighter.

The bus was crowded – buses in Yugoslavia always are – but I found a seat three-quarters of the way back and gripped the seat bar ahead of me with both hands. When Katz and I had crossed Yugoslavia, it had been nothing if not exciting. The roads through the mountains were perilous beyond words, much too narrow for a bus, full of impossible bends and sheer falls from unimaginable heights. Our driver was an escaped lunatic who had somehow talked his way into a job with the bus company. Young and handsome, wearing his cap at a rakish angle, he drove as if cheerfully possessed, passing on blind bends, driving at break-neck speed, honking at everything, slowing for nothing. He sang hearty tunes and carried on lively conversations with the passengers – often turning around in his seat to address them directly – while simultaneously sweeping us along the edge of ragged roads on the brink of sheer-sided cliffs. I remember pressing my face to the window many times and being able to see no road beneath us – just a straight drop and the sort of views you get from an aeroplane. There was never more than an inch of shoulder standing between us and wingless flight.

Katz and I were sitting at the front, and the driver, taking a sudden liking to us, decided to amuse us with some visual jokes – pretending to nod off for a few moments, then jerking back to consciousness just in time to avoid an oncoming truck or acting as if the brakes had failed as we hurtled down a more or less perpendicular incline at the sort of speed usually experienced only by astronauts, causing Katz and me to try to sit on each other's laps.

In the afternoon, after many hours of such bouncing excitement, the bus crested the mountains and began a steep descent into a broad valley of the most inexpressible lushness and beauty. I had never seen such a charmed and dreamy landscape. At every town and village people would emerge from houses as if our arrival were a kind of miracle and trot along with the bus, sometimes passing little bags of cherries through the windows to their friends and the driver and even to Katz and me.

We arrived in Belgrade in the early evening, found by some miracle a cheap and lovely hotel high on a hill, and dined on a rooftop terrace as we watched the sun sink over the Danube and the lights of the city twinkle on. We drank many beers and ate the last of our cherries.

It had been a nearly perfect day and I itched to repeat it now. In a strange way, I was looking forward to the dangers of the mountain road – it was such an exhilarating combination of terror and excitement, like having a heart attack and enjoying it. The bus laboured through the streets of Split and up into the steep, cement-coloured mountains at its back. I was disappointed to discover that the roads had been improved in my long absence – in many places they had been widened and crash barriers had been installed on the more dangerous bends – and that the driver was not obviously psychotic. He drove with both hands and kept his eyes on the road.

Clearly any drama I was to find would come from the landscape, though of this there was plenty. Most people are unaware of the richness and beauty of Yugoslavia's interior. It is as green as England and as stunningly scenic as Austria, but almost wholly untouristed. Within an hour or two of leaving the baking coastline, with its teeming resorts and cereal-box hotels, you find yourself descending from the empty mountains into this lush, lost world of orchards and fields, lakes and woodlands, tidy farmhouses and snug villages – a corner of Europe lost to time. In the fields people cut and gathered hay by hand, with scythes and wooden pitchforks, and crossed their fields behind horse-drawn ploughs. In the villages the elderly women were almost all dressed in black, with scarves around their heads. It was like a picture out of the distant past.

Seven slow, hot hours after leaving Split we rolled into Sarajevo, capital of the republic of Bosnia-Hercegovina. I truly was in another world now. There were minarets everywhere and the writing on shops and street signs was in Cyrillic. Sarajevo is surrounded by steep hills – the 1984 Winter Olympics were held there – and bisected by a narrow, swift, very straight river, the Miljacka. The street along one side of it, connecting the new part of town near the bus station with the old town a mile or so away, was the scene of Sarajevo's most famous incident, the assassination in June 1914 of Archduke Franz Ferdinand.

I got a room in the Hotel Europa, a dark and faded establishment still clinging to a hint of former grandness. There was no television in the room and only about fourteen watts of illumination with all the lights on, but the bed looked comfortable enough and the bath, I noted with a sigh of gratitude, issued steaming water. I had a long soak and, much refreshed, went out to see the town.

Sarajevo was a wonderful surprise, with lots of small parks and leafy squares. In the centre of town is one of Europe's largest bazaars, a series of alleyways lined with tiny shops selling hand-worked brass and copperware. But because there are no tourists, there are none of those irksome little gits tugging at your sleeve and thrusting goods in your face as you find in the more famous bazaars of Istanbul and Tangier. Here no one paid any attention to me at all.

I took a steep walk up into the hills, where old, sometimes tumbledown houses were packed together in a dense and picturesque jumble along roughly cobbled streets that were sometimes all but vertical. It was a strenuous climb – even locals could be seen pausing for breath, a hand against a wall – but the views from the higher points were memorable and exotic, with the setting sun crowning a skyline of minarets, and the muezzins' tortured calls to prayer echoing over the rooftops.

I returned to town in time to join the nightly promenade along the main street – the only time, it appeared, the Yugoslavs get cheerful. I examined restaurant menus along the way and settled on the dining-room of the Hotel Central, which had much the same faded grandeur of the Europa, like a stately home inhabited by an impoverished aristocrat. I was the only customer. Yugoslavia was going through a period of economic upheaval. Inflation was in the hundreds of per cent and the dinar was being devalued daily, sometimes two or three times daily, to the almost embarrassing benefit of the tourist and the detriment of the locals. A generous dinner of soup, steak, vegetables, salad, bread, beer and a coffee cost just $8, and yet I was evidently the only person in town who could afford it.

The service, as everywhere in Yugoslavia, was indifferent – not so much hostile as just past caring. The waiter dribbled my soup across the carpet and tablecloth and disappeared for long periods between courses, leaving me to stare at empty bowls and plates, but I couldn't entirely blame him. The difficulty with being a visitor in a place where you can live like a prince is that your wealth makes a menial of everyone you deal with. In Split, I had noticed some Germans tipping a waiter as if it were play money, almost teasing him with it, and I trusted he had had the sense to add some spittle to their meal. I just hoped that this wasn't what was keeping my waiter now.

In the morning I returned to the station and tried to find out about a bus to Belgrade, but the girl behind the information window was having such a delightful conversation with someone on the telephone that she was clearly not going to answer any enquiries. I waited for many minutes, and even said a few words to her through the mouth-hole in the glass, but she just looked at me blankly and carried on talking, curling the flex around her finger. Eventually I trudged off and found a bus by asking around among the drivers.

The trip to Belgrade took eight hours, and it was even hotter, slower, duller and more crowded than the bus the day before. I sat beside a man whose concern for personal hygiene was rather less than obsessive and spent much of the day wishing I knew the Serbo-Croat for 'Pardon me, but your feet are a trifle malodorous. I wonder if you would be good enough to stick them out of the window.' Gradually, to escape the smell, I fell into the mindless oblivion that seemed more and more to sustain me on these periods of getting from place to place, and patiently awaited the appearance of Belgrade through the front window.

I stepped off the bus in Belgrade feeling cheated. The trip had taken two days and had offered none of the reckless speed and adventure I had been hankering after. I found a room in an old-fashioned hotel called the Excelsior, rather expensive but comfortable, and immediately embarked on the usual business of acquainting myself with the city. I spent two days wandering around and found I remembered almost nothing about Belgrade. For old times' sake, I tried to locate the hotel where Katz and I had stayed, thinking I might dine on the rooftop terrace if it was still there, but I soon realised the quest was hopeless. I didn't remember enough to know where to begin to look in such a sprawling city.

Still, I was rather taken with Belgrade. It is the quintessential Mittel European city – long avenues of stolid, gloomy, five- and six-storey buildings, interspersed with parks and monumental buildings with copper domes. There was a certain indefinable sense of the dead hand of central planning everywhere, but alongside it a refreshing shortage of Western enterprises – McDonald's, Benetton and the like.

There was not a great deal to do in Belgrade. I strolled through the main shopping streets to an inner-city park called Kalemegdan, built around an old fortress and neatly arrayed with trees and benches and statues of Yugoslavian, and more particularly Serbian, heroes.

Most of the benches were taken up with men hunched intently over chessboards, each of them with a congregation of onlookers freely offering advice to both players. At the park's edge was a high terrace with an unobstructed view of the city and of the spot where the Sava and Danube rivers flow together to make one truly monumental river.

One afternoon, I walked some distance out to Hajd Park, a wooded and rolling estate where Tito had his executive compound and where he is buried now. A long paved path led up to his mausoleum. I was the only visitor and there wasn't much to see. Tito was not, as I had hoped, preserved in a glass case. He was safely hidden beneath a marble slab covered with scores of fresh wreaths and flowers. A lone soldier, looking desperately young and bored and uncomfortable, stood at attention beside the tomb. He was clearly supposed to stare straight ahead, but I could see his eyes following me around the room, and I had the terrible feeling that my visit was the high point of his day. 'Mine too,' I mumbled.

I went outside and felt the sudden weight of not knowing what to do with myself. Before me lay a panoramic view of a city I had no keen urge to explore. I spent most of the afternoon sitting in a park by a playground watching young parents pushing children on swings. I kept telling myself to get up and go do something, but my legs wouldn't respond and anyway all I wanted to do was sit and watch children play. I was, I realised at length, homesick. Oh dear.

I woke the next day in a better frame of mind. Today I would fulfil a little dream. I was going to take a first-class sleeper from one European capital to another. This had long seemed to me the very pinnacle of luxury, and I breakfasted in the dining-room of the Excelsior with the serene composure of a man who knows his time has come. My plan was to buy the ticket directly after breakfast and spend the day going around the museums before heading to the station in the evening to take my place among the dispossessed duchesses, Hercule Poirot look-alikes and other exotic characters I presumed still travelled by first-class sleeping carriage in this part of the world.

The concierge told me not to buy my ticket at the station – 'It is hysterical there,' he said, shaking his head sadly – but to go to the main office of Sputnik, the state-run travel agency, where I could make a reservation in an atmosphere of relative tranquillity.

The Sputnik office was orderly but unfriendly and full of sluggish queues. First I had to stand in a line to find out which line to stand in. Then I had to stand in a line to reserve a sleeping compartment, but these, I was told with withering disdain by a nasty-looking piece of work masquerading as a middle-aged woman, were booked solid for weeks and no amount of money could secure one for me now. Well, there goes another dream whooshing down the sluicepan of life, I thought bleakly. The woman directed me to a third line where I *might* get a seat ticket if I were lucky, but she gave a wave of her hand that told me this was unlikely. She was right.

Without even a seat on the train, I returned to the first line to see if there were any other lines I could usefully stand in. The girl in the first line, who happened to be the only nice person in the place, told me that I should stand in the airline line because flights across Yugoslavia were nearly as cheap as the train. I went and stood in the airline line, which was exceptionally long and slow-moving, and discovered when my turn came that it wasn't the airline line at all – ha, ha, ha – that the airline line was one more line to the left. So I went and stood in the airline line and eventually discovered that there were no airline seats available either, not that day or the next.

A sense of helpless frustration was overcoming me, with weepy panic nipping at its heels. I had been here for nearly two hours. I explained to the girl as patiently as I could that I *had* to be in Sofia the next day on account of my visa. She gave me a look that said, Well, why on earth do you expect me to give a fuck?, but she said she would put my name on the standby list for the evening flight and told me to come back at four.

I went to the bus station, hoping by some miracle that there would be a bus to Sofia. The station was absolute chaos – throngs of people bunched around every ticket window or sitting on piles of suitcases, waiting listlessly or erupting into little localised riots whenever a bus arrived. The babble of a dozen tongues filled the air. All the signs were in Cyrillic. I examined the timetables on the wall, but had no real idea what Sofia would look like in Cyrillic. Suddenly the idea of being innocent and free in a foreign land didn't seem so exotic and appealing. I couldn't even tell which was the information window. I was as helpless as an infant.

It took me most of the afternoon to discover that there were no buses to Sofia. My best hope was to take a bus to Niš and another onward to Dimitrovgrad on the Bulgarian border, and hope that I could find some kind of transport the last forty miles to Sofia. It would take three days at least, but I was so eager by now to get out of Yugoslavia and into any other country that I bought a ticket to Niš for $12, pocketed it and trudged back up the long hill to the Sputnik office.

I arrived two seconds after the stroke of four. A new girl was seated at the airline reservations computer. I told her the situation and she looked through the standby list for my name. After a moment she informed me that my name was not on the list. I looked at her with the expression of a man who has lost his job and had his car stolen and now has learned that his wife has run off with his best pal. I said, 'What?'

She said it didn't matter because there were still plenty of seats left on the evening flight.

I said, 'What?'

She looked at me with manifest indifference. A ticket to Sofia would cost $112. Did I want one?

Did I want a ticket? Is the Pope Catholic? Is Betty Ford a clinic? 'Yes,' I said. She did some tinkering with the computer and at length issued me with a ticket. A wave of relief washed over me. I would be in Sofia for dinner – or at least for a late snack. I was getting out of Belgrade. Hooray!

I went outside and hailed a taxi. 'Take me to the airport!' I said to the driver, falling into the back as he shot away from the kerb. Pulling myself upright, I discovered he was young and cheerful and wore his cap at rakish angle. He drove like a lunatic. It was great.

21. Sofia

I was looking forward to Bulgaria. It had been easily the most interesting, if not the most comfortable, of the places Katz and I had visited.

I remembered Sofia as being a city of broad boulevards so empty of traffic that people walked down the middle of them, stepping aside only to make room for the occasional black Zill limousine carrying Party functionaries to some dark, Orwellian ministry or other. I have never been in a more timeless city. It could have been any time in the last forty or fifty years. There were simply no clues to suggest what decade it was; the shape of the few cars on the road, the clothes people wore, the looks of the shops and buildings were all curiously uninformed by fashion.

Sofia had a dark and enormous deparment store called TSUM, at least as big as Selfridges in London, spread over five floors and containing not a single product that appeared to have been produced more recently than 1938 – chunky Bakelite radios, big stubby black fountain pens that looked like something Lord Grade would try to smoke, steam-powered washing machines, that sort of thing. I remember standing in the television and radio department in a crowd of people watching some historical drama in which two actors wearing beards that were hooked over their ears sat talking in a study, the walls of which were clearly painted on canvas. The television had – no exaggeration – a four-inch circular black and white screen and *this* was attracting a crowd.

I spent almost a whole day in TSUM, wandering in amazement, not just because the products were so wondrously old-fashioned but because whole families visited it as if it were some sort of marvellous museum of science and technology. I hoped things hadn't changed.

I arrived at Sofia Airport a little after nine. The foreign-exchange office was closed and, as you cannot get Bulgarian money outside of the country, I was effectively penniless. I woke a sleeping cab driver outside the front entrance and asked him if he would take me into the city for dollars. This is illegal, and I had visions of him reporting me to two guys in trench coats, but he was only too pleased to get his hands on hard currency and took me the nine miles into the city for $10. The cab, an ancient Moskvich, was propelled by a series of smoky blue explosions from the exhaust. It would move ten feet, pause and then lurch another ten feet with the aid of a fresh explosion. We were almost the only car on the streets.

He dropped me at the Sheraton on Lenin Square, quite the grandest hotel I had stayed in on this trip, but I had been told that it was the *only* place to stay in Sofia. Until a couple of years earlier it had been the Hotel Balkan, but then Sheraton took it over and the company has done a consummate job of renovating it. It was all shiny marble and plush sofas. I was impressed.

The girl at the check-in desk explained the hard currency system in operation at the hotel, which was very confusing. Some of the hotel's restaurants, bars and shops accepted only hard currency and some accepted only Bulgarian leva and some accepted both. I didn't really take any of it in.

I went straight out for a walk, eager to see the town. I was delighted to find that I remembered so much of it. There across the square was the big statue of Lenin. Facing it was TSUM, as vast as I remembered it and still clearly in business, and around the corner was the Place 9 Septemvri, a boulevard paved in golden bricks and dominated by the massive headquarters of the Communist Party, soon to be sacked by a mob and nearly burned down. I walked down it now and plunged off into the dark and narrow streets of the downtown.

Sofia must be one of the darkest cities in the world. Only the occasional lightning flashes of a tram at the far end of a street revealed the full outlines of the buildings. For the rest there were just weak pools of light beneath the well-spaced lampposts and a little seepage of illumination from the few bars and restaurants that were still open and doing, without exception, a desultory business. Almost every shop window was dark. None the less the streets were crowded with people, many of them evidently having just concluded a night out and now standing in the road trying to flag down the few cabs that flew past.

I made a lazy circuit of the downtown and emerged in front of TSUM. The goods in the darkened windows looked to be distinctly more up to date than on my previous visit, but at least it was still in business. This, I decided, would be my first port of call in the morning.

In the event, TSUM wasn't open when I hit the sunny streets, so I walked instead up a long straight avenue called Vitosha where most of the other main stores seemed to be. None of them were open yet either, but already long queues were forming at most doors. I had read that things were desperate in Bulgaria – that people began queuing for milk at four-thirty in the morning, that the price of some staples had gone up 800 per cent in a year, that the country had $10.8 billion of debt and so little money that there were only funds enough in the central bank to cover seven minutes' worth of imports – but nothing had prepared me for the sight of several hundred people queuing around the block just to buy a loaf of bread or a few ounces of scraggy meat.

When they opened, most shops posted some beefy sourpuss in the doorway who would let the customers in one at a time. The shelves were always bare. Things were sold straight out of a crate on the floor by the till, and presumably when the crate was empty the door was locked and the rest of the queue was sent away. I watched one woman come out of a baker's with a small loaf of bread and immediately join another long queue at a butcher's next door. They must have to do this every day with everything they buy. What a life.

It had been nothing like this in 1973. Then the shops had been full of goods, but no one appeared to have money to buy them. Now everyone was clutching fistfuls of money, but there was nothing to spend it on.

I went into one shop called 1001 СТОКИ. There was no orderly queue, just an almost incredible crush of people around the door. I didn't so much enter of my own volition as get swept in. Inside there was a mob of people around a single glass display case, waving money and jockeying for attention. All the other cases in the shop were empty, though there were salespeople still posted behind them. I slid through the crowd to see what it was the people were so eager to buy and it was just a pathetic assortment of odds and ends – some plastic cruet sets, twenty long-handled brushes with no identifiable function, some small glass ashtrays, and an assortment of tin-foil plates and pie dishes such as you get free in the West when you buy something to heat in the oven.

Clearly people weren't shopping so much as scavenging for purchasable goods. Again and again, as I ventured up Vitosha, I would peer into the impenetrable gloom of shop windows and discover after a moment that I had attracted a small crowd looking over my shoulder to see what I had spotted. But there was nothing to spot. One electrical shop I passed had three Russian hi-fi systems, two stereo and one mono (when was the last time you saw a mono hi-fi?), but they all had knobs missing and didn't look as if they would last five minutes.

Another shop sold nothing but two kinds of tins – yellow tins and green tins, stacked in their hundreds in neat pyramids on every shelf. It was the only well-stocked shop I saw all day. I have no idea what was in the tins – the labels gave no hint – but I can only assume that it must have been pretty dire or they would have sold out long ago. It was the most depressing morning I have spent in a long time.

I went to TSUM fearing the worst and found it. Whole departments were stripped bare, including my beloved TV section. The premier department store in the country couldn't offer its customers a single television, radio or other electrical item. In some departments three salespeople stood by a till with nothing to sell but perhaps a small stack of tea towels, but elsewhere there would be a lone desperate salesgirl trying to deal with throngs of people because a shipment of something desirable had just come in. At one counter on the third floor a big cardboard box full of socks had just arrived – hundreds and hundreds of socks, all an identical mustard-brown colour, all in thin cotton in the same size and all in bundles of a dozen – and people were buying double armloads of them. I suppose you buy what you can and think about what you are going to do with it afterwards – give some to your father-in-law for Christmas, swap some for a hunk of meat, reward a neighbour for queuing for you.

The saddest department was the toys – one shelf full of identical, ineffably cruddy teddy bears made out of synthetic wool, two dozen identical plastic toy trucks with bowed wheels and peeling, crooked labels, and fourteen metal tricycles all painted the same shade of blue and every one of them scraped or bashed in some way.

On the top two floors were whole departments full of boxes of unidentifiable odds and ends. If you have ever taken apart some mechanical contraption – a doorbell or a washing-machine motor – and had it all spring loose on you and 150 mysterious pieces have gone bouncing in every direction, well, those pieces are what they sell upstairs at TSUM – springs and cogs and small oddments of shaped metal that look as if they must fit together in some way. Scores of people were gravely picking through the boxes.

The busiest department was on the ground floor in what I suppose you would call the notions department. It was like a crowd scene in a Godzilla movie after the news has got out that the monster is on his way to town. All they seemed to sell was buttons, wristwatch straps and ribbons, but then I saw that what everyone was queuing for was a freshly arrived consignment of alarm clocks. They were just simple, cheap-looking plastic alarm clocks, but the shoppers were clearly ready to kill to get one. The department was run by two of the most disagreeable-looking women I ever hope to see. I watched with a kind of dumb fascination. A shy-looking young man whom I took to be North Vietnamese finally reached the till and they ignored him. He held out a wad of money with an entreating look and they just dealt with the people behind him. I don't know why. Finally one of the salesladies pushed his money away and told him to clear off. The man looked as if he could cry. I felt almost as if I could too. I don't know why they were so nasty to him. But he put his money in his pocket and melted into the crowd.

Imagine living like that. Imagine coming home from work and your partner saying, 'Honey, guess what? I had the most wonderful day shopping. I found a loaf of bread, six inches of ribbon, a useful-looking metal thingy and a doughnut.'

'*Really?* A doughnut?'

'Well, actually, I was lying about the doughnut.'

The odd thing was that the people looked amazingly stylish. I don't know how they manage it with so little to buy. In the old days the clothes on all the people looked as if they had been designed by the manager of a Russian tractor factory. People constantly came up to me and Katz offering to buy our jeans. One young guy was so dementedly desperate for a pair of Levi's that he actually started taking his trousers off on the street and urging us to do likewise so that we could effect a trade. Katz and I tried to explain that we didn't want his trousers – they were made out of, like, *hemp* – and asked him if he had anything else, a younger sister or some Cyrillic porno, but he appeared to have nothing worth swapping, and we left him desolate on a street corner, his heart broken and his flies gaping. Now, however, everyone was as smartly dressed as anywhere else in Europe – actually more so, since they took such obvious care and pride in their wardrobe. And the women were simply beautiful, all of them with black hair, chocolate eyes and the most wonderful white teeth. Sofia has, without any doubt, the most beautiful women in Europe.

I spent the better part of a week just walking around. Sofia is full of monuments with crushingly socialist names – the Stadium of the People's Army, the Memorial of the Antifascist Campaigners, the National Palace of Culture – but most of these are contained within some quite lovely parks, with long avenues of chestnuts, benches, swings, even sometimes a boating lake, and often attractive views of the green, hazy mountains that stand at the city's back.

I saw the sights. I went to the old royal palace on Place 9 Septemvri, now the home of the National Gallery of Painting and Sculpture, where I suddenly understood why I was unable to name a single Bulgarian artist, and afterwards crossed the street to have a look at the tomb of Georgi Dimitrov, the national hero – or at least he was until the fall of the Iron Curtain. Now the Bulgarians appeared not to be so certain. There was some minor graffiti on his mausoleum – unthinkable even a couple of months before, I would wager – and you could no longer go in and look at his body, preserved under glass in the fashion beloved of Communists. I remember when Katz and I went to see it in '73, Katz leaned close to the case, sniffed in an obvious manner and said to me in a slightly too-loud voice, 'Something smell a bit off to you?', which nearly got us arrested. Dimitrov was treated like a god. Now, with Communism crumbling, people didn't even want to see him any more.

I went too to the National History Museum and the Alexander Nevsky Memorial Church and the National Archaeological Museum and one or two other diversions, but mostly I just went for long walks and waited for evening to come.

Evening was kind to Sofia. When the shops were shut the queues vanished and people took to strolling on the streets, looking much happier. Sometimes there were small political gatherings outside Dimitrov's tomb and you could see that people were enjoying the unaccustomed luxury of being able to talk freely. One evening outside the old royal palace somebody set up along a wall an arrangement of photographs of the exiled royals, King Simeon and his family. Crowds pressed to see the pictures. I thought it odd at first, but you can imagine what it would be like in Britain if the royal family had been banished forty years ago (now there's a thought for you) and people had been denied any official information about them. So suddenly now the Bulgarians could see what had become of their equivalent of Princess Margaret and the Duke of Edinburgh and all the others. I had a look myself, rather hoping to discover that King Simeon was now managing a Dairy Queen in Sweetwater, Texas, but in fact he appeared to be living a life of elegance and comfort in Paris, so I declined the invitation to sign a petition calling for his reinstatement.

Every evening I went looking for the Club Babalu, a nightclub where Katz and I hung out every night of our stay. That wasn't its real name; we just called it that because it looked so much like Desi Arnaz's Club Babalu on *I Love Lucy*. It was like something straight out of the early 1950s, and it was *the* hot spot in Sofia. People went there for their anniversaries.

Katz and I sat nightly in a balcony overlooking the dance floor drinking Polish beer and watching a rock 'n' roll band (I use the phrase in its Bulgarian sense) whose enthusiasm almost made up for its near total lack of talent. The band played songs that had not been heard in the rest of the world for twenty years – 'Fernando's Hideaway', 'Love Letters in the Sand', 'Green Door' – and people our age were dancing to them as if they were the latest thing, which I suppose in Bulgaria they may have been. The best part was that Katz and I were treated like celebrities – American tourists were that

rare in Sofia then. (They still are, come to that.) People joined us at
our table, bought us drinks. Girls asked us to dance with them. We
got so drunk every night that we missed a dozen opportunities for
sexual gratification, but it was wonderful none the less.

I so much wanted to find the Babalu again that I looked all over the
city and even strolled out to the train station, a long and unrewarding
walk, thinking that if I retraced the route Katz and I had taken into
the city, I might kindle my memory, but no such luck. And then on
a Friday evening, as I was strolling past the restaurant of the Grand
Hotel for about the twentieth time that week, I was brought up so
short by the sound of tinny guitars and scratchy amplifiers that I
actually smacked my nose against the glass in turning to look. It
was the Club Babalu! I had walked past it again and again, but
without the awful music I hadn't even noticed it. Now suddenly I
recognised every inch of it. There was the balcony. There was our
table. Even the waitresses looked vaguely familiar, if a tad older.
Happy memories came flooding back.

I went straight in to order a Polish beer, but a guy on the door in
an oversized black suit wouldn't let me enter. He wasn't being nasty,
but he just wouldn't let me in. I didn't understand why. You get used
to not understanding why in Bulgaria after a while, so I continued
with my walk. About twenty minutes later, after my nightly circuit
of the dark hulk of the Nevsky church, I ambled back past the Grand
and realised why I had been denied entrance. They were closing. It
was nine-thirty on a Friday night and this was the liveliest place
in town. Bulgaria, I reflected as I walked back to the hotel, isn't a
country; it's a near-death experience.

I was lucky that I could retreat whenever I wanted to the luxurious
sanctum of the Sheraton, where I could get cold beers and decent
food and watch CNN on the TV in my room. I cravenly took all
my meals there. I tried hard to find a local restaurant that looked
half-way decent and could not. Sofia has the most unlively bars and
restaurants – plain, poorly lit, with maybe just a factory calendar
on the wall and every surface covered in Formica. I did stop once
at a place out near Juzen Park, but the menu was in Cyrillic and
I couldn't understand a thing. I looked around to see what other

people were eating, thinking I might just point to something on someone else's table, but they were eating foods that didn't even look like food – all gruel and watery vegetables – and I fled back to the hotel, where the menu was in English and the food was appealing.

But I paid for my comfort with a twice-daily dose of guilt. Each time I dined in the Sheraton, I was glumly aware that I was eating better than nine million Bulgarians. I found this economic apartheid repugnant, if irresistible. How can you have a country in which your own citizens are forbidden to go into certain places? If a Bulgarian was by some miracle of thrift and enterprise sufficiently well-heeled, he could go into two of the hotel's restaurants, the Wiener Café and Melnik Grill, but the entrances were on a side street. You couldn't get to them through the hotel. You had to go out of the front door and walk around the corner. Common people couldn't come into the hotel proper, as I could. Hundreds of them must walk by it every working day and wonder what it's like inside. Well, it's wonderful – to a Bulgarian it would seem to offer a life of richness and comfort almost beyond conception: a posh bar where you could get cocktails with ice cubes, restaurants serving foods that haven't been seen elsewhere in the country for years, a shop selling chocolates, brandy and cigarettes and other luxuries so unattainable that the average Bulgarian would be foolish even to dream of them.

It amazed me that I didn't get beaten up every time I emerged from the hotel – *I'd* want to beat me up and I know what a sweet guy I am – but no one showed me anything but kindness and friendship. People would come up to me constantly and ask if I wanted to change money, but I didn't, I couldn't. It was illegal and besides I didn't want any more Bulgarian money than I had: there was nothing to buy with it. Why should I stand in a queue for two hours to buy a pack of cigarettes with leva when I could get better cigarettes for less money in ten seconds in my own hotel? 'I'm really sorry,' I kept saying, and they seemed to understand.

I began to get obsessed with trying to spend some money, but there was nothing to spend it on, nothing. One of the parks, I discovered one Sunday morning, was full of artists selling their own work and I thought, Great! I'll buy a picture. But they were all terrible. Most of them were technically accomplished, but the subjects were just so awful – vivid sunsets with orange and pink clouds, and surreal, Salvador Dali-like paintings of melted objects. It was as if they were so far out of touch with the world that they didn't know what to paint.

The further you roam in Sofia the better it gets. I took to going for day-long walks out into the hilly districts on the south-east side of the city, an area of forests, parks, neighbourhoods of rather grand apartment buildings, winding tranquil streets, some nice homes. As I was walking back into the city, over a footbridge across the Slivnica River and down some anonymous residential street, it struck me that this really was quite a beautiful city. More than that, it was the most European of all the cities I had been to. There were no modern shopping centres, no big gas stations, no McDonald's or Pizza Huts, no revolving signs for Coca-Cola. No city I had ever been to had more thoroughly resisted the blandishments of American culture. It was completely, comprehensively European. This was, I realised with a sense of profound unease, the Europe I had dreamed of as a child.

It is hard to know what will become of Bulgaria. A couple of weeks after my visit, the people of the country, in a moment of madness, freely voted for a Communist regime, the only country in eastern Europe to voluntarily retain the old form of government.

This was 1990, the year that Communism died in Europe, and it seemed to me strange that in all the words that were written about the fall of the Iron Curtain nobody anywhere lamented that it was the end of a noble experiment. I know Communism never worked and I would have hated living under it myself, but it seems to me none the less that there is a kind of sadness in the thought that the only economic system that appears to work is one based on self-interest and greed.

Communism in Bulgaria won't last. It can't last. No people will retain a government that can't feed them or let them provide toys for their children. I'm certain that if I come back to Sofia in five years it will be full of Pizza Huts and Laura Ashleys and the streets will be clogged with BMWs, and all the people will be much happier. I can't blame them a bit, but I'm glad I saw it before it changed.

22. Istanbul

Katz and I went from Sofia to Istanbul on the Orient Express. I had thought that it would be full of romance – I rather imagined some turbanned servant coming round with cups of sweet coffee and complimentary hot towels – but in fact it was awful in every way: hot, foetid, airless, threadbare, crowded, old, slow. By 1973, the Orient Express was just a name on a rusty piece of metal on the side of any old train between Belgrade and Istanbul. A couple of years later it was discontinued altogether.

We had a compartment to ourselves as we left Sofia, but about two stops later the door slid brusquely open and an extended family of noisy fat people, looking like a walking testimonial to the inadvisability of chronic inbreeding, barged in laden with cardboard suitcases and string bags of evil-smelling food. They plonked themselves down, forcing me and Katz into opposite corners, and immediately began delving in the food bags, passing round handkerchiefs full of little dead fish, hunks of dry bread, runny boiled eggs and dripping slabs of pungent curdled cheese whose smell put me in mind of the time my family returned from summer vacation to discover that my mother had inadvertently locked the cat in the broom cupboard for the three hottest weeks of the year. They ate with smacking lips, wiping their stubby fingers on their shirts, before sinking one by one into deep and spluttering comas. By some quirk of Balkan digestion, they expanded as they slept, squeezing us further and further into our respective corners until we were pressed against the wall like lumps of Blu-Tack. We had twenty-two hours of this to get through.

By this point on our trip Katz and I had spent nearly four months together and were thoroughly sick of each other. We had long days in which we either bickered endlessly or didn't speak. On this day, as I recall, we hadn't been speaking, but late in the night, as the train trundled sluggishly across the scrubby void that is western Turkey, Katz disturbed me from a light but delirious slumber by tapping me on the shoulder and saying accusingly, 'Is that dog shit on the bottom of your shoe?'

I sat up a fraction. 'What?'

'Is that dog shit on the bottom of your shoe?'

'I don't know, the lab report's not back yet,' I replied drily.

'I'm serious, is that dog shit?'

'How should I know?'

Katz leaned far enough forward to give it a good look and a cautious sniff. 'It *is* dog shit,' he announced with an odd tone of satisfaction.

'Well, keep quiet about it or everybody'll want some.'

'Go and clean it off, will ya? It's making me nauseous.'

And here the bickering started, in intense little whispers.

'You go and clean it off.'

'It's your shoes.'

'Well, I kind of like it. Besides, it kills the smell of this guy next to me.'

'Well, it's making me nauseous.'

'Well, I don't give a shit.'

'Well, I think you're a fuck-head.'

'Oh, you do, do you?'

'Yes, as a matter of fact. You've been a fuck-head since Austria.'

'Well, you've been a fuck-head since birth.'

'*Me?*' A wounded look. 'That's rich. You were a fuck-head in the *womb*, Bryson. You've got three kinds of chromosomes: X, Y and fuck-head.'

And so it went. Istanbul clearly was not destined to be a success for us. Katz hated it and he hated me. I mostly hated Katz, but I didn't much care for Istanbul either. It was, like the train that took us there, hot, foetid, crowded and threadbare. The streets were full of urchins who snatched anything you didn't cling to with both hands and the food was simply dreadful, all foul-smelling cheese and mysterious lumps of goo. One night Katz nearly got us killed when he enquired of a waiter, 'Tell me, do you have cows shit straight onto the plate or do you scoop it on afterwards?'

One of the sustaining pleasures for Katz in the later stages of the trip was talking candidly in this way to people who could not understand him, making smiling enquiries of a policeman concerning the celebrated tininess of his penis or telling a surly waiter, 'Can we have the bill, Boris? We've got to run because your wife's promised to give us both blow jobs.'

But in this instance it turned out that the waiter had worked in a little place off the Tottenham Court Road for thirteen years and he understood Katz's question only too well. He directed us to the door with the aid of a meat cleaver, making wholly justified remarks about the nobility of Turkish cuisine and the insolence of young tourists.

With this final pleasure denied him on the grounds of prudence and a sincere threat from me that I would kill him myself if an English-speaking Turk didn't do it first, Katz spent the remainder of our time in Istanbul in a moody silence, except for growling at touts in the Grand Bazaar to fuck off and leave him alone, but this I excused on the basis of justified provocation. We had reached the end of the road in every sense. It was a long week.

I wondered now, as I rode a taxi in from the airport through the hot, airless, teeming streets of Istanbul, whether my attitude would be more receptive this time.

Things did not start well. I had made a reservation at the Sheraton through the company's internal reservation system in Sofia, but the hotel turned out to be miles away from the Golden Horn and old town. The room was clean and passably swank, but the television didn't work, and when I went to the bathroom to wash my hands and face, the pipes juddered and banged like something from a poltergeist movie and then, with a series of gasps, issued a steady brown soup. I let the water run for ten minutes, but it never cleared or even thinned. For this I was paying $150 a night.

I sat on the toilet, watching the water run, thinking what an odd thing tourism is. You fly off to a strange land, eagerly abandoning all the comforts of home, and then expend vast quantities of time and money in a largely futile effort to recapture the comforts that you wouldn't have lost if you hadn't left home in the first place.

Sighing, I smeared a little of the brown water around my face, then went out to see Istanbul. It is the noisiest, dirtiest, busiest city I've ever seen. Everywhere there is noise — car horns tooting, sirens shrilling, people shouting, muezzins wailing, ferries on the Bosphorus sounding their booming horns. Everywhere, too, there is ceaseless activity – people pushing carts, carrying trays of food or coffee, humping huge and ungainly loads (I saw one guy with a sofa on his back), people every five feet selling something: lottery tickets, wristwatches, cigarettes, replica perfumes.

Every few paces people come up to you wanting to shine your shoes, sell you postcards or guidebooks, lead you to their brother's carpet shop or otherwise induce you to part with some trifling sum of money. Along the Galata Bridge, swarming with pedestrians, beggars and load bearers, amateur fishermen stood pulling the most poisoned-looking fish I ever hope to see from the oily waters below. At the end of the bridge two guys were crossing the street to Sirkeci Station, threading their way through the traffic leading brown bears on leashes. No one gave them a second glance. Istanbul is, in short, one of those great and exhilarating cities where almost anything seems possible.

The one truly unbearable thing in the city is the Turkish pop music. It is inescapable. It assaults you from every restaurant doorway, from every lemonade stand, from every passing cab. If you can imagine a man having a vasectomy without anaesthetic to a background accompaniment of frantic sitar-playing, you will have some idea of what popular Turkish music is like.

I wandered around for a couple of hours, impressed by the tumult, amazed that in one place there could be so much activity. I walked past the Blue Mosque and Aya Sofia, peeling postcard salesmen from my sleeve as I went, and tried to go to Topkapi, but it was closed. I headed instead for what I thought was the national archaeological museum, but I somehow missed it and found myself presently at the entrance to a large, inviting and miraculously tranquil park, the Gülhane. It was full of cool shade and happy families. There was a free zoo, evidently much loved by children, and somewhere a café playing Turkish torture music, but softly enough to be tolerable.

At the bottom of a gently sloping central avenue, the park ended in a sudden and stunning view of the Bosphorus, glittery and blue. I took a seat at an open-air taverna, ordered a Coke and gazed across the water to the white houses gleaming on the brown hillside of

Üsküdar two miles across the strait. Distant cars glinted in the hot sunshine and ferries plied doggedly back and forth across the Bosphorus and on out to the distant Princes' Islands, adrift in a bluish haze. It was beautiful and a perfect place to stop.

I had clearly come to the end of my own road. That was Asia over there; this was as far as I could go in Europe. It was time to go home. My long-suffering wife was pregnant with her semi-annual baby. The younger children, she had told me on the phone, were beginning to call any grown man 'Daddy'. The grass was waist-high. One of the field walls was tumbling down. The sheep were in the meadow. The cows were in the corn. There was a lot for me to do.

And I was, I admit, ready to go. I missed my family and the comfortable familiarities of home. I was tired of the daily drudgery of keeping myself fed and bedded, tired of trains and buses, tired of existing in a world of strangers, tired of being forever perplexed and lost, tired above all of my own dull company. How many times in recent days I had sat trapped on buses or trains listening to my idly prattling mind and wished that I could just get up and walk out on myself?

At the same time, I had a quite irrational urge to keep going. There is something about the momentum of travelling that makes you want to just keep moving, to never stop. That was Asia over there, after all – right there in my view. *Asia*. The thought of it seemed incredible. I could be there in minutes. I still had money left. An untouched continent lay before me.

But I didn't go. Instead I ordered another Coke and watched the ferries. In other circumstances I think I might have gone. But that of course is neither here nor there.